# THE BEST
# AMERICAN
# MAGAZINE
# WRITING

# 2011

# THE BEST AMERICAN MAGAZINE WRITING

# 2011

**Compiled by the American Society of Magazine Editors**

Columbia University Press   New York

Columbia University Press
*Publishers Since 1893*
New York   Chichester, West Sussex
Copyright © 2011 Columbia University Press
All rights reserved

Library of Congress Cataloging-in-Publication Data
ISSN 1541-0978
ISBN 978-0-231-15940-1 (pbk.)

♾

Columbia University Press books are printed on permanent and durable
acid-free paper.
This book is printed on paper with recycled content.
Printed in the United States of America
p 10 9 8 7 6 5 4 3 2 1

# Contents

Jim Nelson

# Introduction: The Future Is Now, What Will It Look Like?

Having read enough pieces prognosticating on the future of magazines to gag a media critic, finger-swiped my way through enough manifestos on Our Digital Century to fill a thousand Kindle Singles, and listened to enough NPR's *On the Media* to make my ears bleed (and yet I keep listening/bleeding, Brooke Gladstone!), I've often been left to wonder if the future of media might actually be talking about the future of media. I'd bet a media empire on it. Hardly a week goes by when a story involving misbehaving mavens or June iPad sales or some passing zinger from George Lois doesn't become, through a mirror-gazing, self-churning process, a story about the Very Future of Media itself: Does Rupert Murdoch's *News of the Word* scandal, we inevitably ask, mean the end of Fleet Street as we know and hate it? Does Tina Brown's If Lady Di Hadn't Died cover mean newsweeklies are officially kaput and all that will soon be left are websites run by Tina Brown?

So this is the part where we skip right past the hand-wringing over the fate of Print and its archenemy or potential BFF, Digital, or pretend to know even half the answers. This is the part where we resist the urge to use words like "whither." There will be no pining here for the Golden Era of Picture-Books That Made Your Fingers Smudgy. Ideas that will not be discussed in this essay include: the explosive growth and alarming faux-intimacy of

Twitter; the need for twenty-first-century cross-platform branding; are the bandwiths of our attention spans getting perilously frayed?; should all content be free? (short answer: not until Barack Obama completes the socialist-agrarian revolution); and Do Magazines Matter? because, brother, if you have to ask that one, whither your perilously frayed attention span?

This was the year, it is my anthology-introducing duty to remind you, that a magazine article led to the firing of the general in charge of the war in Afghanistan—as dramatic a reaction to any magazine piece since Kim Kardashian revealed the secrets of How She Rolls. When Michael Hastings's piece "The Runaway General" came out and garnered the reaction it did ("as huge as the Pentagon Papers!" seemed to sum it up), you could almost feel the collective heave and sigh among magazine editors. It wasn't high-fiving or back patting; we editors have had the cocksurety long since knocked out of us. It was more like stunned Egyptians reacting to their own people power: *Wow! Did we just do that?*

The truth is we were doing it all the time, albeit not always with the heads of American generals rolling in the wake of our work. I admit that "Give it up for the state of magazines in 2011, people!" is not the most exciting cheerleading line, and I will not ask anyone to chant it. But I cheerfully believe that magazines (and from here on out I will use that term to refer to all periodicals, meaty websites, long-form blogs, content farms with actual farmers, and in-app purchases that require more than three minutes of engagement) do the best big-picture job of any media in targeting and mining the mood, anxieties, and abiding concerns of the culture. So: Can I get a little Jane Mayer love?! Because this was also the year that magazine writers reached about as deeply and meaningfully into the dark, unexplored alleyways of American politics as any journalism can: Mayer's reporting on this country's tortured torture policies and shadowy political networks, collected here in just one of her many stunning *New Yorker* pieces,

"Covert Operations," will, I humbly submit, be taught in American classrooms and no doubt reviled in American Tea Party parlors for decades.

But there was more, is more, and always will be more going on with great magazines and the fine Americans who read them. The breaking-news stories get most of the attention, but for every shocking exposé, there's a piece that rocks your world and wins your heart and maybe even changes what you look for and hope for in writing. I certainly hope Michael Paterniti's "The Suicide Catcher," which we published in *GQ* and which moves me to no end no matter how many times I read it, does that for you, shedding light and understanding where neither is easily shed. (I return to that piece like it's a fairy tale I keep learning from, like some German *mutter* reading Grimm's to her *kinder*.) Or take John Jeremiah Sullivan's wildly original—because everything Sullivan writes is half-wild and wholly original—"Mister Lytle: An Essay," about his unusual relationship with a brilliant ninety-two-year-old Southern literary mentor who teeters on the edge of dementia, has a fondness for the body ("He, for his part, called me boy, and beloved, and once, in a letter, "Breath of My Nostrils'"), and who will live on in your head long after Mister Lytle takes off for the Sweet Hereafter. You read that piece and it slightly rewires the receptors of What Is Possible in your magazine brain, and not a single public official gets fired for it.

I'd even go further and say that at their best, magazines do more than inform, entertain, and waste tons of your valuable time. They create—and I'm going to sound a little Wendell Berry here—a community. By community I don't mean the buzz phrase that sprang up a few years ago when webheads were trying to articulate what everyone was looking for on the Internet. I mean something a little more connective still: that the act of reading great writing lands and lives where the cerebral mixes with the emotional and becomes, if constantly nurtured, almost tribal, feeding a fealty that a sports fan would recognize. It's the only way I've ever read magazines—madly, loyally, almost monogamously—scouring many but devouring the ones that deserve my madness.

True Story That May Explain All, including that loyalty and strange connectivity I'm talking about but which will take three minutes of said valuable time:

When I was a scant ten years old living in an (extremely) planned-community suburb outside D.C., my parents drove me to New York City for the first time, to visit my Katz's-deli-loving relatives and "take in the sights." Like any adolescent, I had a few essential requests: I wanted to tour the entire New York subway system, preferably with a civil engineer. I wanted to see what a real New York newsstand looked like. In my little town, we only had a dusty tobacco shop full of comic books and *Tiger Beats*, and this meager supply could not sustain a boy. Finally and crucially, I wanted to visit the swanky Madison Avenue offices of *Mad Magazine*, which was, to my ten-year-old mind, one of the greatest works of art that Western civilization had ever created, and surely a place where intelligent children would be greeted with respect, Milk Duds, and Alfred E. Newman photo opportunities.

"How about the Statue of Liberty?" my mom asked excitedly.

"Sure, if it's on the way."

Nothing about the trip panned out quite as I expected. Because the underground was "dirty and dangerous," I was given a brief tour of the greasy stairwell of the Thirty-fourth Street subway station then whisked away before the ascending A-trainers could trample me. Was I granted a visit to the offices of *Mad Magazine*, and did I there shake the hands of legendary, heavily bearded publisher William M. Gaines, as per my request? Ha! Dad just steered our station wagon up Madison Avenue, pointing up at buildings and saying: "There it is! There's *Mad*. Oh, look there's Alfred E. Newman in the window. Wave, Jimmy. Wave!" But this was not a joke, and I would not be openly mocked like the cast of *Poseidon Adventure*, so brilliantly parodied that summer in *Mad* issue 161.

At least, I consoled myself, I had been promised a visit to a real New York newsstand, like the salty sidewalk gazebo I'd seen on *The Odd Couple*. I needed to know if there were other publications out there like my favorites, not just *Mad* but *Cracked* and *Sick* and (the underrated) *Crazy*. What would these magazines look like, and would they be even more psycho-sardonically bent: *Wacko* and *Bonkers* and *Wholly Neurotic*?

At last, Mom spotted a crowded little newsstand near Forty-second Street and we got out and ran rushing toward it like kids to a carnival. I sped to the front and took in the outrageous bounty before me—a dizzying array of newsies, French gossip rags, bloody Mafia pictorals, and alarmingly graphic tabloids. Jesus, New York practically *lived* on magazines. But where was the funny stuff? Where were the uproarious sendups of Ser-pig-o? I looked up. Nothing but row after row of open-mouthed nudies and violently shaved Swedes. I recall that a certain beefcake Blueboy repeatedly attempted to molest my eyes. My mother let out an audible gasp, but she did not, bless her, squire me away. She placed her hand firmly on my head and nudged it in the general direction of *Reader's Digest*.

And yep, I found something amazing that day—issue no. 2 of a little gem called *Grin*, "The American Funny Book," with irreverent parodies of Marcus Welby (natch) and *A Clockwork Orange* and, oddly, a "Bonus! Naughty Santa Poster," which is probably why my uncle stole it away from me that night at Katz's, calling it too "risqué" for a ten-year-old, and maybe why he kept on flipping through it all night ("Yep. Awfully, awfully *risqué*"). But I didn't care. I'd discovered that day that a whole world of culture existed and thrived outside of Greenbelt, Maryland, and I could have it all, read it all, if I could just get my hands on it.

And sure, I no longer actually *run* to newsstands, nor to my home computer—to be honest, I really don't run to anything—but a remnant of that feeling or, rather, those feelings has stuck with me: of outbound curiosity for what might be lurking somewhere unread and undiscovered; a steady appetite for writing that says something new or vital in an insightful or gorgeous or surprising way; and loyalty to the magazines that consistently give it to me. My *Mad/Sick/Crazy* loyalty was soon followed by high school devotion to *Creem* and Annie-era *Rolling Stone* (naked John Lennon and repentant Elvis Costello: still wrapped in cellophane somewhere in my Mom's attic). By college, *Rolling Stone* was "corporate," and I was pretentious and did not know it, but I could not live without my poncy little *NME*s and *Melody Maker*s. Post-college and prestarving, I could no longer afford British magazines and lived on *Harper's*, subsisting on steady rations of David Foster Wallace and E. Annie Proulx. I spent way too many caffeinated nights seeing if I could write like Lewis Lapham. (I could not.)

And yes, in those magazines I came to love I found something more: a sense that I was part of a community of readers who together in the moment were reading *the right stuff*, the vital work, the Things That Need to Be Read. The magazines that do it for me today–*New York*, *The Believer*, *Longreads*, *Mojo*, *Tong*, *Fantastic Man*, *The Awl*, and many more, too many to mention—give that same communal rush.

What you hold in your hands is the best of what we magazine editors do—and, it's worth saying, it is *why* most of us do what we do, why we got into this field, and why most of us will do some form or another of it for the rest of our lives, whether we end up working for a food blog, Steve Jobs, or *The New Yorker*: Great stories, amazing writing, pieces that get under your skin, live in your memory, and have a life of their own.

May it give you a rush.

Sid Holt,
chief executive,
American Society of
Magazine Editors

# Acknowledgments

The year 2010 was an extraordinary one for magazine journalism, and this book proves it. Here are timely and important stories on politics and media, the rise of the Tea Party, our war in Afghanistan, the performance of our health care system, and the growing threat of climate change. Here, too, are stories about subjects that touch millions every day: obesity, cancer, autism, suicide. And there are stories about the things many magazine readers love to read about most: movies, television, music, and sports (LeBron, how could you?).

In this book there are stories about the news and stories—like *The New Yorker*'s "Covert Operations" and *Rolling Stone*'s "Runaway General"—that made news. Also here are stories about injustice at home and abroad, including the *Texas Monthly* investigation that won an innocent man his freedom and the *Harper's Magazine* story that asks whether three prisoners at Guantánamo were tortured to death. There is even a poem about the oil spill in the Gulf of Mexico.

*Best American Magazine Writing 2011* draws from work published in 2010 and entered in the National Magazine Awards. Founded in 1966, the National Magazine Awards are sponsored by the American Society of Magazine Editors in association with the Columbia University Graduate School of Journalism. Most of the stories collected here were either finalists for awards or won them.

This year nearly 300 magazines, both print and digital, participated in the awards, submitting 1,783 entries in 34 categories. A list of the categories, finalists, and winners is printed at the back of this book, and a searchable database of previous finalists and winners appears on the ASME website at http://magazine .org/asme. The winner in each category receives a reproduction of Alexander Calder's stabile "Elephant"—which explains why the National Magazine Awards are also known as the Ellies.

The National Magazine Award finalists and winners are decided by judges chosen impartially by ASME. This year there were 359 judges, including distinguished writers, editors, and educators from around the country. They are also listed at the back of this book. ASME is indebted to these judges for devoting so much time and energy to the awards. Their dedication guarantees the integrity of the National Magazine Awards.

ASME thanks the writers, editors, and magazines that permitted their work to be published in *Best American Magazine Writing 2011*. Also to be thanked are all the editors who chose to participate in the National Magazine Awards and the staff who performed the time-consuming and sometimes seemingly thankless task of entering the articles.

To the ASME board of directors, who are chiefly responsible for the success of the National Magazine Awards, thank you. Special thanks to Larry Hackett, the managing editor of *People* and president of ASME.

On behalf of ASME, I want to thank our colleagues at the Columbia Graduate School of Journalism; the dean of the school and Henry R. Luce Professor, Nicholas Lemann; and the associate dean of programs and prizes, Arlene Notoro Morgan.

I am grateful to Jim Nelson, the editor in chief of *GQ*, for writing the introduction to this edition of *Best American Magazine Writing*. Running a magazine is job enough—even if it means sometimes jetting to Europe to hobnob with *il bel mondo*—without having to think about stories that ran in other places last year. I also thank Jim for his continuing support of ASME and the National Magazine Awards.

The members of ASME are indebted to our agent, David Mc-Cormick of McCormick & Williams, for his skillful representation of our interests, and I continue to be especially thankful for the enthusiasm and the patience of our editors at the Columbia University Press, Philip Leventhal and Michael Haskell.

On behalf of ASME, I want to thank our colleagues at MPA—the Association of Magazine Media, especially the chair of the board of directors, Michael Clinton of Hearst Magazines. Thanks also to Nina Link, the president and CEO of MPA, and to Howard Polskin, Cristina Dinozo, Ja-Shin Tsang, Sarah Hansen, and Felicity Crew.

Without Nina Fortuna, the National Magazine Awards would not happen. My thanks to her are immeasurable. Finally, I want to acknowledge my predecessors at ASME, Marlene Kahan and the late Robert Kenyon, without whom the National Magazine Awards would not be the success they are today.

People in the magazine business ask me all the time if I like my job. I guess the idea of running the National Magazine Awards doesn't sound like a lot of fun (or they don't think I'm doing a good job). But I think the real reason they ask me that question is that they can't imagine doing a job that isn't writing for magazines or editing one. They're journalists, after all, and they love what they do. All you have to do is read this book to find out why.

# THE BEST
# AMERICAN
# MAGAZINE
# WRITING

# 2011

## The New York Times Magazine

WINNER—PROFILE WRITING

A reporter in the Washington bureau of the New York Times, Mark Leibovich is well known for his cutting profiles of politicians and the journalists who follow them—pieces like his cover stories for the Times Magazine on Chris Matthews in April 2008 and Glenn Beck in September 2010. Headlined "The Insider's Insider" when it ran in the magazine in April 2010, Leibovich's profile of Mike Allen explains the rise of Politico, the website and magazine where Allen was the first reporter hired after it was founded. As the National Magazine Award judges said, "The Man the White House Wakes Up To" is "both a compelling depiction of an eccentric and an adrenaline-packed tour through Washington's new nexus of news and power." Before joining the Times in 2006, Leibovich was a reporter for the Washington Post (where he was once said to have "put his fangs" into the especially talkative spouse of one hapless politician) and the San Jose Mercury News.

Mark Leibovich

# The Man the White House Wakes Up To

Beffore he goes to sleep, between eleven and midnight, Dan Pfeiffer, the White House communications director, typically checks in by e-mail with the same reporter: Mike Allen of *Politico*, who is also the first reporter Pfeiffer corresponds with after he wakes up at 4:20. A hyperactive former Eagle Scout, Allen will have been up for hours, if he ever went to bed. Whether or not he did is one of the many little mysteries that surround him. The abiding certainty about Allen is that sometime between 5:30 and 8:30 A.M., seven days a week, he hits "send" on a mass e-mail newsletter that some of America's most influential people will read before they say a word to their spouses.

Allen's e-mail tipsheet, *Playbook*, has become the principal early-morning document for an elite set of political and news-media thrivers and strivers. *Playbook* is an insider's hodgepodge of predawn news, talking-point previews, scooplets, birthday greetings to people you've never heard of, random sightings ("spotted") around town and inside jokes. It is, in essence, Allen's morning distillation of the Nation's Business in the form of a summer-camp newsletter.

Like many in Washington, Pfeiffer describes Allen with some variation on "the most powerful" or "important" journalist in the capital. The two men exchange e-mail messages about six or eight times a day. Allen also communes a lot with Rahm Emanuel, the White House chief of staff; Robert Gibbs, the press secretary; David Axelrod, President Obama's senior adviser; and about two dozen other White House officials. But Pfeiffer is likely Allen's main point of contact, the one who most often helps him arrive at a "West Wing Mindmeld," as *Playbook* calls it, which is essentially a pro-Obama take on that day's news. (Allen gets a similar fill from Republicans, which he also disseminates in *Playbook*.)

Pfeiffer tells Allen the message that the Obama administration is trying to "drive" that morning—"drive" being the action verb of choice around the male-dominated culture of *Politico*, a three-year-old publication, of which the oft-stated goal is to become as central to political addicts as ESPN is to sports junkies. "Drive" is a stand-in for the stodgier verb "influence." If, say, David S. Broder and R. W. Apple Jr. were said to "influence the political discourse" through the *Washington Post* and the *New York Times* in the last decades of the twentieth century, *Politico* wants to "drive the conversation" in the new-media landscape of the twenty-first. It wants to "win" every news cycle by being first with a morsel of information, whether or not the morsel proves relevant, or even correct, in the long run—and whether the long run proves to be measured in days, hours, or minutes.

In Politico parlance, "influence" is less a verb than the root of a noun. *Politico*'s top editors describe "influentials" (or "compulsives") as their target audience: elected officials, political operatives, journalists, and other political-media functionaries. Since early 2007, Allen's "data points," as he calls the items in *Playbook*, have become the cheat sheet of record for a time-starved city in which the power-and-information hierarchy has been upended. It is also a daily totem for those who deride Washington as a clubby little town where Usual Suspects talk to the same Usual Suspects in a feedback loop of gamesmanship, trivia, conventional wisdom, and personality cults.

•　　　•　　　•

Allen refers to his readership as "the *Playbook* community." He appeared wounded one morning in March when I suggested to him that his esoteric chronicle may reinforce a conceit that Washington is a closed conclave. No, no, he protested. *Playbook* is open, intimate. No one even edits it before it goes out, he said, which adds to his "human connection" to "the community." Political insiderdom—or the illusion thereof—has moved from Georgetown salons or cordoned-off security zones to a mass e-mail list administrated by a never-married forty-five-year-old grind known as Mikey.

"He is part mascot and part sleepless narrator of our town," Tracy Sefl, a Democratic media consultant and a close aide to Terry McAuliffe, the former Democratic National Committee chairman, told me by e-mail. "He is an omnipresent participant-observer, abundantly kind, generous and just unpredictable enough to make him an object of curiosity to even the most self-interested. Everything about him is literary."

Allen darts through the political world much the way he writes *Playbook*: in abbreviated steps, more like chops. You can spot him from far away, his shiny head darting up and often straight down into his BlackBerry. He says he gets 2,000 e-mail messages a day, tries to answer all that are addressed to him personally, some while walking. He is always bumping into things.

In 1993, Allen was covering a trial in Richmond, Va., for the *New York Times* (as a stringer) and the *Richmond Times-Dispatch* (which employed him). He found a pay phone, darted into the street and got whacked by a car. Allen composed himself, filed stories for both papers, and then found his way to the hospital with a broken elbow. This is one of the many "Mikey Stories" that Washingtonians share with awe and some concern. A corollary are "Mikey Sightings," a bipartisan e-mail chain among prominent people who track Allen's stutter-stepping whereabouts—his showing up out of nowhere, around corners, at odd hours, sometimes a few time zones away.

He bursts in and out of parties, at once manic and serene, chronically toting gifts, cards, and flower arrangements that seem to consume much of an annual income that is believed to exceed $250,000. Allen—who is childless and owns no cars or real estate—perpetually picks up meal and beverage tabs for his friend-sources (the dominant hybrid around Mikey). He kisses women's hands and thanks you so much for coming, even though the party is never at his home, which not even his closest friends have seen. It is as if Mikey is the host of one big party, and by showing up anywhere in Washington, you have served the *Playbook* community and are deserving of the impresario's thanks (or "Hat Tip" in *Playbook*ese).

Allen also has a tendency to suddenly vanish. But then he will pop up on a TV screen a few minutes later. Or you then learn via e-mail that he is racing through O'Hare or via *Playbook* that he took an excursion to the circus (with "Owen and Grace Gallo, ages three and four, who especially liked: doggies on a slide") or Maine ("where an eagle might grab one of your fish while you're focused on the grill").

Or that it's Mark Paustenbach's birthday, whoever he is.

Allen was the first reporter hired by *Politico*'s founding editors, John F. Harris and Jim VandeHei, when they left the *Washington Post* to start the website and newspaper in 2006. He is considered a *Politico* "founding father," in the words of Harris, who, like VandeHei, tends to place great weight and mission onto the organization. Another construct (originating outside *Politico*) is that Harris and VandeHei are God and Jesus—it's unclear who is who—and that Allen is the Holy Ghost. When I mentioned this to Allen recently, he was adamant that it is meant to be facetious and that no one at *Politico* really believes that. Allen, an observant Christian, said the line could be misconstrued. But "Holy Ghost" does seem a particularly apt description of Allen's ubiquity and inscrutability. "I get that what I do is a little elusive, ambiguous," Allen told me. "I try to be a force for good. And I try to be everywhere."

$$• \qquad • \qquad •$$

I met Allen on a hot April night at the basement bar of the Hay-Adams hotel, across from the White House. I headed downstairs, and there he was, startling me in a back stairwell, reading his BlackBerry an inch from his wire-rim glasses. As we entered the bar, Allen greeted two Democratic operatives at a corner table and noted that his friend-source Kevin Madden, a Republican consultant, was at that moment on CNN.

Allen's public bearing combines the rumpledness of an old-school print reporter with the sheen of a new-school "cross-platform brand" who has become accustomed to performing on camera. Every time Allen starts to speak—in person or on air—his eyes bulge for a split second, as if he has just seen a light go on. His mannerisms resemble an almost childlike mimicry of a politician—the incessant thanking, deference, greetings, teeth-clenched smiles, and ability to project belief in the purity of his own voice and motivations. He speaks in quick and certain cadences, on message, in sound bites, karate-chopping the table for emphasis. (His work is "joyful, exciting," he says. It is a "privilege" to work at *Politico* with young reporters. "I love this company. I love what I'm doing." And all that.) Over several discussions, Allen repeated full paragraphs almost to the word.

"The people in this community, they all want to read the same ten stories," he said, table-chopping in the Hay-Adams. "And to find all of those, you have to read 1,000 stories. And we do that for you."

As a practical matter, here is how Allen's ten stories influence the influentials. Cable bookers, reporters and editors read *Play-book* obsessively, and it's easy to pinpoint exactly how an item can spark copycat coverage that can drive a story. Items become segment pieces on *Morning Joe*, the MSNBC program, where there are ten *Politico Playbook* segments each week, more than half of them featuring Allen. This incites other cable hits, many featuring *Politico* reporters, who collectively appear on television about 125 times a week. There are subsequent links to *Politico* stories on the *Drudge Report*, the *Huffington Post*, and other web aggregators that newspaper assigning editors and network news producers check regularly. "Washington narratives and impressions are no longer shaped by the grand pronouncements of big news organizations," said Allen, a former reporter for three of them—the *Washington Post*, the *New York Times*, and *Time* magazine. "The smartest people in politics give us the kindling, and we light the fire."

By "we," Allen is referring to either *Playbook* or *Politico*. But many influentials draw a distinction. They will work to get a little twig into Mikey's kindling and read him faithfully. *Politico*, however, is more fraught.

Nowhere is Washington's ambivalence over *Politico* more evident than in the White House. The Obama and *Politico* enterprises have had parallel ascendancies to an extent: they fashioned themselves as tech-savvy upstarts bent on changing the established order—of politics (Obama) and of how it is covered (*Politico*). They started around the same time, early 2007, and their clashing agendas were apparent early. On the day that *Politico* published its first print edition, Barack Obama's campaign manager, David Plouffe, walked into the campaign's offices and slammed a copy of the new publication on Dan Pfeiffer's keyboard. "This," Plouffe declared, "is going to be a problem."

*Politico* today remains a White House shorthand for everything the administration claims to dislike about Washington—Beltway myopia, politics as daily sport. Yet most of the president's top aides are as steeped in this culture as anyone else—and work hard to manipulate it. "What's notable about this administration is how ostentatiously its people proclaim to be uninterested in things they are plainly interested in," Harris, *Politico*'s editor in chief, told me in an e-mail message.

That *Politico* has been so vilified inside the White House is itself a sign of its entry into "the bloodstream" (another *Politico* phrase). It is, White House officials say, an indictment of the "Washington mentality" that the city is sustaining *Politico* and letting it "drive the conversation" to the extent it does. In early March, Axelrod was sitting in his West Wing office, complaining to me about the "palace-intrigue pathology" of Washington and why he missed Chicago. "I prefer living in a place where people don't discuss the *Politico* over dinner," he said.

But morning is another matter, a solitary, on-the-go cram session in which *Playbook* has become the political-media equivalent of those food pills that futurists envision will replace meals. "*Playbook* is an entity unto itself, far more influential than anything in the rest of the *Politico*," Pfeiffer says.

If, for example, Axelrod can't read the papers before rushing off to the White House, he will scroll through *Playbook* during his six-block ride to work and probably be safe in his 7:30 meeting. At this pivotal hour, Allen is the oddball king of a changing political and media order—the frenetic epitome of a moment in which Washington can feel both exhilarating and very, very small.

. . .

I should disclose a few things: I have known Mike Allen for more than a decade. We worked together at the *Washington Post*, where I spent nine years and where I came to know VandeHei and Harris. We all have the same friends and run into each other a lot, and I have told them how much I admire what they have achieved at *Politico*. I like them all.

In other words, I write this from within the tangled web of "the community." I read *Playbook* every morning on my BlackBerry, usually while my copies of the *New York Times* and the *Washington Post* are in plastic bags. When Allen links to my stories, I see a happy uptick in readership. I have also been a source: after I "spotted" Treasury Secretary Tim Geithner at an organic Chinese restaurant in my neighborhood last year—picking up kung pao chicken with brown rice ("for Tim")—I dutifully e-mailed Allen with the breaking news.

*Playbook* is a descendant of political synopses like *National Journal*'s Hotline, ABC News's Note, and NBC News's First Read, all of which still enjoy junkie followings. But nothing of the ilk has embedded itself in the culture of Washington like *Playbook*—to a point where if somebody in Pfeiffer's department is celebrating a birthday, he is sure to send word to Allen so that everybody in the White House will know.

Allen sends out *Playbook* using Microsoft Outlook to a private mailing list of 3,000. A few minutes later, an automatic blast goes out to another 25,000 readers who signed up to receive it. An additional 3,000 or so enter *Playbook* from Politico.com, which adds up to a rough universe of 30,000 interested drivers, passengers, and eavesdroppers to the conversation.

*Playbook* started three years ago as a chatty "what's happening" memo that Allen sent to his *Politico* bosses. Eventually he started sending it to presidential-campaign officials—the first outside recipient was Howard Wolfson of Hillary Clinton's campaign. Soon Allen would send it to non-*Politico* journalists, White House officials, and, before long, anyone who asked. While most *Playbook* subscribers live around Washington, significant numbers work on Wall Street, in state capitals, and at news and entertainment companies on both coasts. Major retailers (Starbucks) and obscure lobbies (Catfish Farmers of America) pay $15,000 a week to advertise in *Playbook*, a figure that is expected to rise.

Readers describe their allegiance with a conspicuous degree of oversharing. "I definitely read it in bed," Katie Couric told me.

"Doesn't everybody read it in bed?" Margaret Carlson, a columnist for Bloomberg News and the Washington editor at large for *The Week* magazine, said in a video tribute to Allen for his forty-fifth birthday party last June. (For the record, the Republican lobbyist and party hostess Juleanna Glover said in the video that she reads *Playbook* "in my boudoir and while I'm blow-drying my hair.")

"I'd like to thank the Lord for the many blessings he brings me," Allen said at the party. "VandeHei thinks that's a reference to him."

·　　·　　·

"You don't have to do anything else, just read Mike Allen," Bob Woodward declared in February on *Morning Joe* in one of those statements that jab squarely into the ribs of traditional newspaper purveyors. Allen harbors a deep fondness and knowledge of the newspaper industry he might be helping to kill. Peter Watkins, a former press aide for President George W. Bush, recalls that when he told Allen he was from Davis County, Utah, Allen's instant reply was, "Oh, you must have read the *Davis County Clipper.*"

Part of the appeal and the absurdity of *Playbook* is that it imposes a small-town, small-paper sensibility onto a big, complicated city—Lake Wobegon with power. It is expressed in a dialect of "Sirens," "Shots" and "Chasers" that might as well be Mongolian to 99.9 percent of the electorate. To skim *Playbook* is to experience Washington in the midst of an attention-deficited conversation that can bounce from the Congressional Budget Office's score of the health care bill to news of a "state visit" from Feldman's parents (Jud and Sunny) to an all-caps directive that we all "ask Hari about his new puppy." And members of the *Playbook* community— which includes a former president, two former vice presidents,

CEOs, and network anchors—are assumed to know exactly who all these people are.

Allen is a master aggregator, which leads some to dismiss *Playbook* as a cut-and-paste exercise. But that ignores Allen's ability to break news (even if by only fifteen minutes), to cull from e-mail only *he* is receiving, to get early copies of books and magazines, and to pick out the prime nugget from the bottom of a pool report. He has a knack for selecting the "data points" that an info-saturated clan cares most about and did not know when it went to bed. *Playbook*'s politics are "aggressively neutral," and Allen says his are, too—he refuses to vote.

Just as many sources talk to Woodward because they assume everyone is, the White House will leak early talking points to Allen because they know that, for instance, Dick Cheney seems to have made Allen the go-to outlet for many of his criticisms of the current administration. Like Woodward, Allen can be tagged with the somewhat loaded moniker of "access journalist." Clearly the political and news establishments love him. The feeling is mutual and somewhat transactional. They use him and vice versa ("love" and "use" being mutually nonexclusive in Washington). He seems to know everyone and works at it.

Pfeiffer met Allen a decade ago. Over the years, Allen has sent Pfeiffer e-mail messages about things that he knew interested him (Georgetown basketball), just as Allen has served as a one-man Google-alert service for hundreds of friend-sources around town: news about the Redskins (to the Pentagon spokesman Geoff Morrell), about cuff links (to the Washington lawyer Robert Barnett, who collects them). I heard of a low-level economist who has met Allen only once or twice and yet receives from him forwarded wire stories about Asian currency.

Before there was e-mail, Allen would do this by fax; before there were fax machines, he would drop off newspaper clips (or entire out-of-town papers) to his friends' doorsteps. "He operates at such a faster speed than any of us and carries on many more relationships than any of us and so many more simultaneous conversations than any of us," Morrell says.

"The most successful journalists have their own unique brand and circle of friends," VandeHei, *Politico*'s executive editor, told me by e-mail. "This is the Facebook-ization of politics and D.C. The more friends or acquaintances you have, the more time you spend interacting with them via e-mail and I.M., the more information you get, move and market." VandeHei's conceit seems to equate Allen's circle of friends to a commodity—exactly the kind of mutual back-scratching undercurrent that gives "friendship" in Washington its quotation marks. It also reflects *Politico*'s penchant for placing itself at the vanguard of new media when in fact its business has been heavily sustained by ads in its print edition, distributed free in Washington. "*Playbook* is D.C.'s Facebook," VandeHei concluded. "And Mike's the most popular friend."

Allen spent his childhood in Seal Beach, Calif., in Orange County, the oldest of four—two boys, two girls. He told me he had an apolitical upbringing but wanted to attend college near Washington. He enrolled at Washington and Lee University in Lexington, Va., which he said seemed close to D.C. on a map. When he got there, Allen told me, he learned that the college was at least a five-hour Greyhound ride from the capital. He has told this story before, just the kind of recurring lore—a fun tale, a bit dubious—that surrounds Allen and that he surely cultivates. Until recently, the dominant spectacle of his cubicle at *Politico*'s Arlington, Va., offices was a giant birthday card signed by many members of the *Playbook* community. It featured a color cartoon of Allen as the mythological Sphinx and loomed over the real version as he typed, and typed.

•     •     •

People routinely wonder whether Allen actually lives somewhere besides the briefing rooms, newsrooms, campaign hotels, or going-away dinners for Senator So-and-So's press secretary that seem to be his perpetual regimen. And they wonder, "Does Mikey ever sleep?"

The query tires him. He claims he tries to sleep six hours a night, which seems unrealistic for someone who says he tries to wake at two or three A.M. to start *Playbook* after evenings that can include multiple stops (and trails of midnight-stamped e-mail). He supervises four predawn *Playbook* offshoots—*Pulse* (devoted to health care), *Morning Money* (financial news), *Morning Score* (midterm Congressional races), and *Huddle* (Congress)—often writes multiple stories a week for *Politico*, speaks all over the country, and makes relentless TV and radio appearances. I asked Allen if he slept during the day, and he said no.

Allen has been spotted dozing in public—campaign planes, parties—clutching his BlackBerry with two hands against his chest like a teddy bear. He has also been seen asleep over his laptop, only to snap awake into a full and desperate type, as if momentary slumber were just a blip in the 24/7 political story Mikey is writing. "I once called him with a client," Barnett told me in an e-mail message. "He was sound asleep. I am convinced he did the interview fully asleep. Nevertheless, he got every quote right."

Allen delights in being the cheerfully frantic public man. He refers to himself interchangeably with *Playbook*. "*Playbook* made our CBS hit this a.m. by slipping a Benjamin to a plow driver," Allen wrote to his readers on a snowy February morning. "Thank you, Ray."

No shortage of friends will testify to Mikey's thoughtful gestures, some in the extreme. They involve showing up at a friend's son's baseball game (in South Carolina) or driving from Richmond to New York to visit a fraternity brother and heading back the same night (dropping off the morning New York tabloids to friends in Richmond). When Watkins lost his grandfather, Allen appeared at the funeral in Kaysville, Utah, and filed a "pool report" for Watkins's friends and family.

He attends a nondenominational Protestant church and a Bible-study group. During the George W. Bush presidency, which Allen covered for the *Post*, he drew closer to some people in the administration through worship. "He is one of the most thoughtful people I have ever met," Josh Deckard, a former White House press aide, says. "Philippians 2:3 said, 'In humility, consider others better than yourselves,' and I think Mike exemplifies that better than anyone."

Yet even Allen's supposed confidants say that there is a part of Mikey they will never know or even ask about. He is obsessively private. He has given different dates to different friends for the date of his birthday. I asked three of Allen's close friends if they knew what his father did. One said "teacher," another said "football coach," and the third said "newspaper columnist." A 2000 profile of Allen in *The Columbia Journalism Review* described his late father as an "investor."

It is almost impossible to find anyone who has seen his home (a rented apartment, short walk to the office). "Never seen the apartment," volunteered Robert L. Allbritton, *Politico*'s publisher, midinterview. "No man's land." When sharing a cab, Allen is said to insist that the other party be dropped off first. One friend describes driving Allen home and having him get out at a corner; in the rearview mirror, the friend saw him hail a cab and set off in another direction. I've heard more than one instance of people who sent holiday cards to Allen's presumed address only to have them returned unopened. One former copy editor at *Politico*, Campbell Roth, happened to buy a Washington condominium a few years ago that Allen had just vacated. She told me the neighbors called the former tenant "brilliant but weird" and were "genuinely scared about some fire-code violation" based on the mountains of stuff inside.

Allen is known as a legendary hoarder and pack rat. At the *Post*, enormous piles of yellowing papers, clothes, bags and detritus leaned ominously above his cubicle. While reporters are rarely neat freaks (I remember hearing rumors about Nixon-era sandwiches that are still being excavated from David Broder's office), Allen's work areas have been egregious. It got so bad at *Time*, where Allen was given his own office, that it became difficult to even open the door. His chair was raised at a crooked angle, as if it were not touching the floor, and the debris rose so high in some places that it blocked a portion of light coming through a picture window. Colleagues took pictures, as if the place were an archaeological site. It was disturbing to those who cared about Allen, especially after a photo of the office in a seemingly uninhabitable state made the rounds of the press corps and George W. Bush's White House.

Friends and employers have taken on a kind of in-loco-parentis approach to some of Allen's needs—making sure he fills out forms to get his press credentials renewed and encouraging him to slow down. Allbritton says he will sometimes ask Harris and VandeHei: "Are you checking up on Mikey? Is he OK?" Allen's bosses at the *Post* helped him to recover some of the thousands of dollars in unclaimed expenses that he accrued during the 2004 presidential campaign. Close friends have intervened with him on occasion, worried that he is working nonstop and looking dreadful and that his life appears in disarray. Allen thanks them and tells them not to worry.

I asked Allen about his hoarding and clutter issues, and he wanted no part of the discussion. He assured me that the Internet had cured him. "Everything is online now," he explained, smiling, never mind that he was terrorizing building-maintenance types long after the Internet was here.

Allen has achieved a merger of life and work, family and *Playbook*. He is deeply committed to his mother, younger brother, two younger sisters, and eight nieces and nephews scattered on both coasts. They make *Playbook* cameos. He describes Harris and VandeHei as his two closest friends. Both are fiercely protective of Mikey and are students of him. "I've always felt he just, like, operates at levels that I couldn't even begin to fathom with my simple Wisconsin mind," says VandeHei, an Oshkosh native.

A former editor at the *Post* told me that Allen today seems to have taken refuge in his status as a public "brand." He deploys *Playbook* as a protective alter ego. It reminded me of something a senator said to me once—that a lot of politicians are shy, private people and that they enter the business because it allows them to remain shy and private behind a public persona. In a recent phone call, I asked Allen what his hobbies were. He paused, went off the record, and then came back with an unrevealing sound bite. "I'm a well-rounded person," he said, "who is interested in the community, interested in family, interested in sports, interested in the arts, interested in restaurants." I asked him what sports teams he roots for. "I'm not gonna do that," Allen said. "*Playbook* is ecumenical." He allowed that "an astute reader of *Playbook* will notice frequent references to the Packers, Red Sox, and Florida Gators."

·       ·       ·

At one point, I asked Allen if he would ever consider taking *Playbook* elsewhere. Surely he could sell the franchise for a sum that could easily exceed seven figures. (If *Politico* sells $15,000 in ads a week for *Playbook*, then Allen's newsletter alone brings an estimated $780,000 a year.) He was aghast at the question.

*Politico*'s offices are housed in the same place as Washington's ABC affiliate, owned by *Politico*'s corporate parent, Allbritton Communications. They feel more like a television studio than a newsroom. *Politico* reporters dart to and from their "hits" at the newsroom's TV camera. Kim Kingsley, the *Politico* executive vice president (and a former *Post* colleague of mine) is a tireless promoter of *Politico* stories, its reporters, and its brand. The publication has clearly exceeded the expectations of its founders and its naysayers. Copies of favorable press articles are framed on VandeHei's office wall, along with keepsakes from *Politico*'s mainstream incursion (a photo of himself moderating a presidential debate on CNN). VandeHei was elected last year to the Pulitzer Prize board.

Harris and VandeHei discussed the idea of starting an all-politics website while at the *Washington Post*. Harris, who is forty-six, had distinguished himself as a top-notch White House reporter during the Clinton years while VandeHei, who previously worked at the *Wall Street Journal* and *Roll Call*, was an aggressive and ambitious beat reporter. Allbritton, the forty-one-year-old scion to a Washington banking and media empire, approached VandeHei in 2006 about running a new Capitol Hill publication. VandeHei told Allbritton about his and Harris's idea, which Allbritton agreed to back. VandeHei's wife, Autumn, coined the name *Politico*.

Harris and VandeHei were bold in trying to lure journalistic "brands." Their "messaging" brimmed with sports analogies and swagger. VandeHei told the *New York Observer* before the site's debut that he had e-mail messages from reporters "begging for jobs" and that *Politico* would "show we're better than the *New York Times* and the *Washington Post*."

Their first target was Allen, an emerging presence on the web at *Time*. Throughout his career, he has been known as an unfailingly fair, fast, and prolific reporter with an insatiable need to be in the newspaper. "The worst thing you could say to Mike Allen was, 'We don't have space for that story,'" says Maralee Schwartz, the longtime political editor at the *Post*. "It was like telling a child he couldn't have his candy." Allen also struggled to write the front-page analytical stories that were the traditional preserve of newspaper "stars." Harris, who wrote many of these during his twenty-one years at the *Post*, says that the whirling production demands of today's news environment have caught up to Allen's sleepless, spaceless peculiarities.

Before I covered politics, I wrote about Silicon Valley. Hearing Harris talk, I was reminded of the engineers at the height of the web explosion in the 1990s—socially eccentric geniuses who suddenly became the wealthy kings of the culture. Technology had caught up to their wiring. They often worked through several nights straight and never seemed to notice or mind. They were mostly male and single. The real prodigies appeared to achieve total synergy with the machines, just as Allen seems the perfect mental and metabolic match for today's news cycle.

*Politico's* start-up culture tolerates idiosyncrasies better than more established businesses do, Allbritton told me. "It's like you understand a little more," he said. "We all have the wacky uncle."

·　　·　　·

VandeHei, who is thirty-nine, reminds me more of a venture capitalist these days. His mind appears to be constantly somersaulting with business models and management philosophies. A boyish-faced Packers fanatic, he is the more emotional and excitable half of the duo known as VandeHarris. He wears a chip on his shoulder plainly about established news organizations, and you sense that he takes the White House's apparent disregard for *Politico* personally.

"The Obama theory seems to be that the New York Times, big-name opinion writers and big shots on network news still largely shape how people think about policy, politics and news," Vande-Hei wrote to me in an e-mail message. "It's why White House officials spend so much time on the phone with your reporters

(N.Y.T.)—and yet has had little effect on how the public sees the president."

By any measure, *Politico* employs several top-rank journalists, including the political writer Ben Smith, the Congressional reporter David Rogers, and the political reporter Jonathan Martin. Allen has broken some of *Politico*'s biggest stories. He reported that the *Post* was planning to hold paid salons for lobbyists at the home of its publisher, Katharine Weymouth, setting off a firestorm. During the 2008 campaign, he asked John McCain how many homes he owned (eight properties, and it proved a major embarrassment to McCain when he could not immediately answer).

*Politico*'s comprehensive aims can make it goofy and unapologetically trivial at times. A recent item by a Congressional blogger for the site consisted of the following: "Lights are out throughout much of the Longworth House Office Building, a denizen tells me. UPDATE: They are back on."

The site's reporters are mostly young, eager to impress, and driven hard. Predawn why-don't-we-have-this? e-mail messages from editors are common. Working for *Politico* is "like tackle football," VandeHei reminds people, which might explain why most of *Politico*'s best-known bylines are male. The main players have Little League nicknames (Vandy, JMart), use the same terminology, and, strangely, share the same speech affect. I noticed that at least five of them (Allbritton, Harris, VandeHei, Allen, and Martin), when trying to make a point, tended to elongate their vowels in a half-mouthed Midwesternish twang—think Bob Dylan working a wad of chewing tobacco.

In early March, a Web site called Xtranormal featured a spoof about life at the "Politicave," starring computerized automatons of VandeHei and Allen (dressed in a superhero costume). After the VandeHei cartoon addressed Allen as "Mike," Allen replied: "Jim, for the last time, I am not Mike Allen. I am News Cycle Man, here to win the morning!" Allen went on to inform VandeHei about "that unpaid intern who is still crying about when you told her she would never make it in this business if she insists on taking bathroom breaks every day." The spot gave voice to a belief that *Politico*'s cultlike mission demands a freakish devotion that only an action-hero workaholic could achieve. "A page-view sweat-shop" is how one *Politico* writer described the place to me.

Several current and former *Politico* employees were eager to relay their resentment of the place to me, though with a few exceptions, none for attribution. "It's not so much the sweatshoppery itself that I minded," said Ryan Grim, a former *Politico* reporter who is now at the *Huffington Post*. "It was the arbitrary nature of how it was applied." Kingsley, the *Politico* executive vice president, e-mailed me an unsolicited defense: "In my experience, the people who whine about working at *Politico* shouldn't be at *Politico*," she wrote. "They likely lack the metabolism and professional drive it takes to thrive here. For those of us who love a fast pace and a tough challenge, this place is a calling, not a job."

Harris readily acknowledges that *Politico* is "not for everybody," and VandeHei said they have begun focusing their recruiting on New York because "the city produces reporters who are fearless, fast, and ruthlessly competitive."

While journalism breeds a higher-than-average population of bellyachers, turnover was especially high at *Politico* in late March and early April—five reporters and one editor announced they were leaving, including the White House reporter Nia-Malika Henderson (to the *Washington Post*), who had been the only African American on a staff of about fifty reporters. "The natural order of things" is how Harris describes the departures. He said *Politico* is trying to "mature from start-up mode" in a number of areas, including diversity.

*Politico*'s gold standard is a reporter's "metabolism," measured by speed, proficiency and the ephemeral currency of "buzz." But *Politico*'s buzz can also derive from provocative headlines placed atop thinly sourced stories. In February, for instance, *Politico* published a story about apparent tension between President

Obama and Nancy Pelosi. The story—bylined by Allen and Patrick O'Connor—made its assertions based largely on a single anonymous source and was refuted or seriously played down by two on-the-record sources. Nonetheless, *Politico* played it big on its website, under the headline "Family Feud," and multiple stories ensued on cable and online.

More recently, Allen asked in his April 10 *Playbook*: "Good Saturday morning: For brunch convo: Why isn't Secretary Clinton on the media short lists for the Court?" By Monday, the convo had moved from the brunch table to *Morning Joe* (where the host, Joe Scarborough, advocated for her) and *Today* (where the Republican senator Orrin Hatch mentioned her, too). Later that day, *Politico*'s Ben Smith quoted a State Department spokesman who "threw some coolish water on the Clinton-for-Scotus buzz in an e-mail." By then, the cable and blog chatter was fully blown. The White House issued a highly unusual statement that Secretary Clinton would not be nominated. *Politico* then sent out a "breaking news alert," and Smith reported that the White House had "hurriedly punctured the trial balloon." End of convo.

For what it's worth, Philippe Reines, a Clinton adviser, says that he told another *Politico* reporter the previous Friday that the chances of his boss's being nominated were "less than none" and added, "Something being a sexy media story shouldn't be confused with truth."

Political operatives I speak to tend to deploy the word "use" a lot in connection with *Politico*; as in, they "use" the publication to traffic certain stories they know they could not or would not get published elsewhere. I was also struck by how freely VandeHei threw out the word "market" in connection with how newsmakers and sources interacted with *Politico*. "If you want to move data or shape opinion," VandeHei wrote to me by e-mail, "you market it through Mikey and Playbook, because those tens of thousands that matter most all read it and most feed it. Or you market it through someone else at Politico, which will make damn sure its audience of insiders and compulsives read it and blog about it; and that it gets linked around and talked about on TV programs."

By and large, the most common rap against *Politico* concerns its modeled-on-ESPN sensibility. While Harris and VandeHei say—rightly—that *Politico* has devoted lots of space and effort to, say, the health-care debate, many of its prominent stories on the subject followed a reductive, who's-up-who's-down formula. ("No Clear Winner in Seven-Hour Gabfest," read the headline over the main article about President Obama's health-care meeting.) Harris and VandeHei have clearly succeeded in driving the conversation, although the more complicated question is exactly where they are driving it.

"I've been in Washington about thirty years," Mark Salter, a former chief of staff and top campaign aide to John McCain, says. "And here's the surprising reality: On any given day, not much happens. It's just the way it is." Not so in the world of *Politico*, he says, where meetings in which senators act like themselves (maybe sarcastic or short) become "tension filled" affairs. "They have taken every worst trend in reporting, every single one of them, and put them on rocket fuel," Salter says. "It's the shortening of the news cycle. It's the trivialization of news. It's the gossipy nature of news. It's the self-promotion."

Salter asked that if I quoted him, I also mention that he likes and respects many *Politico* reporters, beginning with Mike Allen.

·       ·       ·

On a recent Friday night, a couple hundred influentials gathered for a Mardi Gras–themed birthday party for Betsy Fischer, the executive producer of *Meet the Press*. Held at the Washington home of the lobbyist Jack Quinn, the party was a classic Suck-Up

City affair in which everyone seemed to be congratulating one another on some recent story, book deal, show, or haircut (and, by the way, your boss is doing a swell job, and maybe we could do an interview).

McAuliffe, the former Democratic National Committee chairman, arrived after the former Republican National Committee chairman Ed Gillespie left. Fox News's Greta Van Susteren had David Axelrod pinned into a corner near a tower of cupcakes. In the basement, a very white, bipartisan Soul Train was getting down to hip-hop. David Gregory, the *Meet the Press* host, and *Newsweek*'s Jon Meacham gave speeches about Fischer. Over by the jambalaya, Alan Greenspan picked up some Mardi Gras beads and placed them around the neck of his wife, NBC's Andrea Mitchell, who bristled and quickly removed them. Allen was there too, of course, but he vanished after a while—sending an e-mail message later, thanking me for coming.

In late March, we met for breakfast at Washington's Mayflower Hotel. He brought with him two recent copies of the *San Jose Mercury News* because he knew I used to work there, and he had just been in the Bay Area. He became animated when discussing a long-ago reporting job in Fredericksburg, Va. His favorite story there was headlined, "Hot Dog: A Meal or a Snack?" The county board of supervisors was debating whether hot-dog sales should include a meal tax. "Every single thing that I've written since then," Allen said, "whether it's about a mayor or a governor or senator or president, it all boils down to, 'Hot Dog: A Meal or a Snack?' All great questions come from small questions."

Like a lot of reporters, Allen would much rather ask the questions than answer them. He led off with one: "What's the most surprising thing you learned about me?"

It was what I learned about his father, I told him. Gary Allen was an icon of the far right in the 1960s and 1970s. He was affiliated with the John Birch Society and railed against the "big lies" that led to U.S. involvement in World Wars I and II. He denounced the evils of the Trilateral Commission and "Red Teachers." Rock'n'roll was a "Pavlovian Communist mind-control plot." He wrote speeches for George Wallace, the segregationist governor of Alabama and presidential candidate. "Gary Allen is one of the most popular writers that John Birchites read and believe with a zeal that is nervous-making," wrote Nicholas von Hoffman in a 1972 *Washington Post* column. He wrote mail-order books and pamphlets distributed through a John Birch mailing list.

None of Mike Allen's friends seemed to know any of this about his father, or they were diverting me with other monikers (like "football coach," which he indeed was; Gary Allen coached a Pop Warner team that included Mike, who played center, badly). In an earlier phone interview, Allen said his mother was a first-grade teacher and his dad was a "writer" and "speaker." After I mentioned his father at breakfast, Allen flashed a sudden, teeth-clenched smile that stayed frozen as I spoke. He had described his upbringing to me as nonpolitical. And maybe it was. People who knew Gary Allen, who died of complications from diabetes in 1986, described him as quiet and introspective. "He was more outspoken in his writing," says Dan Lungren, a Republican member of Congress, who represented Orange County back then and knew the family. Lungren, who now represents a district that includes parts of Sacramento, said that the Allens hosted a meet-and-greet at their home for one of his early campaigns.

I asked Mike Allen what it was like being his father's son. "We have a very close family," he said slowly. "I'm very close to all my siblings, and I'm very grateful to my parents for all the emphasis they put on education and family and sports and Scouts." He called his father "a great dad." How did he make his living? "I don't know the details of it," Allen said. He did some teaching, but Allen said he was not sure where or what age groups, whether elementary school or high school or something else. He had an office at home. "To me, he was my dad. So that's what I knew." He says he never read anything his father wrote.

After some fidgety minutes, I asked Allen how he became an Eagle Scout. His eyes softened and stopped blinking as much as they had been, and his voice took on the cadence of solemn recital. He uttered the Boy Scout Law: "A scout is trustworthy," Allen proclaimed, "loyal, helpful, friendly, courteous, kind, obedient, cheerful, thrifty, brave, clean, and reverent."

I asked Allen if I could talk to his siblings. He said he would consider it and maybe set up a conference call but never did. I did not press. It felt intrusive. Nor did I want to overreach for a Rosebud. "Life isn't binary," Allen said a few times at breakfast, in the context of whether a hot dog is a meal or a snack and later in the context of what his father was like. But I could not help being struck by the contrast between father and son.

Gary Allen's writings conveyed great distrust of the established order. He saw conspiracies in both parties, despised Richard Nixon and Henry Kissinger for their internationalism and the "establishment media" for enabling the "communist conspiracy." Mike Allen traverses politics with a boyish and almost star-struck quality toward the assumed order. He is diligent in addressing leaders by proper titles, ranks, "Madam Speakers" and "Mr. Presidents" (a scout is reverent). Friends said he seemed particularly enthralled to be covering the White House during the Bush years and was spotted at all hours around the briefing room and press area.

Allen views *Playbook* as a respite from the chaos and invective of the daily news cycle. And at the end of our discussion about his father, he made a point of ending on a sweet and orderly data point. After Gary Allen died, at fifty, many of his former Pop Warner players filled the church in tribute. Allen said he recalled no talk of his father's political work at the memorial, but he will never forget one detail: a giant blue and gold floral arrangement in the shape of a football was placed onstage, a gift from the kids on Gary Allen's team, the Phantoms.

•        •        •

One of the few times I can recall Allen stepping out of his friendly scoutmaster persona in *Playbook* was when he dismissed a Sunday column by the public editor in the *New York Times* as "a bit of a snore." The column was about how reporters should not use the *Times* to, among other things, plug their friends. "O.K., then!" Allen wrote to conclude the item.

Allen clearly plugs his friends in *Playbook*—quoting from press releases announcing their new jobs ("Taylor Griffin Joins Hamilton Place Strategies as Partner"), referring to pal Katie Couric as a "media icon," reporting that the model car built by Ethan Gibbs, the six-year-old son of Robert Gibbs, finished second in the Cub Scouts' Pinewood Derby. Isn't part of the function of *Playbook* to plug Mike Allen's friends? "I wouldn't agree with that," Allen told me. "*Playbook* is to serve its audience and community, and we serve them by giving them information they need and want. If it were the way you describe it, people wouldn't read it." Recognition of a friend's milestone can also be a data point. People in this tiny world care if two of their own (say, the Democratic operatives Phil Singer and Kim Molstre) have a baby ("Introducing Max George Singer," *Playbook*, March 18).

Allen's focus is customer service. He wants to "spread joy" as the Holy Ghost of the Almighty News Cycle. "I am fortunate," he keeps saying. (Hat Tip: God.)

In early March, I was meeting with Harris in his office when Allen walked in. He welcomed me, thanked me for coming, and returned to his desk to finish a story or six. I visited his cubicle, but Allen was gone. His work area was notable for its lack of clutter—there were a few small stacks of magazines and newspapers and a tray of mint Girl Scout cookies on the top of his terminal. To the left of his desktop was a picture of Allen standing upright and asking President Obama a question at a White House news conference.

In the days leading up to a photo shoot for this article, Allen's work area became spotless, surfaces shining, befitting News Cycle Man. The poster of the cartoon sphinx had been removed. I kept asking Kingsley, "Who cleaned up Mikey's room?" but neither she nor Allen would say. All great questions come from small questions. And some just hang there, until they vanish.

## Rolling Stone

FINALIST—REPORTING

*If fury is any gauge, 2010 was an extraordinary year for magazine reporting. Each of the five finalists for the National Magazine Award for Reporting elicited strong reactions, but only one led directly to the resignation of a four-star general. Michael Hastings was a thirty-year-old reporter best known for his reporting from Iraq—where his fiancée, Andrea Parhamovich, had died in an insurgents' ambush—when he got the opportunity to spend several days with General Stanley McChrystal and his aides while they were grounded in Europe by the eruption of the volcano Eyjafjallajökull. The story that resulted caused an explosion of its own, not only toppling McChrystal but inspiring debate on journalistic ethics (had Hastings broken the rules of the game, or did his story betray the corruption of the establishment media?). Yet as the National Magazine Award judges said, Hastings's real subject wasn't McChrystal at all "but our ill-considered war in Afghanistan— a story he pursued with insight and energy."*

Michael Hastings

# The Runaway General

"How'd I get screwed into going to this dinner?" demands Gen. Stanley McChrystal. It's a Thursday night in mid-April, and the commander of all U.S. and NATO forces in Afghanistan is sitting in a four-star suite at the Hôtel Westminster in Paris. He's in France to sell his new war strategy to our NATO allies—to keep up the fiction, in essence, that we actually *have* allies. Since McChrystal took over a year ago, the Afghan war has become the exclusive property of the United States. Opposition to the war has already toppled the Dutch government, forced the resignation of Germany's president, and sparked both Canada and the Netherlands to announce the withdrawal of their 4,500 troops. McChrystal is in Paris to keep the French, who have lost more than forty soldiers in Afghanistan, from going all wobbly on him.

"The dinner comes with the position, sir," says his chief of staff, Col. Charlie Flynn.

McChrystal turns sharply in his chair.

"Hey, Charlie," he asks, "does this come with the position?"

McChrystal gives him the middle finger.

The general stands and looks around the suite that his traveling staff of ten has converted into a full-scale operations center. The tables are crowded with silver Panasonic Toughbooks, and blue cables crisscross the hotel's thick carpet, hooked up to satellite dishes to provide encrypted phone and e-mail communications. Dressed in off-the-rack civilian casual—blue tie, button-down shirt, dress slacks—McChrystal is way out of his comfort zone. Paris, as one of his advisers says, is the "most anti-McChrystal city you can imagine." The general hates fancy restaurants, rejecting any place with candles on the tables as too "Gucci." He prefers Bud Light Lime (his favorite beer) to Bordeaux, *Talladega Nights* (his favorite movie) to Jean-Luc Godard. Besides, the public eye has never been a place where McChrystal felt comfortable: Before President Obama put him in charge of the war in Afghanistan, he spent five years running the Pentagon's most secretive black ops.

"What's the update on the Kandahar bombing?" McChrystal asks Flynn. The city has been rocked by two massive car bombs in the past day alone, calling into question the general's assurances that he can wrest it from the Taliban.

"We have two KIAs, but that hasn't been confirmed," Flynn says.

McChrystal takes a final look around the suite. At fifty-five, he is gaunt and lean, not unlike an older version of Christian Bale in *Rescue Dawn*. His slate-blue eyes have the unsettling ability to *drill down* when they lock on you. If you've fucked up or disappointed him, they can destroy your soul without the need for him to raise his voice.

"I'd rather have my ass kicked by a roomful of people than go out to this dinner," McChrystal says.

He pauses a beat.

"Unfortunately," he adds, "no one in this room could do it."

With that, he's out the door.

"Who's he going to dinner with?" I ask one of his aides.

"Some French minister," the aide tells me. "It's fucking gay."

The next morning, McChrystal and his team gather to prepare for a speech he is giving at the École Militaire, a French military academy. The general prides himself on being sharper and ballsier than anyone else, but his brashness comes with a price: Although McChrystal has been in charge of the war for only a year, in that short time he has managed to piss off almost everyone with a stake in the conflict. Last fall, during the question-and-answer session following a speech he gave in London, McChrystal dismissed the counterterrorism strategy being advocated by Vice President Joe Biden as "shortsighted," saying it would lead to a state of "Chaos-istan." The remarks earned him a smackdown from the president himself, who summoned the general to a terse private meeting aboard Air Force One. The message to McChrystal seemed clear: *Shut the fuck up, and keep a lower profile.*

Now, flipping through printout cards of his speech in Paris, McChrystal wonders aloud what Biden question he might get today, and how he should respond. "I never know what's going to pop out until I'm up there, that's the problem," he says. Then, unable to help themselves, he and his staff imagine the general dismissing the vice president with a good one-liner.

"Are you asking about Vice President Biden?" McChrystal says with a laugh. "Who's that?"

"Biden?" suggests a top adviser. "Did you say: Bite Me?"

$\bullet$     $\bullet$     $\bullet$

When Barack Obama entered the Oval Office, he immediately set out to deliver on his most important campaign promise on foreign policy: to refocus the war in Afghanistan on what led us to invade in the first place. "I want the American people to understand," he announced in March 2009. "We have a clear and focused goal: to disrupt, dismantle, and defeat Al Qaeda in Pakistan and Afghanistan." He ordered another 21,000 troops to Kabul, the largest increase since the war began in 2001. Taking the advice of both the Pentagon and the Joint Chiefs of Staff, he also fired Gen. David McKiernan—then the U.S. and NATO commander in Afghanistan—and replaced him with a man he didn't know and had met only briefly: Gen. Stanley McChrystal. It was the first time a top general had been relieved from duty during wartime in more than fifty years, since Harry Truman fired Gen. Douglas MacArthur at the height of the Korean War.

Even though he had voted for Obama, McChrystal and his new commander in chief failed from the outset to connect. The general first encountered Obama a week after he took office, when the president met with a dozen senior military officials in a room at the Pentagon known as the Tank. According to sources familiar with the meeting, McChrystal thought Obama looked "uncomfortable and intimidated" by the roomful of military brass. Their first one-on-one meeting took place in the Oval Office four months later, after McChrystal got the Afghanistan job, and it didn't go much better. "It was a ten-minute photo op," says an adviser to McChrystal. "Obama clearly didn't know anything about him, who he was. Here's the guy who's going to run his fucking war, but he didn't seem very engaged. The Boss was pretty disappointed."

From the start, McChrystal was determined to place his personal stamp on Afghanistan, to use it as a laboratory for a controversial military strategy known as counterinsurgency. COIN, as the theory is known, is the new gospel of the Pentagon brass, a doctrine that attempts to square the military's preference for high-tech violence with the demands of fighting protracted wars in failed states. COIN calls for sending huge numbers of ground troops to not only destroy the enemy, but to live among the civilian population and slowly rebuild, or build from scratch, another nation's government—a process that even its staunchest advocates admit requires years, if not decades, to achieve. The theory essentially rebrands the military, expanding its authority (and its funding) to encompass the diplomatic and political sides of warfare: Think the Green Berets as an armed Peace Corps. In 2006, after Gen. David Petraeus beta-tested the theory during his "surge" in Iraq, it quickly gained a hardcore following of think-tankers, journalists, military officers, and civilian officials. Nicknamed "COINdinistas" for their cultish zeal, this influential cadre believed the doctrine would be the perfect solution for Afghanistan. All they needed was a general with enough charisma and political savvy to implement it.

As McChrystal leaned on Obama to ramp up the war, he did it with the same fearlessness he used to track down terrorists in Iraq: Figure out how your enemy operates, be faster and more ruthless than everybody else, then take the fuckers out. After arriving in Afghanistan last June, the general conducted his own policy review, ordered up by Defense Secretary Robert Gates. The now-infamous report was leaked to the press, and its conclusion was dire: If we didn't send another 40,000 troops—swelling the number of U.S. forces in Afghanistan by nearly half—we were in danger of "mission failure." The White House was furious. McChrystal, they felt, was trying to bully Obama, opening him up to charges of being weak on national security unless he did what the general wanted. It was Obama versus the Pentagon, and the Pentagon was determined to kick the president's ass.

Last fall, with his top general calling for more troops, Obama launched a three-month review to reevaluate the strategy in Afghanistan. "I found that time painful," McChrystal tells me in one of several lengthy interviews. "I was selling an unsellable position." For the general, it was a crash course in Beltway politics—a battle that pitted him against experienced Washington insiders like Vice President Biden, who argued that a prolonged counterinsurgency campaign in Afghanistan would plunge America into a military quagmire without weakening international terrorist networks. "The entire COIN strategy is a fraud perpetuated on the American people," says Douglas Macgregor, a retired colonel and leading critic of counterinsurgency who attended West Point with McChrystal. "The idea that we are going to spend a trillion dollars to reshape the culture of the Islamic world is utter nonsense.

In the end, however, McChrystal got almost exactly what he wanted. On December 1, in a speech at West Point, the president laid out all the reasons why fighting the war in Afghanistan is a bad idea: It's expensive; we're in an economic crisis; a decade-long commitment would sap American power; Al Qaeda has shifted its base of operations to Pakistan. Then, without ever using the words "victory" or "win," Obama announced that he would send an additional 30,000 troops to Afghanistan, almost as many as McChrystal had requested. The president had thrown his weight, however hesitantly, behind the counterinsurgency crowd.

Today, as McChrystal gears up for an offensive in southern Afghanistan, the prospects for any kind of success look bleak. In June, the death toll for U.S. troops passed 1,000, and the number of IEDs has doubled. Spending hundreds of billions of dollars on the fifth-poorest country on earth has failed to win over the civilian population, whose attitude toward U.S. troops ranges from intensely wary to openly hostile. The biggest military operation of the year—a ferocious offensive that began in February to retake the southern town of Marja—continues to drag on, prompting McChrystal himself to refer to it as a "bleeding ulcer." In June, Afghanistan officially outpaced Vietnam as the longest war in American history—and Obama has quietly begun to back away from the deadline he set for withdrawing U.S. troops in July of next year. The president finds himself stuck in something even more insane than a quagmire: a quagmire he knowingly walked into, even though it's precisely the kind of gigantic, mind-numbing, multigenerational nation-building project he explicitly said he didn't want.

Even those who support McChrystal and his strategy of counterinsurgency know that whatever the general manages to accomplish in Afghanistan, it's going to look more like Vietnam than Desert Storm. "It's not going to look like a win, smell like a win, or taste like a win," says Maj. Gen. Bill Mayville, who serves as chief of operations for McChrystal. "This is going to end in an argument."

.    .    .

The night after his speech in Paris, McChrystal and his staff head to Kitty O'Shea's, an Irish pub catering to tourists, around the corner from the hotel. His wife, Annie, has joined him for a rare visit: Since the Iraq War began in 2003, she has seen her husband less than thirty days a year. Though it is his and Annie's thirty-third wedding anniversary, McChrystal has invited his inner circle along for dinner and drinks at the "least Gucci" place his staff could find. His wife isn't surprised. "He once took me to a Jack in the Box when I was dressed in formalwear," she says with a laugh.

The general's staff is a handpicked collection of killers, spies, geniuses, patriots, political operators, and outright maniacs. There's a former head of British Special Forces, two Navy Seals, an Afghan Special Forces commando, a lawyer, two fighter pilots, and at least two dozen combat veterans and counterinsurgency experts. They jokingly refer to themselves as Team America, taking the name from the *South Park*–esque sendup of military cluelessness, and they pride themselves on their can-do attitude and their disdain for authority. After arriving in Kabul last summer, Team America set about changing the culture of the International Security Assistance Force, as the NATO-led mission is known. (U.S. soldiers had taken to deriding ISAF as short for "I Suck at Fighting" or "In Sandals and Flip-Flops.") McChrystal banned alcohol on base, kicked out Burger King and other symbols of American excess, expanded the morning briefing to include thousands of officers, and refashioned the command center into a Situational Awareness Room, a free-flowing information hub modeled after Mayor Mike Bloomberg's offices in New York.

He also set a manic pace for his staff, becoming legendary for sleeping four hours a night, running seven miles each morning, and eating one meal a day. (In the month I spend around the general, I witness him eating only once.) It's a kind of super-human narrative that has built up around him, a staple in almost every media profile, as if the ability to go without sleep and food translates into the possibility of a man single-handedly winning the war.

By midnight at Kitty O'Shea's, much of Team America is completely shitfaced. Two officers do an Irish jig mixed with steps from a traditional Afghan wedding dance, while McChrystal's top advisers lock arms and sing a slurred song of their own invention. "*Afghanistan!*" they bellow. "*Afghanistan!*" They call it their Afghanistan song.

McChrystal steps away from the circle, observing his team. "All these men," he tells me. "I'd die for them. And they'd die for me."

The assembled men may look and sound like a bunch of combat veterans letting off steam, but in fact this tight-knit group represents the most powerful force shaping U.S. policy in Afghanistan. While McChrystal and his men are in indisputable command of all military aspects of the war, there is no equivalent position on the diplomatic or political side. Instead, an assortment of administration players compete over the Afghan portfolio: U.S. Ambassador Karl Eikenberry, Special Representative to Afghanistan Richard Holbrooke, National Security Advisor Jim Jones, and Secretary of State Hillary Clinton, not to mention forty or so other coalition ambassadors and a host of talking heads who try to insert themselves into the mess, from John Kerry to John McCain. This diplomatic incoherence has effectively allowed McChrystal's team to call the shots and hampered efforts to build a stable and credible government in Afghanistan. "It jeopardizes the mission," says Stephen Biddle, a senior fellow at the Council on Foreign Relations who supports McChrystal. "The military cannot by itself create governance reform."

Part of the problem is structural: The Defense Department budget exceeds $600 billion a year while the State Department receives only $50 billion. But part of the problem is personal: In private, Team McChrystal likes to talk shit about many of Obama's top people on the diplomatic side. One aide calls Jim Jones, a retired four-star general and veteran of the Cold War, a "clown" who remains "stuck in 1985." Politicians like McCain and Kerry, says another aide, "turn up, have a meeting with Karzai, criticize him at the airport press conference, then get back for the Sunday talk shows. Frankly, it's not very helpful." Only Hillary Clinton receives good reviews from McChrystal's inner circle. "Hillary had Stan's back during the strategic review," says an adviser. "She said, 'If Stan wants it, give him what he needs.'"

McChrystal reserves special skepticism for Holbrooke, the official in charge of reintegrating the Taliban. "The Boss says he's like a wounded animal," says a member of the general's team. "Holbrooke keeps hearing rumors that he's going to get fired, so that makes him dangerous. He's a brilliant guy, but he just comes in, pulls on a lever, whatever he can grasp onto. But this is COIN, and you can't just have someone yanking on shit."

At one point on his trip to Paris, McChrystal checks his Black-Berry. "Oh, not another e-mail from Holbrooke," he groans. "I don't even want to open it." He clicks on the message and reads the salutation out loud, then stuffs the BlackBerry back in his pocket, not bothering to conceal his annoyance.

"Make sure you don't get any of that on your leg," an aide jokes, referring to the e-mail.

•   •   •

By far the most crucial—and strained—relationship is between McChrystal and Eikenberry, the U.S. ambassador. According to those close to the two men, Eikenberry—a retired three-star general who served in Afghanistan in 2002 and 2005—can't stand that his former subordinate is now calling the shots. He's also furious that McChrystal, backed by NATO's allies, refused to put Eikenberry in the pivotal role of viceroy in Afghanistan, which would have made him the diplomatic equivalent of the general. The job instead went to British Ambassador Mark Sedwill—a move that effectively increased McChrystal's influence over diplomacy by shutting out a powerful rival. "In reality, that position needs to be filled by an American for it to have weight," says a U.S. official familiar with the negotiations.

The relationship was further strained in January, when a classified cable that Eikenberry wrote was leaked to the *New York Times*. The cable was as scathing as it was prescient. The ambassador offered a brutal critique of McChrystal's strategy, dismissed President Hamid Karzai as "not an adequate strategic partner," and cast doubt on whether the counterinsurgency plan would be "sufficient" to deal with Al Qaeda. "We will become more deeply engaged here with no way to extricate ourselves," Eikenberry warned, "short of allowing the country to descend again into lawlessness and chaos."

McChrystal and his team were blindsided by the cable. "I like Karl, I've known him for years, but they'd never said anything like that to us before," says McChrystal, who adds that he felt "betrayed" by the leak. "Here's one that covers his flank for the history books. Now if we fail, they can say, 'I told you so.'"

The most striking example of McChrystal's usurpation of diplomatic policy is his handling of Karzai. It is McChrystal, not diplomats like Eikenberry or Holbrooke, who enjoys the best relationship with the man America is relying on to lead Afghanistan. The doctrine of counterinsurgency requires a credible government, and since Karzai is not considered credible by his own people, McChrystal has worked hard to make him so. Over the past few months, he has accompanied the president on more than ten trips around the country, standing beside him at political meetings, or *shuras*, in Kandahar. In February, the day before the doomed offensive in Marja, McChrystal even drove over to the president's palace to get him to sign off on what would be the largest military operation of the year. Karzai's staff, however, insisted that the president was sleeping off a cold and could not be disturbed. After several hours of haggling, McChrystal finally enlisted the aid of Afghanistan's defense minister, who persuaded Karzai's people to wake the president from his nap.

This is one of the central flaws with McChrystal's counterinsurgency strategy: The need to build a credible government puts us at the mercy of whatever tin-pot leader we've backed—a danger that Eikenberry explicitly warned about in his cable. Even Team McChrystal privately acknowledges that Karzai is a less-than-ideal partner. "He's been locked up in his palace the past year," laments one of the general's top advisers. At times, Karzai himself has actively undermined McChrystal's desire to put him in charge. During a recent visit to Walter Reed Army Medical Center, Karzai met three U.S. soldiers who had been wounded in Uruzgan province. "General," he called out to McChrystal, "I didn't even know we were fighting in Uruzgan!"

.       .       .

Growing up as a military brat, McChrystal exhibited the mixture of brilliance and cockiness that would follow him throughout his career. His father fought in Korea and Vietnam, retiring as a two-star general, and his four brothers all joined the armed services. Moving around to different bases, McChrystal took solace in baseball, a sport in which he made no pretense of hiding his superiority: in Little League, he would call out strikes to the crowd before whipping a fastball down the middle.

McChrystal entered West Point in 1972, when the U.S. military was close to its all-time low in popularity. His class was the last to graduate before the academy started to admit women. The "Prison on the Hudson," as it was known then, was a potent mix of testosterone, hooliganism, and reactionary patriotism. Cadets repeatedly trashed the mess hall in food fights, and birthdays were celebrated with a tradition called "rat fucking," which often left the birthday boy outside in the snow or mud, covered in shaving cream. "It was pretty out of control," says Lt. Gen. David Barno, a classmate who went on to serve as the top commander in Afghanistan from 2003 to 2005. The class, filled with what Barno calls "huge talent" and "wild-eyed teenagers with a strong sense of idealism," also produced Gen. Ray Odierno, the current commander of U.S. forces in Iraq.

The son of a general, McChrystal was also a ringleader of the campus dissidents—a dual role that taught him how to thrive in a rigid, top-down environment while thumbing his nose at authority every chance he got. He accumulated more than one hundred hours of demerits for drinking, partying, and insubordination—a record that his classmates boasted made him a "century man." One classmate, who asked not to be named, recalls finding McChrystal passed out in the shower after downing a case of beer he had hidden under the sink. The troublemaking almost got him kicked out, and he spent hours subjected to forced marches in the Area, a paved courtyard where unruly cadets were disciplined. "I'd come visit, and I'd end up spending most of my time in the library, while Stan was in the Area," recalls Annie, who began dating McChrystal in 1973.

McChrystal wound up ranking 298 out of a class of 855, a serious underachievement for a man widely regarded as brilliant. His most compelling work was extracurricular: As managing editor of *The Pointer*, the West Point literary magazine, McChrystal wrote seven short stories that eerily foreshadow many of the issues he would confront in his career. In one tale, a fictional officer complains about the difficulty of training foreign troops to fight; in another, a nineteen-year-old soldier kills a boy he mistakes for a terrorist. In "Brinkman's Note," a piece of suspense fiction, the unnamed narrator appears to be trying to stop a plot to assassinate the president. It turns out, however, that the narrator himself is the assassin, and he's able to infiltrate the White House: "The President strode in smiling. From the right coat pocket of the raincoat I carried, I slowly drew forth my 32-caliber pistol. In Brinkman's failure, I had succeeded."

After graduation, 2nd Lt. Stanley McChrystal entered an army that was all but broken in the wake of Vietnam. "We really felt we were a peacetime generation," he recalls. "There was the Gulf War, but even that didn't feel like that big of a deal." So McChrystal spent his career where the action was: He enrolled in Special Forces school and became a regimental commander of the Third Ranger Battalion in 1986. It was a dangerous position, even in peacetime—nearly two dozen rangers were killed in training accidents during the eighties. It was also an unorthodox career path: Most soldiers who want to climb the ranks to general don't go into the rangers. Displaying a penchant for transforming systems he considers outdated, McChrystal set out to revolutionize the training regime for the rangers. He introduced mixed martial arts, required every soldier to qualify with night-vision goggles on the rifle range, and forced troops to build up their endurance with weekly marches involving heavy backpacks.

In the late 1990s, McChrystal shrewdly improved his inside game, spending a year at Harvard's Kennedy School of Government and then at the Council on Foreign Relations, where he coauthored a treatise on the merits and drawbacks of humanitarian interventionism. But as he moved up through the ranks, McChrystal relied on the skills he had learned as a troublemaking kid at West Point: knowing precisely how far he could go in a rigid military hierarchy without getting tossed out. Being a highly intelligent badass, he discovered, could take you far—especially in the political chaos that followed September 11. "He was very focused," says Annie. "Even as a young officer he seemed to know what he wanted to do. I don't think his personality has changed in all these years."

.    .    .

By some accounts, McChrystal's career should have been over at least two times by now. As Pentagon spokesman during the invasion of Iraq, the general seemed more like a White House mouthpiece than an up-and-coming commander with a reputation for speaking his mind. When Defense Secretary Donald Rumsfeld made his infamous "stuff happens" remark during the looting of Baghdad, McChrystal backed him up. A few days later, he echoed the president's Mission Accomplished gaffe by insisting that major combat operations in Iraq were over. But it was during his next stint—overseeing the military's most elite units, including the rangers, Navy Seals and Delta Force—that McChrystal took part in a cover-up that would have destroyed the career of a lesser man.

After Cpl. Pat Tillman, the former-NFL-star-turned-ranger, was accidentally killed by his own troops in Afghanistan in April 2004, McChrystal took an active role in creating the impression that Tillman had died at the hands of Taliban fighters. He signed off on a falsified recommendation for a Silver Star that suggested Tillman had been killed by enemy fire. (McChrystal would later claim he didn't read the recommendation closely enough—a strange excuse for a commander known for his laser-like attention to minute details.) A week later, McChrystal sent a memo up the chain of command, specifically warning that President Bush should avoid mentioning the cause of Tillman's death. "If the circumstances of Corporal Tillman's death become public," he wrote, it could cause "public embarrassment" for the president.

"The false narrative, which McChrystal clearly helped construct, diminished Pat's true actions," wrote Tillman's mother, Mary, in her book *Boots on the Ground by Dusk*. McChrystal got away with it, she added, because he was the "golden boy" of Rumsfeld and Bush, who loved his willingness to get things done, even if it included bending the rules or skipping the chain of command. Nine days after Tillman's death, McChrystal was promoted to major general.

Two years later, in 2006, McChrystal was tainted by a scandal involving detainee abuse and torture at Camp Nama in Iraq. According to a report by Human Rights Watch, prisoners at the camp were subjected to a now-familiar litany of abuse: stress positions, being dragged naked through the mud. McChrystal was not disciplined in the scandal, even though an interrogator at the camp reported seeing him inspect the prison multiple times. But the experience was so unsettling to McChrystal that he tried to prevent detainee operations from being placed under his command in Afghanistan, viewing them as a "political swamp," according to a U.S. official. In May 2009, as McChrystal prepared for his confirmation hearings, his staff prepared him for hard questions about Camp Nama and the Tillman cover-up. But the scandals barely made a ripple in Congress, and McChrystal was soon on his way back to Kabul to run the war in Afghanistan.

The media, to a large extent, have also given McChrystal a pass on both controversies. Where Gen. Petraeus is kind of a dweeb, a teacher's pet with a ranger's tab, McChrystal is a snake-eating rebel, a "Jedi" commander, as *Newsweek* called him. He didn't care when his teenage son came home with blue hair and a mohawk. He speaks his mind with a candor rare for a high-ranking official. He asks for opinions and seems genuinely interested in the response. He gets briefings on his iPod and listens to books on tape. He carries a custom-made set of nunchucks in his convoy engraved with his name and four stars, and his itinerary often bears a fresh quote from Bruce Lee. ("There are no limits. There are only plateaus, and you must not stay there, you must go beyond them.") He went out on dozens of nighttime raids during his time in Iraq, unprecedented for a top commander, and turned up on missions unannounced, with almost no entourage. "The fucking lads love Stan McChrystal," says a British officer who serves in Kabul. "You'd be out in Somewhere, Iraq, and someone would take a knee beside you, and a corporal would be like 'Who the fuck is that?' And it's fucking Stan McChrystal."

It doesn't hurt that McChrystal was also extremely successful as head of the Joint Special Operations Command, the elite forces that carry out the government's darkest ops. During the Iraq surge, his team killed and captured thousands of insurgents, including Abu Musab al-Zarqawi, the leader of Al Qaeda in Iraq. "JSOC was a killing machine," says Maj. Gen. Mayville, his chief of operations. McChrystal was also open to new ways of killing. He systematically mapped out terrorist networks, targeting specific insurgents and hunting them down—often with the help of cyberfreaks traditionally shunned by the military. "The Boss would find the twenty-four-year-old kid with a nose ring, with some fucking brilliant degree from MIT, sitting in the corner with sixteen computer monitors humming," says a Special Forces commando who worked with McChrystal in Iraq and now serves on his staff in Kabul. "He'd say, 'Hey—you fucking muscleheads couldn't find lunch without help. You got to work together with these guys.'"

Even in his new role as America's leading evangelist for counterinsurgency, McChrystal retains the deep-seated instincts of a terrorist hunter. To put pressure on the Taliban, he has upped the number of Special Forces units in Afghanistan from four to nineteen. "You better be out there hitting four or five targets tonight," McChrystal will tell a Navy Seal he sees in the hallway at headquarters. Then he'll add, "I'm going to have to scold you in the morning for it, though." In fact, the general frequently finds himself apologizing for the disastrous consequences of counterinsurgency. In the first four months of this year, NATO forces killed some ninety civilians, up 76 percent from the same period in 2009—a record that has created tremendous resentment among the very population that COIN theory is intent on winning over. In February, a Special Forces night raid ended in the deaths of two pregnant Afghan women and allegations of a cover-up, and in April, protests erupted in Kandahar after U.S. forces accidentally shot up a bus, killing five Afghans. "We've shot an amazing number of people," McChrystal recently conceded.

Despite the tragedies and miscues, McChrystal has issued some of the strictest directives to avoid civilian casualties that the U.S. military has ever encountered in a war zone. It's "insurgent math," as he calls it—for every innocent person you kill, you create ten new enemies. He has ordered convoys to curtail their reckless driving, put restrictions on the use of air power, and severely limited night raids. He regularly apologizes to Hamid Karzai when civilians are killed, and berates commanders responsible for civilian deaths. "For a while," says one U.S. official, "the most dangerous place to be in Afghanistan was in front of McChrystal after a 'civ cas' incident." The ISAF command has even discussed ways to make *not* killing into something you can win an award for: There's talk of creating a new medal for "courageous restraint," a buzzword that's unlikely to gain much traction in the gung-ho culture of the U.S. military.

But however strategic they may be, McChrystal's new marching orders have caused an intense backlash among his own troops. Being told to hold their fire, soldiers complain, puts them in greater danger. "Bottom line?" says a former Special Forces operator who has spent years in Iraq and Afghanistan. "I would love to kick McChrystal in the nuts. His rules of engagement put soldiers' lives in even greater danger. Every real soldier will tell you the same thing."

In March, McChrystal traveled to Combat Outpost JFM—a small encampment on the outskirts of Kandahar—to confront such accusations from the troops directly. It was a typically bold move by the general. Only two days earlier, he had received an e-mail from Israel Arroyo, a twenty-five-year-old staff sergeant who asked McChrystal to go on a mission with his unit. "I am writing because it was said you don't care about the troops and have made it harder to defend ourselves," Arroyo wrote.

Within hours, McChrystal responded personally: "I'm sad-
dened by the accusation that I don't care about soldiers, as it
is something I suspect any soldier takes both personally and
professionally—at least I do. But I know perceptions depend upon
your perspective at the time, and I respect that every soldier's view
is his own." Then he showed up at Arroyo's outpost and went on
a foot patrol with the troops—not some bullshit photo-op stroll
through a market, but a real live operation in a dangerous war
zone.

Six weeks later, just before McChrystal returned from Paris,
the general received another e-mail from Arroyo. A twenty-three-
year-old corporal named Michael Ingram—one of the soldiers
McChrystal had gone on patrol with—had been killed by an IED
a day earlier. It was the third man the twenty-five-member platoon had lost in a year, and Arroyo was writing to see if the general would attend Ingram's memorial service. "He started to look
up to you," Arroyo wrote. McChrystal said he would try to make
it down to pay his respects as soon as possible.

The night before the general is scheduled to visit Sgt. Arroyo's
platoon for the memorial, I arrive at Combat Outpost JFM to
speak with the soldiers he had gone on patrol with. JFM is a small
encampment, ringed by high blast walls and guard towers. Almost
all of the soldiers here have been on repeated combat tours in
both Iraq and Afghanistan, and have seen some of the worst fighting of both wars. But they are especially angered by Ingram's
death. His commanders had repeatedly requested permission
to tear down the house where Ingram was killed, noting that it
was often used as a combat position by the Taliban. But due to
McChrystal's new restrictions to avoid upsetting civilians, the
request had been denied. "These were abandoned houses," fumes
Staff Sgt. Kennith Hicks. "Nobody was coming back to live in
them."

One soldier shows me the list of new regulations the platoon
was given. "Patrol only in areas that you are reasonably certain

that you will not have to defend yourselves with lethal force," the laminated card reads. For a soldier who has traveled halfway around the world to fight, that's like telling a cop he should only patrol in areas where he knows he won't have to make arrests. "Does that make any fucking sense?" asks Pfc. Jared Pautsch. "We should just drop a fucking bomb on this place. You sit and ask yourself: What are we doing here?"

The rules handed out here are not what McChrystal intended—they've been distorted as they passed through the chain of command—but knowing that does nothing to lessen the anger of troops on the ground. "Fuck, when I came over here and heard that McChrystal was in charge, I thought we would get our fucking gun on," says Hicks, who has served three tours of combat. "I get COIN. I get all that. McChrystal comes here, explains it, it makes sense. But then he goes away on his bird, and by the time his directives get passed down to us through Big Army, they're all fucked up—either because somebody is trying to cover their ass, or because they just don't understand it themselves. But we're fucking losing this thing."

McChrystal and his team show up the next day. Underneath a tent, the general has a forty-five-minute discussion with some two dozen soldiers. The atmosphere is tense. "I ask you what's going on in your world, and I think it's important for you all to understand the big picture as well," McChrystal begins. "How's the company doing? You guys feeling sorry for yourselves? Anybody? Anybody feel like you're losing?" McChrystal says.

"Sir, some of the guys here, sir, think we're losing, sir," says Hicks.

McChrystal nods. "Strength is leading when you just don't want to lead," he tells the men. "You're leading by example. That's what we do. Particularly when it's really, really hard, and it hurts inside." Then he spends twenty minutes talking about counterinsurgency, diagramming his concepts and principles on a whiteboard. He makes COIN seem like common sense, but he's careful not to bullshit the men. "We are knee-deep in the decisive year," he tells them. The Taliban, he insists, no longer has the initiative—"but I don't think we do, either." It's similar to the talk he gave in Paris, but it's not winning any hearts and minds among the soldiers. "This is the philosophical part that works with think tanks," McChrystal tries to joke. "But it doesn't get the same reception from infantry companies."

During the question-and-answer period, the frustration boils over. The soldiers complain about not being allowed to use lethal force, about watching insurgents they detain be freed for lack of evidence. They want to be able to fight—like they did in Iraq, like they had in Afghanistan before McChrystal. "We aren't putting fear into the Taliban," one soldier says.

"Winning hearts and minds in COIN is a coldblooded thing," McChrystal says, citing an oft-repeated maxim that you can't kill your way out of Afghanistan. "The Russians killed 1 million Afghans, and that didn't work."

"I'm not saying go out and kill everybody, sir," the soldier persists. "You say we've stopped the momentum of the insurgency. I don't believe that's true in this area. The more we pull back, the more we restrain ourselves, the stronger it's getting."

"I agree with you," McChrystal says. "In this area, we've not made progress, probably. You have to show strength here, you have to use fire. What I'm telling you is, fire costs you. What do you want to do? You want to wipe the population out here and resettle it?"

A soldier complains that under the rules, any insurgent who doesn't have a weapon is immediately assumed to be a civilian. "That's the way this game is," McChrystal says. "It's complex. I can't just decide: It's shirts and skins, and we'll kill all the shirts."

As the discussion ends, McChrystal seems to sense that he hasn't succeeded at easing the men's anger. He makes one last-ditch effort to reach them, acknowledging the death of Cpl. Ingram. "There's no way I can make that easier," he tells them. "No way I can pretend it won't hurt. No way I can tell you not to feel that. . . . I will tell you, you're doing a great job. Don't let the frustration get to you." The session ends with no clapping and no real resolution. McChrystal may have sold President Obama on counterinsurgency, but many of his own men aren't buying it.

•　　　•　　　•

When it comes to Afghanistan, history is not on McChrystal's side. The only foreign invader to have any success here was Genghis Khan—and he wasn't hampered by things like human rights, economic development, and press scrutiny. The COIN doctrine, bizarrely, draws inspiration from some of the biggest Western military embarrassments in recent memory: France's nasty war in Algeria (lost in 1962) and the American misadventure in Vietnam (lost in 1975). McChrystal, like other advocates of COIN, readily acknowledges that counterinsurgency campaigns are inherently messy, expensive, and easy to lose. "Even Afghans are confused by Afghanistan," he says. But even if he somehow manages to succeed, after years of bloody fighting with Afghan kids who pose no threat to the U.S. homeland, the war will do little to shut down Al Qaeda, which has shifted its operations to Pakistan. Dispatching 150,000 troops to build new schools, roads, mosques, and water-treatment facilities around Kandahar is like trying to stop the drug war in Mexico by occupying Arkansas and building Baptist churches in Little Rock. "It's all very cynical, politically," says Marc Sageman, a former CIA case officer who has extensive experience in the region. "Afghanistan is not in our vital interest—there's nothing for us there."

In mid-May, two weeks after visiting the troops in Kandahar, McChrystal travels to the White House for a high-level visit by Hamid Karzai. It is a triumphant moment for the general, one that demonstrates he is very much in command—both in Kabul and in Washington. In the East Room, which is packed with journalists and dignitaries, President Obama sings the praises of Karzai. The two leaders talk about how great their relationship is, about the pain they feel over civilian casualties. They mention the word "progress" sixteen times in under an hour. But there is no mention of victory. Still, the session represents the most forceful commitment that Obama has made to McChrystal's strategy in months. "There is no denying the progress that the Afghan people have made in recent years—in education, in health care and economic development," the president says. "As I saw in the lights across Kabul when I landed—lights that would not have been visible just a few years earlier."

It is a disconcerting observation for Obama to make. During the worst years in Iraq, when the Bush administration had no real progress to point to, officials used to offer up the exact same evidence of success. "It was one of our first impressions," one GOP official said in 2006, after landing in Baghdad at the height of the sectarian violence. "So many lights shining brightly." So it is to the language of the Iraq War that the Obama administration has turned—talk of progress, of city lights, of metrics like health care and education. Rhetoric that just a few years ago they would have mocked. "They are trying to manipulate perceptions because there is no definition of victory—because victory is not even defined or recognizable," says Celeste Ward, a senior defense analyst at the RAND Corporation who served as a political adviser to U.S. commanders in Iraq in 2006. "That's the game we're in right now. What we need, for strategic purposes, is to create the perception that we didn't get run off. The facts on the ground are not great, and are not going to become great in the near future."

But facts on the ground, as history has proven, offer little deterrent to a military determined to stay the course. Even those closest to McChrystal know that the rising antiwar sentiment at home doesn't begin to reflect how deeply fucked up things are in Afghanistan. "If Americans pulled back and started paying attention to this war, it would become even less popular," a senior

adviser to McChrystal says. Such realism, however, doesn't prevent advocates of counterinsurgency from dreaming big: Instead
of beginning to withdraw troops next year, as Obama promised,
the military hopes to ramp up its counterinsurgency campaign
even further. "There's a possibility we could ask for another surge
of U.S. forces next summer if we see success here," a senior military official in Kabul tells me.

Back in Afghanistan, less than a month after the White House
meeting with Karzai and all the talk of "progress," McChrystal
is hit by the biggest blow to his vision of counterinsurgency. Since
last year, the Pentagon had been planning to launch a major military operation this summer in Kandahar, the country's second-
largest city and the Taliban's original home base. It was supposed
to be a decisive turning point in the war—the primary reason for
the troop surge that McChrystal wrested from Obama late last
year. But on June 10, acknowledging that the military still needs
to lay more groundwork, the general announced that he is postpon-
ing the offensive until the fall. Rather than one big battle, like
Fallujah or Ramadi, U.S. troops will implement what McChrystal
calls a "rising tide of security." The Afghan police and army will
enter Kandahar to attempt to seize control of neighborhoods,
while the U.S. pours $90 million of aid into the city to win over
the civilian population.

Even proponents of counterinsurgency are hard-pressed to
explain the new plan. "This isn't a classic operation," says a U.S.
military official. "It's not going to be Black Hawk Down. There
aren't going to be doors kicked in." Other U.S. officials insist that
doors *are* going to be kicked in, but that it's going to be a kinder,
gentler offensive than the disaster in Marja. "The Taliban have a
jackboot on the city," says a military official. "We have to remove
them, but we have to do it in a way that doesn't alienate the population." When Vice President Biden was briefed on the new plan
in the Oval Office, insiders say he was shocked to see how much
it mirrored the more gradual plan of counterterrorism that he

advocated last fall. "This looks like CT-plus!" he said, according to U.S. officials familiar with the meeting.

Whatever the nature of the new plan, the delay underscores the fundamental flaws of counterinsurgency. After nine years of war, the Taliban simply remains too strongly entrenched for the U.S. military to openly attack. The very people that COIN seeks to win over—the Afghan people—do not want us there. Our supposed ally, President Karzai, used his influence to delay the offensive, and the massive influx of aid championed by McChrystal is likely only to make things worse. "Throwing money at the problem exacerbates the problem," says Andrew Wilder, an expert at Tufts University who has studied the effect of aid in southern Afghanistan. "A tsunami of cash fuels corruption, delegitimizes the government and creates an environment where we're picking winners and losers"—a process that fuels resentment and hostility among the civilian population. So far, counterinsurgency has succeeded only in creating a never-ending demand for the primary product supplied by the military: perpetual war. There is a reason that President Obama studiously avoids using the word "victory" when he talks about Afghanistan. Winning, it would seem, is not really possible. Not even with Stanley McChrystal in charge.

# The New Yorker

FINALIST—REPORTING

*The National Magazine Awards were founded in 1966; that year* The New Yorker *received a special citation for reporting for Truman Capote's* In Cold Blood. *The first award for reporting was presented in 1970; that year* The New Yorker *was the winner for work by David Harris and Daniel Lang (including Lang's story about the rape and murder of a Vietnamese girl by four American soldiers, which became Brian DePalma's movie* Casualties of War). *All told,* The New Yorker *has been nominated thirty-seven times for reporting and won ten times. Yet the subjects of "Covert Operations," Charles and David H. Koch, felt so strongly that they were victims of journalistic malpractice that they wrote ASME to say that Jane Mayer's story was "agenda-driven advocacy masquerad[ing] as objective reporting." The National Magazine Award judges saw it differently, praising Mayer for her reliance on "court documents, tax returns and old friends" to link the Kochs to "the crusade against climate-change science and the tea party revolt."*

Jane Mayer

# Covert Operations

On May 17, a black-tie audience at the Metropolitan Opera House applauded as a tall, jovial-looking billionaire took the stage. It was the seventieth annual spring gala of American Ballet Theatre, and David H. Koch was being celebrated for his generosity as a member of the board of trustees; he had recently donated $2.5 million toward the company's upcoming season and had given many millions before that. Koch received an award while flanked by two of the gala's co-chairs, Blaine Trump, in a peach-colored gown, and Caroline Kennedy Schlossberg, in emerald green. Kennedy's mother, Jacqueline Kennedy Onassis, had been a patron of the ballet and, coincidentally, the previous owner of a Fifth Avenue apartment that Koch had bought, in 1995, and then sold, eleven years later, for 32 million dollars, having found it too small.

The gala marked the social ascent of Koch, who, at the age of seventy, has become one of the city's most prominent philanthropists. In 2008, he donated 100 million dollars to modernize Lincoln Center's New York State Theatre building, which now bears his name. He has given 20 million to the American Museum of Natural History, whose dinosaur wing is named for him. This spring, after noticing the decrepit state of the fountains outside the Metropolitan Museum of Art, Koch pledged at least ten million dollars for their renovation. He is a trustee of the museum, perhaps the most coveted social prize in the city, and serves on the board of Memorial Sloan-Kettering Cancer Center, where, after he donated more than 40 million dollars, an endowed chair and a research center were named for him.

One dignitary was conspicuously absent from the gala: the event's third honorary co-chair, Michelle Obama. Her office said that a scheduling conflict had prevented her from attending. Yet had the first lady shared the stage with Koch it might have created an awkward tableau. In Washington, Koch is best known as part of a family that has repeatedly funded stealth attacks on the federal government, and on the Obama administration in particular.

With his brother Charles, who is seventy-four, David Koch owns virtually all of Koch Industries, a conglomerate, headquartered in Wichita, Kansas, whose annual revenues are estimated to be 100 billion dollars. The company has grown spectacularly since their father, Fred, died in 1967 and the brothers took charge. The Kochs operate oil refineries in Alaska, Texas, and Minnesota, and control some 4,000 miles of pipeline. Koch Industries owns Brawny paper towels, Dixie cups, Georgia-Pacific lumber, Stainmaster carpet, and Lycra, among other products. *Forbes* ranks it as the second-largest private company in the country, after Cargill, and its consistent profitability has made David and Charles Koch—who, years ago, bought out two other brothers— among the richest men in America. Their combined fortune of 35 billion dollars is exceeded only by those of Bill Gates and Warren Buffett.

The Kochs are longtime libertarians who believe in drastically lower personal and corporate taxes, minimal social services for the needy, and much less oversight of industry—especially environmental regulation. These views dovetail with the brothers' corporate interests. In a study released this spring, the University of Massachusetts at Amherst's Political Economy Research

Institute named Koch Industries one of the top ten air polluters in the United States. And Greenpeace issued a report identifying the company as a "kingpin of climate science denial." The report showed that, from 2005 to 2008, the Kochs vastly outdid Exxon-Mobil in giving money to organizations fighting legislation related to climate change, underwriting a huge network of foundations, think tanks, and political front groups. Indeed, the brothers have funded opposition campaigns against so many Obama administration policies—from health-care reform to the economic-stimulus program—that, in political circles, their ideological network is known as the Kochtopus.

In a statement, Koch Industries said that the Greenpeace report "distorts the environmental record of our companies." And David Koch, in a recent, admiring article about him in *New York*, protested that the "radical press" had turned his family into "whipping boys," and had exaggerated its influence on American politics. But Charles Lewis, the founder of the Center for Public Integrity, a nonpartisan watchdog group, said, "The Kochs are on a whole different level. There's no one else who has spent this much money. The sheer dimension of it is what sets them apart. They have a pattern of lawbreaking, political manipulation, and obfuscation. I've been in Washington since Watergate, and I've never seen anything like it. They are the Standard Oil of our times."

• • •

A few weeks after the Lincoln Center gala, the advocacy wing of the Americans for Prosperity Foundation—an organization that David Koch started, in 2004—held a different kind of gathering. Over the July Fourth weekend, a summit called Texas Defending the American Dream took place in a chilly hotel ballroom in Austin. Though Koch freely promotes his philanthropic ventures, he did not attend the summit, and his name was not in evidence. And on this occasion the audience was roused not by a dance performance but by a series of speakers denouncing President Barack Obama. Peggy Venable, the organizer of the summit, warned that administration officials "have a socialist vision for this country."

Five hundred people attended the summit, which served, in part, as a training session for Tea Party activists in Texas. An advertisement cast the event as a populist uprising against vested corporate power. "Today, the voices of average Americans are being drowned out by lobbyists and special interests," it said. "But you can do something about it." The pitch made no mention of its corporate funders. The White House has expressed frustration that such sponsors have largely eluded public notice. David Axelrod, Obama's senior adviser, said, "What they don't say is that, in part, this is a grassroots citizens' movement brought to you by a bunch of oil billionaires."

In April 2009, Melissa Cohlmia, a company spokesperson, denied that the Kochs had direct links to the Tea Party, saying that Americans for Prosperity is "an independent organization and Koch companies do not in any way direct their activities." Later, she issued a statement: "No funding has been provided by Koch companies, the Koch foundations, or Charles Koch or David Koch specifically to support the tea parties." David Koch told *New York*, "I've never been to a tea-party event. No one representing the tea party has ever even approached me."

At the lectern in Austin, however, Venable—a longtime political operative who draws a salary from Americans for Prosperity, and who has worked for Koch-funded political groups since 1994—spoke less warily. "We love what the Tea Parties are doing, because that's how we're going to take back America!" she declared as the crowd cheered. In a subsequent interview, she described herself as an early member of the movement, joking, "I was part of the Tea Party before it was cool!" She explained that the role of Americans for Prosperity was to help "educate" Tea Party activists on policy details and to give them "next-step training" after their rallies so that their political energy could be channeled "more effectively." And she noted that Americans for Prosperity had provided Tea Party activists with lists of elected officials to target. She said of the Kochs, "They're certainly our people. David's the chairman of our board. I've certainly met with them, and I'm very appreciative of what they do."

Venable honored several Tea Party "citizen leaders" at the summit. The Texas branch of Americans for Prosperity gave its Blogger of the Year Award to a young woman named Sibyl West. On June 14, West, writing on her site, described Obama as the "cokehead in chief." In an online thread, West speculated that the president was exhibiting symptoms of "demonic possession (aka schizophrenia, etc.)." The summit featured several paid speakers, including Janine Turner, the actress best known for her role on the television series *Northern Exposure*. She declared, "They don't want our children to know about their rights. They don't want our children to know about a God!"

During a catered lunch, Venable introduced Ted Cruz, a former solicitor general of Texas, who told the crowd that Obama was "the most radical president ever to occupy the Oval Office" and had hidden from voters a secret agenda—"the government taking over our economy and our lives." Countering Obama, Cruz proclaimed, was "the epic fight of our generation!" As the crowd rose to its feet and cheered, he quoted the defiant words of a Texan at the Alamo: "Victory, or death!"

Americans for Prosperity has worked closely with the Tea Party since the movement's inception. In the weeks before the first Tax Day protests, in April 2009, Americans for Prosperity hosted a website offering supporters "Tea Party Talking Points." The Arizona branch urged people to send tea bags to Obama; the

Missouri branch urged members to sign up for "Taxpayer Tea Party Registration" and provided directions to nine protests. The group continues to stoke the rebellion. The North Carolina branch recently launched a "Tea Party Finder" website, advertised as "a hub for all the Tea Parties in North Carolina."

The antigovernment fervor infusing the 2010 elections represents a political triumph for the Kochs. By giving money to "educate," fund, and organize Tea Party protesters, they have helped turn their private agenda into a mass movement. Bruce Bartlett, a conservative economist and a historian, who once worked at the National Center for Policy Analysis, a Dallas-based think tank that the Kochs fund, said, "The problem with the whole libertarian movement is that it's been all chiefs and no Indians. There haven't been any actual people, like voters, who give a crap about it. So the problem for the Kochs has been trying to create a movement." With the emergence of the Tea Party, he said, "everyone suddenly sees that for the first time there are Indians out there—people who can provide real ideological power." The Kochs, he said, are "trying to shape and control and channel the populist uprising into their own policies."

A Republican campaign consultant who has done research on behalf of Charles and David Koch said of the Tea Party, "The Koch brothers gave the money that founded it. It's like they put the seeds in the ground. Then the rainstorm comes, and the frogs come out of the mud—and they're our candidates!"

The Kochs and their political operatives declined requests for interviews. Instead, a prominent New York public-relations executive who is close with the Kochs put forward two friends: George Pataki, the former governor of New York, and Mortimer Zuckerman, the publisher and real-estate magnate. Pataki, a Republican who received campaign donations from David Koch, called him "a patriot who cares deeply about his country." Zuckerman praised David's "gentle decency" and the "range of his public interests."

The Republican campaign consultant said of the family's political activities, "To call them under the radar is an understatement. They are underground!" Another former Koch adviser said, "They're smart. This right-wing, redneck stuff works for them. They see this as a way to get things done without getting dirty themselves." Rob Stein, a Democratic political strategist who has studied the conservative movement's finances, said that the Kochs are "at the epicenter of the anti-Obama movement. But it's not just about Obama. They would have done the same to Hillary Clinton. They did the same with Bill Clinton. They are out to destroy progressivism."

. . .

Oddly enough, the fiercely capitalist Koch family owes part of its fortune to Joseph Stalin. Fred Koch was the son of a Dutch printer who settled in Texas and ran a weekly newspaper. Fred attended MIT, where he earned a degree in chemical engineering. In 1927, he invented a more efficient process for converting oil into gasoline, but, according to family lore, America's major oil companies regarded him as a threat and shut him out of the industry. Unable to succeed at home, Koch found work in the Soviet Union. In the 1930s, his company trained Bolshevik engineers and helped Stalin's regime set up fifteen modern oil refineries. Over time, however, Stalin brutally purged several of Koch's Soviet colleagues. Koch was deeply affected by the experience and regretted his collaboration. He returned to the United States. In the headquarters of his company, Rock Island Oil & Refining, in Wichita, he kept photographs aimed at proving that some of those Soviet refineries had been destroyed in the Second World War. Gus diZerega, a former friend of Charles Koch, recalled, "As the Soviets became a stronger military power, Fred felt a certain amount of guilt at having helped build them up. I think it bothered him a lot."

In 1958, Fred Koch became one of the original members of the John Birch Society, the arch-conservative group known, in part, for a highly skeptical view of governance and for spreading fears of a communist takeover. Members considered President Dwight D. Eisenhower to be a communist agent. In a self-published broadside, Koch claimed that "the Communists have infiltrated both the Democrat and Republican Parties." He wrote admiringly of Benito Mussolini's suppression of communists in Italy and disparagingly of the American Civil Rights Movement. "The colored man looms large in the Communist plan to take over America," he warned. Welfare was a secret plot to attract rural blacks to cities, where they would foment "a vicious race war." In a 1963 speech that prefigures the Tea Party's talk of a secret socialist plot, Koch predicted that communists would "infiltrate the highest offices of government in the U.S. until the President is a Communist, unknown to the rest of us."

Koch married Mary Robinson, the daughter of a Missouri physician, and they had four sons: Freddie, Charles, and twins David and William. John Damgard, the president of the Futures Industry Association, was David's schoolmate and friend. He recalled that Fred Koch was "a real John Wayne type." Koch emphasized rugged pursuits, taking his sons big-game hunting in Africa and requiring them to do farm labor at the family ranch. The Kochs lived in a stone mansion on a large compound across from Wichita's country club; in the summer, the boys could hear their friends splashing in the pool, but they were not allowed to join them. "By instilling a work ethic in me at an early age, my father did me a big favor, although it didn't seem like a favor back then," Charles has written. "By the time I was eight, he made sure work occupied most of my spare time." David Koch recalled that his father also indoctrinated the boys politically. "He was constantly speaking to us children about what was wrong with government," he told Brian Doherty, an editor of the libertarian magazine *Reason* and the author of *Radicals for Capitalism*, a 2007 history of the libertarian movement. "It's something I grew up with—a fundamental point of view that big government was bad, and imposition of government controls on our lives and economic fortunes was not good."

David attended Deerfield Academy, in Massachusetts, and Charles was sent to military school. Charles, David, and William all earned engineering degrees at their father's alma mater, MIT, and later joined the family company. Charles eventually assumed control, with David as his deputy; William's career at the company was less successful. Freddie went to Harvard and studied playwriting at the Yale School of Drama. His father reportedly disapproved of him and punished him financially. (Freddie, through a spokesperson, denied this.)

In 1967, after Fred Koch died, of a heart attack, Charles renamed the business Koch Industries, in honor of his father. Fred Koch's will made his sons extraordinarily wealthy. David Koch joked about his good fortune in a 2003 speech to alumni at Deerfield, where, after pledging 25 million dollars, he was made the school's sole "lifetime trustee." He said, "You might ask: How does David Koch happen to have the wealth to be so generous? Well, let me tell you a story. It all started when I was a little boy. One day, my father gave me an apple. I soon sold it for five dollars and bought two apples and sold them for ten. Then I bought four apples and sold them for twenty. Well, this went on day after day, week after week, month after month, year after year, until my father died and left me three hundred million dollars!"

David and Charles had absorbed their father's conservative politics, but they did not share all his views, according to diZerega, who befriended Charles in the midsixties, after meeting him while browsing in a John Birch Society bookstore in Wichita. Charles eventually invited him to the Kochs' mansion, to participate in an informal political-discussion group. "It was pretty clear that Charles thought some of the Birch Society was bullshit," diZerega recalled.

DiZerega, who has lost touch with Charles, eventually abandoned right-wing views and became a political-science professor.

He credits Charles with opening his mind to political philosophy, which set him on the path to academia; Charles is one of three people to whom he dedicated his first book. But diZerega believes that the Koch brothers have followed a wayward intellectual trajectory, transferring their father's paranoia about Soviet Communism to a distrust of the U.S. government and seeing its expansion, beginning with the New Deal, as a tyrannical threat to freedom. In an essay, posted on Beliefnet, diZerega writes, "As state socialism failed . . . the target for many within these organizations shifted to any kind of regulation at all. 'Socialism' kept being defined downwards."

Members of the John Birch Society developed an interest in a school of Austrian economists who promoted free-market ideals. Charles and David Koch were particularly influenced by the work of Friedrich von Hayek, the author of *The Road to Serfdom* (1944), which argued that centralized government planning led, inexorably, to totalitarianism. Hayek's belief in unfettered capitalism has proved inspirational to many conservatives and to anti-Soviet dissidents; lately, Tea Party supporters have championed his work. In June, the talk-radio host Glenn Beck, who has supported the Tea Party rebellion, promoted *The Road to Serfdom* on his show; the paperback soon became a no. 1 best-seller on Amazon. (Beck appears to be a fan of the Kochs; in the midst of a recent on-air parody of Al Gore, Beck said, without explanation, "I want to thank Charles Koch for this information." Beck declined to elaborate on the relationship.)

Charles and David also became devotees of a more radical thinker, Robert LeFevre, who favored the abolition of the state but didn't like the label "anarchist"; he called himself an "autarchist." LeFevre liked to say that "government is a disease masquerading as its own cure." In 1956, he opened an institution called the Freedom School, in Colorado Springs. Brian Doherty, of *Reason*, told me that "LeFevre was an anarchist figure who won Charles's heart," and that the school was "a tiny world of people who thought the New Deal was a horrible mistake." According to diZerega, Charles supported the school financially and even gave him money to take classes there.

Throughout the seventies, Charles and David continued to build Koch Industries. In 1980, William, with assistance from Freddie, attempted to take over the company from Charles, who, they felt, had assumed autocratic control. In retaliation, the company's board, which answered to Charles, fired William. ("Charles runs it all with an iron hand," Bruce Bartlett, the economist, told me.) Lawsuits were filed, with William and Freddie on one side and Charles and David on the other. In 1983, Charles and David bought out their brothers' share in the company for nearly a billion dollars. But the antagonism remained, and litigation continued for seventeen more years, with the brothers hiring rival private investigators; in 1990, they walked past one another with stony expressions at their mother's funeral. Eventually, Freddie moved to Monaco, which has no income tax. He bought historic estates in France, Austria, and elsewhere, filling them with art, antiques, opera scores, and literary manuscripts. William founded his own energy company, Oxbow, and turned to yachting; he spent an estimated 65 million dollars to win the America's Cup in 1992.

With Charles as the undisputed chairman and CEO, Koch Industries expanded rapidly. Roger Altman, who heads the investment-banking firm Evercore, told me that the company's performance has been "beyond phenomenal." Charles remained in Wichita, with his wife and two children, guarding his privacy while supporting community charities. David moved to New York City, where he is an executive vice president of the company and the CEO of its Chemical Technology Group. A financial expert who knows Koch Industries well told me, "Charles is the company. Charles runs it." David, described by associates as "affable" and "a bit of a lunk," enjoyed for years the life of a wealthy bachelor. He rented a yacht in the South of France and bought a waterfront home in Southampton, where he threw parties that the website New York Social Diary likened to an "East Coast version of Hugh Hefner's soirées." In 1996, he married Julia Flesher, a fashion assistant. They live in a 9,000 square-foot duplex at 740 Park Avenue with their three children. Though David's manner is more cosmopolitan, and more genial, than that of Charles, Brian Doherty, who has interviewed both brothers, couldn't think of a single issue on which the brothers disagreed.

As their fortunes grew, Charles and David Koch became the primary underwriters of hard-line libertarian politics in America. Charles's goal, as Doherty described it, was to tear the government "out at the root." The brothers' first major public step came in 1979, when Charles persuaded David, then thirty-nine, to run for public office. They had become supporters of the Libertarian Party and were backing its presidential candidate, Ed Clark, who was running against Ronald Reagan from the right. Frustrated by the legal limits on campaign donations, they contrived to place David on the ticket in the vice-presidential slot; upon becoming a candidate, he could lavish as much of his personal fortune as he wished on the campaign. The ticket's slogan was "The Libertarian Party has only one source of funds: You." In fact, its primary source of funds was David Koch, who spent more than 2 million dollars on the effort.

Many of the ideas propounded in the 1980 campaign presaged the Tea Party movement. Ed Clark told *The Nation* that libertarians were getting ready to stage "a very big tea party," because people were "sick to death" of taxes. The Libertarian Party platform called for the abolition of the FBI and the CIA, as well as of federal regulatory agencies, such as the Securities and Exchange Commission and the Department of Energy. The party wanted to end Social Security, minimum-wage laws, gun control, and all personal and corporate income taxes; it proposed the legalization of prostitution, recreational drugs, and suicide. Government should be reduced to only one function: the protection of individual rights. William F. Buckley Jr., a more traditional conservative, called the movement "Anarcho-Totalitarianism."

That November, the Libertarian ticket received only 1 percent of the vote. The brothers realized that their brand of politics didn't sell at the ballot box. Charles Koch became openly scornful of conventional politics. "It tends to be a nasty, corrupting business," he told a reporter at the time. "I'm interested in advancing libertarian ideas." According to Doherty's book, the Kochs came to regard elected politicians as merely "actors playing out a script." A longtime confidant of the Kochs told Doherty that the brothers wanted to "supply the themes and words for the scripts." In order to alter the direction of America, they had to "influence the areas where policy ideas percolate from: academia and think tanks."

•     •     •

After the 1980 election, Charles and David Koch receded from the public arena. But they poured more than 100 million dollars into dozens of seemingly independent organizations. Tax records indicate that in 2008 the three main Koch family foundations gave money to thirty-four political and policy organizations, three of which they founded and several of which they direct. The Kochs and their company have given additional millions to political campaigns, advocacy groups, and lobbyists. The family's subterranean financial role has fueled suspicion on the left; Lee Fang, of the liberal blog *ThinkProgress*, has called the Kochs "the billionaires behind the hate."

Only the Kochs know precisely how much they have spent on politics. Public tax records show that between 1998 and 2008 the Charles G. Koch Charitable Foundation spent more than 48 million dollars. The Claude R. Lambe Charitable Foundation, which is controlled by Charles Koch and his wife, along with two company employees and an accountant, spent more than 28 million.

The David H. Koch Charitable Foundation spent more than 120 million. Meanwhile, since 1998 Koch Industries has spent more than 50 million dollars on lobbying. Separately, the company's political-action committee, KochPAC, has donated some 8 million dollars to political campaigns, more than 80 percent of it to Republicans. So far in 2010, Koch Industries leads all other energy companies in political contributions, as it has since 2006. In addition, during the past dozen years the Kochs and other family members have personally spent more than 2 million dollars on political contributions. In the second quarter of 2010, David Koch was the biggest individual contributor to the Republican Governors Association, with a million-dollar donation. Other gifts by the Kochs may be untraceable; federal tax law permits anonymous personal donations to politically active nonprofit groups.

In recent decades, members of several industrial dynasties have spent parts of their fortunes on a conservative agenda. In the 1980s, the Olin family, which owns a chemicals and manufacturing conglomerate, became known for funding right-leaning thinking in academia, particularly in law schools. And during the nineties Richard Mellon Scaife, a descendant of Andrew Mellon, spent millions attempting to discredit President Bill Clinton. Ari Rabin-Havt, a vice president at the Democratic-leaning website Media Matters, said that the Kochs' effort is unusual in its marshalling of corporate and personal funds: "Their role, in terms of financial commitments, is staggering."

Of course, Democrats give money, too. Their most prominent donor, the financier George Soros, runs a foundation, the Open Society Institute, that has spent as much as 100 million dollars a year in America. Soros has also made generous private contributions to various Democratic campaigns, including Obama's. But Michael Vachon, his spokesman, argued that Soros's giving is transparent, and that "none of his contributions are in the service of his own economic interests." The Kochs have given millions of dollars to nonprofit groups that criticize environmental regulation and support lower taxes for industry. Gus diZerega, the former friend, suggested that the Kochs' youthful idealism about libertarianism had largely devolved into a rationale for corporate self-interest. He said of Charles, "Perhaps he has confused making money with freedom."

Some critics have suggested that the Kochs' approach has subverted the purpose of tax-exempt giving. By law, charitable foundations must conduct exclusively nonpartisan activities that promote the public welfare. A 2004 report by the National Committee for Responsive Philanthropy, a watchdog group, described the Kochs' foundations as being self-serving, concluding, "These foundations give money to nonprofit organizations that do research and advocacy on issues that impact the profit margin of Koch Industries."

The Kochs have gone well beyond their immediate self-interest, however, funding organizations that aim to push the country in a libertarian direction. Among the institutions that they have subsidized are the Institute for Justice, which files lawsuits opposing state and federal regulations; the Institute for Humane Studies, which underwrites libertarian academics; and the Bill of Rights Institute, which promotes a conservative slant on the Constitution. Many of the organizations funded by the Kochs employ specialists who write position papers that are subsequently quoted by politicians and pundits. David Koch has acknowledged that the family exerts tight ideological control. "If we're going to give a lot of money, we'll make darn sure they spend it in a way that goes along with our intent," he told Doherty. "And if they make a wrong turn and start doing things we don't agree with, we withdraw funding."

• • •

The Kochs' subsidization of a pro-corporate movement fulfills, in many ways, the vision laid out in a secret 1971 memo that Lewis

Powell, then a Virginia attorney, wrote two months before he was nominated to the Supreme Court. The antiwar movement had turned its anger on defense contractors, such as Dow Chemical, and Ralph Nader was leading a public-interest crusade against corporations. Powell, writing a report for the U.S. Chamber of Commerce, urged American companies to fight back. The greatest threat to free enterprise, he warned, was not communism or the New Left but, rather, "respectable elements of society"— intellectuals, journalists, and scientists. To defeat them, he wrote, business leaders needed to wage a long-term, unified campaign to change public opinion.

Charles Koch seems to have approached both business and politics with the deliberation of an engineer. "To bring about social change," he told Doherty, requires "a strategy" that is "vertically and horizontally integrated," spanning "from idea creation to policy development to education to grassroots organizations to lobbying to litigation to political action." The project, he admitted, was extremely ambitious. "We have a radical philosophy," he said.

In 1977, the Kochs provided the funds to launch the nation's first libertarian think tank, the Cato Institute. According to the Center for Public Integrity, between 1986 and 1993 the Koch family gave 11 million dollars to the institute. Today, Cato has more than 100 full-time employees, and its experts and policy papers are widely quoted and respected by the mainstream media. It describes itself as nonpartisan, and its scholars have at times been critical of both parties. But it has consistently pushed for corporate tax cuts, reductions in social services, and laissez-faire environmental policies.

When President Obama, in a 2008 speech, described the science on global warming as "beyond dispute," the Cato Institute took out a full-page ad in the *Times* to contradict him. Cato's resident scholars have relentlessly criticized political attempts to stop global warming as expensive, ineffective, and unnecessary.

Ed Crane, the Cato Institute's founder and president, told me that "global-warming theories give the government more control of the economy."

Cato scholars have been particularly energetic in promoting the Climategate scandal. Last year, private e-mails of climate scientists at the University of East Anglia, in England, were mysteriously leaked, and their exchanges appeared to suggest a willingness to falsify data in order to buttress the idea that global warming is real. In the two weeks after the e-mails went public, one Cato scholar gave more than twenty media interviews trumpeting the alleged scandal. But five independent inquiries have since exonerated the researchers, and nothing was found in their e-mails or data to discredit the scientific consensus on global warming.

Nevertheless, the controversy succeeded in spreading skepticism about climate change. Even though the National Oceanic and Atmospheric Administration recently issued a report concluding that the evidence for global warming is unequivocal, more Americans are convinced than at any time since 1997 that scientists have exaggerated the seriousness of global warming. The Kochs promote this statistic on their company's website but do not mention the role that their funding has played in fostering such doubt.

In a 2002 memo, the Republican political consultant Frank Luntz wrote that so long as "voters believe there is no consensus about global warming within the scientific community" the status quo would prevail. The key for opponents of environmental reform, he said, was to question the science—a public-relations strategy that the tobacco industry used effectively for years to forestall regulation. The Kochs have funded many sources of environmental skepticism, such as the Heritage Foundation, which has argued that "scientific facts gathered in the past 10 years do not support the notion of catastrophic human-made warming." The brothers have given money to more obscure groups, too, such as the Independent Women's Forum, which opposes the presentation of global warming as a scientific fact in American public schools. Until 2008, the group was run by Nancy Pfotenhauer, a former lobbyist for Koch Industries. Mary Beth Jarvis, a vice president of a Koch subsidary, is on the group's board.

Naomi Oreskes, a professor of history and science studies at the University of California, San Diego, is the coauthor of *Merchants of Doubt*, a new book that chronicles various attempts by American industry to manipulate public opinion on science. She noted that the Kochs, as the heads of "a company with refineries and pipelines," have "a lot at stake." She added, "If the answer is to phase out fossil fuels, a different group of people are going to be making money, so we shouldn't be surprised that they're fighting tooth and nail."

David Koch told *New York* that he was unconvinced that global warming has been caused by human activity. Even if it has been, he said, the heating of the planet will be beneficial, resulting in longer growing seasons in the Northern Hemisphere. "The Earth will be able to support enormously more people because far greater land area will be available to produce food," he said.

· · ·

In the mideighties, the Kochs provided millions of dollars to George Mason University, in Arlington, Virginia, to set up another think tank. Now known as the Mercatus Center, it promotes itself as "the world's premier university source for market-oriented ideas—bridging the gap between academic ideas and real-world problems." Financial records show that the Koch family foundations have contributed more than 30 million dollars to George Mason, much of which has gone to the Mercatus Center, a nonprofit organization. "It's ground zero for deregulation policy in Washington," Rob Stein, the Democratic strategist, said. It is an unusual arrangement. "George Mason is a public university, and receives public funds," Stein noted. "Virginia is hosting an institution that the Kochs practically control."

The founder of the Mercatus Center is Richard Fink, formerly an economist. Fink heads Koch Industries' lobbying operation in Washington. In addition, he is the president of the Charles G. Koch Charitable Foundation, the president of the Claude R. Lambe Charitable Foundation, a director of the Fred C. and Mary R. Koch Foundation, and a director and cofounder, with David Koch, of the Americans for Prosperity Foundation.

Fink, with his many titles, has become the central nervous system of the Kochtopus. He appears to have supplanted Ed Crane, the head of the Cato Institute, as the brothers' main political lieutenant. Though David remains on the board at Cato, Charles Koch has fallen out with Crane. Associates suggested to me that Crane had been insufficiently respectful of Charles's management philosophy, which he distilled into a book called *The Science of Success* and trademarked under the name Market-Based Management, or MBM. In the book, Charles recommends instilling a company's corporate culture with the competitiveness of the marketplace. Koch describes MBM as a "holistic system" containing "five dimensions: vision, virtue and talents, knowledge processes, decision rights and incentives." A top Cato Institute official told me that Charles "thinks he's a genius. He's the emperor, and he's convinced he's wearing clothes." Fink, by contrast, has been far more embracing of Charles's ideas. (Fink, like the Kochs, declined to be interviewed.)

At a 1995 conference for philanthropists, Fink adopted the language of economics when speaking about the Mercatus Center's purpose. He said that grant makers should use think tanks and political-action groups to convert intellectual raw materials into policy "products."

The *Wall Street Journal* has called the Mercatus Center "the most important think tank you've never heard of," and noted that fourteen of the twenty-three regulations that President George

W. Bush placed on a "hit list" had been suggested first by Mercatus scholars. Fink told the paper that the Kochs have "other means of fighting [their] battles" and that the Mercatus Center does not actively promote the company's private interests. But Thomas McGarity, a law professor at the University of Texas who specializes in environmental issues, told me that "Koch has been constantly in trouble with the EPA, and Mercatus has constantly hammered on the agency." An environmental lawyer who has clashed with the Mercatus Center called it "a means of laundering economic aims." The lawyer explained the strategy: "You take corporate money and give it to a neutral-sounding think tank," which "hires people with pedigrees and academic degrees who put out credible-seeming studies. But they all coincide perfectly with the economic interests of their funders."

In 1997, for instance, the EPA moved to reduce surface ozone, a form of pollution caused, in part, by emissions from oil refineries. Susan Dudley, an economist who became a top official at the Mercatus Center, criticized the proposed rule. The EPA, she argued, had not taken into account that smog-free skies would result in more cases of skin cancer. She projected that if pollution were controlled it would cause up to 11,000 additional cases of skin cancer each year.

In 1999, the District of Columbia Circuit Court took up Dudley's smog argument. Evaluating the EPA rule, the court found that the EPA had "explicitly disregarded" the "possible health benefits of ozone." In another part of the opinion, the court ruled, 2-1, that the EPA had overstepped its authority in calibrating standards for ozone emissions. As the Constitutional Accountability Center, a think tank, revealed, the judges in the majority had previously attended legal junkets, on a Montana ranch, that were arranged by the Foundation for Research on Economics and the Environment—a group funded by Koch family foundations. The judges have claimed that the ruling was unaffected by their attendance.

•     •     •

"Ideas don't happen on their own," Matt Kibbe, the president of FreedomWorks, a Tea Party advocacy group, told me. "Throughout history, ideas need patrons." The Koch brothers, after helping to create Cato and Mercatus, concluded that think tanks alone were not enough to effect change. They needed a mechanism to deliver those ideas to the street and to attract the public's support. In 1984, David Koch and Richard Fink created yet another organization, and Kibbe joined them. The group, Citizens for a Sound Economy, seemed like a grassroots movement, but according to the Center for Public Integrity it was sponsored principally by the Kochs, who provided $7.9 million between 1986 and 1993. Its mission, Kibbe said, "was to take these heavy ideas and translate them for mass America. . . . We read the same literature Obama did about nonviolent revolutions—Saul Alinsky, Gandhi, Martin Luther King. We studied the idea of the Boston Tea Party as an example of nonviolent social change. We learned we needed boots on the ground to sell ideas, not candidates." Within a few years, the group had mobilized fifty paid field workers, in twenty-six states, to rally voters behind the Kochs' agenda. David and Charles, according to one participant, were "very controlling, very top down. You can't build an organization with them. They run it."

Around this time, the brothers faced a political crisis. In 1989, the Senate Select Committee on Indian Affairs investigated their business and released a scathing report accusing Koch Oil of "a widespread and sophisticated scheme to steal crude oil from Indians and others through fraudulent mismeasuring." The Kochs admitted that they had improperly taken 31 million dollars' worth of crude oil but said that it had been accidental. Charles Koch told committee investigators that oil measurement is "a very uncertain art."

To defend its reputation, Koch Industries hired Robert Strauss, then a premier Washington lobbyist; the company soon opened an office in the city. A grand jury was convened to investigate the allegations, but it eventually disbanded without issuing criminal charges. According to the Senate report, after the committee hearings Koch operatives delved into the personal lives of committee staffers, even questioning an ex-wife. Senate investigators were upset by the Kochs' tactics. Kenneth Ballen, the counsel to the Senate committee, said, "These people have amassed such unaccountable power!"

By 1993, when Bill Clinton became president, Citizens for a Sound Economy had become a prototype for the kind of corporate-backed opposition campaigns that have proliferated during the Obama era. The group waged a successful assault on Clinton's proposed BTU tax on energy, for instance, running advertisements, staging media events, and targeting opponents. And it mobilized antitax rallies outside the Capitol—rallies that NPR described as "designed to strike fear into the hearts of wavering Democrats." Dan Glickman, a former Democratic congressman from Wichita, who supported the BTU tax, recalled, "I'd been in Congress eighteen years. The Kochs actually engaged against me and funded my opponent. They used a lot of resources and effort—their employees, too." Glickman suffered a surprise defeat. "I can't prove it, but I think I was probably their victim," he said.

The Kochs continued to disperse their money, creating slippery organizations with generic-sounding names, and this made it difficult to ascertain the extent of their influence in Washington. In 1990, Citizens for a Sound Economy created a spinoff group, Citizens for the Environment, which called acid rain and other environmental problems "myths." When the *Pittsburgh Post-Gazette* investigated the matter, it discovered that the spinoff group had "no citizen membership of its own."

In 1997, another Senate investigation began looking into what a minority report called "an audacious plan to pour millions of dollars in contributions into Republican campaigns nationwide without disclosing the amount or source," in order to evade campaign-finance laws. A shell corporation, Triad Management, had paid more than 3 million dollars for attack ads in twenty-six House races and three Senate races. More than half of the advertising money came from an obscure nonprofit group, the Economic Education Trust. The Senate committee's minority report suggested that "the trust was financed in whole or in part by Charles and David Koch of Wichita, Kansas." The brothers were suspected of having secretly paid for the attack ads, most of which aired in states where Koch Industries did business. In Kansas, where Triad Management was especially active, the funds may have played a decisive role in four of six federal races. The Kochs, when asked by reporters if they had given the money, refused to comment. In 1998, however, the *Wall Street Journal* confirmed that a consultant on the Kochs' payroll had been involved in the scheme. Charles Lewis, of the Center for Public Integrity, described the scandal as "historic. Triad was the first time a major corporation used a cutout"—a front operation—"in a threatening way. Koch Industries was the poster child of a company run amok."

·　　·　　·

During the Clinton administration, the energy industry faced increased scrutiny and regulation. In the midnineties, the Justice Department filed two lawsuits against Koch Industries, claiming that it was responsible for more than 300 oil spills, which had released an estimated 3 million gallons of oil into lakes and rivers. The penalty was potentially as high as 214 million dollars. In a settlement, Koch Industries paid a record 30-million-dollar civil fine and agreed to spend 5 million dollars on environmental projects.

In 1999, a jury found Koch Industries guilty of negligence and malice in the deaths of two Texas teenagers in an explosion that resulted from a leaky underground butane pipeline. (In 2001, the company paid an undisclosed settlement.) And in the final months of the Clinton presidency the Justice Department leveled a ninety-seven-count indictment against the company for covering up the discharge of ninety-one tons of benzene, a carcinogen, from its refinery in Corpus Christi, Texas. The company was liable for 350 million dollars in fines, and four Koch employees faced up to 35 years in prison. The Koch Petroleum Group eventually pleaded guilty to one criminal charge of covering up environmental violations, including the falsification of documents, and paid a 20-million-dollar fine. David Uhlmann, a career prosecutor who, at the time, headed the environmental-crimes section at the Justice Department, described the suit as "one of the most significant cases ever brought under the Clean Air Act." He added, "Environmental crimes are almost always motivated by economics and arrogance, and in the Koch case there was a healthy dose of both."

During the 2000 election campaign, Koch Industries spent some 900,000 dollars to support the candidacies of George W. Bush and other Republicans. During the Bush years, Koch Industries and other fossil-fuel companies enjoyed remarkable prosperity. The 2005 energy bill, which Hillary Clinton dubbed the Dick Cheney Lobbyist Energy Bill, offered enormous subsidies and tax breaks for energy companies. The Kochs have cast themselves as deficit hawks, but, according to a study by Media Matters, their companies have benefitted from nearly 100 million dollars in government contracts since 2000.

In 2004, Citizens for a Sound Economy was accused of illegitimately throwing its weight behind Bush's reelection. The group's Oregon branch had attempted to get Ralph Nader on the presidential ballot in order to dilute Democratic support for John Kerry. Critics argued that it was illegal for a tax-exempt nonprofit organization to donate its services for partisan political purposes. (A complaint was filed with the Federal Election Commission; it was dismissed.)

That year, internal rivalries at Citizens for a Sound Economy caused the organization to split apart. David Koch and Fink started a new group, Americans for Prosperity, and they hired Tim Phillips to run it. Phillips was a political veteran who had worked with Ralph Reed, the evangelical leader and Republican activist, cofounding Century Strategies, a campaign-consulting company that became notorious for its ties to the disgraced lobbyist Jack Abramoff. Phillips's online biography describes him as an expert in "grasstops" and "grassroots" political organizing. The Kochs' choice of Phillips signaled an even greater toughness. The conservative operative Grover Norquist, who is known for praising "throat slitters" in politics, called Phillips "a grownup who can make things happen."

Last year, Phillips told the *Financial Times* that Americans for Prosperity had only 8,000 registered members. Currently, its website claims that the group has "1.2 million activists." Whatever its size, the Kochs' political involvement has been intense; a former employee of the Cato Institute told me that Americans for Prosperity "was micromanaged by the Kochs." And the brothers' investment may well have paid off: Americans for Prosperity, in concert with the family's other organizations, has been instrumental in disrupting the Obama presidency.

In January 2008, Charles Koch wrote in his company newsletter that America could be on the verge of "the greatest loss of liberty and prosperity since the 1930s." That October, Americans for Prosperity held a conference of conservative operatives at a Marriott hotel outside Washington. Erick Erickson, the editor in chief of the conservative blog *RedState.com*, took the lectern, thanked David Koch, and vowed to "unite and fight . . . the armies of the left!" Soon after Obama assumed office, Americans for Prosperity launched "Porkulus" rallies against Obama's stimulus-spending measures. Then the Mercatus Center released a report claiming that stimulus funds had been directed disproportionately toward Democratic districts; eventually, the author was forced to correct the report, but not before Rush Limbaugh, citing the paper, had labeled Obama's program "a slush fund," and Fox News and other conservative outlets had echoed the sentiment. (Phil Kerpen, the vice president for policy at Americans for Prosperity, is a contributor to the Fox News website. Another officer at Americans for Prosperity, Walter Williams, often guest-hosts for Limbaugh.)

Americans for Prosperity also created an offshoot, Patients United Now, which organized what Phillips has estimated to be more than 300 rallies against health-care reform. At one rally, an effigy of a Democratic congressman was hung; at another, protesters unfurled a banner depicting corpses from Dachau. The group also helped organize the "Kill the Bill" protests outside the Capitol in March, where Democratic supporters of health-care reform alleged that they were spat on and cursed at. Phillips was a featured speaker.

Americans for Prosperity has held at least eighty events targeting cap-and-trade legislation, which is aimed at making industries pay for the air pollution that they create. Speakers for the group claimed, with exaggeration, that even back-yard barbecues and kitchen stoves would be taxed. The group was also involved in the attacks on Obama's "green jobs" czar, Van Jones, and waged a crusade against international climate talks. Casting his group as a champion of ordinary workers who would be hurt by environmentalists, Phillips went to Copenhagen last year and staged a protest outside the United Nations conference on climate change, declaring, "We're a grassroots organization. . . . I think it's unfortunate when wealthy children of wealthy families . . . want to send unemployment rates in the United States up to 20 percent."

Grover Norquist, who holds a weekly meeting for conservative leaders in Washington, including representatives from Americans for Prosperity, told me that last summer's raucous rallies were pivotal in undermining Obama's agenda. The Republican leadership in Congress, he said, "couldn't have done it without August,

when people went out on the streets. It discouraged deal makers"—
Republicans who might otherwise have worked constructively
with Obama. Moreover, the appearance of growing public opposition to Obama affected corporate donors on K Street. "K Street
is a three-billion-dollar weathervane," Norquist said. "When
Obama was strong, the Chamber of Commerce said, 'We can work
with the Obama administration.' But that changed when thousands of people went into the street and 'terrorized' congressmen.
August is what changed it. Now that Obama is weak, people are
getting tough."

As the first anniversary of Obama's election approached,
David Koch came to the Washington area to attend a triumphant
Americans for Prosperity gathering. Obama's poll numbers were
falling fast. Not a single Republican senator was working with
the administration on health care, or much else. Pundits were
writing about Obama's political ineptitude, and Tea Party groups
were accusing the president of initiating "a government takeover."
In a speech, Koch said, "Days like today bring to reality the vision of our board of directors when we started this organization,
five years ago." He went on, "We envisioned a mass movement, a
state-based one, but national in scope, of hundreds of thousands
of American citizens from all walks of life standing up and fighting for the economic freedoms that made our nation the most
prosperous society in history. . . . Thankfully, the stirrings from
California to Virginia, and from Texas to Michigan, show that
more and more of our fellow citizens are beginning to see the
same truths as we do."

While Koch didn't explicitly embrace the Tea Party movement
that day, more recently he has come close to doing so, praising it
for demonstrating the "powerful visceral hostility in the body
politic against the massive increase in government power, the massive efforts to socialize this country." Charles Koch, in a newsletter
sent to his 70,000 employees, compared the Obama administration to the regime of the Venezuelan strongman Hugo Chávez.

The Kochs' sense of imperilment is somewhat puzzling. Income inequality in America is greater than it has been since the 1920s, and since the seventies the tax rates of the wealthiest have fallen more than those of the middle class. Yet the brothers' message has evidently resonated with voters: a recent poll found that 55 percent of Americans agreed that Obama is a socialist.

Americans for Prosperity, meanwhile, has announced that it will spend an additional 45 million dollars before the midterm elections, in November. Although the group is legally prohibited from directly endorsing candidates, it nonetheless plans to target some fifty House races and half a dozen Senate races, staging rallies, organizing door-to-door canvassing, and running ads aimed at "educating voters about where candidates stand."

Though the Kochs have slowed Obama's momentum, their larger political battle is far from won. Richard Fink, interviewed by FrumForum.com this spring, said, "If you look at where we've gone from the year 2000 to now, with the expansion of government spending and a debt burden that threatens to bankrupt the country, it doesn't look very good at all." He went on, "It looks like the infrastructure that was built and nurtured has not carried the day." He suggested that the Kochs needed "to get more into the practical, day-to-day issues of governing."

•　　•　　•

In 1991, David Koch was badly injured in a plane crash in Los Angeles. He was the sole passenger in first class to survive. As he was recovering, a routine physical exam led to the discovery of prostate cancer. Koch received treatment, settled down, started a family, and reconsidered his life. As he told *Portfolio*, "When you're the only one who survived in the front of the plane and everyone else died—yeah, you think, 'My God, the good Lord spared me for some greater purpose.' My joke is that I've been busy ever since, doing all the good work I can think of, so He can have confidence in me."

Koch began giving spectacularly large donations to the arts and sciences. And he became a patron of cancer research, focusing on prostate cancer. In addition to his gifts to Sloan-Kettering, he gave 15 million dollars to New York–Presbyterian Hospital, 125 million to MIT for cancer research, 20 million to Johns Hopkins University, and 25 million to the M. D. Anderson Cancer Center, in Houston. In response to his generosity, Sloan-Kettering gave Koch its Excellence in Corporate Leadership Award. In 2004, President Bush named him to the National Cancer Advisory Board, which guides the National Cancer Institute.

Koch's corporate and political roles, however, may pose conflicts of interest. For example, at the same time that David Koch has been casting himself as a champion in the fight against cancer, Koch Industries has been lobbying to prevent the EPA from classifying formaldehyde, which the company produces in great quantities, as a "known carcinogen" in humans.

Scientists have long known that formaldehyde causes cancer in rats, and several major scientific studies have concluded that formaldehyde causes cancer in human beings—including one published last year by the National Cancer Institute, on whose advisory board Koch sits. The study tracked 25,000 patients for an average of forty years; subjects exposed to higher amounts of formaldehyde had significantly higher rates of leukemia. These results helped lead an expert panel within the National Institutes of Health to conclude that formaldehyde should be categorized as a known carcinogen and be strictly controlled by the government. Corporations have resisted regulations on formaldehyde for decades, however, and Koch Industries has been a large funder of members of Congress who have stymied the EPA, requiring it to defer new regulations until more studies are completed.

Koch Industries became a major producer of the chemical in 2005 after it bought Georgia-Pacific, the paper and wood-products company, for 21 billion dollars. Georgia-Pacific manufactures formaldehyde in its chemical division and uses it to produce various wood products, such as plywood and laminates. Its annual production capacity for formaldehyde is 2.2 billion pounds. Last December, Traylor Champion, Georgia-Pacific's vice president of environmental affairs, sent a formal letter of protest to federal health authorities. He wrote that the company "strongly disagrees" with the NIH panel's conclusion that formaldehyde should be treated as a known human carcinogen. David Koch did not recuse himself from the National Cancer Advisory Board or divest himself of company stock while his company was directly lobbying the government to keep formaldehyde on the market. (A board spokesperson said that the issue of formaldehyde had not come up.)

James Huff, an associate director at the National Institute for Environmental Health Sciences, a division of the NIH, told me that it was "disgusting" for Koch to be serving on the National Cancer Advisory Board: "It's just not good for public health. Vested interests should not be on the board." He went on, "Those boards are very important. They're very influential as to whether NCI goes into formaldehyde or not. Billions of dollars are involved in formaldehyde."

Harold Varmus, the director of the National Cancer Institute, knows David Koch from Memorial Sloan-Kettering, which he used to run. He said that, at Sloan-Kettering, "a lot of people who gave to us had large business interests. The one thing we wouldn't tolerate in our board members is tobacco." When told of Koch Industries' stance on formaldehyde, Varmus said that he was "surprised."

•      •      •

The David H. Koch Hall of Human Origins, at the Smithsonian's National Museum of Natural History, is a multimedia exploration of the theory that mankind evolved in response to climate change. At the main entrance, viewers are confronted with a giant graph charting the Earth's temperature over the past ten million years, which notes that it is far cooler now than it was ten thousand years ago. Overhead, the text reads, "HUMANS EVOLVED IN RESPONSE TO A CHANGING WORLD." The message, as amplified by the exhibit's website, is that "key human adaptations evolved in response to environmental instability." Only at the end of the exhibit, under the headline "OUR SURVIVAL CHALLENGE," is it noted that levels of carbon dioxide are higher now than they have ever been and that they are projected to increase dramatically in the next century. No cause is given for this development; no mention is made of any possible role played by fossil fuels. The exhibit makes it seem part of a natural continuum. The accompanying text says, "During the period in which humans evolved, Earth's temperature and the amount of carbon dioxide in the atmosphere fluctuated together." An interactive game in the exhibit suggests that humans will continue to adapt to climate change in the future. People may build "underground cities," developing "short, compact bodies" or "curved spines," so that "moving around in tight spaces will be no problem."

Such ideas uncannily echo the Koch message. The company's January newsletter to employees, for instance, argues that "fluctuations in the earth's climate predate humanity," and concludes, "Since we can't control Mother Nature, let's figure out how to get along with her changes." Joseph Romm, a physicist who runs the website ClimateProgress.org, is infuriated by the Smithsonian's presentation. "The whole exhibit whitewashes the modern climate issue," he said. "I think the Kochs wanted to be seen as some sort of high-minded company, associated with the greatest natural-history and science museum in the country. But the truth is, the exhibit is underwritten by big-time polluters, who are underground funders of action to stop efforts to deal with this threat to humanity. I think the Smithsonian should have drawn the line."

Cristián Samper, the museum's director, said that the exhibit is not about climate change and described Koch as "one of the best donors we've had, in my tenure here, because he's very interested in the content, but completely hands off." He noted, "I don't know all the details of his involvement in other issues."

The Kochs have long depended on the public's not knowing all the details about them. They have been content to operate what David Koch has called "the largest company that you've never heard of." But with the growing prominence of the Tea Party and with increased awareness of the Kochs' ties to the movement, the brothers may find it harder to deflect scrutiny. Recently, President Obama took aim at the Kochs' political network. Speaking at a Democratic National Committee fund raiser, in Austin, he warned supporters that the Supreme Court's recent ruling in the Citizens United case—which struck down laws prohibiting direct corporate spending on campaigns—had made it even easier for big companies to hide behind "groups with harmless-sounding names like Americans for Prosperity." Obama said, "They don't have to say who, exactly, Americans for Prosperity are. You don't know if it's a foreign-controlled corporation"—or even, he added, "a big oil company."

## Harper's Magazine

WINNER—REPORTING

*Few National Magazine Awards could have been as controversial as the one* Harper's Magazine *garnered for "The Guantánamo 'Suicides.'"* Critics argued that Scott Horton's reporting did not support his conclusions (some even suggested that it was unthinkable to question the integrity of military officers). Other readers maintained that Horton's analysis, while speculative, nonetheless raised important questions that the government did not seem interested in answering. Yet the plain fact remained that three prisoners died at Guantánamo on June 9, 2006. According to the official report, they hanged themselves, their hands bound, rags stuffed down their throats, their bodies unnoticed for more then two hours despite regulations requiring guards to inspect their cells every ten minutes. The National Magazine Award judges said that Horton reconstructed "the events of that evening in gripping and convincing detail," leaving readers "with the impression, wholly earned, that the gravest possible miscarriage of justice may have occurred."*

Scott Horton

# The Guantánamo "Suicides"

## 1. "Asymmetrical Warfare"

When President Barack Obama took office last year, he promised to "restore the standards of due process and the core constitutional values that have made this country great." Toward that end, the president issued an executive order declaring that the extraconstitutional prison camp at Guantánamo Naval Base "shall be closed as soon as practicable, and no later than one year from the date of this order." Obama has failed to fulfill his promise. Some prisoners there are being charged with crimes, others released, but the date for closing the camp seems to recede steadily into the future. Furthermore, new evidence now emerging may entangle Obama's young administration with crimes that occurred during the George W. Bush presidency, evidence that suggests the current administration failed to investigate seriously— and may even have continued—a cover-up of the possible homicides of three prisoners at Guantánamo in 2006.

   Late on the evening of June 9 that year, three prisoners at Guantánamo died suddenly and violently. Salah Ahmed Al-Salami, from Yemen, was thirty-seven. Mani Shaman Al-Utaybi, from Saudi Arabia, was thirty. Yasser Talal Al-Zahrani, also from Saudi Arabia, was twenty-two and had been imprisoned at Guantánamo since he was captured at the age of seventeen. None of the men had been charged with a crime, though all three had been engaged in hunger strikes to protest the conditions of their imprisonment. They were being held in a cell block, known as Alpha Block, reserved for particularly troublesome or high-value prisoners.

As news of the deaths emerged the following day, the camp quickly went into lockdown. The authorities ordered nearly all the reporters at Guantánamo to leave and those en route to turn back. The commander at Guantánamo, Rear Admiral Harry Harris, then declared the deaths "suicides." In an unusual move, he also used the announcement to attack the dead men. "I believe this was not an act of desperation," he said, "but an act of asymmetrical warfare waged against us." Reporters accepted the official account, and even lawyers for the prisoners appeared to believe that they had killed themselves. Only the prisoners' families in Saudi Arabia and Yemen rejected the notion.

Two years later, the U.S. Naval Criminal Investigative Service, which has primary investigative jurisdiction within the naval base, issued a report supporting the account originally advanced by Harris, now a vice admiral in command of the Sixth Fleet. The Pentagon declined to make the NCIS report public, and only when pressed with Freedom of Information Act demands did it disclose parts of the report, some 1,700 pages of documents so heavily redacted as to be nearly incomprehensible. The NCIS documents were carefully cross-referenced and deciphered by students and faculty at the law school of Seton Hall University in New Jersey, and their findings, released in November 2009, made clear why the Pentagon had been unwilling to make its conclusions public. The official story of the prisoners' deaths was full of unacknowledged contradictions, and the centerpiece of the report—a reconstruction of the events—was simply unbelievable.

According to the NCIS documents, each prisoner had fashioned a noose from torn sheets and T-shirts and tied it to the top of his cell's eight-foot-high steel-mesh wall. Each prisoner was able somehow to bind his own hands, and, in at least one case, his own feet, then stuff more rags deep down into his own throat. We are then asked to believe that each prisoner, even as he was choking on those rags, climbed up on his washbasin, slipped his head through the noose, tightened it, and leapt from the washbasin to hang until he asphyxiated. The NCIS report also proposes that the three prisoners, who were held in non-adjoining cells, carried out each of these actions almost simultaneously.

Al-Zahrani, according to the report, was discovered first, at 12:39 A.M., and taken by several Alpha Block guards to the camp's detention medical clinic. No doctors could be found there, nor the phone number for one, so a clinic staffer dialed 911. During this time, other guards discovered Al-Utaybi. Still others discovered Al-Salami a few minutes later. Although rigor mortis had already set in—indicating that the men had been dead for at least two hours—the NCIS report claims that an unnamed medical officer attempted to resuscitate one of the men and, in attempting to pry open his jaw, broke his teeth.

The fact that at least two of the prisoners also had cloth masks affixed to their faces, presumably to prevent the expulsion of the rags from their mouths, went unremarked by the NCIS, as did the fact that standard operating procedure at Camp Delta required the navy guards on duty after midnight to "conduct a visual search" of each cell and detainee every ten minutes. The report claimed that the prisoners had hung sheets or blankets to hide their activities and shaped more sheets and pillows to look like bodies sleeping in their beds, but it did not explain where they were able to acquire so much fabric beyond their tightly controlled allotment or why the navy guards would allow such an obvious and immediately observable deviation from permitted behavior. Nor did the report explain how the dead men managed to hang undetected for more than two hours or why the navy guards on duty, having for whatever reason so grievously failed in their duties, were never disciplined.

A separate report, the result of an "informal investigation" initiated by Admiral Harris, found that standard operating procedures were violated that night but concluded that disciplinary action was not warranted, because of the "generally permissive environment" of the cell block and the numerous "concessions" that had been made with regard to the prisoners' comfort, "concessions" that had resulted in a "general confusion by the guard and the JDG staff over many of the rules that applied to the guard force's handling of the detainees." According to Harris, even had standard operating procedures been followed, "it is possible that the detainees could have successfully committed suicide anyway."

This is the official story, adopted by NCIS and Guantánamo command and reiterated by the Justice Department in formal pleadings, by the Defense Department in briefings and press releases, and by the State Department. Now four members of the Military Intelligence unit assigned to guard Camp Delta, including a decorated noncommissioned army officer who was on duty as sergeant of the guard the night of June 9, have furnished an account dramatically at odds with the NCIS report—a report for which they were neither interviewed nor approached.

All four soldiers say they were ordered by their commanding officer not to speak out, and all four soldiers provide evidence that authorities initiated a cover-up within hours of the prisoners' deaths. Army Staff Sergeant Joseph Hickman and men under his supervision have disclosed evidence in interviews with *Harper's Magazine* that strongly suggests that the three prisoners who died on June 9 had been transported to another location prior to their deaths. The guards' accounts also reveal the existence of a previously unreported black site at Guantánamo where the deaths, or at least the events that led directly to the deaths, most likely occurred.

## 2. "Camp No"

The soldiers of the Maryland-based 629th Military Intelligence Battalion arrived at Guantánamo Naval Base in March 2006, assigned to provide security to Camp America, the sector of the base containing the five individual prison compounds that house the prisoners. Camp Delta was at the time the largest of these compounds, and within its walls were four smaller camps, numbered 1 through 4, which in turn were divided into cell blocks. Life at Camp America, as at all prisons, was and remains rigorously routinized for both prisoners and their jailers. Navy guards patrol the cell blocks, and army personnel control the exterior areas of the camp. All observed incidents must be logged. For the army guards who man the towers and "sally ports" (access points), knowing who enters and leaves the camp, and exactly when, is the essence of their mission.

One of the new guards who arrived that March was Joe Hickman, then a sergeant. Hickman grew up in Baltimore and joined the Marines in 1983, at the age of nineteen. When I interviewed him in January at his home in Wisconsin, he told me he had been inspired to enlist by Ronald Reagan, "the greatest president we've ever had." He worked in a military intelligence unit and was eventually tapped for Reagan's Presidential Guard detail, an assignment reserved for model soldiers. When his four years were up, Hickman returned home, where he worked a series of security jobs—prison transport, executive protection, and eventually private investigations. After September 11 he decided to reenlist, at thirty-seven, this time in the Army National Guard.

Hickman deployed to Guantánamo with his friend Specialist Tony Davila, who grew up outside Washington, D.C., and who had himself been a private investigator. When they arrived at Camp Delta, Davila told me, soldiers from the California National Guard unit they were relieving introduced him to some of the curiosities of the base. The most noteworthy of these was an unnamed and officially unacknowledged compound nestled out of sight between two plateaus about a mile north of Camp Delta, just outside Camp America's perimeter. One day, while on patrol, Hickman and Davila came across the compound. It looked like other camps within Camp America, Davila said, only it had no guard towers and was surrounded by concertina wire. They saw no activity, but Hickman guessed the place could house as many as eighty prisoners. One part of the compound, he said, had the same appearance as the interrogation centers at other prison camps.

The compound was not visible from the main road, and the access road was chained off. The guardsman who told Davila about the compound had said, "This place does not exist," and Hickman, who was frequently put in charge of security for all of Camp America, was not briefed about the site. Nevertheless, Davila said, other soldiers—many of whom were required to patrol the outside perimeter of Camp America—had seen the compound, and many speculated about its purpose. One theory was that it was being used by some of the nonuniformed government personnel who frequently showed up in the camps and were widely thought to be CIA agents.

A friend of Hickman's had nicknamed the compound "Camp No," the idea being that anyone who asked if it existed would be told, "No, it doesn't." He and Davila made a point of stopping by whenever they had the chance; once, Hickman said, he heard a "series of screams" from within the compound.

Hickman and his men also discovered that there were odd exceptions to their duties. Army guards were charged with searching and logging every vehicle that passed into and out of Camp Delta. "When John McCain came to the camp, he had to be logged in." However, Hickman was instructed to make no record whatsoever of the movements of one vehicle in particular—a white van, dubbed the "paddy wagon," that navy guards used to transport heavily manacled prisoners, one at a time, into and out of Camp Delta. The van had no rear windows and contained a dog cage large enough to hold a single prisoner. Navy drivers, Hickman came to understand, would let the guards know they had a prisoner in the van by saying they were "delivering a pizza."

The paddy wagon was used to transport prisoners to medical facilities and to meetings with their lawyers. But as Hickman monitored the paddy wagon's movements from the guard tower at Camp Delta, he frequently saw it follow an unexpected route. When the van reached the first intersection to the east, instead of heading right—toward the other camps or toward one of the buildings where prisoners could meet with their lawyers—it made a left. In that direction, past the perimeter checkpoint known as ACP Roosevelt, there were only two destinations. One was a beach where soldiers went to swim. The other was Camp No.

## 3. "Lit Up"

The night the prisoners died, Hickman was on duty as sergeant of the guard for Camp America's exterior security force. When his twelve-hour shift began, at 6:00 P.M., he climbed the ladder to Tower 1, which stood twenty feet above Sally Port 1, the main entrance to Camp Delta. From there he had an excellent view of the camp and much of the exterior perimeter as well. Later he would make his rounds.

Shortly after his shift began, Hickman noticed that someone had parked the paddy wagon near Camp 1, which houses Alpha Block. A moment later, two navy guards emerged from Camp 1, escorting a prisoner. They put the prisoner into the back of the van and then left the camp through Sally Port 1, just below Hickman. He was under standing orders not to search the paddy wagon, so he just watched it as it headed east. He assumed the guards and their charge were bound for one of the other prison camps southeast of Camp Delta. But when the van reached the first intersection, instead of making a right, toward the other camps, it made the left, toward ACP Roosevelt and Camp No.

Twenty minutes later—about the amount of time needed for the trip to Camp No and back—the paddy wagon returned. This time Hickman paid closer attention. He couldn't see the navy guards' faces, but from body size and uniform they appeared to be the same men.

The guards walked into Camp 1 and soon emerged with another prisoner. They departed Camp America, again in the direction of Camp No. Twenty minutes later, the van returned. Hickman, his curiosity piqued by the unusual flurry of activity and guessing that the guards might make another excursion, left Tower 1 and drove the three quarters of a mile to ACP Roosevelt to see exactly where the paddy wagon was headed. Shortly thereafter, the van passed through the checkpoint for the third time and then went another hundred yards, whereupon it turned toward Camp No, eliminating any question in Hickman's mind about where it was going. All three prisoners would have reached their destination before 8:00 P.M.

Hickman says he saw nothing more of note until about 11:30 P.M., when he had returned to his preferred vantage at Tower 1. As he watched, the paddy wagon returned to Camp Delta. This time, however, the navy guards did not get out of the van to enter Camp 1. Instead, they backed the vehicle up to the entrance of the medical clinic, as if to unload something.

At approximately 11:45 P.M.—nearly an hour before the NCIS claims the first body was discovered—Army Specialist Christopher Penvose, preparing for a midnight shift in Tower 1, was approached by a senior navy NCO. Penvose told me that the NCO—who, following standard operating procedures, wore no name tag—appeared to be extremely agitated. He instructed Penvose to go immediately to the Camp Delta chow hall, identify a female senior petty officer who would be dining there, and relay to her a specific code word. Penvose did as he was instructed.

The officer leapt up from her seat and immediately ran out of the chow hall.

Another thirty minutes passed. Then, as Hickman and Penvose both recall, Camp Delta suddenly "lit up"—stadium-style floodlights were turned on, and the camp became the scene of frenzied activity, filling with personnel in and out of uniform. Hickman headed to the clinic, which appeared to be the center of activity, to learn the reason for the commotion. He asked a distraught medical corpsman what had happened. She said three dead prisoners had been delivered to the clinic. Hickman recalled her saying that they had died because they had rags stuffed down their throats and that one of them was severely bruised. Davila told me he spoke to navy guards who said the men had died as the result of having rags stuffed down their throats.

Hickman was concerned that such a serious incident could have occurred in Camp 1 on his watch. He asked his tower guards what they had seen. Penvose, from his position at Tower 1, had an unobstructed view of the walkway between Camp 1 and the medical clinic—the path by which any prisoners who died at Camp 1 would be delivered to the clinic. Penvose told Hickman, and later confirmed to me, that he saw no prisoners being moved from Camp 1 to the clinic. In Tower 4 (it should be noted that army and navy guard-tower designations differ), another army specialist, David Caroll, was forty-five yards from Alpha Block, the cell block within Camp 1 that had housed the three dead men. He also had an unobstructed view of the alleyway that connected the cell block itself to the clinic. He likewise reported to Hickman, and confirmed to me, that he had seen no prisoners transferred to the clinic that night, dead or alive.

## 4. "He Could Not Cry Out"

The fate of a fourth prisoner, a forty-two-year-old Saudi Arabian named Shaker Aamer, may be related to that of the three prisoners who died on June 9. Aamer is married to a British woman and was in the process of becoming a British subject when he was captured in Jalalabad, Afghanistan, in 2001. United States authorities insist that he carried a gun and served Osama bin Laden as an interpreter. Aamer denies this. At Guantánamo, Aamer's fluency in English soon allowed him to play an important role in camp politics. According to both Aamer's attorney and press accounts furnished by army colonel Michael Bumgarner, the Camp America commander, Aamer cooperated closely with Bumgarner in efforts to bring a 2005 hunger strike to an end. He persuaded several prisoners to break their strike for a while, but the settlement collapsed and soon afterward Aamer was sent to solitary confinement. Then, on the night the prisoners from Alpha Block died, Aamer says he himself was the victim of an act of striking brutality.

He described the events in detail to his lawyer, Zachary Katznelson, who was permitted to speak to him several weeks later. Katznelson recorded every detail of Aamer's account and filed an affidavit with the federal district court in Washington, setting it out:

On June 9th, 2006, [Aamer] was beaten for two and a half hours straight. Seven naval military police participated in his beating. Mr. Aamer stated he had refused to provide a retina scan and fingerprints. He reported to me that he was strapped to a chair, fully restrained at the head, arms and legs. The MPs inflicted so much pain, Mr. Aamer said he thought he was going to die. The MPs pressed on pressure points all over his body: his temples, just under his jawline, in the hollow beneath his ears. They choked him. They bent his nose repeatedly so hard to the side he thought it would break. They pinched his thighs and feet constantly. They gouged his eyes. They held his eyes open and shined a mag-lite in them for minutes on end, generating intense heat. They bent his fingers until he screamed. When he screamed, they cut off his airway, then put a mask on him so he could not cry out.

The treatment Aamer describes is noteworthy because it produces excruciating pain without leaving lasting marks. Still, the fact that Aamer had his airway cut off and a mask put over his face "so he could not cry out" is alarming. This is the same technique that appears to have been used on the three deceased prisoners.

The United Kingdom has pressed aggressively for the return of British subjects and persons of interest. Every individual requested by the British has been turned over, with one exception: Shaker Aamer. In denying this request, U.S. authorities have cited unelaborated "security" concerns. There is no suggestion that the Americans intend to charge him before a military commission or in a federal criminal court, and, indeed, they have no meaningful evidence linking him to any crime. American authorities may be concerned that Aamer, if released, could provide evidence against them in criminal investigations. This evidence would include what he experienced on June 9, 2006, and during his 2002 detention in Afghanistan at Bagram Airfield, where he says he was subjected to a procedure in which his head was smashed repeatedly against a wall. This torture technique, called "walling" in CIA documents, was expressly approved at a later date by the Department of Justice.

## 5. "You All Know"

By dawn, the news had circulated through Camp America that three prisoners had committed suicide by swallowing rags. Colonel Bumgarner called a meeting of the guards, and at 7:00 A.M. at least fifty soldiers and sailors gathered at Camp America's open-air theater.

Bumgarner was known as an eccentric commander. Hickman marveled, for instance, at the colonel's insistence that his staff line up and salute him, to music selections that included Beethoven's Fifth Symphony and the reggae hit "Bad Boys," as he entered the command center. This morning, however, Hickman thought Bumgarner seemed unusually nervous and clipped.

According to independent interviews with soldiers who witnessed the speech, Bumgarner told his audience that "you all know" three prisoners in the Alpha Block at Camp 1 committed suicide during the night by swallowing rags, causing them to choke to death. This was a surprise to no one—even servicemen who had not worked the night before had heard about the rags. But then Bumgarner told those assembled that the media would report something different. It would report that the three prisoners had committed suicide by hanging themselves in their cells. It was important, he said, that servicemen make no comments or suggestions that in any way undermined the official report. He reminded the soldiers and sailors that their phone and e-mail communications were being monitored. The meeting lasted no more than twenty minutes. (Bumgarner has not responded to requests for comment.)[1]

That evening, Bumgarner's boss, Admiral Harris, read a statement to reporters:

1. After this report was published on Harpers.org on January 18, Bumgarner did send an e-mail to the Associated Press. "This blatant misrepresentation of the truth infuriates me," he wrote. "I don't know who Sgt. Hickman is, but he is only trying to be a spotlight ranger." In fact, Bumgarner should have no trouble remembering Hickman. As camp commander, he awarded him a commendation medal for defusing a prison riot. In his e-mail, Bumgarner also said Hickman "knows nothing about what transpired in Camp 1, or our medical facility. I do, I was there." By his own sworn testimony, however, Bumgarner did not arrive at Camp 1 until 12:48 A.M. on June 10. "On the night of 09JUN06, I was not in the camp," he told the NCIS. "I had spent the evening at Admiral Harris's house." As of press time, Bumgarner has not returned my calls seeking clarification on the matter.

An alert, professional guard noticed something out of the ordinary in the cell of one of the detainees. The guard's response was swift and professional to secure the area and check on the status of the detainee. When it was apparent that the detainee had hung himself, the guard force and medical teams reacted quickly to attempt to save the detainee's life. The detainee was unresponsive and not breathing. [The] guard force began to check on the health and welfare of other detainees. Two detainees in their cells had also hung themselves.

When he finished praising the guards and the medics, Harris—in a notable departure from traditional military decorum—launched his attack on the men who had died on his watch. "They have no regard for human life," Harris said, "neither ours nor their own." A Pentagon press release issued soon after described the dead men, who had been accused of no crime, as Al Qaeda or Taliban operatives. Lieutenant Commander Jeffrey Gordon, the Pentagon's chief press officer, went still further, telling the *Guardian*'s David Rose, "These guys were fanatics like the Nazis, Hitlerites, or the Ku Klux Klan, the people they tried at Nuremberg." The Pentagon was not the only U.S. government agency to participate in the assault. Colleen Graffy, a deputy assistant secretary of state, told the BBC that "taking their own lives was not necessary, but it certainly is a good P.R. move."

The same day the three prisoners died, Fox News commentator Bill O'Reilly completed a reporting trip to the naval base, where, according to his account on *The O'Reilly Factor*, the Joint Army Navy Task Force "granted the *Factor* near total access to the prison." Although the Pentagon began turning away reporters after news of the deaths had emerged, two reporters from the *Charlotte Observer*, Michael Gordon and photographer Todd Sumlin, had arrived that morning to work on a profile of Bumgarner, and the colonel invited them to shadow him as he dealt with the crisis. A Pentagon spokesman later told the *Observer* it had been expecting a "puff piece," which is why, according to the *Observer*, "Bumgarner and his superiors on the base" had given them permission to remain.

Bumgarner quickly returned to his theatrical ways. As Gordon reported in the June 13, 2006, issue of the *Observer*, the colonel seemed to enjoy putting on a show. "Right now, we are at ground zero," Bumgarner told his officer staff during a June 12 meeting. Referring to the naval base's prisoners, he said, "There is not a trustworthy son of a bitch in the entire bunch." In the same article, Gordon also noted what he had learned about the deaths. The suicides had occurred "in three cells on the same block," he reported. The prisoners had "hanged themselves with strips of knotted cloth taken from clothing and sheets," after shaping their pillows and blankets to look like sleeping bodies. "And Bumgarner said," Gordon reported, "each had a ball of cloth in their mouth either for choking or muffling their voices."

Something about Bumgarner's *Observer* interview seemed to have set off an alarm far up the chain of command. No sooner was Gordon's story in print than Bumgarner was called to Admiral Harris's office. As Bumgarner would tell Gordon in a follow-up profile three months later, Harris was holding up a copy of the *Observer*: "This," said the admiral to Bumgarner, "could get me relieved." (Harris did not respond to requests for comment.) That same day, an investigation was launched to determine whether classified information had been leaked from Guantánamo. Bumgarner was suspended.

Less than a week after the appearance of the *Observer* stories, Davila and Hickman each heard separately from friends in the navy and in the military police that FBI agents had raided the colonel's quarters. The MPs understood from their FBI contacts that there was concern over the possibility that Bumgarner had taken home some classified materials and was planning to share them with the media or to use them in writing a book.

On June 27, two weeks later, Gordon's *Observer* colleague Scott Dodd reported: "A brigadier general determined that 'unclassified sensitive information' was revealed to the public in the days after the June 10 suicides." Harris, according to the article, had already ordered "appropriate administrative action." Bumgarner soon left Guantánamo for a new post in Missouri. He now serves as an ROTC instructor at Virginia Tech in Blacksburg.

Bumgarner's comments appear to be at odds with the official Pentagon narrative on only one point: that the deaths had involved cloth being stuffed into the prisoners' mouths. The involvement of the FBI suggested that more was at issue.

## 6. "An Unmistakable Message"

On June 10, NCIS investigators began interviewing the navy guards in charge of Alpha Block, but after the Pentagon committed itself to the suicide narrative, they appear to have stopped. On June 14, the interviews resumed, and the NCIS informed at least six navy guards that they were suspected of making false statements or failing to obey direct orders. No disciplinary action ever followed.

The investigators conducted interviews with guards, medics, prisoners, and officers. As the Seton Hall researchers note, however, nothing in the NCIS report suggests that the investigators secured or reviewed the duty roster, the prisoner-transfer book, the pass-on book, the records of phone and radio communications, or footage from the camera that continuously monitored activity in the hallways, all of which could have helped them authoritatively reconstruct the events of that evening.

The NCIS did, however, move swiftly to seize every piece of paper possessed by every single prisoner in Camp America, some 1,065 pounds of material, much of it privileged attorney-client correspondence. Several weeks later, authorities sought an after-the-fact justification. The Justice Department—bolstered by sworn statements from Admiral Harris and from Carol Kisthardt, the special agent in charge of the NCIS investigation—claimed in a U.S. district court that the seizure was appropriate because there had been a conspiracy among the prisoners to commit suicide. Justice further claimed that investigators had found suicide notes and argued that the attorney-client materials were being used to pass communications among the prisoners.

David Remes, a lawyer who opposed the Justice Department's efforts, explained the practical effect of the government's maneuvers. The seizure, he said, "sent an unmistakable message to the prisoners that they could not expect their communications with their lawyers to remain confidential. The Justice Department defended the massive breach of the attorney-client privilege on the account of the deaths on June 9 and the asserted need to investigate them."

If the "suicides" were a form of warfare between the prisoners and the Bush administration, as Admiral Harris charged, it was the latter that quickly turned the war to its advantage.


### 7. "Yasser Couldn't Even Make a Sandwich!"

When I asked Talal Al-Zahrani what he thought had happened to his son, he was direct. "They snatched my seventeen-year-old son for a bounty payment," he said. "They took him to Guantánamo and held him prisoner for five years. They tortured him. Then they killed him and returned him to me in a box, cut up."

Al-Zahrani was a brigadier general in the Saudi police. He dismissed the Pentagon's claims, as well as the investigation that supported them. Yasser, he said, was a young man who loved to play soccer and didn't care for politics. The Pentagon claimed that Yasser's frontline battle experience came from his having been a cook in a Taliban camp. Al-Zahrani said that this was preposterous: "A cook? Yasser couldn't even make a sandwich!"

"Yasser wasn't guilty of anything," Al-Zahrani said. "He knew that. He firmly believed he would be heading home soon. Why would he commit suicide?" The evidence supports this argument. Hyperbolic U.S. government statements at the time of Yasser Al-Zahrani's death masked the fact that his case had been reviewed and that he was, in fact, on a list of prisoners to be sent home. I had shown Al-Zahrani the letter that the government says was Yasser's suicide note and asked him whether he recognized his son's handwriting. He had never seen the note before, he answered, and no U.S. official had ever asked him about it. After studying the note carefully, he said, "This is a forgery."

Also returned to Saudi Arabia was the body of Mani Al-Utaybi. Orphaned in his youth, Mani grew up in his uncle's home in the small town of Dawadmi. I spoke to one of the many cousins who shared that home, Faris Al-Utaybi. Mani, said Faris, had gone to Baluchistan—a rural, tribal area that straddles Iran, Pakistan, and Afghanistan—to do humanitarian work, and someone there had sold him to the Americans for $5,000. He said that Mani was a peaceful man who would harm no one. Indeed, U.S. authorities had decided to release Al-Utaybi and return him to Saudi Arabia. When he died, he was just a few weeks shy of his transfer.

Salah Al-Salami was seized in March 2002, when Pakistani authorities raided a residence in Karachi believed to have been used as a safe house by Abu Zubaydah and took into custody all who were living there at the time. A Yemeni, Al-Salami had quit his job and moved to Pakistan with only $400 in his pocket. The U.S. suspicions against him rested almost entirely on the fact that he had taken lodgings, with other students, in a boarding house that terrorists might at one point have used. There was no direct evidence linking him either to Al Qaeda or to the Taliban. On August 22, 2008, the *Washington Post* quoted from a previously secret review of his case: "There is no credible information to suggest [Al-Salami] received terrorist related training or is a member of the Al Qaeda network." All that stood in the way of Al-Salami's release from Guantánamo were difficult diplomatic relations between the United States and Yemen.

## 8. "The Removal of the Neck Organs"

Military pathologists connected with the Armed Forces Institute of Pathology arranged immediate autopsies of the three dead prisoners, without securing the permission of the men's families. The identities and findings of the pathologists remain shrouded in extraordinary secrecy, but the timing of the autopsies suggests that medical personnel stationed at Guantánamo may have undertaken the procedure without waiting for the arrival of an experienced medical examiner from the United States. Each of the heavily redacted autopsy reports states unequivocally that "the manner of death is suicide" and, more specifically, that the prisoner died of "hanging." Each of the reports describes ligatures that were found wrapped around the prisoner's neck, as well as circumferential dried abrasion furrows imprinted with the very fine weave pattern of the ligature fabric and forming an inverted "V" on the back of the head. This condition, the anonymous pathologists state, is consistent with that of a hanging victim.

The pathologists place the time of death "at least a couple of hours" before the bodies were discovered, which would be sometime before 10:30 P.M. on June 9. Additionally, the autopsy of Al-Salami states that his hyoid bone was broken, a phenomenon usually associated with manual strangulation, not hanging.

The report asserts that the hyoid was broken "during the removal of the neck organs." An odd admission, given that these are the very body parts—the larynx, the hyoid bone, and the thyroid cartilage—that would have been essential to determining whether death occurred from hanging, from strangulation, or from choking. These parts remained missing when the men's families finally received their bodies.

All the families requested independent autopsies. The Saudi prisoners were examined by Saeed Al-Ghamdy, a pathologist based in Saudi Arabia. Al-Salami, from Yemen, was inspected by Patrice Mangin, a pathologist based in Switzerland. Both pathologists noted the removal of the structure that would have been the natural focus of the autopsy: the throat. Both pathologists contacted the Armed Forces Institute of Pathology, requesting the missing body parts and more information about the previous autopsies. The institute did not respond to their requests or queries. (It also did not respond to a series of calls I placed requesting information and comment.)

When Al-Zahrani viewed his son's corpse, he saw evidence of a homicide. "There was a major blow to the head on the right side," he said. "There was evidence of torture on the upper torso, and on the palms of his hand. There were needle marks on his right arm and on his left arm." None of these details are noted in the U.S. autopsy report. "I am a law enforcement professional," Al-Zahrani said. "I know what to look for when examining a body."

Mangin, for his part, expressed particular concern about Al-Salami's mouth and throat, where he saw "a blunt trauma carried out against the oral region." The U.S. autopsy report mentions an effort at resuscitation, but this, in Mangin's view, did not explain the severity of the injuries. He also noted that some of the marks on the neck were not those he would normally associate with hanging.

## 9. "I Know Some Things You Don't"

Sergeant Joe Hickman's tour of duty, which ended in March 2007, was distinguished: he was selected as Guantánamo's "NCO of the Quarter" and was given a commendation medal. When he returned to the United States, he was promoted to staff sergeant and worked in Maryland as an army recruiter before eventually settling in Wisconsin. But he could not forget what he had seen at Guantánamo. When Barack Obama became president, Hickman decided to act. "I thought that with a new administration and new ideas I could actually come forward," he said. "It was haunting me."

Hickman had seen a 2006 report from Seton Hall University Law School dealing with the deaths of the three prisoners, and he followed their subsequent work. After Obama was inaugurated in January 2009, he called Mark Denbeaux, the professor who had led the Seton Hall team. "I learned something from your report," he said, "but I know some things you don't."

Within two days, Hickman was in Newark, meeting with Denbeaux. Also at the meeting was Denbeaux's son and sometime coeditor, Josh, a private attorney. Josh Denbeaux agreed to represent Hickman, who was concerned that he could go to prison if he disobeyed Colonel Bumgarner's order not to speak out, even if that order was itself illegal. Hickman did not want to speak to the press. On the other hand, he felt that "silence was just wrong."

The two lawyers quickly made arrangements for Hickman to speak instead with authorities in Washington, D.C. On February 2, they had meetings on Capitol Hill and with the Department of Justice. The meeting with Justice was an odd one. The father-and-son legal team were met by Rita Glavin, the acting head of the Justice Department's Criminal Division; John Morton, who was soon to become an assistant secretary at the Department of Homeland Security; and Steven Fagell, counselor to the head of the Criminal Division. Fagell had been, along with the new attorney general, Eric Holder, a partner at the elite Washington law firm of Covington & Burling, and was widely viewed as "Holder's eyes" in the Criminal Division.

For more than an hour, the two lawyers described what Hickman had seen: the existence of Camp No, the transportation of the three prisoners, the van's arrival at the medical clinic, the lack of evidence that any bodies had ever been removed from Alpha

Block, and so on. The officials listened intently and asked many questions. The Denbeauxes said they could provide a list of witnesses who would corroborate every aspect of their account. At the end of the meeting, Mark Denbeaux recalled, the officials specifically thanked the lawyers for not speaking to reporters first and for "doing it the right way."

Two days later, another Justice Department official, Teresa McHenry, head of the Criminal Division's Domestic Security Section, called Mark Denbeaux and said that she was heading up an investigation and wanted to meet directly with his client. She went to New Jersey to do so. Hickman then reviewed the basic facts and furnished McHenry with the promised list of corroborating witnesses and details on how they could be contacted.

The Denbeauxes did not hear from anyone at the Justice Department for at least two months. Then, in April, an FBI agent called to say she did not have the list of contacts. She asked if this document could be provided again. It was. Shortly thereafter, a Justice official and two FBI agents interviewed Davila, who had left the army, in Columbia, South Carolina.[2] The official asked Davila if he was prepared to travel to Guantánamo to identify the locations of various sites. He said he was. "It seemed like they were interested," Davila told me. "Then I never heard from them again."

Several more months passed, and Hickman and his lawyers became increasingly concerned that nothing was going to happen. On October 27, 2009, they resumed dealings with Congress that

2. After this report was published on Harpers.org on January 18, a Justice Department spokesman wrote to complain that two of the witnesses interviewed by the department had misremembered the names of the lawyers present at those meetings. She refused to address any of the other allegations in the article. Instead, she insisted I note that Justice had "conducted a thorough inquiry into this matter, carefully examined the allegations, found no evidence of wrongdoing and subsequently closed the matter." Then she told me, as she had when I was reporting the story, that she would not arrange an interview with any of the officials involved in the matter.

they had initiated on February 2 and then broken off at the Justice Department's request; they were also in contact with ABC News. Two days later, Teresa McHenry called Mark Denbeaux and asked whether he had gone to Congress and ABC News about the matter. "I said that I had," Denbeaux told me. He asked her, "Was there anything wrong with that?" McHenry then suggested that the investigation was finished. Denbeaux reminded her that she had yet to interview some of the corroborating witnesses. "There are a few small things to do," Denbeaux says McHenry answered. "*Then* it will be finished."

Specialist Christopher Penvose told me that on October 30, the day following the conversation between Mark Denbeaux and Teresa McHenry, an official showed up at Penvose's home in south Baltimore with some FBI agents. She had a "few questions," she told him. Investigators working with her soon contacted two other witnesses.

On November 2, 2009, McHenry called Mark Denbeaux to tell him that the Justice Department's investigation was being closed. "It was a strange conversation," Denbeaux recalled. McHenry explained that "the gist of Sergeant Hickman's information could not be confirmed." But when Denbeaux asked what that "gist" actually was, McHenry declined to say. She just reiterated that Hickman's conclusions "appeared" to be unsupported. Denbeaux asked *what* conclusions exactly were unsupported. McHenry refused to say.

## 10. "They Accomplished Nothing"

One of the most intriguing aspects of this case concerns the use of Camp No. Under George W. Bush, the CIA created an archipelago of secret detention centers that spanned the globe, and authorities at these sites deployed an array of Justice Department–sanctioned torture techniques—including waterboarding, which often entails inserting cloth into the subject's mouth—on prisoners they deemed to be involved in terrorism. The presence of a black site at Guantánamo has long been a subject of speculation among lawyers and human-rights activists, and the experience of Sergeant Hickman and other Guantánamo guards compels us to ask whether the three prisoners who died on June 9 were being interrogated by the CIA and whether their deaths resulted from the grueling techniques the Justice Department had approved for the agency's use—or from other tortures lacking that sanction.

Complicating these questions is the fact that Camp No might have been controlled by another authority, the Joint Special Operations Command, which Bush's defense secretary, Donald Rumsfeld, had hoped to transform into a Pentagon version of the CIA. Under Rumsfeld's direction, JSOC began to take on many tasks traditionally handled by the CIA, including the housing and interrogation of prisoners at black sites around the world. The Pentagon recently acknowledged the existence of one such JSOC black site, located at Bagram Airfield in Afghanistan, and other suspected sites, such as Camp Nama in Baghdad, have been carefully documented by human-rights researchers.

In a Senate Armed Services Committee report on torture released last year, the sections about Guantánamo were significantly redacted. The position and circumstances of these deletions point to a significant JSOC interrogation program at the base. (It should be noted that Obama's order last year to close other secret detention camps was narrowly worded to apply only to the CIA.)

Regardless of whether Camp No belonged to the CIA or JSOC, the Justice Department has plenty of its own secrets to protect. The department would seem to have been involved in the cover-up from the first days, when FBI agents stormed Colonel Bumgarner's quarters. This was unusual for two reasons. When Pentagon officials engage in a leak investigation, they generally use military investigators. They rarely turn to the FBI because they cannot control the actions of a civilian agency. Moreover, when the FBI does open an investigation, it nearly always does so with

great discretion. The Bumgarner investigation was widely tele-
graphed, though, and seemed intended to send a message to the
military personnel at Camp Delta: Talk about what happened at
your own risk. All of which suggests it was not the Pentagon so
much as the White House that hoped to suppress the truth.

In the weeks following the 2006 deaths, the Justice Department decided to use the suicide narrative as leverage against the
Guantánamo prisoners and their troublesome lawyers, who were
pressing the government to justify its long-term imprisonment
of their clients. After the NCIS seized thousands of pages of privileged communications, the Justice Department went to court to
defend the action. It argued that such steps were warranted by
the extraordinary facts surrounding the June 9 "suicides." U.S.
District Court Judge James Robertson gave the Justice Department a sympathetic hearing, and he ruled in its favor, but he also
noted a curious aspect of the government's presentation: its "ci-
tations supporting the fact of the suicides" were all drawn from
media accounts. Why had the Justice Department lawyers who
argued the case gone to such lengths to avoid making any statement under oath about the suicides? Did they do so in order to
deceive the court? If so, they could face disciplinary proceedings
or disbarment.

The Justice Department also faces questions about its larger
role in creating the circumstances that led to the use of so-called
enhanced interrogation and restraint techniques at Guantánamo
and elsewhere. In 2006, the use of a gagging restraint had already
been connected to the death on January 9, 2004, of an Iraqi prisoner, Lieutenant Colonel Abdul Jameel, in the custody of the
Army Special Forces. And the bodies of the three men who died
at Guantánamo showed signs of torture, including hemorrhages,
needle marks, and significant bruising. The removal of their throats
made it difficult to determine whether they were already dead
when their bodies were suspended by a noose. The Justice Department itself had been deeply involved in the process of approving

and setting the conditions for the use of torture techniques, issuing a long series of memoranda that CIA agents and others could use to defend themselves against any subsequent criminal prosecution.

Teresa McHenry, the investigator charged with accounting for the deaths of the three men at Guantánamo, has firsthand knowledge of the Justice Department's role in auditing such techniques, having served at the Justice Department under Bush and having participated in the preparation of at least one of those memos. As a former war-crimes prosecutor, McHenry knows full well that government officials who attempt to cover up crimes perpetrated against prisoners in wartime face prosecution under the doctrine of command responsibility. (McHenry declined to clarify the role she played in drafting the memos.)

As retired rear admiral John Hutson, the former judge advocate general of the navy, told me, "Filing false reports and making false statements is bad enough, but if a homicide occurs and officials up the chain of command attempt to cover it up, they face serious criminal liability. They may even be viewed as accessories after the fact in the original crime." With command authority comes command responsibility, he said. "If the heart of the military is obeying orders down the chain of command, then its soul is accountability up the chain. You can't demand the former without the latter."

The Justice Department thus faced a dilemma; it could do the politically convenient thing, which was to find no justification for a thorough investigation, leave the NCIS conclusions in place, and hope that the public and the news media would obey the Obama administration's dictum to "look forward, not backward"; or it could pursue a course of action that would implicate the Bush Justice Department in a cover-up of possible homicides.

Nearly 200 men remain imprisoned at Guantánamo. In June 2009, six months after Barack Obama took office, one of them, a thirty-one-year-old Yemeni named Muhammed Abdallah Salih, was found dead in his cell. The exact circumstances of his death, like those of the deaths of the three men from Alpha Block, remain uncertain. Those charged with accounting for what happened—the prison command, the civilian and military investigative agencies, the Justice Department, and ultimately the attorney general himself—all face a choice between the rule of law and the expedience of political silence. Thus far, their choice has been unanimous.

Not everyone who is involved in this matter views it from a political perspective, of course. General Al-Zahrani grieves for his son, but at the end of a lengthy interview he paused and his thoughts turned elsewhere. "The truth is what matters," he said. "They practiced every form of torture on my son and on many others as well. What was the result? What facts did they find? They found nothing. They learned nothing. They accomplished nothing."

## The New Yorker

WINNER—PUBLIC INTEREST

*Death comes, and modern medicine stops it—for a time. Doctors and families struggle against the inevitable, yet at great cost, both financially and emotionally, and against all hope, we prolong the lives of those we love. How and when should we stop? This is the question Atul Gawande asks—and answers—in "Letting Go." As a surgeon at Brigham and Women's Hospital in Boston and an associate professor at the Harvard School of Public Health, Gawande writes with special authority. Indeed, this is the second year in a row that his work has won the National Magazine Award for Public Interest for* The New Yorker. *His story "The Cost Conundrum," which was reported to have influenced President Obama's campaign for health-care reform, earned the same honor in 2010. Of "Letting Go," the National Magazine Award judges said, "The story is a masterful blend of reportage and commentary . . . a moving revelation as well as call to action—the very essence of public-interest journalism."*

Atul Gawande

# Letting Go

Sara Thomas Monopoli was pregnant with her first child when her doctors learned that she was going to die. It started with a cough and a pain in her back. Then a chest X ray showed that her left lung had collapsed and her chest was filled with fluid. A sample of the fluid was drawn off with a long needle and sent for testing. Instead of an infection, as everyone had expected, it was lung cancer, and it had already spread to the lining of her chest. Her pregnancy was thirty-nine weeks along, and the obstetrician who had ordered the test broke the news to her as she sat with her husband and her parents. The obstetrician didn't get into the prognosis—she would bring in an oncologist for that—but Sara was stunned. Her mother, who had lost her best friend to lung cancer, began crying.

The doctors wanted to start treatment right away, and that meant inducing labor to get the baby out. For the moment, though, Sara and her husband, Rich, sat by themselves on a quiet terrace off the labor floor. It was a warm Monday in June 2007. She took Rich's hands, and they tried to absorb what they had heard. Monopoli was thirty-four. She had never smoked or lived with anyone who had. She exercised. She ate well. The diagnosis was bewildering. "This is going to be OK," Rich told her. "We're going to work through this. It's going to be hard, yes. But we'll figure it out. We can find the right treatment." For the moment, though, they had a baby to think about.

"So Sara and I looked at each other," Rich recalled, "and we said, 'We don't have cancer on Tuesday. It's a cancer-free day. We're having a baby. It's exciting. And we're going to enjoy our baby.'" On Tuesday, at 8:55 P.M., Vivian Monopoli, seven pounds nine ounces, was born. She had wavy brown hair, like her mom, and she was perfectly healthy.

The next day, Sara underwent blood tests and body scans. Dr. Paul Marcoux, an oncologist, met with her and her family to discuss the findings. He explained that she had a non-small-cell lung cancer that had started in her left lung. Nothing she had done had brought this on. More than 15 percent of lung cancers— more than people realize—occur in nonsmokers. Hers was advanced, having metastasized to multiple lymph nodes in her chest and its lining. The cancer was inoperable. But there were chemotherapy options, notably a relatively new drug called Tarceva, which targets a gene mutation commonly found in lung cancers of female nonsmokers. Eighty-five percent respond to this drug, and, Marcoux said, "some of these responses can be long-term."

Words like "respond" and "long-term" provide a reassuring gloss on a dire reality. There is no cure for lung cancer at this stage. Even with chemotherapy, the median survival is about a year. But it seemed harsh and pointless to confront Sara and Rich with this now. Vivian was in a bassinet by the bed. They were working hard to be optimistic. As Sara and Rich later told the social worker who was sent to see them, they did not want to focus on survival statistics. They wanted to focus on "aggressively managing" this diagnosis.

Sara was started on the Tarceva, which produced an itchy, acne-like facial rash and numbing tiredness. She also underwent a surgical procedure to drain the fluid around her lung; when the fluid kept coming back, a thoracic surgeon eventually placed a small, permanent tube in her chest, which she could drain whenever fluid accumulated and interfered with her breathing. Three weeks after the delivery, she was admitted to the hospital with severe shortness of breath from a pulmonary embolism—a blood clot in an artery to the lungs, which is dangerous but not uncommon in cancer patients. She was started on a blood thinner. Then test results showed that her tumor cells did not have the mutation that Tarceva targets. When Marcoux told Sara that the drug wasn't going to work, she had an almost violent physical reaction to the news, bolting to the bathroom in mid-discussion with a sudden bout of diarrhea.

Dr. Marcoux recommended a different, more standard chemotherapy, with two drugs called carboplatin and paclitaxel. But the paclitaxel triggered an extreme, nearly overwhelming allergic response, so he switched her to a regimen of carboplatin plus gemcitabine. Response rates, he said, were still very good for patients on this therapy.

She spent the remainder of the summer at home, with Vivian and her husband and her parents, who had moved in to help. She loved being a mother. Between chemotherapy cycles, she began trying to get her life back.

Then, in October, a CT scan showed that the tumor deposits in her left lung and chest and lymph nodes had grown substantially. The chemotherapy had failed. She was switched to a drug called pemetrexed. Studies found that it could produce markedly longer survival in some patients. In reality, however, only a small percentage of patients gained very much. On average, the drug extended survival by only two months—from eleven months to thirteen months—and that was in patients who, unlike Sara, had responded to first-line chemotherapy.

She worked hard to take the setbacks and side effects in stride. She was upbeat by nature, and she managed to maintain her optimism. Little by little, however, she grew sicker—increasingly exhausted and short of breath. By November, she didn't have the wind to walk the length of the hallway from the parking garage to Marcoux's office; Rich had to push her in a wheelchair.

A few days before Thanksgiving, she had another CT scan, which showed that the pemetrexed—her third drug regimen—wasn't working, either. The lung cancer had spread: from the left chest to the right, to the liver, to the lining of her abdomen, and to her spine. Time was running out.

.    .    .

This is the moment in Sara's story that poses a fundamental question for everyone living in the era of modern medicine: What do we want Sara and her doctors to do now? Or, to put it another way, if you were the one who had metastatic cancer—or, for that matter, a similarly advanced case of emphysema or congestive heart failure—what would you want your doctors to do?

The issue has become pressing, in recent years, for reasons of expense. The soaring cost of health care is the greatest threat to the country's long-term solvency, and the terminally ill account for a lot of it. Twenty-five percent of all Medicare spending is for the 5 percent of patients who are in their final year of life, and most of that money goes for care in their last couple of months which is of little apparent benefit.

Spending on a disease like cancer tends to follow a particular pattern. There are high initial costs as the cancer is treated, and then, if all goes well, these costs taper off. Medical spending for a breast-cancer survivor, for instance, averaged an estimated 54,000 dollars in 2003, the vast majority of it for the initial diagnostic testing, surgery, and, where necessary, radiation and chemotherapy. For a patient with a fatal version of the disease, though, the cost curve is U-shaped, rising again toward the end—to an average of 63,000 dollars during the last six months of life with an incurable breast cancer. Our medical system is excellent at trying to stave off death with 8,000-dollar-a-month chemotherapy, 3,000-dollar-a-day intensive care, 5,000-dollar-an-hour surgery. But, ultimately, death comes, and no one is good at knowing when to stop.

The subject seems to reach national awareness mainly as a question of who should "win" when the expensive decisions are made: the insurers and the taxpayers footing the bill or the patient battling for his or her life. Budget hawks urge us to face the fact that we can't afford everything. Demagogues shout about rationing and death panels. Market purists blame the existence of insurance: if patients and families paid the bills themselves, those expensive therapies would all come down in price. But they're debating the wrong question. The failure of our system of medical care for people facing the end of their life runs much deeper. To see this, you have to get close enough to grapple with the way decisions about care are actually made.

Recently, while seeing a patient in an intensive-care unit at my hospital, I stopped to talk with the critical-care physician on duty, someone I'd known since college. "I'm running a warehouse for the dying," she said bleakly. Out of the ten patients in her unit, she said, only two were likely to leave the hospital for any length of time. More typical was an almost-eighty-year-old woman at the end of her life, with irreversible congestive heart failure, who was in the ICU for the second time in three weeks, drugged to oblivion and tubed in most natural orifices and a few artificial ones. Or the seventy-year-old with a cancer that had metastasized to her lungs and bone and a fungal pneumonia that arises only in the final phase of the illness. She had chosen to forgo treatment, but her oncologist pushed her to change her mind, and she was put on a ventilator and antibiotics. Another woman, in her eighties, with end-stage respiratory and kidney failure, had been in the unit for two weeks. Her husband had died after a long illness, with a feeding tube and a tracheotomy, and she had mentioned that she didn't want to die that way. But her children couldn't let her go and asked to proceed with the placement of various devices: a permanent tracheotomy, a feeding tube, and a dialysis catheter. So now she just lay there tethered to her pumps, drifting in and out of consciousness.

Almost all these patients had known, for some time, that they had a terminal condition. Yet they—along with their families and doctors—were unprepared for the final stage. "We are having more conversation now about what patients want for the end of their life, by far, than they have had in all their lives to this point," my friend said. "The problem is that's way too late." In 2008, the national Coping with Cancer project published a study showing that terminally ill cancer patients who were put on a mechanical ventilator, given electrical defibrillation or chest compressions, or admitted, near death, to intensive care had a substantially worse quality of life in their last week than those who received no such interventions. And, six months after their death, their caregivers were three times as likely to suffer major depression. Spending one's final days in an ICU because of terminal illness is for most people a kind of failure. You lie on a ventilator, your every organ shutting down, your mind teetering on delirium and permanently beyond realizing that you will never leave this borrowed, fluorescent place. The end comes with no chance for you to have said goodbye or "It's OK" or "I'm sorry" or "I love you."

People have concerns besides simply prolonging their lives. Surveys of patients with terminal illness find that their top priorities include, in addition to avoiding suffering, being with family, having the touch of others, being mentally aware, and not becoming a burden to others. Our system of technological medical care has utterly failed to meet these needs, and the cost of this failure is measured in far more than dollars. The hard question we face, then, is not how we can afford this system's expense. It is how we can build a health-care system that will actually help dying patients achieve what's most important to them at the end of their lives.

· · ·

For all but our most recent history, dying was typically a brief process. Whether the cause was childhood infection, difficult childbirth, heart attack, or pneumonia, the interval between recognizing that you had a life-threatening ailment and death was often just a matter of days or weeks. Consider how our presidents died before the modern era. George Washington developed a throat infection at home on December 13, 1799, that killed him by the next evening. John Quincy Adams, Millard Fillmore, and Andrew Johnson all succumbed to strokes and died within two days. Rutherford Hayes had a heart attack and died three days later. Some deadly illnesses took a longer course: James Monroe and Andrew Jackson died from the months-long consumptive process of what appears to have been tuberculosis; Ulysses Grant's oral cancer took a year to kill him, and James Madison was bedridden for two years before dying of "old age." But, as the end-of-life researcher Joanne Lynn has observed, people usually experienced life-threatening illness the way they experienced bad weather—as something that struck with little warning—and you either got through it or you didn't.

Dying used to be accompanied by a prescribed set of customs. Guides to *ars moriendi*, the art of dying, were extraordinarily popular; a 1415 medieval Latin text was reprinted in more than a hundred editions across Europe. Reaffirming one's faith, repenting one's sins, and letting go of one's worldly possessions and desires were crucial, and the guides provided families with prayers and questions for the dying in order to put them in the right frame of mind during their final hours. Last words came to hold a particular place of reverence.

These days, swift catastrophic illness is the exception; for most people, death comes only after long medical struggle with an incurable condition—advanced cancer, progressive organ failure (usually the heart, kidney, or liver), or the multiple debilities of very old age. In all such cases, death is certain, but the timing isn't. So everyone struggles with this uncertainty—with how, and when, to accept that the battle is lost. As for last words, they hardly seem to exist anymore. Technology sustains our organs until we are well past the point of awareness and coherence. Besides, how do you attend to the thoughts and concerns of the dying when medicine has made it almost impossible to be sure who the dying even are? Is someone with terminal cancer, dementia, incurable congestive heart failure dying, exactly?

I once cared for a woman in her sixties who had severe chest and abdominal pain from a bowel obstruction that had ruptured her colon, caused her to have a heart attack, and put her into septic shock and renal failure. I performed an emergency operation to remove the damaged length of colon and give her a colostomy. A cardiologist stented her coronary arteries. We put her on dialysis, a ventilator, and intravenous feeding, and stabilized her. After a couple of weeks, though, it was clear that she was not going to get much better. The septic shock had left her with heart and respiratory failure as well as dry gangrene of her foot, which would have to be amputated. She had a large, open abdominal wound with leaking bowel contents, which would require twice-a-day cleaning and dressing for weeks in order to heal. She would not be able to eat. She would need a tracheotomy. Her kidneys were gone, and she would have to spend three days a week on a dialysis machine for the rest of her life.

She was unmarried and without children. So I sat with her sisters in the ICU family room to talk about whether we should proceed with the amputation and the tracheotomy. "Is she dying?" one of the sisters asked me. I didn't know how to answer the question. I wasn't even sure what the word "dying" meant anymore. In the past few decades, medical science has rendered obsolete centuries of experience, tradition, and language about our mortality, and created a new difficulty for mankind: how to die.

•     •     •

One Friday morning this spring, I went on patient rounds with Sarah Creed, a nurse with the hospice service that my hospital system operates. I didn't know much about hospice. I knew that it specialized in providing "comfort care" for the terminally ill, sometimes in special facilities, though nowadays usually at home. I knew that, in order for a patient of mine to be eligible, I had to write a note certifying that he or she had a life expectancy of less than six months. And I knew few patients who had chosen it, except maybe in their very last few days, because they had to sign a form indicating that they understood their disease was incurable and that they were giving up on medical care to stop it. The picture I had of hospice was of a morphine drip. It was not of this brown-haired and blue-eyed former ICU nurse with a stethoscope, knocking on Lee Cox's door on a quiet street in Boston's Mattapan neighborhood.

"Hi, Lee," Creed said when she entered the house.

"Hi, Sarah," Cox said. She was seventy-two years old. She'd had several years of declining health due to congestive heart failure from a heart attack and pulmonary fibrosis, a progressive and irreversible lung disease. Doctors tried slowing the disease with steroids, but they didn't work. She had cycled in and out of the hospital, each time in worse shape. Ultimately, she accepted hospice care and moved in with her niece for support. She was dependent on oxygen and unable to do the most ordinary tasks. Just answering the door, with her thirty-foot length of oxygen tubing trailing after her, had left her winded. She stood resting for a moment, her lips pursed and her chest heaving.

Creed took Cox's arm gently as we walked to the kitchen to sit down, asking her how she had been doing. Then she asked a series of questions, targeting issues that tend to arise in patients with terminal illness. Did Cox have pain? How was her appetite, thirst, sleeping? Any trouble with confusion, anxiety, or restlessness? Had her shortness of breath grown worse? Was there chest pain or heart palpitations? Abdominal discomfort? Trouble with bowel movements or urination or walking?

She did have some new troubles. When she walked from the bedroom to the bathroom, she said, it now took at least five minutes to catch her breath, and that frightened her. She was also getting chest pain. Creed pulled a stethoscope and a blood-pressure cuff from her medical bag. Cox's blood pressure was acceptable, but her heart rate was high. Creed listened to her heart, which had a normal rhythm, and to her lungs, hearing the fine crackles of her pulmonary fibrosis but also a new wheeze. Her ankles were swollen with fluid, and when Creed asked for her pillbox she saw that Cox was out of her heart medication. She asked to see Cox's oxygen equipment. The liquid-oxygen cylinder at the foot of the neatly made bed was filled and working properly. The nebulizer equipment for her inhaler treatments, however, was broken.

Given the lack of heart medication and inhaler treatments, it was no wonder that she had worsened. Creed called Cox's pharmacy to confirm that her refills had been waiting, and had her arrange for her niece to pick up the medicine when she came home from work. Creed also called the nebulizer supplier for same-day emergency service.

She then chatted with Cox in the kitchen for a few minutes. Her spirits were low. Creed took her hand. Everything was going to be all right, she said. She reminded her about the good days she'd had—the previous weekend, for example, when she'd been able to go out with her portable oxygen cylinder to shop with her niece and get her hair colored.

I asked Cox about her previous life. She had made radios in a Boston factory. She and her husband had two children and several grandchildren.

When I asked her why she had chosen hospice care, she looked downcast. "The lung doctor and heart doctor said they couldn't help me anymore," she said. Creed glared at me. My questions had made Cox sad again.

"It's good to have my niece and her husband helping to watch me every day," she said. "But it's not my home. I feel like I'm in the way."

Creed gave her a hug before we left and one last reminder. "What do you do if you have chest pain that doesn't go away?" she asked.

"Take a nitro," Cox said, referring to the nitroglycerin pill that she can slip under her tongue.

"And?"

"Call you."

"Where's the number?"

She pointed to the twenty-four-hour hospice call number that was taped beside her phone.

Outside, I confessed that I was confused by what Creed was doing. A lot of it seemed to be about extending Cox's life. Wasn't the goal of hospice to let nature take its course?

"That's not the goal," Creed said. The difference between standard medical care and hospice is not the difference between treating and doing nothing, she explained. The difference was in your priorities. In ordinary medicine, the goal is to extend life. We'll sacrifice the quality of your existence now—by performing surgery, providing chemotherapy, putting you in intensive care—for the chance of gaining time later. Hospice deploys nurses, doctors, and social workers to help people with a fatal illness have the fullest possible lives right now. That means focusing on objectives like freedom from pain and discomfort, or maintaining mental awareness for as long as possible, or getting out with family once in a while. Hospice and palliative-care specialists aren't much concerned about whether that makes people's lives longer or shorter.

Like many people, I had believed that hospice care hastens death because patients forgo hospital treatments and are allowed high-dose narcotics to combat pain. But studies suggest otherwise. In one, researchers followed 4,493 Medicare patients with either terminal cancer or congestive heart failure. They found no difference in survival time between hospice and nonhospice patients with breast cancer, prostate cancer, and colon cancer. Curiously, hospice care seemed to extend survival for some patients; those with pancreatic cancer gained an average of three weeks, those with lung cancer gained six weeks, and those with congestive heart failure gained three months. The lesson seems almost Zen: you live longer only when you stop trying to live longer. When Cox was transferred to hospice care, her doctors thought that she wouldn't live much longer than a few weeks. With the supportive hospice therapy she received, she had already lived for a year.

Creed enters people's lives at a strange moment—when they have understood that they have a fatal illness but have not necessarily acknowledged that they are dying. "I'd say only about a quarter have accepted their fate when they come into hospice," she said. When she first encounters her patients, many feel that they have simply been abandoned by their doctors. "Ninety-nine percent understand they're dying, but one hundred percent hope they're not," she says. "They still want to beat their disease." The initial visit is always tricky, but she has found ways to smooth things over. "A nurse has five seconds to make a patient like you and trust you. It's in the whole way you present yourself. I do not come in saying, 'I'm so sorry.' Instead, it's: 'I'm the hospice nurse, and here's what I have to offer you to make your life better. And I know we don't have a lot of time to waste.'"

That was how she started with Dave Galloway, whom we visited after leaving Lee Cox's home. He was forty-two years old. He and his wife, Sharon, were both Boston firefighters. They had a three-year-old daughter. He had pancreatic cancer, which had spread; his upper abdomen was now solid with tumor. During the past few months, the pain had become unbearable at times, and he was admitted to the hospital several times for pain crises. At his most recent admission, about a week earlier, it was found that the tumor had perforated his intestine. There wasn't even a temporary fix for this problem. The medical team started him on intravenous nutrition and offered him a choice between going to the intensive-care unit and going home with hospice. He chose to go home.

"I wish we'd gotten involved sooner," Creed told me. When she and the hospice's supervising doctor, Dr. JoAnne Nowak, evaluated Galloway upon his arrival at home, he appeared to have only a few days left. His eyes were hollow. His breathing was labored. Fluid swelled his entire lower body to the point that his skin blistered and wept. He was almost delirious with abdominal pain.

They got to work. They set up a pain pump with a button that let him dispense higher doses of narcotic than he had been allowed. They arranged for an electric hospital bed, so that he could sleep with his back raised. They also taught Sharon how to keep Dave clean, protect his skin from breakdown, and handle the crises to come. Creed told me that part of her job is to take the measure of a patient's family, and Sharon struck her as unusually capable. She was determined to take care of her husband to the end, and, perhaps because she was a firefighter, she had the resilience and the competence to do so. She did not want to hire a private-duty nurse. She handled everything, from the IV lines and the bed linens to orchestrating family members to lend a hand when she needed help.

Creed arranged for a specialized "comfort pack" to be delivered by FedEx and stored in a minirefrigerator by Dave's bed. It contained a dose of morphine for breakthrough pain or shortness of breath, Ativan for anxiety attacks, Compazine for nausea, Haldol for delirium, Tylenol for fever, and atropine for drying up the upper-airway rattle that people can get in their final hours. If any such problem developed, Sharon was instructed to call the twenty-four-hour hospice nurse on duty, who would provide instructions about which rescue medications to use and, if necessary, come out to help.

Dave and Sharon were finally able to sleep through the night at home. Creed or another nurse came to see him every day, sometimes twice a day; three times that week, Sharon used the emergency hospice line to help her deal with Dave's pain crises or hallucinations. After a few days, they were even able to go out to a favorite restaurant; he wasn't hungry, but they enjoyed just being there, and the memories it stirred.

The hardest part so far, Sharon said, was deciding to forgo the two-liter intravenous feedings that Dave had been receiving each day. Although they were his only source of calories, the hospice staff encouraged discontinuing them because his body did not seem to be absorbing the nutrition. The infusion of sugars, proteins, and fats made the painful swelling of his skin and his shortness of breath worse—and for what? The mantra was live for now. Sharon had balked, for fear that she'd be starving him. The night before our visit, however, she and Dave decided to try going without the infusion. By morning, the swelling was markedly reduced. He could move more, and with less discomfort. He also began to eat a few morsels of food, just for the taste of it, and that made Sharon feel better about the decision.

When we arrived, Dave was making his way back to bed after a shower, his arm around his wife's shoulders and his slippered feet taking one shuffling step at a time.

"There's nothing he likes better than a long hot shower," Sharon said. "He'd live in the shower if he could."

Dave sat on the edge of his bed in fresh pajamas, catching his breath, and then Creed spoke to him as his daughter, Ashlee, ran in and out of the room in her beaded pigtails, depositing stuffed animals in her dad's lap.

"How's your pain on a scale of one to ten?" Creed asked.

"A six," he said.

"Did you hit the pump?"

He didn't answer for a moment. "I'm reluctant," he admitted.

"Why?" Creed asked.

"It feels like defeat," he said.

"Defeat?"

"I don't want to become a drug addict," he explained. "I don't want to need this."

Creed got down on her knees in front of him. "Dave, I don't know anyone who can manage this kind of pain without the medication," she said. "It's not defeat. You've got a beautiful wife and daughter, and you're not going to be able to enjoy them with the pain."

"You're right about that," he said, looking at Ashley as she gave him a little horse. And he pressed the button.

Dave Galloway died one week later—at home, at peace, and surrounded by family. A week after that, Lee Cox died, too. But, as if to show just how resistant to formula human lives are, Cox had never reconciled herself to the incurability of her illnesses. So when her family found her in cardiac arrest one morning they followed her wishes and called 911 instead of the hospice service. The emergency medical technicians and firefighters and police rushed in. They pulled off her clothes and pumped her chest, put a tube in her airway and forced oxygen into her lungs, and tried to see if they could shock her heart back. But such efforts rarely succeed with terminal patients, and they did not succeed with her.

Hospice has tried to offer a new ideal for how we die. Although not everyone has embraced its rituals, those who have are helping to negotiate an *ars moriendi* for our age. But doing so represents a struggle—not only against suffering but also against the seemingly unstoppable momentum of medical treatment.

·    ·    ·

Just before Thanksgiving of 2007, Sara Monopoli, her husband, Rich, and her mother, Dawn Thomas, met with Dr. Marcoux to discuss the options she had left. By this point, Sara had undergone three rounds of chemotherapy with limited, if any, effect. Perhaps Marcoux could have discussed what she most wanted as death neared and how best to achieve those wishes. But the signal he got from Sara and her family was that they wished to talk only about the next treatment options. They did not want to talk about dying.

Recently, I spoke to Sara's husband and her parents. Sara knew that her disease was incurable, they pointed out. The week after she was given the diagnosis and delivered her baby, she spelled out her wishes for Vivian's upbringing after she was gone. She had told her family on several occasions that she did not want to die in the hospital. She wanted to spend her final moments peacefully at home. But the prospect that those moments might be coming soon, that there might be no way to slow the disease, "was not something she or I wanted to discuss," her mother said.

Her father, Gary, and her twin sister, Emily, still held out hope for a cure. The doctors simply weren't looking hard enough, they felt. "I just couldn't believe there wasn't something," Gary said. For Rich, the experience of Sara's illness had been disorienting: "We had a baby. We were young. And this was so shocking and so odd. We never discussed stopping treatment."

Marcoux took the measure of the room. With almost two decades of experience treating lung cancer, he had been through many of these conversations. He has a calm, reassuring air and a native Minnesotan's tendency to avoid confrontation or over-intimacy. He tries to be scientific about decisions.

"I know that the vast majority of my patients are going to die of their disease," he told me. The data show that, after failure of second-line chemotherapy, lung-cancer patients rarely get any added survival time from further treatments and often suffer significant side effects. But he, too, has his hopes.

He told them that, at some point, "supportive care" was an option for them to think about. But, he went on, there were also experimental therapies. He told them about several that were under trial. The most promising was a Pfizer drug that targeted one of the mutations found in her cancer's cells. Sara and her family instantly pinned their hopes on it. The drug was so new that it didn't even have a name, just a number—PF0231006—and this made it all the more enticing.

There were a few hovering issues, including the fact that the scientists didn't yet know the safe dose. The drug was only in a Phase I trial—that is, a trial designed to determine the toxicity of a range of doses, not whether the drug worked. Furthermore, a test of the drug against her cancer cells in a petri dish showed no effect. But Marcoux didn't think that these were decisive obstacles—just negatives. The critical problem was that the rules of the trial excluded Sara because of the pulmonary embolism she had developed that summer. To enroll, she would need to wait two months, in order to get far enough past the episode. In the meantime, he suggested trying another conventional chemotherapy, called Navelbine. Sara began the treatment the Monday after Thanksgiving.

It's worth pausing to consider what had just happened. Step by step, Sara ended up on a *fourth* round of chemotherapy, one with a minuscule likelihood of altering the course of her disease and a great likelihood of causing debilitating side effects. An opportunity to prepare for the inevitable was forgone. And it all happened because of an assuredly normal circumstance: a patient and family unready to confront the reality of her disease.

I asked Marcoux what he hopes to accomplish for terminal lung-cancer patients when they first come to see him. "I'm thinking, Can I get them a pretty good year or two out of this?" he said. "Those are my expectations. For me, the long tail for a patient like her is three to four years." But this is not what people want to hear. "They're thinking ten to twenty years. You hear that time and time again. And I'd be the same way if I were in their shoes."

You'd think doctors would be well equipped to navigate the shoals here, but at least two things get in the way. First, our own views may be unrealistic. A study led by the Harvard researcher Nicholas Christakis asked the doctors of almost 500 terminally ill patients to estimate how long they thought their patient would survive and then followed the patients. Sixty-three percent of doctors overestimated survival time. Just 17 percent under-estimated it. The average estimate was 530 percent too high. And the better the doctors knew their patients, the more likely they were to err.

Second, we often avoid voicing even these sentiments. Studies find that although doctors usually tell patients when a cancer is not curable, most are reluctant to give a specific prognosis, even when pressed. More than 40 percent of oncologists report offering treatments that they believe are unlikely to work. In an era in which the relationship between patient and doctor is increasingly miscast in retail terms—"the customer is always right"—doctors are especially hesitant to trample on a patient's expectations. You worry far more about being overly pessimistic than you do about being overly optimistic. And talking about dying is enormously fraught. When you have a patient like Sara Monopoli, the last thing you want to do is grapple with the truth. I know, because Marcoux wasn't the only one avoiding that conversation with her. I was, too.

Earlier that summer, a PET scan had revealed that, in addition to her lung cancer, she also had thyroid cancer, which had spread to the lymph nodes of her neck, and I was called in to decide whether to operate. This second, unrelated cancer was in fact operable. But thyroid cancers take years to become lethal. Her lung cancer would almost certainly end her life long before her thyroid cancer caused any trouble. Given the extent of the surgery that would have been required and the potential complications, the best course was to do nothing. But explaining my reasoning to Sara meant confronting the mortality of her lung cancer, something that I felt ill prepared to do.

Sitting in my clinic, Sara did not seem discouraged by the discovery of this second cancer. She seemed determined. She'd read about the good outcomes from thyroid-cancer treatment. So she was geared up, eager to discuss when to operate. And I found myself swept along by her optimism. Suppose I was wrong, I wondered, and she proved to be that miracle patient who survived metastatic lung cancer?

My solution was to avoid the subject altogether. I told Sara that the thyroid cancer was slow-growing and treatable. The priority was her lung cancer, I said. Let's not hold up the treatment for that. We could monitor the thyroid cancer and plan surgery in a few months.

I saw her every six weeks, and noted her physical decline from one visit to the next. Yet even in a wheelchair, Sara would always arrive smiling, makeup on and bangs bobby-pinned out of her eyes. She'd find small things to laugh about, like the tubes that created strange protuberances under her dress. She was ready to try anything, and I found myself focusing on the news about experimental therapies for her lung cancer. After one of her chemotherapies seemed to shrink the thyroid cancer slightly, I even raised with her the possibility that an experimental therapy could work against both her cancers, which was sheer fantasy. Discussing a fantasy was easier—less emotional, less explosive, less prone to misunderstanding—than discussing what was happening before my eyes.

Between the lung cancer and the chemo, Sara became steadily sicker. She slept most of the time and could do little out of the house. Clinic notes from December describe shortness of breath, dry heaves, coughing up blood, severe fatigue. In addition to the drainage tubes in her chest, she required needle-drainage procedures in her abdomen every week or two to relieve the severe pressure from the liters of fluid that the cancer was producing there.

A CT scan in December showed that the lung cancer was spreading through her spine, liver, and lungs. When we met in January, she could move only slowly and uncomfortably. Her lower body had become swollen. She couldn't speak more than a sentence without pausing for breath. By the first week of February, she needed oxygen at home to breathe. Enough time had elapsed since her pulmonary embolism, however, that she could start on Pfizer's experimental drug. She just needed one more set of scans for clearance. These revealed that the cancer had spread to her brain, with at least nine metastatic growths across both hemispheres. The experimental drug was not designed to cross the blood-brain barrier. PF0231006 was not going to work.

And still Sara, her family, and her medical team remained in battle mode. Within twenty-four hours, Sara was scheduled to see a radiation oncologist for whole-brain radiation to try to reduce the metastases. On February 12, she completed five days of radiation treatment, which left her immeasurably fatigued, barely able get out of bed. She ate almost nothing. She weighed twenty-five pounds less than she had in the fall. She confessed to Rich that, for the past two months, she had experienced double vision and was unable to feel her hands.

"Why didn't you tell anyone?" he asked her.

"I just didn't want to stop treatment," she said. "They would make me stop."

She was given two weeks to recover her strength after the radiation. Then she would be put on another experimental drug from a small biotech company. She was scheduled to start on February 25. Her chances were rapidly dwindling. But who was to say they were zero?

In 1985, the paleontologist and writer Stephen Jay Gould published an extraordinary essay entitled "The Median Isn't the Message," after he had been given a diagnosis, three years earlier, of

abdominal mesothelioma, a rare and lethal cancer usually associated with asbestos exposure. He went to a medical library when
he got the diagnosis and pulled out the latest scientific articles
on the disease. "The literature couldn't have been more brutally
clear: mesothelioma is incurable, with a median survival of only
eight months after discovery," he wrote. The news was devastating.
But then he began looking at the graphs of the patient-survival
curves.

Gould was a naturalist, and more inclined to notice the variation around the curve's middle point than the middle point itself.
What the naturalist saw was remarkable variation. The patients
were not clustered around the median survival but, instead,
fanned out in both directions. Moreover, the curve was skewed
to the right, with a long tail, however slender, of patients who lived
many years longer than the eight-month median. This is where
he found solace. He could imagine himself surviving far out in
that long tail. And he did. Following surgery and experimental
chemotherapy, he lived twenty more years before dying, in 2002,
at the age of sixty, from a lung cancer that was unrelated to his
original disease.

"It has become, in my view, a bit too trendy to regard the acceptance of death as something tantamount to intrinsic dignity," he
wrote in his 1985 essay. "Of course I agree with the preacher of
Ecclesiastes that there is a time to love and a time to die—and
when my skein runs out I hope to face the end calmly and in my
own way. For most situations, however, I prefer the more martial
view that death is the ultimate enemy—and I find nothing re-
proachable in those who rage mightily against the dying of the
light."

I think of Gould and his essay every time I have a patient with
a terminal illness. There is almost always a long tail of possibility,
however thin. What's wrong with looking for it? Nothing, it seems
to me, unless it means we have failed to prepare for the outcome
that's vastly more probable. The trouble is that we've built our

medical system and culture around the long tail. We've created a multi-trillion-dollar edifice for dispensing the medical equivalent of lottery tickets—and have only the rudiments of a system to prepare patients for the near certainty that those tickets will not win. Hope is not a plan, but hope is our plan.

.     .     .

For Sara, there would be no miraculous recovery, and, when the end approached, neither she nor her family was prepared. "I always wanted to respect her request to die peacefully at home," Rich later told me. "But I didn't believe we could make it happen. I didn't know how."

On the morning of Friday, February 22, three days before she was to start her new round of chemo, Rich awoke to find his wife sitting upright beside him, pitched forward on her arms, eyes wide, struggling for air. She was gray, breathing fast, her body heaving with each open-mouthed gasp. She looked as if she were drowning. He tried turning up the oxygen in her nasal tubing, but she got no better.

"I can't do this," she said, pausing between each word. "I'm scared."

He had no emergency kit in the refrigerator. No hospice nurse to call. And how was he to know whether this new development was fixable?

We'll go to the hospital, he told her. When he asked if they should drive, she shook her head, so he called 911, and told her mother, Dawn, who was in the next room, what was going on. A few minutes later, firemen swarmed up the stairs to her bedroom, sirens wailing outside. As they lifted Sara into the ambulance on a stretcher, Dawn came out in tears.

"We're going to get ahold of this," Rich told her. This was just another trip to the hospital, he said to himself. The doctors would figure this out.

At the hospital, Sara was diagnosed with pneumonia. That troubled the family, because they thought they'd done everything to keep infection at bay. They'd washed hands scrupulously, limited visits by people with young children, even limited Sara's time with baby Vivian if she showed the slightest sign of a runny nose. But Sara's immune system and her ability to clear her lung secretions had been steadily weakened by the rounds of radiation and chemotherapy as well as by the cancer.

In another way, the diagnosis of pneumonia was reassuring because it was just an infection. It could be treated. The medical team started Sara on intravenous antibiotics and high-flow oxygen through a mask. The family gathered at her bedside, hoping for the antibiotics to work. This could be reversible, they told one another. But that night and the next morning her breathing only grew more labored.

"I can't think of a single funny thing to say," Emily told Sara as their parents looked on.

"Neither can I," Sara murmured. Only later did the family realize that those were the last words they would ever hear from her. After that, she began to drift in and out of consciousness. The medical team had only one option left: to put her on a ventilator. Sara was a fighter, right? And the next step for fighters was to escalate to intensive care.

·    ·    ·

This is a modern tragedy, replayed millions of times over. When there is no way of knowing exactly how long our skeins will run—and when we imagine ourselves to have much more time than we do—our every impulse is to fight, to die with chemo in our veins or a tube in our throats or fresh sutures in our flesh. The fact that we may be shortening or worsening the time we have left hardly seems to register. We imagine that we can wait until the doctors tell us that there is nothing more they can do. But rarely is there *nothing* more that doctors can do. They can give toxic drugs of unknown efficacy, operate to try to remove part of the tumor, put in a feeding tube if a person can't eat: there's always something. We want these choices. We don't want anyone—certainly not bureaucrats or the marketplace—to limit them. But that doesn't mean we are eager to make the choices ourselves. Instead, most often, we make no choice at all. We fall back on the default, and the default is: Do Something. Is there any way out of this?

In late 2004, executives at Aetna, the insurance company, started an experiment. They knew that only a small percentage of the terminally ill ever halted efforts at curative treatment and enrolled in hospice, and that, when they did, it was usually not until the very end. So Aetna decided to let a group of policyholders with a life expectancy of less than a year receive hospice services *without* forgoing other treatments. A patient like Sara Monopoli could continue to try chemotherapy and radiation, and go to the hospital when she wished—but also have a hospice team at home focusing on what she needed for the best possible life now and for that morning when she might wake up unable to breathe. A two-year study of this "concurrent care" program found that enrolled patients were much more likely to use hospice: the figure leaped from 26 percent to 70 percent. That was no surprise, since they weren't forced to give up anything. The surprising result was that they did give up things. They visited the emergency room almost half as often as the control patients did. Their use of hospitals and ICUs dropped by more than two-thirds. Overall costs fell by almost a quarter.

This was stunning, and puzzling: it wasn't obvious what made the approach work. Aetna ran a more modest concurrent-care program for a broader group of terminally ill patients. For these patients, the traditional hospice rules applied—in order to qualify for home hospice, they had to give up attempts at curative treatment. But, either way, they received phone calls from palliative-care nurses who offered to check in regularly and help them find services for anything from pain control to making out a living will. For these patients, too, hospice enrollment jumped to seventy percent, and their use of hospital services dropped sharply. Among elderly patients, use of intensive-care units fell by more than 85 percent. Satisfaction scores went way up. What was going on here? The program's leaders had the impression that they had simply given patients someone experienced and knowledgeable to talk to about their daily needs. And somehow that was enough—just talking.

The explanation strains credibility, but evidence for it has grown in recent years. Two-thirds of the terminal-cancer patients in the Coping with Cancer study reported having had no discussion with their doctors about their goals for end-of-life care, despite being, on average, just four months from death. But the third who did were far less likely to undergo cardiopulmonary resuscitation or be put on a ventilator or end up in an intensive-care unit. Two-thirds enrolled in hospice. These patients suffered less, were physically more capable, and were better able, for a longer period, to interact with others. Moreover, six months after the patients died their family members were much less likely to experience persistent major depression. In other words, people who had substantive discussions with their doctor about their end-of-life preferences were far more likely to die at peace and in control of their situation, and to spare their family anguish.

Can mere discussions really do so much? Consider the case of La Crosse, Wisconsin. Its elderly residents have unusually low end-of-life hospital costs. During their last six months, according to Medicare data, they spend half as many days in the hospital as the national average, and there's no sign that doctors or patients are halting care prematurely. Despite average rates of obesity and smoking, their life expectancy outpaces the national mean by a year.

I spoke to Dr. Gregory Thompson, a critical-care specialist at Gundersen Lutheran Hospital, while he was on ICU duty one recent evening, and he ran through his list of patients with me. In most respects, the patients were like those found in any ICU— terribly sick and living through the most perilous days of their lives. There was a young woman with multiple organ failure from a devastating case of pneumonia, a man in his midsixties with a ruptured colon that had caused a rampaging infection and a heart attack. Yet these patients were completely different from those in other ICUs I'd seen: none had a terminal disease; none battled the final stages of metastatic cancer or untreatable heart failure or dementia.

To understand La Crosse, Thompson said, you had to go back to 1991, when local medical leaders headed a systematic campaign to get physicians and patients to discuss end-of-life wishes. Within a few years, it became routine for all patients admitted to a hospital, nursing home, or assisted-living facility to complete a multiple-choice form that boiled down to four crucial questions. At this moment in your life, the form asked:

1. Do you want to be resuscitated if your heart stops?
2. Do you want aggressive treatments such as intubation and mechanical ventilation?
3. Do you want antibiotics?
4. Do you want tube or intravenous feeding if you can't eat on your own?

By 1996, 85 percent of La Crosse residents who died had written advanced directives, up from 15 percent, and doctors almost always knew of and followed the instructions. Having this system in place, Thompson said, has made his job vastly easier. But it's not because the specifics are spelled out for him every time a sick patient arrives in his unit.

"These things are not laid out in stone," he told me. Whatever the yes/no answers people may put on a piece of paper, one will find nuances and complexities in what they mean. "But, instead of having the discussion when they get to the ICU, we find many times it has already taken place."

Answers to the list of questions change as patients go from entering the hospital for the delivery of a child to entering for complications of Alzheimer's disease. But, in La Crosse, the system means that people are far more likely to have talked about what they want and what they don't want before they and their relatives find themselves in the throes of crisis and fear. When wishes aren't clear, Thompson said, "families have also become much more receptive to having the discussion." The discussion, not the list, was what mattered most. Discussion had brought La Crosse's end-of-life costs down to just over half the national average. It was that simple—and that complicated.

·     ·     ·

One Saturday morning last winter, I met with a woman I had operated on the night before. She had been undergoing a procedure for the removal of an ovarian cyst when the gynecologist who was operating on her discovered that she had metastatic colon cancer. I was summoned, as a general surgeon, to see what could be done. I removed a section of her colon that had a large cancerous mass, but the cancer had already spread widely. I had not been able to get it all. Now I introduced myself. She said a resident had told her that a tumor was found and part of her colon had been excised.

Yes, I said. I'd been able to take out "the main area of involvement." I explained how much bowel was removed, what the recovery would be like—everything except how much cancer there was. But then I remembered how timid I'd been with Sara

Monopoli, and all those studies about how much doctors beat around the bush. So when she asked me to tell her more about the cancer, I explained that it had spread not only to her ovaries but also to her lymph nodes. I said that it had not been possible to remove all the disease. But I found myself almost immediately minimizing what I'd said. "We'll bring in an oncologist," I hastened to add. "Chemotherapy can be very effective in these situations."

She absorbed the news in silence, looking down at the blankets drawn over her mutinous body. Then she looked up at me. "Am I going to die?"

I flinched. "No, no," I said. "Of course not."

A few days later, I tried again. "We don't have a cure," I explained. "But treatment can hold the disease down for a long time." The goal, I said, was to "prolong your life" as much as possible.

I've seen her regularly in the months since, as she embarked on chemotherapy. She has done well. So far, the cancer is in check. Once, I asked her and her husband about our initial conversations. They don't remember them very fondly. "That one phrase that you used—'prolong your life'—it just . . ." She didn't want to sound critical.

"It was kind of blunt," her husband said.

"It sounded harsh," she echoed. She felt as if I'd dropped her off a cliff.

I spoke to Dr. Susan Block, a palliative-care specialist at my hospital who has had thousands of these difficult conversations and is a nationally recognized pioneer in training doctors and others in managing end-of-life issues with patients and their families. "You have to understand," Block told me. "A family meeting is a procedure, and it requires no less skill than performing an operation."

One basic mistake is conceptual. For doctors, the primary purpose of a discussion about terminal illness is to determine what people want—whether they want chemo or not, whether they want to be resuscitated or not, whether they want hospice or not. They focus on laying out the facts and the options. But that's a mistake, Block said.

"A large part of the task is helping people negotiate the overwhelming anxiety—anxiety about death, anxiety about suffering, anxiety about loved ones, anxiety about finances," she explained. "There are many worries and real terrors." No one conversation can address them all. Arriving at an acceptance of one's mortality and a clear understanding of the limits and the possibilities of medicine is a process, not an epiphany.

There is no single way to take people with terminal illness through the process, but, according to Block, there are some rules. You sit down. You make time. You're not determining whether they want treatment X versus Y. You're trying to learn what's most important to them under the circumstances—so that you can provide information and advice on the approach that gives them the best chance of achieving it. This requires as much listening as talking. If you are talking more than half of the time, Block says, you're talking too much.

The words you use matter. According to experts, you shouldn't say, "I'm sorry things turned out this way," for example. It can sound like pity. You should say, "I wish things were different." You don't ask, "What do you want when you are dying?" You ask, "If time becomes short, what is most important to you?"

Block has a list of items that she aims to cover with terminal patients in the time before decisions have to be made: what they understand their prognosis to be; what their concerns are about what lies ahead; whom they want to make decisions when they can't; how they want to spend their time as options become limited; what kinds of trade-offs they are willing to make.

Ten years ago, her seventy-four-year-old father, Jack Block, a professor emeritus of psychology at the University of California at Berkeley, was admitted to a San Francisco hospital with symptoms from what proved to be a mass growing in the spinal cord of his neck. She flew out to see him. The neurosurgeon said that the procedure to remove the mass carried a 20 percent chance of leaving him quadriplegic, paralyzed from the neck down. But without it he had a 100 percent chance of becoming quadriplegic.

The evening before surgery, father and daughter chatted about friends and family, trying to keep their minds off what was to come, and then she left for the night. Halfway across the Bay Bridge, she recalled, "I realized, 'Oh, my God, I don't know what he really wants.'" He'd made her his health-care proxy, but they had talked about such situations only superficially. So she turned the car around.

Going back in "was really uncomfortable," she said. It made no difference that she was an expert in end-of-life discussions. "I just felt awful having the conversation with my dad." But she went through her list. She told him, "'I need to understand how much you're willing to go through to have a shot at being alive and what level of being alive is tolerable to you.' We had this quite agonizing conversation where he said—and this totally shocked me— 'Well, if I'm able to eat chocolate ice cream and watch football on TV, then I'm willing to stay alive. I'm willing to go through a lot of pain if I have a shot at that.'"

"I would never have expected him to say that," Block went on. "I mean, he's a professor emeritus. He's never watched a football game in my conscious memory. The whole picture—it wasn't the guy I thought I knew." But the conversation proved critical, because after surgery he developed bleeding in the spinal cord. The surgeons told her that, in order to save his life, they would need to go back in. But he had already become nearly quadriplegic and would remain severely disabled for many months and possibly forever. What did she want to do?

"I had three minutes to make this decision, and, I realized, he had already made the decision." She asked the surgeons whether, if her father survived, he would still be able to eat chocolate ice cream and watch football on TV. Yes, they said. She gave the OK to take him back to the operating room.

"If I had not had that conversation with him," she told me, "my instinct would have been to let him go at that moment, because it just seemed so awful. And I would have beaten myself up. Did I let him go too soon?" Or she might have gone ahead and sent him to surgery, only to find—as occurred—that he survived only to go through what proved to be a year of "very horrible rehab" and disability. "I would have felt so guilty that I condemned him to that," she said. "But there was no decision for me to make." He had decided.

During the next two years, he regained the ability to walk short distances. He required caregivers to bathe and dress him. He had difficulty swallowing and eating. But his mind was intact and he had partial use of his hands—enough to write two books and more than a dozen scientific articles. He lived for ten years after the operation. This past year, however, his difficulties with swallowing advanced to the point where he could not eat without aspirating food particles, and he cycled between hospital and rehabilitation facilities with the pneumonias that resulted. He didn't want a feeding tube. And it became evident that the battle for the dwindling chance of a miraculous recovery was going to leave him unable ever to go home again. So, this past January, he decided to stop the battle and go home.

"We started him on hospice care," Block said. "We treated his choking and kept him comfortable. Eventually, he stopped eating and drinking. He died about five days later."

·     ·     ·

Susan Block and her father had the conversation that we all need to have when the chemotherapy stops working, when we start needing oxygen at home, when we face high-risk surgery, when the liver failure keeps progressing, when we become unable to dress ourselves. I've heard Swedish doctors call it a "breakpoint discussion," a systematic series of conversations to sort out when they need to switch from fighting for time to fighting for the other things that people value—being with family or traveling or enjoying chocolate ice cream. Few people have this discussion, and there is good reason for anyone to dread these conversations. They can unleash difficult emotions. People can become angry or overwhelmed. Handled poorly, the conversations can cost a person's trust. Handled well, they can take real time.

I spoke to an oncologist who told me about a twenty-nine-year-old patient she had recently cared for who had an inoperable brain tumor that continued to grow through second-line chemotherapy. The patient elected not to attempt any further chemotherapy, but getting to that decision required hours of discussion—for this was not the decision he had expected to make. First, the oncologist said, she had a discussion with him alone. They reviewed the story of how far he'd come, the options that remained. She was frank. She told him that in her entire career she had never seen third-line chemotherapy produce a significant response in his type of brain tumor. She had looked for experimental therapies, and none were truly promising. And although she was willing to proceed with chemotherapy, she told him how much strength and time the treatment would take away from him and his family.

He did not shut down or rebel. His questions went on for an hour. He asked about this therapy and that therapy. And then, gradually, he began to ask about what would happen as the tumor got bigger, the symptoms he'd have, the ways they could try to control them, how the end might come.

The oncologist next met with the young man together with his family. That discussion didn't go so well. He had a wife and small children, and at first his wife wasn't ready to contemplate stopping chemo. But when the oncologist asked the patient to explain in his own words what they'd discussed, she understood. It was the same with his mother, who was a nurse. Meanwhile, his father sat quietly and said nothing the entire time.

A few days later, the patient returned to talk to the oncologist. "There should be something. There *must* be something," he said. His father had shown him reports of cures on the Internet. He confided how badly his father was taking the news. No patient wants to cause his family pain. According to Block, about two-thirds of patients are willing to undergo therapies they don't want if that is what their loved ones want.

The oncologist went to the father's home to meet with him. He had a sheaf of possible trials and treatments printed from the Internet. She went through them all. She was willing to change her opinion, she told him. But either the treatments were for brain tumors that were very different from his son's or else he didn't qualify. None were going to be miraculous. She told the father that he needed to understand: time with his son was limited, and the young man was going to need his father's help getting through it.

The oncologist noted wryly how much easier it would have been for her just to prescribe the chemotherapy. "But that meeting with the father was the turning point," she said. The patient and the family opted for hospice. They had more than a month together before he died. Later, the father thanked the doctor. That last month, he said, the family simply focused on being together, and it proved to be the most meaningful time they'd ever spent.

Given how prolonged some of these conversations have to be, many people argue that the key problem has been the financial incentives: we pay doctors to give chemotherapy and to do surgery but not to take the time required to sort out when doing so is unwise. This certainly is a factor. (The new health-reform act was to have added Medicare coverage for these conversations, until it was deemed funding for "death panels" and stripped out of the legislation.) But the issue isn't merely a matter of financing.

It arises from a still unresolved argument about what the function of medicine really is—what, in other words, we should and should not be paying for doctors to do.

The simple view is that medicine exists to fight death and disease, and that is, of course, its most basic task. Death is the enemy. But the enemy has superior forces. Eventually, it wins. And in a war that you cannot win, you don't want a general who fights to the point of total annihilation. You don't want Custer. You want Robert E. Lee, someone who knew how to fight for territory when he could and how to surrender when he couldn't, someone who understood that the damage is greatest if all you do is fight to the bitter end.

More often, these days, medicine seems to supply neither Custers nor Lees. We are increasingly the generals who march the soldiers onward, saying all the while, "You let me know when you want to stop." All-out treatment, we tell the terminally ill, is a train you can get off at any time—just say when. But for most patients and their families this is asking too much. They remain riven by doubt and fear and desperation; some are deluded by a fantasy of what medical science can achieve. But our responsibility, in medicine, is to deal with human beings as they are. People die only once. They have no experience to draw upon. They need doctors and nurses who are willing to have the hard discussions and say what they have seen, who will help people prepare for what is to come—and to escape a warehoused oblivion that few really want.

•     •     •

Sara Monopoli had had enough discussions to let her family and her oncologist know that she did not want hospitals or ICUs at the end—but not enough to have learned how to achieve this. From the moment she arrived in the emergency room that Friday morning in February, the train of events ran against a peaceful ending. There was one person who was disturbed by this, though, and who finally decided to intercede—Chuck Morris, her primary physician. As her illness had progressed through the previous year, he had left the decision making largely to Sara, her family, and the oncology team. Still, he had seen her and her husband regularly and listened to their concerns. That desperate morning, Morris was the one person Rich called before getting into the ambulance. He headed to the emergency room and met Sara and Rich when they arrived.

Morris said that the pneumonia might be treatable. But, he told Rich, "I'm worried this is it. I'm really worried about her." And he told him to let the family know that he said so.

Upstairs in her hospital room, Morris talked with Sara and Rich about the ways in which the cancer had been weakening her, making it hard for her body to fight off infection. Even if the antibiotics halted the infection, he said, he wanted them to remember that there was nothing that would stop the cancer.

Sara looked ghastly, Morris told me. "She was so short of breath. It was uncomfortable to watch. I still remember the attending"— the oncologist who admitted her for the pneumonia treatment. "He was actually kind of rattled about the whole case, and for him to be rattled is saying something."

After her parents arrived, Morris talked with them, too, and when they were finished Sara and her family agreed on a plan. The medical team would continue the antibiotics. But if things got worse they would not put her on a breathing machine. They also let him call the palliative-care team to visit. The team prescribed a small dose of morphine, which immediately eased her breathing. Her family saw how much her suffering diminished, and suddenly they didn't want any more suffering. The next morning, they were the ones to hold back the medical team.

"They wanted to put a catheter in her, do this other stuff to her," her mother, Dawn, told me. "I said, 'No. You aren't going to do anything to her.' I didn't care if she wet her bed. They wanted to do lab tests, blood-pressure measurements, finger sticks. I was very uninterested in their bookkeeping. I went over to see the head nurse and told them to stop."

In the previous three months, almost nothing we'd done to Sara—none of our chemotherapy and scans and tests and radiation—had likely achieved anything except to make her worse. She may well have lived longer without any of it. At least she was spared at the very end.

That day, Sara fell into unconsciousness as her body continued to fail. Through the next night, Rich recalled, "there was this awful groaning." There is no prettifying death. "Whether it was with inhaling or exhaling, I don't remember, but it was horrible, horrible, horrible to listen to."

Her father and her sister still thought that she might rally. But when the others had stepped out of the room, Rich knelt down weeping beside Sara and whispered in her ear. "It's OK to let go," he said. "You don't have to fight anymore. I will see you soon."

Later that morning, her breathing changed, slowing. At 9:45 A.M., Rich said, "Sara just kind of startled. She let a long breath out. Then she just stopped."

## Men's Health

WINNER—PERSONAL
SERVICE

*Here's another way to look at modern medicine—or rather what modern medicine can do to you. A founding editor at* Men's Health, *Laurence Roy Stains was diagnosed with stage II prostate cancer in 2008; this story begins as he lies on a table as his prostate is removed by a robot (readers may find the robot touch especially alarming). Instead of celebrating his good fortune—after all, more than 27,000 men die of prostate cancer each year—Stains soon has second thoughts and begins to investigate both the risks and remedies of prostate cancer. His conclusion: "Overdetection. Overdiagnosis. Overtreatment. These are the new buzzwords of twenty-first-century cancer research." The National Magazine Award for Personal Service honors magazines for stories that serve readers' needs and aspirations—which often means answers. "I Want My Prostate Back" knows it can't give you that, and that may be the best answer of all.*

Laurence Roy Stains

# I Want My Prostate Back

It's June 20, the first day of summer in 2008. I'm knocked out on an operating table and a robot is removing my prostate gland. In April I learned I had stage II prostate cancer, and after questioning experts and survivors, I've decided surgery is the way to go. Let's git 'er done. My mom died of cancer, but not me. No way.

Now, almost two years later, I'm not going to say, "thank god they caught it in time . . . I'm so blessed, each new morning is a miracle . . . Blah blah blah blah."

No, what I'm thinking is more along the lines of: *I want my prostate back.*

Your prostate gland labors in obscurity. The size of a golf ball, it's tucked away under your bladder, biding its time until you and your reproductive system decide to emit the sacred seed. Then the semen assembly line kicks in: The sperm swim up from your testicles to the seminal vesicles, and there they are mixed in a happy bath of fructose, vitamin C, and prostaglandins. This brew then proceeds to your prostate, which tops it off with enzymes, citric acid, and zinc before your man milk is propelled out of your body and into hers with rather pleasant smooth-muscle contractions. This long bomb triumphantly delivers your DNA into the end zone.

Ah, glory days.

But around the time in your life when you start to think more about your 401(k) than foreplay, your prostate starts to misfire. It swells in size, and the swelling clamps your urethra in a vise grip. If the cause of the swelling is benign, you're lucky. That's what those running-to-the-men's-room commercials for Flomax are all about. But some of the very same symptoms can also be caused by a prostate-cancer tumor.

Prostate cancer is the second most common cancer among men; only some skin cancers are more rampant. In 2009, it caused an estimated 27,360 deaths—long, slow, embattled deaths, as the cancer spread beyond men's prostates to nearby bones, notably their spines. Once the cancer advances past your prostate, you have only a 30 percent chance of surviving five years. But catch it early, before the cancer cells escape, and your chance of surviving five years is 100 percent.

Here's the good news about prostate cancer: Deaths are down because it is being diagnosed much earlier. In fact, 94 percent of all diagnoses these days peg the malignancy at stage I or stage II, before it metastasizes beyond the prostate. (Stage III cancers have begun to break out of the prostate; stage IV cancers have invaded nearby tissue and bone.) That has resulted in a steadily declining death rate of 4 percent a year since 1994. The declining mortality has generally been attributed to the widespread use—starting in the 1990s—of a simple test for the prostate-specific antigen, or PSA.

•     •     •

These days, the PSA test is so routine for middle-aged men that your doctor might order one for you without even asking. My internist did that for me in the summer of 2007, as part of a regular physical. Mostly he was worried about my cholesterol levels. The results showed mildly troubling cholesterol—but a very troubling PSA number. Standards in place at the time held that it should be less than 4; some evidence has suggested that it should be less than 2.5 if you're younger than fifty. Mine was 12.6.

My doctor sent me to a urologist, who suspected that my high number was caused by a prostate infection. The only way to confirm those suspicions, unfortunately, was by collecting some prostatic fluid. He sat there grinning apologetically as he held up one gloved and well-lubricated index finger and asked me to bend over a chair. Then he stuck his finger up my ass and pushed on my prostate like it was a doorbell on Halloween night. About ten minutes later, after I'd recovered, he gave me a scrip for an antibiotic and told me to come back at the end of the summer so he could retest my PSA.

I really didn't want to go back. So I didn't.

I put it off repeatedly until the night, months later, when I met the person I later called, only half jokingly, the Angel on the Train. I was sitting in the dining car having chicken a la Amtrak with my wife and son when suddenly a disheveled old man tottered up the aisle carrying a little plastic bag full of pills. The steward swung him around and plopped him into the booth with us. Nobody said a word for fifteen minutes. Awkward! Then I started talking to him, and before I knew it we were comparing prostates. My wife ratted me out: "He had a high PSA reading," she said, waving her fork in my direction. "But he won't go back to the doctor."

The old guy turned to me. And, establishing eye contact for the first time, he said, "You really need to have that checked out."

When I returned home I had another PSA test. It was 9.2. That's better, right?

Well, as it turns out, nothing about the PSA test is accurate, starting with the name. The letters stand for a protein produced by the prostate. When PSA was first identified, the prostate appeared to be its only source, but it has even been detected, albeit in smaller amounts, in women. Clearly, there are non-prostate sources of PSA.

When your prostate is healthy, PSA is mostly contained within it, but if there is trouble in the tissue, more PSA can leak into the blood. By the time cancer has ransacked and spread beyond the gland, PSA levels can soar into the thousands. But the PSA test is so exquisitely fine-tuned that it picks up leaking PSA at the very lowest levels, measuring it in nanograms per milliliter of blood. That's right: nanogram, as in one-billionth of a gram.

As it turns out, the common threshold of 4 nanograms per milliliter is rather arbitrary. You can have cancer even if your PSA reading is below 4. That was definitively shown by a 2004 study of 2,950 men who were followed for seven years as part of the Prostate Cancer Prevention Trial. These men never had a PSA level above 4, or an abnormal digital rectal exam, for the entire length of the study. They all underwent a prostate biopsy—and cancer was found in 449 of them, or 15.2 percent.

On the other hand, you can have a PSA reading above 4, and it could be caused by two common maladies: prostatitis, which is an inflammation usually caused by an infection, and benign prostatic hyperplasia (BPH), which is the fancy name for the benign swelling that plagues aging glands. Both can cause PSA leakage. In fact, the majority of high PSA readings are due to these noncancerous causes. Only one man in four with a PSA level between 4 and 10 will be found to have cancer after a subsequent biopsy.

So what good is this PSA test, anyway? Even its defenders admit, sheepishly, that it's no pregnancy test. And its detractors say it's useless. In 2004, a team of Stanford urologists looked at pathology results of more than 1,300 surgically removed prostates and found that the PSA number predicted nothing more than the gland's size. The lead author, Thomas Stamey, M.D., now retired, declared at the time, "The PSA era is probably over." Which is noteworthy: Dr. Stamey is one of the inventors of the method used to prepare PSA for testing, and in 1987 he published the first study linking increased PSA levels to prostate cancer.

But nobody listened, and a lot of men continue to get biopsies they don't really need. If an estimated 192,280 men were diagnosed with prostate cancer in 2009, you can bet another 575,000 men endured biopsies that turned up nothing. If that statistic makes you shrug, you've never had a doctor come after you with a biopsy gun.

●     ●     ●

April 11, 2008. I'm lying on my left side on a gurney in my urologist's office. As instructed, I've lowered my pants to my knees. I'm here for a biopsy, but first comes the ultrasound. My doctor lubricates the ultrasound wand, which is about the size of my son's Spider-Man toothbrush, and slides it into my rectum. All is well until he starts to muscle it into various positions to improve the camera angles; then it feels less like a medical device and more like a broom handle.

Can a biopsy be any worse? Yes, it can. He inserts a syringe into my rectum to inject lidocaine into my prostate—six shots, in six separate locations, and all I can say is, never have a prostate biopsy without serious sedation. But by the time my doctor goes back up there to grab his twelve tissue samples, I don't feel a thing. I just hear the spring-loaded biopsy gun go off, bang, each time.

Then I go home to rest. And hope. Only a one in four chance they'll find something. I like those odds.

Five days later, the report comes back. Two of the twelve tissue cores are positive for cancer. I talk to people, even though the last thing I want to do is talk to people. Why are women so much better at this? They have "races for the cure" and that pink ribbon. A freakin' logo for their cancer! It must be a girl thing.

As for me, I just quietly call some strangers whose names have been passed along to me—by women, of course. One guy, John, had a biopsy that came back with only 1 percent cancer in one core. But his father had died of prostate cancer, so after two years of "watchful waiting," he finally went under the knife. I could opt for watchful waiting, but . . . waiting for what? For cancer to colonize my spine?

I have three treatment options: (1) surgery to remove my prostate, (2) external beams of radiation, or (3) brachytherapy, which involves implanting radioactive pellets in my prostate. Radiation treatments and their side effects can stretch out over months. I just want this to end. I'm in my fifties, so I'll recover from surgery, no problem. I choose surgery.

Besides, some 75,000 radical prostatectomies were performed robotically in the United States in 2008. The surgeon sits across the room at a console that looks like a video-game booth, manipulating a set of robotic arms over the patient. Unlike traditional surgery, there's no eight-inch incision and not as much blood loss; instead, the procedure is done through six dime-sized cuts in and below the navel. The best part, of course, is that the surgeon can be incredibly accurate, because he's seeing the tissues magnified ten times and controlling the arms to make micro-sized movements. And if he sneezes, hey, no problem! As two doctors wrote in the British medical journal *The Lancet*, a nice feature here is the "elimination of a surgeon's physiological tremor."

Oh, yeah. I like that feature. When the whole point is to remove my prostate while sparing the surrounding nerves that create my erections, I totally love that feature.

It's June 18, 2008, two nights before surgery. I'm in bed with my wife, and I miss my prostate already. I tell her that if and when we have sex again, there will be no ejaculate, no man milk, no wet spot. Henceforth I shall be seedless. You can see where I was going with this, can't you, guys? I was hoping I'd receive a happy send-off.

My wife says, "You should talk to your doctor about that."

Gosh, honey. Thanks.

•     •     •

Here's what patients think their doctors say: If you undergo the relatively new "nerve-sparing" prostate surgery, you will eventually return to the level of erectile function you enjoyed before you had the surgery. It may take weeks, months, or a couple of years, depending on age and prostate size—but that mojo will return. That's what patients want to hear, too, so maybe they miss the doctors' qualifiers about "most men," and "in certain cases . . ."

Unfortunately, that's just not the truth, says John L. Gore, M.D., an assistant professor of urology at the University of Washington. "Even with a perfect surgery there's going to be some shutdown."

Dr. Gore is qualified to say this; he conducted one of the most recent studies of prostate-cancer patients and how surgery affects them. He and his UCLA colleague, Mark Litwin, M.D., followed 475 prostate-cancer patients for four years. These patients received more scrutiny than the typical so-how's-your-erection questions from their doctors. They filled out a twenty-minute questionnaire in the privacy of their homes before surgery and at 1, 2, 4, 8, 12, 18, 24, 30, 36, 42, and 48 months afterward. And, no, things were not as they had been before.

"We're not saying sexual function is terrible after surgery," says Dr. Gore. "We're saying the likelihood of that function being exactly what it was before surgery is essentially zero." And, he adds, you'll recover what you're going to recover within two years. "Beyond that, it is what it is."

Okay, so . . . just how messed up are prostate patients? That question was answered by a nine-hospital study of 1,201 men, led by Martin Sanda, M.D., director of the prostate-cancer center at Beth Israel Deaconess Medical Center. After two years, radiation and brachytherapy patients complained most about urinary and bowel troubles; the 603 prostatectomy patients (93 percent of whom had nerve-sparing surgery) complained more about sexual function. To be blunt: 64 percent of them said their erections were not firm enough for penetration (compared with 17 percent who had erection trouble before surgery), and just under half did not recover erections suitable for sex. This is, remember, two years after their surgery.

"One problem is that doctors often don't spend enough time with their patients to fully explain that sexual recovery typically takes years, not months, and often does not occur," Dr. Sanda says. "Men might assume that as long as they can have a nerve-sparing procedure, their sexuality will be fine. In reality, nerve sparing provides a reasonable chance for erection recovery, but it by no means guarantees it."

I'm not trying to pick a fight with urologic or cancer surgeons, but rather to help prostate-cancer patients have expectations that are more realistic. "Patients live a long time after treatment and many die with, rather than from, prostate cancer," notes Dr. Gore. "It's critical that they participate in shared decision making with their physicians so they don't come out of the process with regret."

•     •     •

I had no regrets. At first. I spent one night in the hospital, and five days later I taught a three-hour class. Soon I'd quit inserting pink panty liners into my boxers. And urination became a reclaimed pleasure: I could piss like a racehorse, just like in my teens.

As for what's clinically called "restoration of sexual function," here's my official report: I dunno. My marriage was a mess, so you can imagine the amount of sexual healing that didn't happen. But plenty of guys' marriages are, you know, *meh*—just okay. So I wonder: Do a lot of wives think this is a dandy time to close up shop? How many other wives make it a habit to come to bed long after he's asleep?

I also wonder how much of the sexual wreckage is more than just nerve damage. Without any ejaculate, I feel like a broken toy. Like a water pistol that squirts jelly. (Or nothing.) If love ever comes my way again, I'll sort of dread it. I'll be a spectator at my own sexual rehab, and we all know what that does for an erection.

While wondering whether I'd ever again throw the high hard one, I read everything I could about prostate cancer. Within weeks I was filled with remorse. In early August—less than two months post-op—the U.S. Preventive Services Task Force, the nation's leading independent panel of experts in prevention and primary care, said doctors should no longer screen for prostate cancer in men age seventy-five and older. At that age, the panel reasoned, the harms from treating the cancer outweigh the benefits.

This was a big deal: As recently as 2002, the panel was neutral on the topic. But the evidence of the last several years led the panel to conclude that the benefits of screening in the seventy-five-and-older age group are "small to none," while the harms from treatment are "moderate to substantial."

As a recent cancer patient, I was totally confused. *Wait a minute*, I'm thinking. *This is cancer we're talking about. If you don't kill it, it kills you. Right?*

Wrong.

As it turns out, prostate cancer is "heterogeneous," as the panel's report puts it. That is, one man's prostate cancer differs from another's. Some prostate cancer is aggressive, spreads rapidly, and will kill you. But screening tends to pick up the more slow-growing cancers. They can stop growing. You can live with them for years, symptom-free. Some may even regress on their own, says one theory, without nuclear bullets or robot intervention. I'm not seventy-five, but I still had reason to wonder: Was my cancer the dangerous kind, or the benign kind?

Here's the real problem with screening based on the PSA test: It can't tell the difference! So why operate on a seventy-six-year-old man who is more likely to die of something else? By age eighty, most men have some cancer in their prostate. And the question is even harder to answer for younger men.

PSA screening is *too* good. The panel concluded that in the seventy-five-and-up crowd, screening finds cancer that "will never cause symptoms during the patient's lifetime." Here's a jarring thought: In 1980, a white man's lifetime risk of a prostate-cancer diagnosis was one in eleven; today it's one in six. Yet his chance of dying of cancer is *lower*, not higher. So we're finding more cancer, with fewer fatalities. Just how much cancer is not worth finding? The panel wasn't sure, but noted this: "Incidence data suggest overdiagnosis rates ranging from 29 percent to 44 percent of all prostate-cancer cases detected by PSA screening."

Almost eight months later, with my toy still broken and my heart breaking, I read the results of two huge trials that assessed regular screening—similar to what I received. They were published in the *New England Journal of Medicine* (*NEJM*), accompanied by an editorial by Michael J. Barry, M.D., a prostate disease outcomes researcher and the chief of general medicine at Massachusetts General Hospital. His conclusion: "Serial PSA screening has at best a modest effect on prostate-cancer mortality during the first decade of follow-up. This benefit comes at the cost of substantial overdiagnosis and overtreatment."

Overdetection. Overdiagnosis. Overtreatment. These are the new buzzwords of twenty-first-century cancer research—not just on prostate cancer, but on breast cancer, too.

Here are the particulars. In one of the *NEJM* studies, nearly 77,000 men from ten U.S. study centers were divided into two groups. Either they received an annual PSA test and a digital rectal exam, or they received "usual care," which may or may not have included screening. After ten years, there was no reduction in the death rate for the screened group.

The other study followed 182,000 men in seven European countries. The 73,000 men who were screened an average of every four years for prostate cancer underwent 17,000 biopsies and had a 70 percent higher rate of disease. They also, not surprisingly, received much more treatment. According to estimates, 277 per 10,000 of those men underwent radical prostatectomy (versus 100 in the control group), and another 220 per 10,000 had radiation therapy (versus 123 per 10,000 in the control group). That's a lot of treatment—with few lives saved. The study's conclusion: If you aggressively screened 1,410 men, and cut or irradiated 48 of them, you'd save exactly one man's life.

Were those my odds? I hate those odds.

Did I need surgery or not? Because if I didn't, I want my prostate back.

.    .    .

I'm in the hospital's pathology lab to visit my prostate, or what remains of it. After my surgery it was sent here, where it was sliced up like prosciutto. Then twenty-four tissue slices, each just three millimeters thick, were stained bubblegum pink and made into microscope-friendly slides. We look at slide F-4 because I want to see what cancer—my cancer, specifically—looks like. It doesn't look like anything. It looks like the Blob.

"It's actually not very interesting," the pathologist is telling me. It's just a ho-hum, garden-variety cancer. If I had left it in my body, she thinks it would have begun to bother me in another four or five years.

"Probably," she says. She thinks a moment, then tells me: "You made the right choice."

The surgical pathology report on my operation notes that a fifty-seven-year-old white male received a robotic prostatectomy. Several specimens were examined, including surrounding fat tissue, vas deferens, and seminal vesicles. All were cancer-free. Finally, the prostate itself arrived: forty grams. With plenty of cancer to go around. There is tumor present on the left and right sides of the gland, in nine of the twenty-four sections, and most worrisome of all, it's present at the margin of the prostate on the lower left side.

It's given a Gleason score of seven (on a ten-point scale), which means it's moderately abnormal. It's staged at T2c, the last stage before cancer begins to spread beyond the prostate gland.

I call someone who will know what it all means: Eric Klein, M.D., chairman of the Glickman Urological and Kidney Institute at the Cleveland Clinic. He thinks I might have gone another decade without symptoms. But based on the grade and volume of the tumor, "I would say, yes, you definitely needed to have that tumor removed."

In another decade, I'll still be in my sixties. My father is ninety-two.

I wonder what my urologist thinks; he knows my prostate better than anyone. After all, he's the man who removed it. So I make my one-year follow-up appointment. Maybe he's completely changed his position on prostate cancer. Maybe he's prescribing herbal teas these days. Who knows?

My urologist sits down with me and patiently looks over my pathology report. Yes, there was a lot of tumor volume. Furthermore, it was on both sides of the gland. Furthermore, it was at the margin of the gland in one spot. Then he notes a detail I'd neglected to tell Dr. Klein: The cancer was located at the bottom of the gland, a site where, according to a Vanderbilt University study, small margins of cancerous prostate cells commonly remain after surgery.

"By age 70, you would probably have had metastatic disease," he concludes. "Or earlier."

"When would I have begun to feel pain?"

He's silent.

"What are you thinking?"

He's slow to answer. "I'm thinking, dying of prostate cancer is horrible," he finally says. The cancer, once it spreads, causes immense pain. It can obstruct the bladder and everything else down below, so the patient needs to have tubes inserted. Multiple tubes. Requiring multiple hospital stays. And there's the hormone therapy, which is so often in vain.

"If we could know whose cancer is going to progress, and whose won't," he says, "that would be great."

Great for him, I have the feeling, as much as for his patients. He tries to be helpful. We talk about the odds of recurrence, and PSA doubling time, and various treatments, and what works best. But again, there's nothing you can hang your hat on.

I tilt my head back and scream at his ceiling tiles: "There's nothing about prostate cancer you can hang your hat on!"

Except for this fact: Nobody wants to die of it. So I guess it was a good thing my prostate was taken out.

My friend John is not so sure. Here it is, eighteen months later, and he still has erectile problems, leaky bladder problems. Does he regret it? "A lot of times, yes," he says.

As for you? I hope you or your father or one of your friends will not be among the unlucky many to receive a diagnosis of prostate cancer. And this year, there will be enough men to fill nearly three Superdomes. Picture it: row upon row of silent men with full agendas and empty stares. And no place to hang a hat.

**O, The Oprah Magazine**

In 2008, Paige Williams's story
"You Have Thousands of Angels
Around You" won the National
Magazine Award for Feature
Writing for Atlanta magazine
(the story was also anthologized
in Best American Magazine
Writing that year). Even then,
her life was falling apart. As the
headline writers at O explained,
Williams was "eighty pounds
overweight, divorced, out of work,
and deeply in debt." The solution?
Bikram yoga. In "My Bra's Too
Tight" and "It's Never Too Late,"
Williams used her skills as a master
of narrative journalism not only to
trace her path to physical and
spiritual recovery but also to give
readers the kinds of practical
advice they turn to magazine to
get. "By sharing her story of bad
health and worse decisions with
humility and grace," the National
Magazine Award judges said,
"Williams inspires readers and
shows them how to improve their
lives for the better." Williams now
teaches narrative writing at the
Nieman Foundation for Journalism
at Harvard University.

Paige Williams

# My Bra's Too Tight *and* It's Never Too Late

## My Bra's Too Tight

The teacher wants me to make a Japanese ham sandwich. To my knowledge, I've never seen a Japanese ham sandwich, but as I understand it, I'm to stand bent with my face to my shins and chest to my thighs in perfect vertical union—I *am* the sandwich.

I would say I look more like a jelly roll. My flabby abdomen won't let my forehead anywhere near my knees, and my legs tremble as I try contorting myself into a position my body neither recognizes nor endorses. The goal is to concentrate on stretching and breathing, but I'm fixating on my unpedicured toenails. And the neon paleness of my legs. And the fact that I probably should have shaved.

The students around me are tanned and toned and very nearly nude. Every body glistens. We're in a Bikram yoga studio, after all, where the heat is set to 105 degrees and the humidity to 40 percent, to facilitate flexibility. The men wear nothing but shorts; the women rock hot pants and halters. Because I'd rather lick the sweat-soaked carpet than bare my wretched flesh, I have on the hot-yoga equivalent of a snowsuit: calf-length sweatpants, a jog bra, and a T-shirt. I'm huffing harder than a serial killer. And we're only on posture number one.

Posture number one of class one of day one. Assuming I survive, I'll make the ham sandwich and about two dozen other postures every single day for the next two months, for the notorious sixty-day Bikram challenge. I'm subjecting myself to "Bikram's torture chamber," as founder Bikram Choudhury himself calls this insanely intense regimen, because the program promises renewal from the inside out—because suffering inside this hot room may be my surest path to survival out in the world.

I need to change so many things about my life, it's hard to know where to start. I need physical and spiritual transformation, from the mental to the muscular to the molecular. I need to stop treating my body like a landfill. I need stability, which I haven't seen in so long, I've forgotten how it feels. I need a reset button.

This won't be easy. As I start the challenge, I'm divorced, in debt, and eighty pounds overweight. Wellbutrin and Lexapro, in their little amber bottles, rattle around in my life like maracas. My career? Mr. Toad's Wild Ride. One minute I'm winning the magazine industry's top honor for feature writing, the next I'm taking a new job out West, and the next I'm losing that job, moving all my stuff into storage, and living back home with my mother, in Mississippi.

"Do this yoga for sixty days and it will change your body, your mind, and your life," says Choudhury, a former Indian yoga champion who lives in Los Angeles and who is, depending on your viewpoint, either a beloved lifesaving guru or just a really flexible guy who got lucky, and rich, with an idea and a persona. Bikram students believe, and I hope they're right, that Choudhury's heat-centric, copyrighted sequence of ancient hatha yoga postures is a transformative agent like no other; testimonials the world over suggest this yoga eases the symptoms of a range of maladies—depression, diabetes, carpal tunnel syndrome, fibromyalgia, migraines, arthritis, back pain, and heart disease, for instance—while relaxing the mind and slimming the body.

"Can't you just do all that by, like, *running* every day for sixty days?" a friend asks. Good question, but the answer doesn't interest me. None of my past fitness activities—racquet sports, cycling, jogging, gym circuit training, kickboxing—seem catalytic enough for the depth of change I'm after.

I'm not a renovation; I'm a teardown. And I'm hoping Bikram is my bulldozer.

### Anatomy of a Meltdown

Is it possible to pinpoint the moment a life swings out of balance? For me it happened "gradually and then suddenly," to borrow from Hemingway.

The slope started getting slippery when my father died in 1995. After my marriage failed a few years later, I left the beauty and comfort of Charlotte, North Carolina, and began my peripatetic period, living and working in ten cities (and one European country) within ten years. Along the way, I stockpiled debt by following divorce with graduate school (expensive) in New York (super-expensive) and by self-medicating my depression with stuff—I overpaid for rent, I indulged, I shopped. I have always believed quality of life can turn on a pretty, new set of cotton sheets.

The debt left me anxious and mentally exhausted. Then my body began throwing me strange new curves: Fibroid tumors grew in my uterus and surgeons had to cut them out. My eggs and estrogen bailed on me, making chaos of my hormones. As I worked harder and longer to get out of debt, I convinced myself that I was too busy and too tired to tend to my own wellness. Raised an athlete, I now exercised less often than Thomas Pynchon appeared in public. By the time I left New York for Atlanta, in the spring of 2006, a pattern had set in: anxiety, work, self-isolation, medication, and protracted sobbing mixed with flurries of rage.

You know what helps in painful situations? Pie. Also Big Macs. Publicly, I ate properly if at all, but nighttime triggered a junk food free-for-all. Because I ate poorly and didn't exercise, I slept badly. Because I slept badly, I woke up harried and late, so I never had time for breakfast. By noon, as I caffeinated instead of hydrated and often skipped lunch, I was already thinking about what I'd eat that night. I wasn't a snacker; I was a volume eater. Food was all I looked forward to.

For a while, my career was the one thing I managed to hold together. In the fall of 2008, I assumed the editorship of a small magazine out West. I treated magazine editing like neurosurgery—we didn't just have to be good, we had to be perfect, even as the economy imploded, even as the publishing industry took a particularly big hit. For a bajillion reasons, the situation didn't work out. I'd say the center couldn't hold, but I'm not sure there ever was a center. Wherever my slide started, it ended here: Stress + sugar + carbohydrate overload − exercise + insomnia − adequate water + self-loathing − romantic intimacy + regret = meltdown. One particularly fraught Friday morning I reached my limit with the magazine's publisher and failed, completely, to hold my tongue. By Monday morning, I was in the unemployment office.

The depression that had held me down for so long now dropped me into a well. My whole body ached. My hair fell out in the shower. For three months, I had a headache every day, often so painful that I'd lie with a cold cloth on my forehead, just trying not to throw up. Most nights, I went to bed with a heated terrycloth beanbag around my neck like a boa, like I was eighty. If I managed to sleep, I'd reflexively grind my teeth worse than ever. (It was an old problem: Years ago, when I was married, my then-husband woke me one night and said: "Are you eating *candy?*")

While looking for a new job, I had time to start exercising again, and to eat right, and to drink plenty of water, but I didn't. It was easier to relocate permanently to the land of dim rooms, dark chocolate, and all-day television, to outfit my wardrobe entirely in caftans. To paraphrase novelist Richard Ford, I was learning what's at the end of my rope and what it felt like to be there.

But there are problems and there are Problems. I wasn't dealing with a debilitating condition or an abusive husband or unremitting poverty or the death of a child or a male population that wanted me dead just because I wear lipstick; the only war zone I've ever lived in is the one in my head. My situation was self-imposed. I had choices. It was time to start making some good ones.

While lying fully clothed in my childhood bed in the middle of a beautiful and utterly wasted Mississippi summer day, I realized it was either get up—I mean really get up—or die. I don't know why, but I thought of Bikram yoga. I had tried Bikram a few times. I remembered appreciating most of all the permission to be quiet. I recalled the yoga room as a place where I could breathe.

## Hard Numbers

As I start the sixty-day challenge, I need to know the depth of the damage. I can't just keep saying I feel lousy; I need raw, supporting data on why I feel lousy.

My sister, Tracey, tells me about Lifesigns, a Memphis-based clinic that performs extensive physicals. In the days before my workup, I hit one last gastro-nostalgic round of Burger King, Wendy's, and Taco Bell, and if there were a Dairy Queen within twenty-five miles, buddy, I'd hit that, too. I'm eating leftover Papa John's breadsticks even as I ring up Lifesigns to *make the appointment*—and I don't even like breadsticks.

Although I've experienced clean-eating periods in my life, good nutrition doesn't come naturally to me. In my home state of Mississippi, the fattest state in the nation, 32.5 percent of adults are obese and a vegetable isn't considered edible unless you've cooked it in a half-pound of bacon grease.

All this history shows up on the Lifesigns scale, of course. Before checking me for heart disease (clear), a thyroid condition (clear), cancer (clear), and diabetes (see below), the nurse weighs me in at an astonishing 208 pounds—83 pounds more than I'd like to weigh (I'm fifty-five). "Your physical exam," the detailed report from Felix Caldwell, MD, will say, "reveals . . . evidence of obesity."

*Obesity?*

I probably should have known this, but federal guidelines say you are clinically obese and therefore in danger of liver and heart disease, diabetes, sleep problems, osteoarthritis, and cancer if your body mass index (BMI) is 30 or higher. Your risk for chronic disease increases significantly when your BMI surpasses even 25; mine comes back as 34.6. For a woman my age, overall body fat should be between 23 and 33.9 percent; mine is 42.1. I am basically a gel. Your health risks increase even further if your waist circumference measures more than thirty-five inches (forty for men); mine measures thirty-seven.

I ring up Mehmet Oz, MD, the cardiothoracic surgeon, author, and *O* magazine contributing editor, for help understanding the nine-page report. "The obesity is gonna cost you some life expectancy," he tells me flatly as he looks over my test results. "Your blood pressure is almost perfect, but your fasting blood sugar is ninety-nine [milligrams per deciliter]—if it were over a hundred, I'd start calling you a prediabetic. So, you're close. I can almost guarantee that if you maintained this lifestyle another five years, the sugar would slowly rise."

My LDL cholesterol, the bad one, should be 100 or less but measures 149—"high enough that we actually would start to treat that, normally," Oz goes on to say. High cholesterol, he explains, is an early indicator of metabolic syndrome: belly fat leading to a series of negative health changes. "The belly fat squeezes the kidneys, which can lead to high blood pressure; the fat can also poison your liver. The fact that your kidneys are a little abnormal reflects changes to kidney function from the inflammatory effects of the obesity. And you're developing foie gras of your liver."

Oz makes it clear that I need to improve my diet immediately and exercise at least thirty minutes a day—for the rest of my life. He singles out breathing and stretching as particularly beneficial—which, as it happens, are central to Bikram yoga.

## Stretch, Sweat, Repeat × 60

Bikram Yoga Memphis, the studio closest to my mother's home in Tupelo, Mississippi, is cruelly located a few doors down from Muddy's Bake Shop, which some consider the best cupcake pusher in the city. For the first seven of the sixty days, my goal is twofold: Stay out of Muddy's and do not throw up in class.

On day one, BYM founder Lori Givens stands up front, on a carpeted podium. The goal for beginners, she says, is just to stay in the room, to learn to breathe. "Feet together, heels and toes touching, let's begin," she says. In a Bikram studio, only the teacher speaks, delivering Choudhury's almost incessant and incantatory instructions. Class takes place in a large, rectangular studio with thin carpeting and a floor-to-ceiling mirror on one long wall. The lights—*so bright.* They are, in fact, fluorescent. In the mirror, I look not only gargantuan but also slightly green.

This essential setup can be found in every Bikram yoga studio from Memphis to Jakarta, on the theory that the more minimalist and standardized the practice, the deeper the potential for focused hard work. "If you want a dark room and incense, go find another yoga—we don't do that," teacher and BYM co-owner and codirector Gregg Williams tells us one day. "Bikram wants the room bright so you can see yourself." The idea is to meet your own eyes as you move through the postures—to develop a relationship with your mirrored self and start being kind to her.

Although Lori and her instructors continually refer to Bikram as basic, nothing about it feels basic to me as day after day I blunder through twenty-six postures and two breathing exercises, including physical impersonations of a rabbit, a camel, a perfect human bridge, a flower petal blooming, an eagle, a cobra, a corpse, a triangle, a pearl necklace, and more. My body simply won't bend. My breath is so loud, I'm attracting attention, and I truly worry that I'll pass out. Even lying in savasana—flat on my back with my arms by my side—feels strenuous, because my heels won't touch and the junk in my trunk puts a pinching arch in my back. Obviously, this is going to be a little more complicated than sweating some, stretching some, and—voilà!—solace and skinny jeans.

But it's not only the extra weight that interferes; my brain never shuts up: *My bra's too tight. My ponytail's too high. This carpet stinks. Is that cellulite on my biceps? I'm thirsty. Maybe it'll rain today. Why does everybody in here have a tattoo? Do I need a tattoo? If I got a tattoo, what would it look like and where would I put it? I might be having a heart attack. I'm exhausted—I'm done with this posture. I'm gonna bake me some chicken tonight.*

It's amazing how many irritants you can find even in such a controlled environment. If I weren't so desperate to change my life, the sweat alone would keep me far, far away from this room. Other people's sweat freaks me out, as does any breach of my personal space. I need a two-foot circumference in all situations, especially those involving the potential slinging and mingling of human effluvia. The sweat dripping on towels and mats looks to me like biotoxic rain. Day after day, I try distancing my mat from others or holing up in a back corner, until Lori sighs and diagnoses me with control issues. "This is something we'll need to work on," she says.

Perfectionism gets no points, either. Just having expectations is a mistake. Though every posture of every class is the same, I realize over time that it's also potentially different, a hard concept to grasp for someone who tends to see the world as either yin or yang, who has always measured success in terms of ground gained.

To execute a decent balancing stick on Monday and completely flub it on Tuesday unsettles me, and my classroom emotions start to veer like mountain switchbacks:

confidence

panic

euphoria

despair.

One day Gregg is leading us through the standing series—the first fifty minutes of class, where the heart rate rises—when all of a sudden I'm pretty sure I'm going to projectile-vomit my lunch onto the bare heels of the woman in front of me. This is not unusual—the heat and exertion can come down on you quickly, especially if you're new or not drinking enough water. The feeling is so overpowering, I attempt to flee the room.

Fleeing the room, like talking or whispering in class, is not allowed.

"Sit back down! Sit back down!" Gregg says.

"You'd rather I throw up on the carpet?" I say.

"You're not going to throw up," he says. "Lie down. Just breathe."

This panicked feeling is what they call the "yoga truck." When the yoga truck hits, all you want to do is get out, or lie in savasana and count ceiling tiles. After fifteen days, I am sore and discouraged and sick of being wringing wet, and I feel utterly overwhelmed by everything I'm supposed to remember, sometimes all of it at once: Lock your knee, contract your abdominal muscles, chin down, chest up, focus only on yourself in the mirror, quiet your breath, pulling is the object of stretching, if you're falling out of the posture you're not kicking hard enough, chin up, eyes open, let it go, just be here, have compassion for yourself, kick harder—kick, kick, kick, kick, kick, kick, kick! I can't even get through the full ninety minutes without standing or sitting out certain postures.

Flat on my back, I silently rant at myself. *I hate you. I hate this class. I hate this stupid stomach and these enormous boobs. I hate Ben and Jerry and KFC and the Lay's potato chip company. My car smells like a yoga studio, and for what? After nearly three weeks, my clothes aren't any looser. I may as well go on a cupcake crime spree for all the good this is doing . . .*

"Get out of your head," the teachers say.

This, for me, is becoming the most important instruction of all, far more important than "Suck in your stomach." I'm stuck in self-flagellating old thought patterns and focusing on what's not happening rather than on what is. All I can think—and talk—about is my weight, which is a little like worrying about a leaky roof when the foundation is cracked.

"How long did it take you to get yourself into this mess?" Gregg asks me one day.

"Years," I say.

"Well, then," he says, "it'll take a while to fix it."

Gregg should know. He weighed 435 pounds and was at the point of suicide when he started Bikram four years ago. He has lost more than 200 pounds and is now engaged to Lori. Bikram is Lori and Gregg's business but also their lifestyle. The same is true of all the teachers—they are my leaders as well as my classmates. They learned, as I am learning, that the body begins to crave Bikram—the heat, the moves, the comfort of healthy discomfort. When I started the sixty days, I wanted to kill the already-dead yogi who came up with standing bow-pulling posture, but I'm actually starting to look forward to it—not much, mind you, but some.

"Elbow hurt? Arms hurt? Back hurt? Hair hurt? Hands hurt? Good for you," Choudhury has been known to say to his students during particularly challenging moments in class. "All the pain in the world is not going to take happiness, peace away from you. If anybody can make you angry, you are the loser. If anyone can steal your happiness, peace, away from you, you are the loser."

You'd have to be in the studio to understand the power of words like these. The teachers' instructions and insights become like a mantra, and the teachers themselves like coaches, or beloved shrinks. As I lie in savasana, half-dead with exhaustion, just listening to Lori, Gregg, Kerri, Shannon, Jyo, or Kristy talk about strength and determination—about the integrity of the *attempt*—propels me through the remaining postures. I may not do the moves perfectly or even well, but by week four I'm doing them. I've stayed in the room, which calls upon reserves of calm I didn't even know I had. The blood flows, and whether the Bikram claims about health benefits are true or not, I do start to feel different and to cultivate better thoughts. Instead of thinking, *I can't do this*, an alternative occurs to me: *I am doing this.*

"Emotions first," Lori keeps telling me. "Then the body will follow."

The first demon to go is the stiffness. The second is the headaches. As I reach the halfway mark of thirty days, I feel more relaxed. I stand straighter. I can touch my toes. People tell me my skin looks great, my eyes brighter. One day in the parking lot, a woman driving a Mercedes cuts me off, and instead of fuming, I simply let it go—lady wants to be a jerk, let her be a jerk; it's got nothing to do with me.

I'm drinking water now—not enough but more than before. I've completely changed my diet to lean meats and vegetables and have set myself back only once—with a pair of chewy Chips Ahoy cookies (120 calories) one particularly rough night alone at a cousin's house. The food changes don't feel like sacrifice. In fact, I was hungrier on the drive-through diet of probably 3,000 calories a day than I am now on half that amount.

On day sixty, I'm scheduled to return to Lifesigns for a back-end battery of tests, but on day thirty I do a few measurements of my own. My weight has dropped to 198—a long way from my personal goal of 125, but I'll take it. Wii Fit tells me my BMI has fallen from 34.6 to 32.7. I've lost 2.5 inches in my hips, 2.5 in my bust, and 1 inch in the all-important waistline.

Also, I got a job—a terrific one. Another city, another magazine. I'll start work after I finish the Bikram challenge, assuming I finish the Bikram challenge.

At one point, Choudhury himself swings through Memphis to promote his book *Bikram Yoga: The Guru Behind Hot Yoga Shows the Way to Radiant Health and Personal Fulfillment*. Lori and Gregg arrange for me to talk with him before a crowded Borders book signing, a conversation that encompasses the fifth dimension, Jupiter, and a parable about a wooden bird. Choudhury, who routinely mentions having trained and befriended public figures like Shirley MacLaine, Richard Nixon, Madonna, and Kareem Abdul-Jabbar, has just taken an emotional tour of Graceland and keeps talking about Elvis. "He was my best friend. I could have saved Elvis's life."

Choudhury is sixty-three and looks fifty. He is petite and compact (I've seen his abs—I know). For the book signing, he dresses in a salmon-colored, formfitting V-neck sweater and creased white pants that look like something a cruise director might wear. His Rolex is as blingy as anything Elvis wore circa 1975.

"What's the most important thing in your life?" Choudhury asks me. His rhetoric is well practiced—the question lives in his repertoire, just as the Japanese ham sandwich lives in his lineup of postures.

"Is it bad that I can't answer that question?" I say.

"I ask the same question around the globe," he tells me. "They say the most important thing is God, water, wind, family, children, love—all bull. The most important thing in your life is you."

By day sixty, I hope to understand what he means.

# It's Never Too Late

## I Am Such a Cheater

In a couple of hours, I'm supposed to unfurl my yoga mat at Bikram Yoga Memphis, yet here I am at Karen Wilder Fitness, considering a fling with the exercise machines. The Bikram studio still seems a little alien to me, but being in Karen's gym feels like being among old friends: There's Elliptical Trainer and Free Weights and Smith—and I'm so happy to see Kettlebell I want to pick him up and swing him like a favorite child. I haven't exactly hung out with these guys lately, but I'm pretty sure we could pick up where we left off, maybe even bump our relationship up a notch, get into some real commitment.

For more than four weeks, as I've settled into the sixty-day Bikram challenge, my teachers have been telling me that this yoga is all my body needs, that a class per day for two months will renew me "from the inside out." According to them, and to founder Bikram Choudhury, I'm getting all the weight resistance and cardio (yes, cardio) I need, plus the active meditation of hatha, a centuries-old style of yoga. The deeper I get into the challenge, the more limber, focused, cleansed, and relaxed I feel, but I've started worrying to the point of obsession that I'm not losing weight fast enough and that others agree.

I sense that they're looking me up and down in a certain way, judging. I started out eighty pounds overweight, and I'm losing one to two pounds per week—the healthiest and most maintainable kind of weight loss, doctors say—but nobody wants to hear this. All people seem to care about is what they see, not the process behind it. Reading doubt on their faces, I'm hurt, angry, ashamed. And now panicked.

A little weepily, I explain all this to calm, lovely Karen, who listens and nods, as if she understands perfectly the maniac sitting in front of her. As I babble on, I'm pawing through my absurdly enormous Timbuk2 messenger bag for a tissue and yanking out lipsticks and ponytail holders and free-floating receipts and a tattered *Runner's World* that I borrowed days ago from my brother-in-law and still haven't read. Later, when I listen to a tape of the conversation, I hear myself speaking in breathless bursts, barely letting Karen talk.

"Hold on," I say at one point, "I need to breathe."

"It's amazing you just recognized that," Karen says. "So you're already good at catching yourself in your breathing patterns. Now, every day, I want you to look at yourself in the mirror with kind eyes and with thankfulness and patience. Just allow yourself to do that."

Sentimentality usually triggers my gag reflex, but in this moment I make a decision not to go cynical. If I need to trade in my critical eyes for some kind ones, I may as well start today. While I'm at it, I'll stop what a psychologist would refer to as my "all-or-nothing thinking": If I'm still wearing gigantic jeans, Bikram must not work; if my most recent job was a disaster, I must be terrible at what I do; if my marriage didn't take, I'll never love or be loved again. "Your first prescription is, renew your mind every day," Karen says. "That sets the template. That will create harmony in your body."

Good. But what will create a *waistline* in my body? That's what I still want to know.

## You'd Better Not Scream for Ice Cream

This body can't be rebuilt by Bikram alone. Living well also involves eating well, and I'm not talking about bibbing up for lobster every night. I changed my diet on day one of the challenge and have stuck to it. I'm in this to refresh and destress, and half of that transformation involves eating like a sane person, not like a lumberjack with one hour left to live.

Yet there's so much information out there about how to eat right, it's hard to know which stuff to pay attention to and which will just fog your life with cabbage odor. I've never been a fad freak, but I have, at various points, tried Atkins, the Zone, Slim-Fast, Weight Watchers, and Herbalife. And I'm still not immune. My cousin Jill and I have spent the last few weeks melting "virgin coconut oil" and drizzling it on salads and oatmeal because we've heard it shrinks belly fat.

I'm also well versed in all the clever diet strategies: Make a week's worth of meals in advance, freeze them, and "when you get home just pop one in the microwave!" Or organize ingredients into carefully Sharpied Tupperware and Ziplocs so all you have to do is combine and bake, or combine and stir-fry. Etc. The problem is, when you lack the energy even to care what you put in your mouth, it's easiest just to call Domino's, no matter what's in the pantry.

Now that my energy level is changing and I'm more active, I do care. At this point, I want a credible source to make me a nutrition map, and I want that person to be Lori Givens, who owns Bikram Yoga Memphis with her fiancé, Gregg Williams.

Lori is a nutrition freak without the annoying behavior of a nutrition freak. She is long and lean and gorgeous and strong, but she doesn't walk around boring everyone to death with talk about bee pollen or vanadium or wild yam. I've asked her to show me what to buy and to tell me why. I already know that trans fats are poison and that I should stay away from all things white (white pasta, white bread, potatoes = pudge), but the knowledge that baby greens trump tortellini has done me zero good. I've spent most of my postdivorce adulthood filling my fridge with freshness, only to watch (and smell) it all go to waste. Broccoli morphs into sordid soup. Kale shrinks and pales to the point that I can't even remember what it used to be. Rancid meats, moldy fruits . . . in my culinary history, perishables just perish.

With Lori as my guide, I might make choices that stick. To that end, Jill and I hit Whole Foods with her one afternoon early on in the Bikram regimen. First, Lori schools us on the benefits of salsa and Wasa crackers, kale and salmon and spelt, but as we head toward Dairy she starts gunning for outlaws. Women pull their children out of the way; a tumbleweed rolls through; somewhere, a horse whinnies. When Lori reaches the case of beautifully wrapped Cheddar wedges and Boursin and Brie, she looks me hard in the eye.

"No more cheese," she says.

Which is not even funny. The words *cheese shop* thrill me the way *bubble bath* and *touchdown* thrill other people. I'm a goat girl all the way. Or was. So long, chèvre.

"Cheese has a happiness protein in it," Lori says, explaining that, like refined sugar, cheese comforts with an immediate (and ultimately false) chemical lift. For similar reasons, she also shoots down my other favorite thing: cereal. I have at times lived on raisin bran, Honey Nut Cheerios, and granola, but Lori says, "Never eat cereal after noon. You know what? Just don't eat cereal at all."

The salad bar seems like safe enough territory until Lori lays waste to the wasabi peas ("They're fried"), to too much egg, and to chickpeas—too many chickpeas will equal too much Paige. "If you gotta have beans, go for kidney over garbanzo," she says. "Less fat, more fiber."

Gloppy dressings: like, never. You'll want red wine or balsamic vinegar, Lori says, and very little or no oil. You'll want the baby greens or the romaine lettuce, not the iceberg, because the darker and leafier the vegetable, the healthier it is. Sunflower seeds—okay, a few. Croutons? Dream on. Cheese topping? Nice try; see above.

We eventually build a day's menu that uses all the food groups without blowing more than 1,500 calories. We have organic chicken, organic sliced turkey breast, and mahimahi, which Lori likes to bake on aluminum foil spritzed with olive oil–flavored cooking spray. We have Kashi GoLean hot cereal and Mr. Krispers, which are chips baked in sea salt and pepper—you can eat, like, five million of them for 120 calories. We've got Amy's organic frozen lasagna and frozen palak paneer and a cart full of kombucha—fermented tea @ $3.99 per.

We've also got a price tag of about $100. And I am not an heiress.

"How long will this last us?" I ask.

"The perishable stuff, about a week," Lori says. The Olave first-cold-pressed extra-virgin olive oil, the Bragg apple cider vinegar, the Nasoya fat-free faux mayonnaise, the mineral-rich Redmond sea salt ("Don't be afraid to use it!")—all that will last a bit longer. I have a feeling my cost-to-cart ratio is far different from a cost-to-cart ratio at Costco. Then again, a lot of these items aren't available at places like that. If they were, a lot more people would be healthy, right?

Not until they can make Wasa taste like dark chocolate, at which point the answer is: Maybe, but probably not even then.

## This Is Your Brain on Bikram

Anyway, I've got other worries. For five weeks, I've behaved like a yoga mouse in class—hugging the baseboards, sticking to the back wall—but one day, Gregg's in a mood. He yanks me out of my comfort zone, sticks me up in front of everybody, and says, "You're not gonna hide in the corner anymore."

I'd been thinking he might go easier on me as the weeks pass, but the opposite has happened. He seems to wake up in the morning with me on his mind—and not in the good way. The more progress I make, the harder he pushes. "Some teachers come from a place of sympathy. I don't," Gregg says when I ask why he's gotta hate on me constantly. "I come from a place of 'You need to work hard all the time, every time.'"

In the first month, as I learned the twenty-six postures and two breathing exercises, my goal was not to become some golden goddess of yoga; my goal was to stay in the room and learn to breathe.

This second month, I'm working on more than the poses. I'm working on committing, which is hard for an inveterate leaver. I've left cities and jobs and dear friends and good men. I've left my family over and over again. I've been in such a hurry to flee some situations and get on to the next, I've left clothes in the closet, food in the fridge. In Bikram class, I've already tried to leave once, but that didn't work. So knowing that I can't leave, I quietly protest my captivity by pretending.

The yogis call this the games stage. I'll do anything to buy myself a break. One day, I could do triangle posture if I wanted to, but I don't want to, so I breathe dramatically and pretend to be near collapse. (Result: I kind of really *do* feel near collapse.)

The teachers recognize the tricks because they've tried them all themselves. If I say I don't feel well, Gregg shakes his head and says, "Do yoga like a champion." If I admit (or claim) that I'm exhausted, he says, "No mercy." I've heard an urban myth about an instructor in California who was in the middle of teaching a class when a rat showed up in the back of the room. "Rat! Rat!" the students yelled, and the teacher said, "That's not a rat. That's the manifestation of your fears."

When Choudhury passed through town recently, he told me, "Your mind is supposed to be your best friend, but it's the number one enemy. Mind can make you Hitler or Mother Teresa." He has repeated this line all over the world, to students like John McEnroe and Madonna and to students like me. "It's never too late, you're never too bad, never too old, never too sick to start from scratch and begin again," he said. This is the thought that drives me back into that 105-degree room day after day.

One afternoon in the middle of ustrasana, or camel pose—a killer backbend that some consider the toughest posture in the whole practice—it occurs to me that if I can remain calm and focused while in such a physically stressful state, I can get through anything. The studio around me is full of people who know just what I mean. They practice not because a Bikram studio is a particularly lovely place to spend ninety minutes a day but because without it, they would be angry, inflexible, immobilized, fatigued, intolerant, petty, pained, and maybe even dead. The type-A personalities feel calmer. Every student has a story.

At the beginning of the challenge, a sixty-day goal felt daunting. Around day twenty, it felt impossible. Around day fifty, I started getting that giddy, generous feeling that comes when the bad date (or vacation or visit) is almost over and you can sense freedom. Only I don't want freedom.

On day sixty, as the final class ends, I would like to say the clouds part and the angels weep. When Gregg utters his final words and we as a class take our last measured breath, I expect a rush of emotion, but Bikram is not about the big display. It's about powerfully careful moves. What I feel in that last moment is calm, and satisfied, and certain that I now have a refuge, a resource—a blueprint.

## Hard Numbers, Part II

I'm so eager to see what the diagnostics will show, I hardly even notice the needle sucking blood out of my arm.

My last Bikram class ended just an hour ago and I'm already back at Lifesigns. Before I started the challenge, the clinic tested everything from my lung capacity to my body fat to my cholesterol, with some alarming results. My LDL, or "bad" cholesterol, was 149 when it should have been less than 100. My triglycerides suggested an abysmal diet. My body-fat test showed I was nearly half made up of fat, and my body mass index (BMI) was 34.6 when it should've been 25 or less. My blood glucose level was 99, one point away from prediabetes. On the treadmill stress test, I barely got to a workout intensity level of eight METS, when I should've been able to do ten.

For depression, I was taking (and had been taking for years) the highest possible combination dosage of Wellbutrin and Lexapro. I slept miserably if at all. I had headaches every day. I had plenty of reasons to be happy, but I couldn't see any of them.

The sixty-day challenge got me out of bed and out of my own head and showed me the futility of self-flagellation and regret. I've stopped taking the Wellbutrin and Lexapro, and, while the depression is still with me, it feels manageable. I've still been turning like a rotisserie chicken at night when I sleep, but I must not be grinding my teeth anymore because I no longer wake up with a headache. Now I'm ready to see what Bikram has done for my body. The results:

Weight: I've lost fourteen pounds.

Waist: five inches, gone.

LDL cholesterol: 108.

BMI: 32.3—down 7 percent.

Treadmill stress test: I get to 11.5 METS this time.

Fasting blood glucose: It's dropped to 73.

"Everything changed," says Felix Caldwell, MD, "and in the right direction."

All except for one thing.

For the second round of blood tests, I ask Caldwell to check my hormones. A few years ago, another doctor checked them. I'd recently had surgery to remove fibroid tumors, and I wanted to make sure I could still have children. I hadn't been feeling well for a while, though, and my symptoms—hot flashes, mood swings—sounded like the dreaded menopause. And sure enough, the blood work even back then suggested I was headed in that direction more quickly than usual; the fertility specialist told me she could probably still help me, but I'd have to hurry.

Instead of hurrying to have children, I hurried off to work. And now my Lifesigns numbers show not perimenopause, but full-blown menopause. At age forty-two.

Menopause means that my body is making much less estrogen and progesterone, hormones that are critical to bone density and reproductive health, among other things. Onset depends on life circumstances and genes; women generally can expect meno-pause to occur at the age their mothers went through it, which in my case would have been around age fifty-two. Until now, I'd thought I had at least a decade before onset; and because friends of mine had given birth in their early forties, I thought I had a few seconds left on the kid clock.

"So definitely no children," I say to Dr. Mehmet Oz when I get him on the phone. Oz is director of the Cardiovascular Institute at Columbia University and a regular *O* magazine contributor. He's looking at my diagnostics as we talk, just as he did with the pre-Bikram set.

"You're not having kids," he says. "But maybe that's a good thing."

"Maybe for them," I say.

We laugh. It isn't funny.

"Well, at least this explains a lot," I say. The miserably sleep-less nights. The exhaustion. The face flushes so severe I'm powder-dry one minute and glistening the next. The suddenly thick waist after a lifetime with a flat stomach. The irritability. The fa-tigue. The overbearing stress. "Progesterone is like Valium," Oz explains, "so when you lower your progesterone levels—this hormone that keeps you calm and collected, that helps you deal with the slights that occur to women in our society—you're a lot more stressed out."

"Did I do something wrong?" I ask. "Did I do something to cause this?"

"We're not sure how weight affects menopause," he says. "It certainly throws off your hormones. Stress could affect meno-pause. Physical activity slows down menopause; if you're inac-tive, you'll get menopause earlier. I think stress and inactivity are the big things driving this."

It's stunningly painful to hear once again that I may have been the chief architect of my own decline and that even as I claw my way out of my self-made mess there'll be something new to worry about: an earlier risk of cardiovascular disease, thinning bones, a premature invitation to AARP.

I ask: What now? Oz recommends bioidentical hormone therapy and refers me to his friend Erika Schwartz, MD, a New York specialist in the treatment.

"The life that you happen to be in has thrown you a lot of curveballs," Schwartz tells me by phone a few days later. "Because you didn't have the tools you needed to fend off these curveballs, you absorbed them. We need to replenish your hormones and then see what your body does with the information. The body has a beautiful way of healing itself."

She prescribes an FDA-approved cream called EstroGel (bioidentical estrogen); her own Pro-Cream, a low-dose, nonprescription bioidentical progesterone topical; and a low-dose thyroid medication. (My thyroid level, as it turned out, fell on the low end of the normal range.) She suggests that I add supplements, including vitamin D, which I've actually been taking since the pre-Bikram round of diagnostics.

"By the way, none of this is because you are menopausal—I hate that term," Schwartz says. "You feel this way because you're hormonally out of balance. That's it. When people say 'menopause' it's like, 'Whoa, I'm old; it's over.' But you're not. You're not. You're not."

Which is what I most want, and need, to hear. This attitude feels absolutely necessary to my ability to move forward. Now I'm armed with a trio of defenses: hormone replacements, a new way of thinking about what's happening to my body, and, of course, Bikram. At first, this yoga felt exploratory, optional, but now that I know what's really going on, it feels essential to managing my day-to-day happiness and improving my overall well-being.

I've found a great yoga studio in my new city. I recognize none of the other students, of course, but everything about the postures is now familiar—as familiar, in fact, as Kettlebell and all my other old gym friends, which I ultimately never touched throughout the two months of Bikram.

I do not, and will never, love every class. Some days I'd rather stroll through Times Square in a string bikini than spend another ninety minutes in that steam box. Yet the best of Bikram redeems those days. The best of Bikram is like being in love. It's like taking in that first breath of springtime air, seeing green tips on the stems of dogwoods.

One Saturday in Memphis, I walked out of class and into a golden morning. Everything I saw seemed urgent and worthy and beautiful. I passed two old men hauling four small horses. I saw a field of yellow wildflowers. I swear to you, at a traffic light I pulled up behind a LOVE WINS bumper sticker. At the grocery, as I wheeled my empty cart back to the corral, an old man said, "Baby, let me push that over there for you. It'll be my good turn for the day." When I got in the car, Lloyd Cole was singing—again, not even kidding—that song about Eva Marie Saint in *On the Waterfront: "All you need is love is all you need."* The whole sixty-day experience was worth one euphoric morning. Because I'd forgotten I could even feel that way.

## New York

New York *is widely considered to be one of the best magazines being published today. This year the magazine was nominated for nine National Magazine Awards and received two, for Magazine Section (for "Strategist") and General Excellence. Jonathan Van Meter's work for* New York *helps to explain the magazine's success. Van Meter's profile of Joan Rivers is in fact the second time the magazine has been nominated for one of his pieces. Last year his story "A Nonfiction Marriage"— about Gay and Nan Talese, one a celebrated writer, the other a highly regarded book editor—was also nominated for the National Magazine Award for Profile Writing. The National Magazine Award judges described Van Meter's story about Rivers as an "unusually intimate profile . . . a meet-up of candid writing and colorful subject." The subhead of "Joan Rivers Always Knew She Was Funny" was "It's the Rest of the World That Sometimes Forgot." You won't after you read this story.*

Jonathan Van Meter

# Joan Rivers Always Knew She Was Funny

E xpect nothing and you won't be disappointed. This is the mantra of the pessimist and the persecuted alike, the preemptive strike of those who tend to paint the picture a little blacker than it is. And then there is Joan Rivers, the orneriest creature ever to darken Hollywood's door. She once told me that her husband, Edgar Rosenberg, who killed himself in 1987, lived by the heartwarming motto "Fuck them over before they fuck you over first."

I have known Rivers for twenty-two years, long enough to know that she does not exactly share this view of the world, even if she likes to muck around in it from time to time. In fact, she considers it a flaw in her late husband's character, one that set in motion the chain reaction that almost destroyed her career: In the mideighties, Rivers was one of the most successful comedians in the world. She was the highest-paid entertainer on the Vegas Strip and Johnny Carson's permanent guest host on the *Tonight Show*, until she was lured away to Fox to host her own late-night talk show. Edgar, she says, was a toxic presence on the set of her show, fighting bitterly with Barry Diller and Rupert Murdoch over everything from office furniture to money. Joan and Edgar were fired after only seven months, and the fallout was devastating. She was excommunicated by Carson, her mentor, for leaving; she was effectively banned from late night, hardly ever invited to appear on Letterman, Leno, Conan. Her marriage fell apart and then Edgar swallowed a bottle of pills. Her daughter, Melissa, stopped speaking to her. Rivers fell into a deep depression, became bulimic, and considered suicide herself.

When I first met Rivers it was 1988, just a year after Edgar had killed himself. She was moving back to New York after fourteen years in Los Angeles and taking over Linda Lavin's role in *Broadway Bound*, a gig that she says pulled her life out of its nosedive. It wouldn't be the last time she found redemption through her work.

On a recent morning in early May, we are sitting in her study eating cake. It has been served to us by Kevin and Debbie, her butler and housekeeper, who have been living with her for twenty years in their own quarters in her grand apartment, a mini-Versailles on East Sixty-second Street. ("Marie Antoinette would have lived here," Rivers likes to say, "if she had money.") Joan loves cake, loves anything sweet. The Joan Rivers diet: You can eat anything you want before three P.M. and then nothing for the rest of the day. When she goes out to dinner, she puts a small pile of Altoids on the table next to her plate, which she eats one after another while barely touching her food.

We are talking about the peculiar turn of events her life has taken recently, how she is suddenly squarely at the center of the culture again—something that has escaped her since her Fox debacle. At the age of seventy-six, it seems, she has been rediscovered. Much of it has to do with a new documentary about her life, *Joan Rivers: A Piece of Work*, which opens in theaters on June 11. Roger Ebert wrote, in one of the film's many rave reviews, that it is "one of the most truthful documentaries about show business I've seen. Also maybe the funniest." The film comes at the end of a remarkable year for Rivers, one that began when she won *The Celebrity Apprentice* (after one of the uglier reality-TV showdowns), outfoxing all those bimbos, has-beens, and two-bit poker players to emerge—somehow—as the sympathetic character. At long last, not fired! It's unfamiliar territory for Rivers: to be the one people root for.

"It's amazing," says Rivers, shaking her head in disbelief. But then this: "People who have seen the film come up to me and say, 'I never liked you until now.' TV interviewers say, right in front of me, 'Even if you have always hated Joan Rivers . . . you are going to love her and be mesmerized by this film.' They spit right in my face and then spend the next ten minutes wiping it dry." That is when she shows me the pillow she has embroidered that sits on a leather couch in her study: DON'T EXPECT PRAISE WITHOUT ENVY UNTIL YOU ARE DEAD.

If Joan Rivers has a hard time taking a compliment, she has an even tougher time handing one out. "I will only praise someone who can't take anything away from me," she says with a mordant laugh. "People ask me all the time: 'What do you think about Sarah Silverman?'" She switches into a comically polite-insincere voice. "Hmmm. She's nice, I guess. I really haven't seen her."

She shoots me a get-real look. "She's terrific. She's very funny and very pretty. But why should I admit it?"

Even at this late stage in her forty-year career, Rivers is nowhere near ready to cede the stage to a younger generation. (As her former manager Billy Sammeth says in the film, "Right now they see her as a plastic-surgery freak who's past her sell-by date. . . . But God help the next queen of comedy, because this one's not abdicating. Never will.") I am reminded of an e-mail she sent me a couple of years ago, when she was at yet another low point in her career. I asked her what she thought of Kathy Griffin. "I am her friend but also furious," she wrote. "She is the big one now. My club dates have simply vanished and gone to her. She will last as she is very driven. Like me, she *wants* it. But every time a gay man tells me, 'Oh, she is just like you! I love her!' I fucking want to strangle them. But, please God let *someone* give me credit. I feel so totally forgotten. The fucking *New Yorker* did this big piece on the genius of Rickles, who is brilliant but who hasn't changed a line in fifteen years. Meanwhile, I am totally 'old hat' and ignored while in reality I could still wipe the floor with both Kathy and Sarah. Anyhow, fuck them all. Age sucks. It's the final mountain."

•     •     •

In late January, Rivers made her first trip to the Sundance Film Festival in Park City, Utah, to attend the premiere of *A Piece of Work*. Directed by Ricki Stern with Annie Sundberg, whose previous two documentaries were about wrongful convictions and Darfur (go figure), the film is essentially a year in the life of Rivers, who comes across as, if not the hardest-working person in show business, then certainly its most unrelenting practitioner. Ricki Stern is the daughter of her friends Marjorie and Michael Stern, a couple Rivers met five years ago "at a stuffy dinner party" in Connecticut, where she has a country home. "Marjorie was the only person who laughed out loud when someone said Demi Moore was talented," jokes Rivers.

At Sundance, Rivers wears a slight variation of the same all-black outfit every day. Today: Donna Karan sweater, Chanel slacks, Manolo boots, full-length sable fur, huge sunglasses. Among the green and crunchy in their polar fleece and turquoise jewelry, she stands out like a whore in church. She knows she is anathema to this crowd, with her ostentatious plastic surgery, conservative streak, and glitzy lifestyle. Though she calls herself an independent and voted for Obama, she is constitutionally Republican. Friends with Nancy Reagan. Thinks we should just bomb the shit out of Iran. Ambivalent about feminism. Detests whining and victimhood and laziness. Hated *Precious*. "I got very annoyed," she says. "I thought, Oh, get a job! Stand up and get a job!"

To Rivers, Sundance is a tribal gathering of the too earnest and the no fun—*artistes* in hypocritically expensive jeans. At one point, she sits down for an interview with the film critic Peter

Travers and he asks her about her first trip to the festival. "Everyone here is an *act*-or," she says. " 'Hi, I'm Deborah, and I am an *act*-or.' Oh, fuck you. You are an actress." Who's funny to you? he asks. "At Sundance? I find no one funny." She cracks up. Are you going to be serious while you're here? he asks. "When I meet Bob Redford I will be serious," she says. "If I recognize him after the face-lift."

She travels around town in a black Escalade bursting with entourage: two assistants, Jocelyn and Graham, hair-and-makeup man Martyn and his boyfriend Digby, as well as Marjorie and Michael Stern. It is a rolling cackle-fest, Rivers slaying the group with metronomic consistency. She is a spoken-word Twitter feed, constantly streaming one-liners: sometimes shocking, sometimes vile, sometimes cruel, always hilarious. Not surprisingly, she is recognized everywhere she goes. As we are heading into a restaurant on Main Street for lunch one day, she is swarmed by a group of very young people with pierced lips and pink hair. Rivers, as a young film-industry guy tells me one night at a party, is considered cool to people too young to know her as anything but the outrageous red-carpet lady. As we head into the restaurant, the strangest-looking chick in the group yells, "I love you, Joan!"

A few weeks before Sundance, I called Rivers to ask about the documentary and I got hit with her don't-expect-anything-and-you-won't-be-disappointed voodoo. Asked about Ricki and Annie, she cracked, "They don't wear makeup." Do you like the movie? Long pause. "They forgot to show that I actually enjoy my life."

But now, in Utah, it is finally sinking in that the movie is good. The premiere is at a synagogue, funnily enough, and after a long wait in a makeshift greenroom there is a silly press conference and photo op, where Rivers, off the top of her head, makes the joke, since repeated, that she should have made a documentary about her life selling jewelry on QVC called *Semi-Precious*.

Rivers seems nervous on her way in to the theater. It is the first time she is seeing the film on a big screen in front of an audience.

As we wait for it to start, she tells me a story about Prince Charles, with whom she has been friends for several years. ("Not inner circle," she says. "Outer-inner circle.") HRH sends her a Christmas gift every year, which, more than once, has been two very fancy teacups. "One year," she says, "I took a picture under my Christmas tree with the teacups and wrote, 'How could you send me two teacups when I'm *alone*?' Another time I wrote, 'I'm enjoying tea with my best friend!' and I sent a picture of me in a cemetery. And he never acknowledges it! He never says to me when I see him"—doing his accent perfectly—"'Ohhhh, funny funny funny!' So this year I thought, I'm just going to write him a nice thank-you note. And the other day our mutual friend calls and says, 'Just spoke to Charles! He said, "I can't *wait* to see Joan's note this year!"'"

As the theater fills up, a steady stream of fans and well-wishers stop to chat. A woman in the aisle in front of us turns around and asks, "Doesn't that bother you?" Rivers says, "Are you kidding? Forty years! Thank God they're still doing it. I have many friends in the business they don't bother with anymore, who are asked to step aside on the red carpet, and that's more embarrassing."

·     ·     ·

Rivers has always got her nose in a book. She devours them, several at a time. On this trip, there is *Game Change*. "Hillary comes off as furious and rightfully so. And you hate Obama in the end. He's weak. Michelle is the tough one. Palin is a moron. McCain is an egocentric fool." The other she is reading is George Carlin's *Last Words*. "It reminds me why I hated him," she says. "The arrogance, the self-congratulatory tone, the superior attitude, and then the selling out for any shitty award."

It is a cliché but it is true. Most comedians are dreary bores: neurotic, self-obsessed, competitive, and no fun when they are not onstage. Not Joanie! She is funny in the way that your funniest friend is: aware of everything, well-read, opinionated. She also asks good questions. "Who do you hate?" is one of her conversation starters, and it always works because there is always someone to hate. At the moment, she hates Oprah, who she thinks is phony. "How can I help out Kitty Kelley," she says. "Should I throw her a book party?"

Her single greatest gift is her ability, in the heat of the moment, to find the funny line. My recent favorite example also highlights the rarefied world in which Rivers sometimes travels. Not long ago she was invited to dinner at Lily Safra's home at 820 Fifth Avenue. Safra owns the most expensive residence in the world, the $500 million Villa Leopolda in the south of France. Rivers was seated next to Carroll Petrie, a rich society lady who is deaf as a post, and the two of them were marveling over, oh, I don't know, the dozens of Fabergé clocks in Safra's house. Petrie said, too loud, "Doesn't it just make you feel *poor*?" To which Rivers replied, "Carroll, name me one other person in this room who is playing Cleveland this weekend."

One of the most consistently subversive things about Rivers is her level of commitment to a spur-of-the-moment prank. I have seen her pull off dozens of them over the years. Once, coming out of Pat Wexler's office, where she goes for her Botox and filler, she crawled on her hands and knees into a waiting room full of socialites and models and, screwing up her face to resemble a stroke victim, moaned out of one side of her mouth, "Look what she did to me!" Another time, she played a practical joke on Marjorie Stern and some unsuspecting diners at Sarabeth's: "It's like three weeks into the Bernie Madoff thing," says Rivers. "I get there first, and there are two tables to pass before you get to our table. And one was like six Jewish ladies and the other was two Jewish couples. You could just tell. Very New York people. I grabbed the waitress and I say, 'Please don't say her name, because Mrs. Madoff doesn't want people to know it's her.' I said it loud enough for the other tables to overhear it." Marjorie, who has a Ruth Madoff aspect, takes the story from here. "I walk in and they are all staring at me. And I look over at Joan to see what the problem is and she says, 'Ruthie! Sit here!' At which point the entire place is stunned speechless. Forks suspended in midair."

"They *hissed* at her," says Rivers, crippled with laughter. When I remind her that there are six Jewish ladies who now think she is friends with Ruth Madoff, she yells, "I know!" and laughs even harder.

Rivers will take the piss out of anything. Shortly after I had lost a big job, she called, and when I answered the phone a bit too quickly she said, "Really? The first ring? So *desperate.*" And then she hung up on me. A few days after 9/11, she called and asked me if I wanted to meet her for lunch at Windows on the Ground. She pushes as far as she can as soon as she can. It's compulsive.

In the film there is a scene where Rivers is playing some lousy casino in Wisconsin, and she does a bit about Helen Keller and a man stands and bellows, "It's not very funny if you have a deaf son!" Rivers lets him have it. "Oh, you stupid ass, let me tell you what comedy is about . . ."

"You go ahead and tell me what," he says.

"Oh, please," she says. "You are so stupid. Comedy is to make everybody laugh at everything, and deal with things, you idiot."

At Sundance, an interviewer asks her about the moment. "If you laugh at it, you can deal with it, and if you don't, you can't deal with it. And don't start telling me that I shouldn't be saying it. That's the way I do it. I would have been laughing at Auschwitz."

One of the great misconceptions about Rivers is that she is mean-spirited and heartless—that there is nothing more to her than her comedy or her red-carpet patter. To the celebrities who are on the receiving end of some of her sharpest material she can seem cruel, but as a civilian she is surprisingly sensitive, someone who cries as easily as she laughs. At Sundance alone, she is brought to tears a half-dozen times. A journalist interviewing her on camera asks if she could sing a few bars of the song that's been in her head lately. She demurs for a moment, saying she can't sing, and then chokes out, in that raspy voice of hers, a few lines from "Send in the Clowns" ("Isn't it rich / Isn't it queer . . ."). When she starts to cry, the guy asks her why. "Because that's life. And I'm very tired. Life is very tough. If you don't laugh, it's tough. And 'Send in the Clowns' is a song that says you need that because it's all . . ." She chokes up again and then says, "Horrible."

One day at Sundance while we are waiting for a screening to end, Rivers is approached by an older gentleman. "Excuse me," he says. "I just have to interrupt." Rivers looks up at him and cautiously smiles. "I want to thank you for bringing me joy in 1960 in Korea." Her body language changes in an instant. "I was a gay soldier in peacetime Korea who was starved for Broadway," he continues, "and you were performing with the USO troop." He pauses to watch the memory dawn on Rivers's face.

"Sheila . . ."

"Sheila Smith! Yes!" says Rivers, stunned.

"Jack . . ."

"Jack Edelman! Yes! Yes! Yes!"

"Patience Cleveland," he says.

Rivers screams, "Patience Cleveland!"

"Richard Nealon."

"And Jeanne . . . Jeanne Beauvais," says Rivers. "The opera singer. . . . How do you remember the names?"

"I was way up above the Thirty-eighth Parallel in Camp Kaiser, Korea, and will never ever forget all of you."

"That was my first traveling job that paid," says Rivers.

"She was an ingenue. A young singer-comedienne. *Light* comedy," says the man to Rivers's entourage, who are hanging on his every word.

When the man leaves, Joan says, "We were on the DMZ line between North and South Korea. It was very scary but it was fabulous. Patience Cleveland was pregnant and was trying to have an abortion. We took hot sea baths in Japan. We got these two crazy marines to ride us over bumpy terrain in Korea. Nothing worked. And she went back to New York, went to a Chinese restaurant on West Forty-sixth Street and went down into the basement and got an abortion."

Michael Stern says, "A Chinese restaurant? Did they do it with MSG?"

Rivers pauses for a nanosecond—wait for it—and finds the line. "Bite down on this egg roll."

What strikes me as this scene unfolds is just how long Rivers has been this radically modern presence. One of the best things about the documentary is that it reminds you, with great archival footage of Rivers's early TV performances, that she is the mother of a certain brand of transgressive female comedy. Would there be a Sandra Bernhard or a Roseanne or a Rosie O'Donnell or a Kathy Griffin or a Sarah Silverman, without Joan Rivers? "When I am onstage, I am every woman's outrage about where they put us," she says to me one day. "We have no control. And that's why I am screaming onstage. We have no control! I am furious about everything. All that anger and madness comes out onstage."

•     •     •

Rivers adored her mother. "She died in my mid-to-late forties," she says. "She was so smart and funny. My friend Alice told me at her funeral that my mother once said to her, so proudly, 'Joan isn't just a star. She's a superstar! And she did it all herself!' It still makes me cry. Both of my parents got to see me host Carson, thank God. That's all anyone wants: to have their parents see they're going to be all right in life."

Her relationship with her own daughter, however, has not gone as smoothly. Some of the more visceral scenes in the documentary are between Joan and Melissa. There is something in their body language, in the way they talk over each other, that gives you a glimpse into the dynamic: classic yenta behavior on Joan's part; stuck in a sullen teenage gear on Melissa's part.

Someone who knows both women well said to me recently, "The greatest thing about Joan is her bravado, her ability to just laugh at everything and push through. But her greatest weakness is that moment when she can't push through and she really takes something in. She can become unreasonable and vindictive. And it usually has to do with Melissa, when she feels that Melissa has been wronged. When Melissa has an enemy it has to be Joan's enemy. But Joan carries it to the level of a crusade."

I ask Melissa if she thinks her mother is still reacting out of guilt over that terrible time in their lives. "I think she does have a lot of unresolved guilt." But, she says, "as an adult I have such a clearer perspective and acceptance of who my mother is and why she does what she does." She also concedes that she has plenty of baggage of her own. "I carry the burden of my father, in his note, saying to me, 'You have to take care of your mother.' I take that very, very seriously. I feel like she is my responsibility." She pauses for a moment. "And yet! I feel like we have a really good relationship. And it's very normal in abnormal circumstances."

Melissa was worried at first about the documentary. "Melissa is a very private person," Joan says. "And she doesn't understand show business. I will do *anything* on camera. You want me to do what?!?! . . . Hmmm. How much? . . . Okay!" When Ricki Stern showed Rivers a rough cut, she sent back three pages of notes. Most of her complaints were about what was *not* in the film: Where's the red carpet? Nothing on QVC? You don't show my triumph in Edinburgh! "And then there were certain things that you really shouldn't put in, that Melissa objected to," she says. "I talked about Edgar one night and it was very late and I was saying what I say very often, which is that I walk past his picture and give him the finger. Fuck you, what you did to us! Which is part of suicide. But it shouldn't maybe be there. Melissa didn't want to see that."

But Melissa seems to be coming around: "The first time I saw the film it was very difficult to watch. She is showing parts of herself that I see and I understand and I was worried that other people wouldn't understand. But from the response the film is getting, I think I was wrong. Because people *do* understand."

This summer, the family begins filming a reality show for WE called *Mother Knows Best*. Rivers has rented out her house in Connecticut for the season and is moving in with Melissa and her nine-year-old son, Cooper, whom Joan is crazy about. "He is funny," she says, handing out her highest praise. "And he gets that I'm funny. He recently told me that he knew that I was famous. And I said to him, 'You know why Grandma is famous? Because I make people happy.'"

Rivers says she is nervous about the show. "I don't know if it's going to wreck our lives. I think it's going to be very hard on us because I don't want it to be one of these stupid reality shows. We want it real, with real mother-daughter conflict and real problems." Like what? "I want her to get married to the boyfriend and they don't want to get married. I'm sorry, I am not comfortable with somebody coming down the stairs in his jockey shorts who is not married to her."

Melissa responds: "She's, like, completely supportive of gay rights and everyone should be able to do whatever they want, live and let live, and whatever makes you happy. She has no problem with, like a rhino and a ferret living together, and yet she can't believe that I don't want to get married again!"

There will be plenty of grist for argument. "Everything she does in the house gets me crazy," says Rivers of her daughter. "The way she lives—very California. Have a sandwich over the sink? Excuse me?"

The way that Rivers lives is very old-fashioned and extremely formal, with her live-in butler and stiff dinner parties with finger bowls. "It comes from the way my mother was raised," she says.

"She came from very rich Russians who had servants. When they came here they were dead broke, but my mother remembered that from childhood. She always lived very formally, or tried to." I tell her that people are surprised when they see the film by how grandly she lives—this foulmouthed comic in her gilded palace. "This business is such a mess. Nothing is set in stone. As I say in the movie, 'You are standing on mud.' So the formality, the rigidness of sitting down to a beautiful table, it's a ritual. My bed is turned down every night. But that's because I've just come from hearing someone say, 'If you've always hated Joan Rivers . . . !' I want things to look pretty. I should have been Martha Stewart. Martha Stewartvitz."

Earlier this year, apropos of nothing, Rivers sent me an e-mail while she was out in L.A. visiting her daughter. "Just bought Melissa three hundred dollars' worth of new place mats. God she must hate me."

"That is a perfect example of what our relationship is like," says Melissa. "So, my place mats are a little worn out! We all get busy. But my mother had the car stop on the way from the airport to my house. And showed up with all sorts of new place mats and napkins. Without asking me. That's stepping over the line a little. I can't take care of myself?" She laughs. "But luckily I needed the place mats."

All this talk of proper homemaking reminds me of something Rivers said to me years ago. She was talking about the scene in one of her favorite movies, *Rebecca*, when Laurence Olivier and Joan Fontaine realize that their relationship is not what they thought it was. "Bad things can happen," said Rivers, "even in a pretty house." When I mention this to her now she says, "Sure did on Ambazac Way"—where they lived in L.A. "We were in *Architectural Digest*." Pause. "Edgar still jumped."

·     ·     ·

Joan Rivers will turn seventy-seven on June 8. "Age is so frustrating," she says to me in her study in New York. "I make deals with God all the time. 'Give me ten more good years and I'll call it a day.' Age is the one thing that is absolutely coming at you. And right now, thank God, everything is working. I have my checkups and the doctors always say, 'I can't get over it!' But I am pedaling as fast as I can. My manager was just here today. He said, 'There's very little left, timewise.' But I can do it! I can do a radio show from anywhere! I just have to keep the pot churning. You cannot stop."

People always ask Rivers why she doesn't just retire, enjoy her old age. "But they don't get that I love it," she says. "All I ever wanted was this. I'm lucky, you idiots." Here, she imitates her society-lady friends. " 'We're going to the Kentucky Derby and then taking cooking lessons in Venice and then we are going on so-and-so's boat and then perhaps *five fun days* with a group to the Galápagos!' And you go, *Why?* I've done all that crap. That's not retirement to me. That's death."

When I ask her how she fell in with that crowd, she says, "Sort of by mistake. I got friendly with C. Z. Guest and through her I met Jerry Zipkin and I had no idea that if Jerry and C. Z. said, 'This Jew is okay,' you were okay. You got in. Immediately. And it's all very glamorous at the beginning. Going to the Metropolitan Opera, taking a table here, being on a committee there. Going out all the time all dressed up."

She levels me with a look. "And then I got bored to *death.* Nobody tells you the truth. I once asked one of the ladies, 'Did you ever have an affair?' And she stared at me like I was crazy. 'Why would I tell you?' she said. Another time, someone had just bought an apartment and I said, 'How much?' And she said, 'That is really none of your business.' And I thought, Fine. Then we are not friends and I don't want to spend any more time with you. I was friendly with one couple who I no longer see at all. They would always say, 'We're such good friends.' And then I found out that their daughter had a complete nervous breakdown. For a year, I was always told everything is wonderful. Well, then what are we wasting our time here at Elaine's or Mortimer's or Swifty's? I don't want to sit in Swifty's and not say anything about anything. I just totally stepped away. Blaine Trump is one of the few people I am friends with out of that period. She's honest. She will sit there and say, 'Life is crap.' All I want you to do, if we are sitting down and it's after six P.M., is tell me the truth. Because we've all lied to each other all day long in business and we've all had these lunches and we've all ass-kissed to the point where I carry Chapstick. If I am going to sit down and eat with you, just tell me the truth and let me say to you, 'Things are lousy and I'm sad.'"

One of the saddest times in Rivers's life since I have known her was when her best friend Tommy Corcoran died a few years ago. Rivers spoke to him three times a day, and he walked Melissa down the aisle at her wedding. When I ask her about the challenges of getting old she says, "The loss of friends. It's the thinning out of people with whom you have a history, whom you adore. I feel amazing. I truly feel like I am twenty-five. I walk everywhere. There's nothing wrong with me. The mind is going better than ever. But I look at my living room at night and I see Tommy and the good times and that just really upsets me. There's no one to call up. Nobody cares that you got home. That's horrible. To go into your apartment and nobody cares that you came off the plane very late. And suddenly you develop tremendous attachments to your dogs. And then you know that it's sick. They are animals and they love me, but it isn't right to say, 'My dogs! I've got to rush home to the dogs!' They'll be just fine without me." There is a long silence as she looks up to keep the tears from ruining her makeup. "And the other thing with age is that you have no tolerance. You just think, *Ugh, don't. I've played this game.* You just want to say to people, 'I've been through it.'"

·    ·    ·

After the first day at Sundance, Rivers insists that I move out of my fleabag hotel and into a giant suite that is connected to her giant suite at the Stein Eriksen Lodge. "It's already paid for," she says, "and I will only use it to put on hair and makeup." And so we become roommates for a couple of days.

When we get home at night, and she closes the door between our suites, I can tell she is staying up late. "My day starts when I get home and it's finally over," she says. "I take my bath and do my crossword. I call it puttering. I may read a book. I go through the *Wall Street Journal*, I watch television. I want two and a half hours with no one talking. I went to bed at four A.M. last night. I do that every night."

In the morning, Rivers comes in wearing her nightgown and no makeup, and she and Martyn begin the lengthy beautification routine. At one point in the film, as Rivers is sitting in a chair getting made up for some event, she says to the camera, "It's very scary when you see yourself totally without any makeup . . . Oh, it gives me the willies. Who is that person? So, I get up in the morning and the first thing I do is I get into makeup. I was never the natural beauty. No man has ever, ever told me I'm beautiful." The insecurity is touching, and perhaps a clue as to why she has availed herself of so much plastic surgery over the years.

Rivers has had three big relationships since Edgar. "Spiros was my first one, my Greek shipping tycoon. That lasted four years." Then there was Bernard, the cheap one. "He wouldn't get a car and driver. A man who had $150 million. I was standing there in the pouring rain at Lincoln Center and he said to me, 'You are so spoiled.' I remember saying to him, 'If you were an *actor*, Bernard, and had no money, we would be on the subway and I wouldn't be saying a word. But you have $150 million, Bernard. And I'm wearing $700 shoes, and this is silly. What are we proving here?' Bernard carried the ketchup back and forth to the Hamptons. Does that tell you everything?"

And then there was Orin Lehman, of the Lehman Brothers family, who served as New York State's parks commissioner. He was a World War II hero who was injured in the Battle of the Bulge and had the use of only one leg and walked with metal braces. Rivers was with him for nine years, until she caught him cheating, in 2001, and threw him out. "I was mad about Orin," she says. "Love of my life. Adored him. People would say, 'Orin Lehman? Blech.' Melissa never got what I liked about him. But he was amazing. A gentleman. He was elegant. He got everything. He was so brave. I loved the bravery. That this man *walked*. He willed himself to walk. I know it sounds strange, but he was very sexy."

I ask her if she still hopes to meet someone. "Yes, but it's very hard at this age. The pickings are so slim. I'd love to have somebody. And my terms are: Pay every bill I have and you've got to understand that I love my life and I love the theater. Talk about set in your ways. I love what I do, I love how I do it. I have my country house, I have my family, and I have my career. Where are you going to fit in? Call me a week from Tuesday."

There is one man in particular she's interested in. "He's coming in February. He's taking me to the dog show." She laughs.

"Very, very rich," says Marjorie.

"He's from Oklahoma City," says Rivers. "So it's over already."

And then she takes it a step further, paints the picture a little darker. "He's a man in his seventies and he's going to meet a very beautiful young woman in her fifties who will move in so fast, and he will feel so good, and she will show him a picture of her twat and it's finished."

Later that day, after a packed screening at the festival ("Listen to them *laugh*," Rivers had said backstage, her eyes lit with joy), Rivers comes into my room and her mood has changed. "This is why everything sucks," she says. "At the end of the day, no such thing as, 'Ain't it going great?' We came here, we're the toast of Sundance, Melissa calls me up beyond happy" about the good reviews for her new book about lessons learned on the red carpet. "The next call is from this man, who I have had dinner with three or four times and really clicked with. He asked me to save the week of February 14 because he's coming in. Now he says, 'Coming with a lady I've met that I know you will love as much as I do. Can't wait to spend the week with you!' My God. How about that? Nothing is ever a hundred percent. There's no such thing as 'everything is going great.'"

·   ·   ·

On the last night in Utah, Rivers and her entourage are going to dinner at an Italian restaurant to celebrate her assistant Jocelyn's birthday. The snow is really coming down, so Jocelyn decides we ought to take the shuttle bus into town. Too dangerous to drive. "The diva is going out in style," she says to her boss. "You can overrule us, but we all feel it's the safest way." We arrive at the restaurant and Rivers immediately begins to kvetch and worry about where we are going to be seated. But as soon as we settle at the table—a big round corner table with a beautiful view of the snow falling on the side of the mountain—her mood lifts. She ignores her mints and actually eats her dinner. She also knocks back a couple of glasses of red wine and before long is on a serious roll, telling funny stories and teasing the waitress ("You are never going to meet a man with that butch haircut").

As we await the arrival of the birthday cake, Rivers launches into a story about a night in the early nineties when she performed at a big star-studded televised Comedy Central event at Radio City Music Hall. What I remember most about that night is how great she looked, how nervous she was in the limo as she ran her lines, and how she roared through her set and the audience went nuts. I have never once heard her brag about a performance. But now, at dinner, she is telling the group, "I walked in there and *killed*." The disappointing part was what happened next.

"They wanted to do, like, an original-cast moment. They wanted to put me up there with the Greats and the Has-Beens, you know what I'm telling you? I thought, *What don't you understand here? Don't you put me out there with Phyllis Diller and Milton Berle. I was so angry that I wouldn't stay for the finale. Into the limo!"* She pauses. "But that night was a big night in my life." And then she says, more quietly, "I was at such a low point then. And they were all coming over to me, all these comediennes, and each one has their own little show and I don't. And they were all"—mockingly—"'Thank you, Joan. I wouldn't be where I am but for *yoooou.'*" She takes a big gulp of her wine. "You want to say to them, 'I will show you how it's done, pussycat. Follow *that.*'"

## Slate

SUBMITTED IN PROFILE
WRITING

*If there's one thing reporters and editors worry about, it's access—especially access to celebrities. Without access, you're nothing. With access, you're still sometimes nothing because you can't always use what you've got or you won't get access again. Luckily, everybody lives in public these days—a fact Jonah Weiner uses to advantage in this clever profile of the famously volatile Kanye West (or as the headline writers at* Slate *put it, "an all-access, totally non-exclusive interview with the would-be king of hip-hop"). Relying solely on blog posts and Twitter feeds, Weiner takes readers inside West's apartment, his jet, even his hungover head. All without having to put up with West himself, much less his publicists. Plus, Weiner got to demonstrate his mastery of the digital tools (take our word for it) that so enliven contemporary journalism. Weiner's editors at* Slate *proudly proclaimed this "the first great profile of the social media era," and many informed readers are inclined to agree.*

Jonah Weiner

# Kanye West Has a Goblet

"Fur pillows are hard to actually sleep on," Kanye West tells me. It's just before noon on an overcast Sunday in late July, and West has invited me into his Manhattan apartment. Three years ago, the rapper hired an interior designer to renovate the place into a stark configuration of right angles and polished stone surfaces. But these days, West's aesthetic has taken a turn for the maximal. "Versailles is the shit," he says. He's in the process, as he puts it, of "turning the crib real Kingish." The pillows are part of the plan.

Interviews with Kanye West have become increasingly rare over the past few years. For a time, the Chicago rapper was unavoidable—on the cover of *Time* in a blazer and jeans, on the cover of *Rolling Stone* in a crown of thorns—but the late 2007 death of his mother Donda knocked him off the radar. There are only a small handful of print interviews West has given since her passing. His silence was presumably—at least in part—a function of grief, but West has also communicated his general ambivalence about journalists. "This is my problem with interviews, you know? What if you did music, and someone else could come in and change your words around and then release it to the radio? And you ain't even get a chance to listen to it before they dropped it to radio? That's how interviews are! You say what you say and then you get paraphrased," he's said. "I wanna get approval over the shit."

So, as West begins the run-up to the release of his fifth album—it's set to come out in November and is currently titled *Dark Twisted Fantasy*—he has launched a new-media-heavy promo offensive, in which his words go straight from his mouth to the public record. So far, this tour has involved impromptu, video-recorded performances at the Silicon Valley offices of Facebook and Twitter, an account opened at the latter site and immediately put to near-constant use, and a real-time interview with fans on a website called UStream. There was a visit to the offices of *Rolling Stone*, too, where he monologued at some editors and allowed them to post a video clip of the visit. An interview on New York's Hot 97 last Wednesday has been the sole old-media throwback.

This way, West's thinking goes, if someone's going to quote him out of context and make him sound like an asshole, it will be him, thank you very much. The strategy brings to mind M.I.A.'s online retaliations in the wake of Lynn Hirschberg's *New York Times Magazine* hit piece, but refigured—far more cannily—as a preemptive strike.

That's one way of looking at it, anyway. Here's another: West has agreed to speak candidly to me on a wide variety of subjects, to run his mouth but remain pithy at the same time, and to grant me virtually round-the-clock access to his life—no publicist popping his head in and telling me there's five minutes left. As conditions go for writing a profile, these are extremely favorable. No, I don't get to ask any questions, but I do get a constantly updating record of West's thoughts, whereabouts, cravings, jokes, meals, flirtations, *bon mots*, and on and on. In the face of a mountainous info dump like West's, isn't the basic work of profiling—building from the raw material of everything someone says and does toward a more focused sense of who they are—as relevant as ever?

Several days before he invited me into his home, West brought me aboard a small plane he referred to as a "babymama" jet (because, he elaborated, like a purse dog, it's the sort of cute, undersized thing a rich guy gets for his mistress). West wore a slim dark suit, unbuttoned rakishly at the cuffs, with a tuxedo collar. "Everything's the right backdrop for a suit," he says. He's been talking a lot about suits recently, presenting them as a sign of some next-level classiness, getting his Glenn O'Brien on. He mentioned a girl who'd recently asked him why he was so dressed up. "I told her, 'cause I'm not headed to the gym right now,'" he said. As we boarded the plane, a couple other guys dressed in their own suits accompanied West, mugging on the tarmac *Reservoir Dogs*–style. (West never saw fit to introduce them.)

Flying back from Silicon Valley to New York, West wanted to show me images of some recent kingish purchases he'd made, along with various treasures he had his eye on. It was a giddy tour of *ancien régime*–looking finery that didn't end until well after the plane had landed. There were two golden goblets— thin-stemmed and etched with an intricate floral pattern—that West said he planned to use for drinking water. He was particularly excited about a bowl that squats regally on a gold base. The bowl is made of milky, hand-painted porcelain, with two grippable gold lions curling up its sides. "I copped this to eat cereal out of," he said, adding that he's been fantasizing about buying a horse. It's hard to say exactly how much, if at all, he was joking.

It's similarly unclear, three days later at his apartment, whether he regrets buying the fur pillows, which cost him god knows how much, or if he regards their impracticality as central to their appeal. Uncomfortable fur pillows represent the kind of problem a plebe would kill to have, after all, and in West's acquisition value system, form left function lying bruised, beaten, and bloody on the mat long ago. At one point West tells me, apropos of nothing, "I jog in Lanvin."

But when West complains about the pillows, it's not just an underhanded brag. It also speaks to a deeper sense that, as life has gotten ever more luxuriously comfortable for him, he has become that much more restive and incapable of truly enjoying it. He fancies himself a king these days, but throughout his career he has frequently come across like a princess tossing and turning atop a pea. It's as though an irritating little voice nags at him from down below, telling him that he still hasn't achieved everything he can, that he still doesn't have all the success he deserves, and that he never will. Sometimes he says he doesn't want to be "limited by the art form of rap," and sometimes he sets his sights higher and says he doesn't want to be limited by the twenty-first century: "When I think of competition it's like I try to create against the past. I think about Michelangelo and Picasso, you know, the pyramids," he says.

Last September, when he interrupted Taylor Swift at the Video Music Awards, West's nagging inner voice enjoyed its biggest platform to date—and suffered its biggest rebuke. As Swift accepted her award for best female video, West stormed the stage, grabbed her mic—and the spotlight—to mount a protest on behalf of Beyonce Knowles, whose "Single Ladies" video was up for the same award.

West had risen to national prominence with a stammering, justice-seeking outburst in 2005, when he interrupted Mike Myers and Chris Tucker on a Katrina telethon and excoriated George W. Bush. Here was a stammering, sort-of-justice-seeking outburst of a different kind—and where the first had been roundly celebrated, this one was decried. "Fuck you Kanye, it's like you stepped on a kitten," Katy Perry said, neatly encapsulating the majority response. Last week, on Hot 97, West—who apologized to Swift then fell into a long, self-imposed exile—likened himself to "a modern day Emmett Till," the fourteen-year-old boy murdered in Mississippi for supposedly whistling at a white woman. Although it'd be naive to say that there had been no racial component to the event or its fallout, the Till comparison proved that West's sense of persecution is alive and well.

At his apartment today, West says he's "working on being a doper person," but he seems to be feeling pretty dope as it is. "This is gonna be a dope ass day," he says. "Life is awesome," he says. "I love me," he says.

West's struggle between self-love and self-doubt has been career-long. He made his 2004 debut as a Louis Vuitton backpack of contradictions, casting himself as a principled "conscious" rapper with a weakness for womanizing and conspicuous consumption. "Always said if I rapped I'd say something significant," a rhyme on one early song went, "but now I'm rapping 'bout money, hoes, and rims again." On another track, West observed, mournfully, "We buy a lot of clothes when we don't really need 'em / Things we buy to cover up what's inside / Cause they make us hate ourself and love they wealth." He identified his materialism—and, by extension, that of the upwardly mobile underclass at large—as the symptom of an inherited, deeply ingrained self-loathing and insecurity.

West has yet to cure himself of that affliction—quite the contrary, as the kingish splurges attest. But he hasn't swept it under the rug, either. (The rug in question is a Persian "with cherub imagery," in case you're wondering). His tendency, in fact, is to inflate his cockiness to the point of grotesquerie, to type it out in ALL CAPS, to render it obscenely over-compensatory, and maybe even to inscribe its plush trappings with a faint tinge of penitent masochism, from the uncomfortable fur pillows to a new song that revolves around a refrain—"My chain heavy, my chain too heavy"—that turns a boast into a statement of suffering.

When West says something like "I love me," the words carry some irony. One of his favorite fictional characters is Ron Burgundy, from *Anchorman*—an arrogant, preening blowhard who exults in his stupidity, blissfully unaware of how ridiculous he is. When West raps, "I don't know how to put this, but I'm kind of a big deal," quoting from *Anchorman*, it's both a boast and a parody of one.

In other words, West has always been an interesting braggart because he lets a brag function as its opposite—he likes to have his cake and poison it, too. "Thoughts is Napoleon," West says, and you wonder if he's comparing his mind-state to the emperor or the complex.

$$\bullet \qquad \bullet \qquad \bullet$$

When West spoke to me last spring, there was more poison in the cake mix than usual. "I never feel like I'm not the underdog. I never felt completely comfortable," he said in March, still reeling, it seemed, from the VMA fallout. As West went on, it became clear that the death of the designer Alexander McQueen had shaken him and added to his funk. Mainstream rappers aren't really supposed to parade their vulnerabilities—at least they weren't until West came along, clearing the way for marquee emoters like Kid Cudi and Drake—but he readily admitted that he empathized with the designer's suicidal torment. (In the video-of-sorts for "See You in My Nightmares," he drives a blade into his stomach, loosing a flurry of confetti and a little claymation beast in a fantastical act of hari-kari.)

"I know how it feels when the night demons come," West told me. "Sometimes when it hurts so bad we have to just lay in the bed. Just lay in bed and don't move." He added that he had begun work on new music, and described the process as gruelingly cathartic: "Sometimes I turn the music up and drink and cry."

Cut to a Thursday in July and West seemed to have banished the night demons, at least for the moment, with the raw force of 10,000 lumens. We were at his apartment and he was showing off his brand-new projection-screen television. At about thirteen feet wide, it takes up a huge chunk of wall space. The image on the screen was a breathtaking overhead view of some vaguely familiar metropolis. It looked like we were peering through a window. "Watching *Dark Knight* in the day!" West said proudly.

By Friday night, the charms of the screen had yet to wear off—he'd hardly had a chance to use the thing between an editing session for the music video for his new single, "Power," and a dinner with Jay-Z. Now he had an audience he seemed especially interested in impressing: some girls visiting him from Stockholm named Helena and Carolina. "Why girls from Stockholm be so fresh?" West asked. He was mixing Grey Goose with Ruby Red grapefruit juice, pouring the cocktails into vintage Versace glassware and hitting them pretty hard. One of girls—I never found out who they were, exactly, or how he knew them—showed West some photos of her mom. The alcohol was making him cheeky. "Hey, I don't know what to say about this," West said. "Let me see more of you!"

The girls were drinking, too, and one of them spoke to me briefly in a garble of English and her native tongue. "Hey, Kayne's nya album ar magiskt. . . . that shit is crazy . . . det basta som gjorts pa lange. . . . lyssna pa det and get back to me!" she said. He'd been playing her some beats that RZA had produced for the upcoming record, and she loved them.

The new album promises a marked change in tone from the last one, *808s and Heartbreak*, a set of brooding electro-dirges written in the aftermath of West's mother's death and his breakup with a longtime girlfriend. On early songs and rhymes he's shared so far, West has restored the uptempo swing and goofball punchlines he deep-sixed last time out. "I'm Socrates but my skin more chocolatey," West raps on "See Me Now," a relentlessly buoyant track he dedicated to "the summer, the BBQs," to fun.

Even "Mama's Boyfriend," an Oedipal stew of jealousy and anger, contains a viciously funny tirade, delivered from the adolescent West's perspective, against the "ol' Old Spice wearin', short-chain wearin', dress-shoes-and-jogging-pants wearin'" new guy his mom's brought home. The song ends with a Nashville-worthy narrative twist when West finds himself caring for a boy whose mom he's dating.

Drinking vodka with the Swedes, West was exultant. He bopped his head hard to his own music, rapped along a little bit. The *Avatar* Blu-ray was playing. West yelled, at no one and everyone, "Nigga my screen is 13 feeeeeet! Don't talk to me!" He raised a toast—"Skal!"—then announced that he was headed off to a club.

I wasn't invited—even an all-access pass has its limits —but from the headache West was nursing the next morning, it seemed like he'd had fun. "Hangovers ain't good man," he said around 10 A.M. on Saturday. It was unclear how much, if any, sleep he'd gotten. He made his way to a closet and began trying on suits again.

## Esquire

FINALIST—COLUMNS
AND COMMENTARY

*Still more Kanye West. And Lord Byron, Edwin Booth, Grace Kelly, Clint Eastwood, Matt Damon, Steven Spielberg and Secretary of Defense Robert M. Gates—all these and more inhabit and inform "A Thousand Words About Our Culture," Stephen Marche's monthly column in* Esquire. *According to his editors, Marche "has a simple mandate—make sense of our damn culture, one topic at a time." In the first of these three columns, "What's Your Favorite War?," Marche writes that "depending on what screen you're watching, war is either a virtuous struggle of good over evil, a moral (and literal) minefield, or a thrilling nightmare." In "Why Is Clint Eastwood Still the Man?," Marche explains Eastwood's deep appeal: "What he embodies more than anything is the definitive virtue for American men: restraint." And in "Why Can't Kanye West Shut the Hell Up?," Marche explicates twenty-first-century celebrity: "A perpetual enterprise of more, with Twitter acting as both the engine and the agent of unending revelation."*

Stephen Marche

# What's Your Favorite War? *and* Why Is Clint Eastwood Still the Man? *and* Why Can't Kanye West Shut the Hell Up?

## What's Your Favorite War?

A friend of mine, a foreign correspondent who used to work for CNN, recently described to me a poster he saw in the back of a cab on the Afghanistan-Pakistan border: bin Laden riding a unicorn with a Kalashnikov in each hand while the Twin Towers explode behind him. Clearly the terrorists are winning the cultural dimension of the war; they know what kind of war movie they want to see, and we do not. At the same time that 30,000 of the country's best young men and women will be deployed to the most desperate corner of the earth, we are surrounded by conflicting depictions of battle. Depending on what screen you're watching, war is either a virtuous struggle of good over evil [*The Pacific*], a moral (and literal) minefield [*Green Zone*], or a thrilling nightmare [*The Hurt Locker*]—and that's not even counting the daily screaming matches on Fox News and MSNBC. After eight long years of bloodshed, and who knows how many more to come, we're still not sure why we fight, and our understanding of war is only growing more blood-dimmed and confused.

*The Pacific* comes to HBO from the same Spielberg-Hanks juggernaut that brought us that other ten-part miniseries about World War II [*Band of Brothers*] back before 9/11. To compare the two epics is to understand just how much has changed over the past decade. At the turn of the century, when Steven Spielberg revolutionized war cinema with his graphic depictions of the visceral and psychological carnage of battle [*Saving Private Ryan*], the audience had the stomach for realism. We were, after all, pretty much at peace at the time. But after years of random death and hollow victory, *The Pacific*'s creators take a softer approach to the devastation of war. In the three episodes that I've seen, the music never stops swelling. The clichés never stop hitting you in the face. You know the first time you see a southerner that he's going to be called "Johnny Reb" by a northerner, and so he is. Anyone whose name ends with a vowel comes from a happy family in which all the women cook nothing but big elaborate meals. These are not soldiers; they are flower arrangements on the theme of soldiers. Similarly, *The Pacific* isn't a war movie; it's a propaganda film about a war that's been over for sixty years. And God, we want to fight that war again, don't we? The enemy wore easily identifiable uniforms, with skulls on them and stuff. The conflict had a clear beginning, middle, and end, throughout which the United States was the ultimate hero. And after the war was all over, America taught the world the true meaning of victory, rebuilding its enemies with magnanimity, generosity, and wisdom. Who wouldn't rather watch that war than the nightly news?

And yet movie studios still insist on churning out films about our current dealings in Afghanistan and Iraq, despite the fact that no one is quite sure how these stories are going to end. (Even Vietnam, right in the middle of Hollywood's great countercultural awakening, didn't inspire great films [*Apocalypse Now*, 1979; *The Deer Hunter*, 1978; *Coming Home*, 1978] until well after the fall of Saigon.) Now joining the list of television shows and movies about the war on terror that nobody bothered to see is *Green Zone*, which goes like this: A warrant officer, stranded in the moral and material chaos of post-invasion Iraq, works against his own government, single-handedly laboring to discover the elusive weapons of mass destruction that would provide belated justification for the quagmire. It's crazy: We've come to expect soldiers to be morally superior to the mission they have been entrusted to execute. In pop culture right now, soldiers exist in an impossible space: part warrior, part saint, part victim.

The basic fact may be that Afghanistan and Iraq make for lousy movies. Unlike World War II, its happy endings and unimpeachable motives so well suited for celluloid, our ongoing struggles are happening in real time, with jarring visuals and Twitter-feed updates. In other words, they're more like video games. The greatest artwork made so far about the war on terror is a first-person-shooter game [Call of Duty: Modern Warfare 2] that broke sales records when it came out in November. I should add that while I admire this game enormously—it might be the first protest game—I don't enjoy playing it much. Controller in hand and eyes on the screen, I keep asking myself: Why am I here? Whom am I killing? Modeled closely on the experience of soldiers in Afghanistan, the game flashes quotations on the screen after you're killed that are even more disturbing. It quotes Confucius—"Before you embark on a journey of revenge, dig two graves"—and Francis Bacon: "In taking revenge a man is but even with his enemy, but in passing it over he is superior." The more you die, the less your dying makes sense, and it's no coincidence that the only satisfying war movie of late is *The Hurt Locker*, which is about as close to a video game as you can get without actually having a controller in your hand. Just like Call of Duty, the movie opens with a quote (". . . war is a drug"—Chris Hedges) and relies on a first-person point of view when navigating the war-torn terrain. If *The Hurt Locker* deserves to win Best Picture—as some believe it does—the victory will be a coup for gamers everywhere.

You can expect to see plenty more where *The Hurt Locker* came from. Movies (and video games) demand heroes, and the U.S. military has plenty of them: a million and a half men and women who have arrived in the middle of a shitstorm with an incomprehensible backstory and an uncertain ending. The secretary of defense [Robert Gates] says 2011 will be the beginning of disengagement in Afghanistan, not the end, and until the last man leaves Iraq and Afghanistan, this story can go pretty much anywhere.

# Why Is Clint Eastwood Still the Man?

Leonard Cohen, that magnificent Canadian Buddhist Jew, once defined a saint this way: "A saint does not dissolve the chaos; if he did, the world would have changed long ago. . . . It is a kind of balance that is his glory. He rides the drifts like an escaped ski." By Cohen's definition, the closest thing that American men have to a patron saint right now is Clint Eastwood. This magazine recently commissioned a survey of twenty- and fifty-year-old American men, and when asked to name the coolest man in the country, both groups chose Eastwood by a wide margin. The guys born in 1960, the ones who grew up growling, "Feeling lucky, punk?" [*Dirty Harry*] to their friends, make sense, but the ones born in 1990? How did they end up picking the old guy from *Space Cowboys* over Clooney and LeBron? The answer is simple, really: During all the real and imagined crises of American masculinity that the past half century has coughed onto our screens, Eastwood has been the one stable figure in the midst of the darkness and the turmoil, a man entirely apart from the boring and draining established types that have dominated movies for four decades—macho pigs [Burt Reynolds, Gerard Butler], lovable schmucks [Woody Allen, Michael Cera], merry pranksters [Chevy

Chase, Adam Sandler], and impossibly cool hipsters [Steve McQueen, Brad Pitt]. Eastwood's endurance is the endurance of saints, and what he embodies more than anything is the definitive virtue for American men both then and now: restraint. He rides the line between his own terrible desires and the world as it is with the grace we all aspire to.

This month, his thirty-first film as a director [*Hereafter*, starring Matt Damon as a man who talks to the dead] arrives in theaters, and, being about life after death, it invites retrospectives on the man. It is incredible to me that Eastwood has been defined throughout his career as an icon of macho. Macho is a preening pose assumed by men who aren't sure they're men and who compensate by needing more, having more, showing more [*The Expendables*]. The explosion of beefcake action movies in the eighties—Schwarzenegger and his gym buddies—coincided neatly with the mass entry of women into the workplace: classic overcompensation. But Eastwood has never needed to compensate for anything. Manhood, for Eastwood, has always been about needing and having and showing less. His gift as an actor and director is his economy of motion and expression; his moral vision is of men who struggle with and eventually master their bloodlust and lust and their desire for booze and self-degradation. At the beginning of his career, in his classic spaghetti westerns [*The Good, the Bad, and the Ugly*], he combined two classic American types—the hard-boiled agent from the crime fiction of Dashiell Hammett and Raymond Chandler and the lonesome cowboy from the long-established western—and created characters who dominated through their utter self-possession. You could fire a gun at their faces and they wouldn't even flinch. A little later, *Dirty Harry*, while somewhat fascistic, was attuned to the urban hellholes of the seventies, the definitive fantasy of control over the uncontrollable. And *Unforgiven*, the masterpiece that set up Eastwood's late career, is the greatest film ever made about the mastery of the violence within. His more recent films grapple with control over fame [*Flags of Our Fathers*], racism [*Gran Torino*], the impulse for revenge [*Mystic River*], and now, in *Hereafter*, life after death.

Eastwood's endurance is one of the rare phenomena that make me genuinely hopeful about men. It's not just that he proves that you can be awesome when you're eighty. He proves that it's possible to be open-minded and creative and daring and still hold on to the old virtues. Unlike his career contemporaries, many of whom dabble in conscious self-parody or unconscious self-parody or the occasional voice-over job, Eastwood has gone only bigger and wider and stranger and better, conquering a dizzying breadth of material: female boxers, World War II veterans, South African rugby players, racist mechanics. And that's just the past six years. Self-control defines his off-screen persona as well as his movies. He appears only in films he directs and stays more or less entirely outside the celebrity-industrial complex, with its necessary surrender of control. Eastwood remains, against all odds, his own man.

And now that we are supposedly entering the next crisis of masculinity—this time the world doesn't need men because we can't listen, we can't sit still in kindergarten, and so all society will shortly be a massive gynocracy in which men's primary role will be as the problem children of successful mothers and wives—we need Eastwood more than ever. Whatever else has changed over the past fifty years, self-mastery and control over our lives are still what we want more than anything. My favorite Eastwood film—and I'm not joking—is the orangutan movie [*Every Which Way but Loose*] from 1978; it was demolished by critics but remains one of his highest-grossing movies ever. A man tied to an ape, driving across America, brawling for money, looking for love. If this film had been made by a French or Serbian director, it would have been hailed as an absurdist parable about how to live well with brute desires in a brutal world. At one point, a woman asks Eastwood's character why he fought so hard and risked so much for the ape, and the answer sounds like a rallying cry for men everywhere: "I really hated to see him in that cage." And in the end, the ape is free.

# Why Can't Kanye West Shut the Hell Up?

If you're in the mood to listen to Kanye West, and you very well might be, you didn't have to wait for his new album that drops this month [Kanye West named his new album *My Beautiful Dark Twisted Fantasy*] to hear his new songs. All fall, every Friday, West has been releasing a new track on his Twitter feed, which is, in almost every possible way, the perfect outlet for his music: equal parts superficial and subversive, occasionally brilliant but mostly fun and forgettable. And the songs we've heard so far are good—witty, catchy, and, in a word, fresh—but they come at a time when Kanye matters less for his music than for the swirl of art and angst he has created around himself on Twitter over the past few years. Forget TMZ and reality TV and the other celebrity death scrums of 2010: Technology has carried Kanye all the way to the other side of fame, where there are no secrets to reveal and there is no reality to show.

As an artist, Kanye is immensely admirable. He doesn't always fare well, but he always fares *forward*. He's taken rap, a daringly self-centered art form, far beyond the standard ego promotion of bald hype. His last album, *808s & Heartbreak*, took the shallow musical gimmickry of Auto-Tune, a program designed to eliminate individuality, and produced a hauntingly personal album. And since the early days of *The College Dropout*, he's resisted the silly thuggishness and tired rants that had long since failed to shock; while other rappers sell a fantasy of brute power through wealth and violence, Kanye sells the complexity of himself as he is, sometimes grand, sometimes pathetic, sometimes gracious, sometimes vicious, sometimes silly, sometimes profound. And he is nothing if not self-aware: "If I'm a douche, then put me in your coochie," he says in "Lord Lord Lord."

The varied poses of his personality have merged seamlessly and effortlessly with the Twitter age. More than a million fans follow him daily, hourly. They inspect the pictures of the presents Cartier sends him. They read his opinions about Mark Twain. They note what he eats for brunch, what pillows he buys, what tracks he's laying down right this instant. One minute ago he posted the following: "At the crib I use really nice napkins instead of paper towels . . . got the idea from the YSL bathroom . . . waaaaay nicer." Other celebrities tweet—some with more wit and some with more followers [Lady Gaga has more Twitter followers than anyone else in the world. In September, she used Twitter to announce her rally to repeal Don't Ask, Don't Tell]—but Kanye, despite being mocked for this obsession with Twitter, has fused the technology with his music in a unique way. Take just one set of lyrics from the first Friday track, "Monster": "Have you ever had sex with a pharaoh? / Put the pussy in a sarcophagus / Now she's claiming that I bruise her esophagus." The song is a tweet and the tweet is a song, and the lack of distinction weakens both sides. Same goes for Kanye's public appearances: The world rewards him for speaking outrageously in his songs, and his songs are his life, and his life is his songs, so why shouldn't he speak outrageously in life? All his scandals of the past few years ["Taylor, I'm really happy for you. Ima let you finish, but Beyonce had one of the best videos of all time!"; "George Bush doesn't care about black people."] occurred because he couldn't distinguish between real life and art. (Incidentally, it was lost in the furor that he was right on both counts.) And yet the guy can't help himself. Even when President Obama called him a "jackass," there was a certain tenderness in the word. The president was talking like Kanye was the nation's troubled cousin who can't shut up about himself, which is more or less what he is.

Since the first celebrities emerged, mixing their work and their lives in powerful dreams of projected personality, the possibility of confusing art and reality has existed. The man considered by some (but not me) to be the world's first celebrity [Lord Byron] was a great poet, but that's not why so many admirers asked for locks of his hair that he reportedly had to start sending out clippings from his dog, Boatswain. Men and women adored Byron because, according to one woman who slept with him, he was "mad, bad, and dangerous to know." The greatest American actor of the nineteenth century [Edwin Booth] thought his career was over when his brother shot President Lincoln. He soon learned that audiences worshipped him more—and worshipped his tortured performances of *Hamlet* and *Julius Caesar* more—because they knew about his personal tragedy. And the great celebrities of the twentieth century [Grace Kelly, Jacqueline Kennedy Onassis, Gwyneth Paltrow] ran away from the cameras, but this only made their fans eager to see more and know more. Today, celebrity has become a perpetual enterprise of more, with Twitter acting as both the engine and the agent of unending revelation. Jump on or jump off.

Kanye has jumped on. Like every hip-hop artist today, Kanye sees himself as a brand and dreams of total integration of himself with everything that can conceivably be consumed. But being a brand involves being both more than a human being and less, which may explain why there's a wild, frantic sadness to his personality, or what Cyril Connolly once described as the "fugitive distress of hedonism." To be a brand is ultimately to be a hollow thing. Like a bell. The hollowness of Kanye West rings out and his distress only makes him more attractive. Being a brand has its own demands, and they are growing more and more pressing by the second. Kanye at least is willing to go all the way. "I'm living in the future so the present is my past. / My presence is a present, kiss my ass," he says in "Monster." All that in just ninety-two characters.

## Sports Illustrated, from Curiously Long Posts

FINALIST—BLOGGING

*Blogging has long been recognized as a distinctive form of journalism—the one form of journalism unique to the web—but last year was the first time that a magazine received a National Magazine Award for Blogging, when* Foreign Policy *was honored for Thomas Ricks's blog* The Best Defense. *Unfortunately, blogs don't always translate to paper and ink. No hyperlinks, of course, but more importantly the immediacy of the web is lost. Joe Posnanski's blog* Curiously Long Posts *is different. On the* Sports Illustrated *website, long blog posts are not uncommon—during football season, readers could while away their Mondays reading SI blogs—but unlike most of his colleagues, Posnanski tends to focus on one topic and explore it with what the National Magazine Award judges called "uncommon writerly gifts." Here Posnanski plumbs one of the most controversial sports decisions of 2010—LeBron James's abandonment of Cleveland and its meaning for those he left behind, including Posnanski's own friends and family.*

# A Boulevard Called Chagrin

CLEVELAND—Angry? You have no idea. Let's just put it this way. Last weekend, when I checked into my Cleveland hotel near the aptly named boulevard of Chagrin, the manager gave me a little gift bag (with water and such) and a letter. When you travel a lot, the managers always give you nondescript letters with multiple exclamation points, letters that look a little something like this:

Dear Valued Customer!

Thank you so much for your business! If there is anything we can do to help you enjoy your stay, please do not hesitate to Dial 0 and ask! We here at the hotel take great pride in our customer service! Please put us to the test! And thank you again for your business! We know there are many options for a busy traveler like you! Thank you!

Sincerely!
The Hotel Staff!

I long ago stopped reading these letters, for obvious reasons. And I did not read this one. That was until my wife glanced at it and said, "Um, have you read this letter?"

"No."

"You might want to take a look at it."

So I looked at it. It welcomed me to the hotel, said how excited they were to have me there, and all the usual stuff.

"Keep reading," my wife said.

Then came this: "I wanted to also let you know that we especially appreciate the articles you have written in the past few weeks regarding LeBron James. I'm not going to expound on the subject, but let me just say that we all applaud the opinions that you have so eloquently shared in your articles."

Angry? You have no idea.

·   ·   ·

The striking part is how many houses are for sale in and around my old neighborhood. *Forbes* magazine this year ranked Cleveland as America's most miserable city, three spots ahead of Detroit, that rival rust-belt city that had been the final punch line of the most recent Hastily Made Cleveland Tourism Video gag on YouTube ("At least we're not Detroit! We're not Detroit!").

Well, people have been saying that sort of misery thing about Cleveland for many, many years, long before I was even born . . . but something about all those "For Sale" signs makes it feel a little bit different. The signs seem to be in every front yard, block after block, like they are political signs, like people want to encourage everyone to vote for RE/MAX or Prudential.

"You don't know," Michael, one of my childhood friends, tells me over corned-beef sandwiches at Corky and Lenny's on that boulevard named Chagrin. "The city is dying."

"Come on," I say, "people always say Cleveland is dying."

"Yeah," he says. "But this time it really is."

·   ·   ·

Angry? You have no idea. There are people who set up at Progressive Field, before Indians games, to sell anti–LeBron James stuff:

T-shirts, hats, voodoo dolls, that sort of thing. This is not new or original. This is exactly the sort of thing that people do after various minor catastrophes.[1] In Lawrence, Kan., I remember them selling "Benedict Williams" shirts after Roy Williams left Kansas to coach at North Carolina. At Stanford, after The Play—the famous five-lateral play where Cal's Kevin Moen finished it by crashing into the end zone and the Stanford band—they sold T-shirts showing all the various penalties that Cal's players had committed but had not been called.

But, eventually, the agony fades. And that's what's different about the anti–LeBron James feeling here: It only seems to be growing. The anger only seems to be rising. When LeBron James humiliated his hometown by going on ESPN to announce to the world that he was taking his talents to South Beach so he could ball it up with a few buddies and try to win the championship he could not come close to winning as the star, well, there was the expected fury. People around the NBA questioned James's heart. Former players questioned his competitiveness. Cavaliers owner Dan Gilbert wrote a Comic Sans screed that called James a quitter and a loser. The *Cleveland Plain Dealer* put up its now-famous front page photo of LeBron James walking away—with an arrow and small print pointing to his still naked championship ring finger. In time around the nation, as was inevitable, the story lost steam. Yes, people were disgusted. But the Miami Heat—starring Dwyane Wade, LeBron James, and Chris Bosh—will be (after all) interesting to watch, to root for or root against, to follow as a sign of the times. Michael Jordan made the point that he never wanted to join Isiah Thomas or Magic Johnson or Larry Bird—he wanted to BEAT them, and that rings true. The Superfriends in Miami

1. Jerry Seinfeld once said that if they had T-shirts in biblical days, people would have sold them after the Ten Plagues ("Boils! I Was There!" "Locusts Descended And All I Got Was This Stupid T-Shirt!").

feels like something new. People will want to know how it turns out.

Only the story will not lose steam in Cleveland. The rage does not dissipate. When a fan showed up to an Indians-Yankees game on Wednesday wearing a LeBron James Miami Heat jersey, he was booed and heckled and taunted so mercilessly by so many hundreds of fans that he was escorted out of the stadium. Maybe the guy thought it would be kind of funny to tweak the Cleveland fans, to draw a little anger, to be the wise guy—some people are like that. And, hey, it's just sports. He badly misunderstood. It's not just sports here. This is no joke here. This is not funny here. Angry? You have no idea.

"Buy your F—— LeBron shirts here!" the man in front of the stadium shouts. And then this: "The kids love them!"

·    ·    ·

I grew up in a circle of immigrants—my parents came to America and Cleveland just a couple of years before I was born. Their friends were immigrants themselves. And as they gather together again all these years later to remember my grandfather, I notice for the first time that each one seems to have a different accent. An English accent. A Hungarian accent. A Polish accent. A Russian accent. And so on. It seemed normal when I was growing up, I never even thought about it. That was just Cleveland to me . . . a flurry of accents, the smell of bread in Little Italy, the kids kicking soccer balls outside Arabica Coffee Shop in Coventry, the Wiener Schnitzel at Balaton, the guy throwing pizza dough in the air at Geraci's, the orthodox Jews walking along Green Road . . .

Now, though, their different accents sound so odd together, because they are all talking about LeBron James.

"I think he purposely lost in the playoffs," says one woman who has known me since I was born and, as far as I can remember, never once before has talked about sports. "I believe it."

"It's true," says another woman in another accent. "He knew that if he won the championship, it would have been harder to leave."

"He just played like a loser," one of the men says. "There is no doubt that he was not trying. Remember that elbow injury?"

Everyone in the room nods. In the deciding game of the playoffs against Chicago, LeBron James's right elbow hurt so much that he shot his final free throw left-handed . . . bricking it badly. The injury was called an elbow strain, and James played every game in the conference semifinals against Boston. But in this room—and all over this town—the elbow injury is just another odd subplot. "I think he knew he was leaving," the man says, putting words to the theory. "And so he faked that elbow injury."

"Why would he do that?"

"So he would have an excuse when he left," the man says.

There is no talk in this room about the seven remarkable seasons of LeBron James in Cleveland, the twenty-eight points, seven rebounds and seven assists he averaged, the two MVP awards he won, the way he dragged the 2007 team to the finals, the pride in basketball that he instilled in a city where the Cavaliers were a nonentity. There is no talk about the joy of watching LeBron James play basketball like no one ever had in Cleveland, and no room for such talk. Not now. Maybe not ever.

"I never want to see anyone get hurt, but . . ." another woman with another accent says, and I have to stop listening.

.     .     .

Angry? You have no idea. Bill Livingston, a sports columnist for the *Plain Dealer* and someone I have been friendly with for twenty years, just this week wrote an entire column under the headline: "Retire LeBron James' No. 23 Jersey with the Cleveland Cavaliers? No Way."

The headline describes Bill's opinion, which is essentially this: Cleveland should never retire LeBron James's jersey. Bill says that James's greatness is indisputable . . . and the cruel way he chose to leave Cleveland is unforgivable. "It took a lot to turn such gold into lead, but he managed it," Bill wrote. He wrote that the other Cleveland sports villains (with the exception of the never-to-be-forgiven Art Modell) were simply victims of the moment, and in that he is right.

- Craig Ehlo may be remembered in town as the guy that Michael Jordan made his famous shot over . . . but hey, the guy was Michael Jordan.

- Brian Sipe may be remembered for throwing the interception in the end zone at the end of the playoff game against Oakland in 1981—Red Right 88 was the play—but Sipe had been the swashbuckling quarterback whose late-game brilliance had led the Browns to that playoff game.

- Earnest Byner may be remembered for the fumble against Denver in the AFC Championship Game that thwarted a remarkable comeback attempt . . . but it was Byner's magnificence that drove that comeback attempt in the first place.

And James, Livingston writes, is "the indisputably great player who left in a manner designed to inflict the most emotional pain on the fans and do the most harm to the franchise." For this, Livingston concludes, James "simply does not belong with men who took pride in the jersey and played to honor the city and its fans."

I have tried to read the column two ways. I have tried to read it the way you might read it if you are not from Cleveland, if you have no emotional attachment to Cleveland, if you view Cleveland as just another city that you've heard jokes about. And I would bet that from that perspective, it reads as petty . . . all of this probably reads as petty. LeBron James, after all, played amazing basketball for seven years in Cleveland, and at age twenty-five he went to Miami, a fabulous city on the water, where he can play with incredible players and schmooze with the biggest stars and perhaps win a title. Yes, you would probably agree, his ESPN show, *The Decision*, was ill-advised and dumb, and you might even grant that it was borderline cruel . . . but you probably would add that even if he had left Cleveland in the classiest way possible, it would not have made a big difference in the reaction. You would probably say that people in Cleveland should just get over it, the city did not have a lifetime contract with him, the guy has a right to follow his own path and all that.

I can certainly see how you would feel these things if you're not from Cleveland.

But, then, if you're not from Cleveland, if you are not connected to Cleveland, you have not lived through forty-five years of uninterrupted sports heartache, season after season. You have not endured a river catching fire, a city going bankrupt, an NBA halftime show called "Fat Guy Eating Beer Cans." You have not lived through a million Cleveland jokes, and endless Cleveland winters, and ten-cent beer night, and the collapse of Cleveland businesses, and the draining of the Cleveland population, and the countless hopes that build and collapse. The feeling in Cleveland was that LeBron James knew about all these things—he grew up in Akron, and he played his whole pro career in Cleveland, and he had to understand what he meant to a city.

Maybe he did understand. Maybe he didn't. Maybe he cared. Maybe he didn't. Either way, he went on television to announce to the world that he was dumping Cleveland for someplace more exciting.

From Livingston's column: "ESPN's suck-up brigades will be out in force . . . accusing Cleveland of eating its young . . . they will say we let 28 minutes of that dreadful, self-serving *The Deci-sion* show, courtesy of the Lapdog Network, erase seven years of excellence."

Angry? You have no idea.

• • •

I have been on Chagrin Blvd. in Cleveland a thousand times in my life. I had never even once considered the meaning of the word. There is a lot of Chagrin in Cleveland—Chagrin Blvd., the Chagrin River, the city of Chagrin Falls. All this actually came from a French trader named Sieur de Saguin, who had built up a good relationship with the American Indians in the area. When he died—as I understand it—they wanted to name the river for him, but did not have an "S" sound in the language. So they went with "Shaguin." Later, a surveyor named Seth Please changed the name to "Chagrin." Anyway, that's what the encyclopedias say. And this led to all the chagrin in Cleveland.

I never fully realized how many depressing word choices per-vade Cleveland. The football team is called the "Browns"—it is named for the legendary coach Paul Brown, but, as Tom Hanks once said, it fits because everything in Cleveland is brown. The most famous building in town is the skyscraper called "The Ter-minal Tower." The Cuyahoga River, the one that caught fire, is thought only to mean "Crooked River." The lake is called "Erie."

And chagrin . . . it means "distress or embarrassment at hav-ing failed or been humiliated." Oh, the city will go on. LeBron James, in the end, is a basketball player, and despite the gigantic billboard of him that overlooked downtown and the joke that the economy was based on him, no, Cleveland will go on. There are always good things. The medical industry in town grows rapidly, and downtown has come back and there are great plans. In sports, the Browns have hired Mike Holmgren to turn things around, the Indians have some young talent, the Cavaliers have a determined owner and a clear mission. In life, Cleveland has come back so many times before, because the place still has the sort of diversity and industriousness of great places. The city will go on.

Still, as I go around, visiting old friends, seeing all the familiar places, counting the "For Sale" signs, noticing the T-shirts ("Born Here, Raised Here, Played Here, Hated Here," is one of those shirts), avoiding the potholes . . . I feel this sadness. Is Cleveland angry? You have no idea. I wish people here could let go. And I understand why people here cannot. And I just keep driving on a street called Chagrin.

## Tablet Magazine, from The Scroll

WINNER—BLOGGING

*Founded in 2009,* Tablet Magazine *describes itself as "a daily online magazine of Jewish news, ideas, and culture." A modest self-depiction for a publication that has already won two National Magazine Awards: the 2010 award for Podcasting and the 2011 award for Blogging. Marc Tracy is not the only contributor to* Tablet*'s award-winning blog* The Scroll, *but his posts far outnumber those of other writers and give the blog its distinctive voice. Tracy's posts range from short comments on news events to extended analysis of political and cultural developments—though he is not above running a simple list like "The Top 10 Jewish-American Athletes" (topped by Sandy Koufax; Sid Luckman is sadly relegated to fourth). In the first of the two blog posts collected here, Tracy investigates the Mossad assassination of a Hamas agent in Dubai. In "Peretz Agonistes," Tracy offers a brief yet insightful assessment of the career of the longtime proprietor of* The New Republic, *Martin Peretz.*

Marc Tracy

# Murder in Dubai
*and* Peretz
# Agonistes

## Murder in Dubai

Mahmoud al-Mabhouh, the Hamas weapons procurer who played
a crucial role facilitating arms shipments from Iran to Gaza, was
murdered in his Dubai hotel room on the night of January 19.
Dubai police claim the assassination was a Mossad operation—
the list of suspects now numbers twenty-six—and basically all
reporting agrees with that assessment. But there are also assorted
oddities that suggest that the Mossad may not have done it, or at
least not alone. The Palestinian Authority, several Arab governments, and maybe some elements within Hamas also wanted al-
Mabhouh dead. The Mossad, per its usual practice, has neither
confirmed nor denied its involvement.

For now, assume it was the Mossad—the rest of the world certainly does. Because the assassins used forgeries of other countries' passports, those nations are ostensibly angry with Israel,
and because the Mossad looks to have been unusually inept
(among other things, the assassins were captured on Dubai's extensive security-camera system), the intelligence agency's reputation has ostensibly suffered. At the end of the day, though, the
Mossad is way too useful to the West for serious diplomatic reper-
cussions to follow (though some strains are possible). And—inept
or not, harmed reputation or not, and Mossad or not—the mission

was certainly accomplished: like Generalissimo Francisco Franco before him, Mahmoud al-Mabhouh is still dead.

The reason, however, that this story has leapt to the front pages of Israeli and British tabloids and received extensive media coverage around the world, including in the United States (and especially on *The Scroll!*), is the less geopolitically significant cloak-and-dagger element—less geopolitically significant, but *totally awesome*. Here's a primer on that fun stuff.

### How Did They Do It?

At least one member of the assassination squad—which according to Judith Miller's reporting for *Tablet Magazine* trailed al-Mabhouh's movements on two previous visits to Dubai—was waiting for al-Mabhouh at the Dubai airport terminal when he flew in from Damascus (where he lived, along with much of Hamas's senior leadership) on January 19. Security cameras captured two assassins, wearing fake beards and looking like typical European tourists, checking into his hotel immediately after he did, even riding up the elevator with him to watch him enter his room, room 230. An hour later, the squad had ascertained that the room opposite his was unoccupied, booked it, and used it as their staging ground. That was room 237—why, yes, that *is* also the room with the creepy old lady in *The Shining*.

At around 8 P.M. on January 19, someone tried to reprogam the lock to al-Mabhouh's door. At 8:24, al-Mabhouh arrived at the hotel after spending several hours out and about. At 8:48, four assassins—big men—departed the hotel. Al-Mabhouh was discovered the next day at 1:30 P.M. Nothing indicated forced entry. And a "Do Not Disturb" sign hung on the door of room 230.

How was al-Mabhouh killed? Reports had suggested a drug-induced heart attack, others electrocution followed by asphyxiation, and still others just asphyxiation. We could always be pretty sure that he did not succumb to cancer, as Hamas initially claimed on January 20, when his corpse was first discovered.

Only yesterday did Dubai police announce that al-Mabhouh was injected with a muscle relaxant and then suffocated.

## What's the Deal with the Passports?

The twenty-six suspects used passports from Britain, Ireland, France, Australia, and Germany. (Those entering Dubai with Israeli passports are, presumably, automatically red-flagged; travelers from those countries are not.) Most if not all of these were forgeries, though at least the single German one appears to be real. Most carried the names of real, innocent Israeli residents, usually ones who were actually, say, dual British-Israeli citizens and carried British passports. (Some of the real-life people are pissed, but at least one is amused.) The *pictures* on the passports (which are now in the public record—see http://media.ida hostatesman.com/smedia/2010/02/24/12/607-Mideast_Dubai_ Hamas_Slaying.sff.embedded.prod_affiliate.36.jpg) are not pictures of those named on the passports. Instead, they are doctored pictures that resemble the assassins who held them enough that they were able to get past customs, but not so much that we can easily identify them now. In other words: well done, whoever you are.

## But Maybe It Wasn't the Mossad?

The assassins' fake passports implicated innocent Israelis—would the Mossad really want to do that? Two of the killers, both holding fake Australian passports, reportedly escaped to Iran afterward, which you would not think would be the most hospitable place for two Mossad assassins on the lam. (Yesterday, we learned that two others entered the United States soon after the killing. That sounds more like it.) And two former Fatah security personnel connected to powerful P.A. official Muhammed Dahlan, who has in the past worked with covert U.S. forces to try to topple Hamas's Gaza leadership, have also been arrested in connection with the plot.

Then there's al-Mabhouh. The guy spent two decades wanted by the Mossad for the 1989 killing of two Israeli soldiers. The Egyptian and Jordanian authorities, to say nothing of the Palestinian Authority (which considers Hamas an enemy almost as much as Israel does), had it in for him, too. (Hamas's initial investigation concluded that al-Mabhouh was killed by an Arab government.) In other words, this is someone used to keeping an anonymous profile. He was given to traveling in disguise, complete with colored contact lenses; it's even rumored that he had cosmetic surgery so as to permit anonymity.

Given all this, he was *astonishingly* careless. He told an aide (since arrested) and his family of his travel plans, in detail. He traveled under his own name, and without bodyguards—a rarity for him. Allegedly, the bodyguards couldn't get plane tickets. (Raise your hand if you remember the part in *The Godfather* when Michael's two bodyguards suddenly flee from the front of his house in Sicily, and that's how Michael knows his car's ignition has been wired.)

All of this points to the prospect that, whether institutional or individual, something or someone that was not the Mossad nonetheless colluded with the Mossad in the killing. That is, assuming it was the Mossad that killed him.

### But It Was Mossad, Right?

That's the smart money. It's not just the clean method of dispatching the target (say what you want about the assassins appearing on the Dubai cameras, that we didn't know how al-Mabhouh was killed until yesterday says something about the professionalism of his killers); or the way al-Mabhouh's death fits perfectly into the Mossad's pattern of assassinating Israel's enemies; or Judith Miller's report that it was the Mossad, the *Times* of London's report that Israeli Prime Minister Benjamin Netanyahu personally approved the job, and the Dubai police chief's assertion that he is "99 percent" sure it was Mossad, followed by his claim that he possesses DNA evidence of at least one assassin. It's all of the above.

There are two major aspects of the job that were uncharacteristic of the Mossad: first, being exposed as they have been, and, second, sending twenty-six people to do the job instead of, like, three. The former fact can be explained simply by Dubai's having an incredibly extensive security-camera system, so that not getting picked up on it would be extremely difficult; and in fact, the assassins gave every indication of knowing they were probably being taped. The large list of suspects could be explained, as *Haaretz* spy correspondent Yossi Melman suggested, as the Dubai police chief's deliberately throwing out false or tenuous evidence. For example, the Mossad agents escaping to Iran: is this something that did not happen, but the Dubai police chief wants us to think happened? Or that Mossad wants us to think happened? Or maybe this was just a really complicated job, one that happened to require the skills of over two dozen operatives?

To believe that it was not the Mossad, you must believe that some country or entity other than Israel had a motive to assassinate al-Mabhouh strong enough to trump fears of being implicated (while also knowing it was so valuable to the rest of the world that diplomatic consquences would be minimal); the information on which dual British-Israeli citizens carry British passports; the manpower and money to orchestrate an extensive, months-long, complex operation; and the training and expertise to stalk and stake out al-Mabhouh, kill him so that his death could not be confirmed for almost twenty-four hours and his murder could not be confirmed for over a week, and manage not

to have a single agent, out of as many as twenty-six, be apprehended. Could Egypt's spies pull it off this well? Could the CIA,
for that matter?

Anyway, the market has spoken: Mossad's job-opening web-
page has never been busier, and sales of "Don't Mess With The
Mossad" t-shirts are up tenfold.

# Peretz Agonistes

The most surprising thing you learn in *New York*'s generally
fantastic profile of longtime *New Republic* owner, editor, and all-
around maven Martin Peretz—assuming you know something
of Peretz's politics and recent controversies (and chances are, if
you have already read the profile, you do)—is that he has been
known to attend the protests in the East Jerusalem neighborhood of Sheikh Jarrah, "in solidarity with Palestinians threatened with eviction." This is astonishing, given that these protests
have become something between a rite of passage and a shibbo-
leth for the Israeli left (Todd Gitlin gave his first-hand account of
the ritual earlier this month in *Tablet Magazine*) and that, on the
question of Israel, Peretz is, shall we say, no dove.

But the profile depicts someone much more complex than the
caricature of Peretz, furthered by his enemies but buttressed by
his own blog posts, as a ranting, right-wing, and—there's really
no denying it—occasionally racist pundit. Partly, this more balanced view of Peretz is the result of a peace process so stagnant
that someone on the right cannot help but seem like a moderate
(Palestinian president Salam Fayyad is "a very modernizing person, but I would doubt that he commands loyalty," Peretz says,
and one can easily imagine someone with opposite views nodding in agreement). And partly, this more balanced view of Peretz may also be the result of the fact that Peretz—despite being,

as the article's title has it, "in Exile" from most of the things that have defined his seven decades (the United States, Harvard, his now-ex-wife, *The New Republic*)—cooperated with the profile and so presumably had some ability to craft the narrative it tells. This is not pure supposition on my part: Earlier this fall, a reporter on assignment for *Tablet Magazine* tried to interview Peretz about his participation in an English-language teaching program in Jaffa (which the profile opens with), only to be told Peretz wanted nothing written about his trip.

The article's most important contribution to the public record is its filling in of the recent controversy surrounding Peretz's remark, "Muslim life is cheap, most notably to Muslims," and the brouhaha it led to at Harvard. There is good reporting about his unhappy childhood and about his long, tapering, and finally finished marriage. There is some choice inside-baseball stuff (longtime literary editor Leon Wieseltier remains a close friend of Peretz's, but they no longer discuss Israel, which makes sense; *TNR* writer John Judis "knows zero" about Israel, Peretz opines, which isn't true). There is one timeless line—"I mean, fuck these fancy Upper West Side rabbis," Peretz complains—and another, from the writer Fouad Ajami, that seems really to get at the man: "Arabs understand Marty. He has that Middle Eastern quality: me against my brother, me and my brother against my cousin, me and my cousin against the world."

And yet the true defense of Martin Peretz (besides the fact that he and his wife funded the presidential campaign of maybe the most worthy politician of the past fifty years, Eugene McCarthy) comes in one of those indelibly *New York*-y sidebars that runs alongside the article. It depicts the chronology of *The New Republic*'s editors: Michael Kinsley, Hendrik Hertzberg, Andrew Sullivan, Peter Beinart, Frank Foer. Those are some of the best and most important journalists of the past quarter-century, and Peretz sponsored them all and in certain cases discovered them. You could add in a dozen or two dozen more writers—Charles

Krauthammer, Margaret Talbot, Jonathan Chait, Hanna Rosin, James Wood, Ruth Franklin—whom we perhaps would not have heard of were it not for Peretz. This is to say nothing of Wieseltier, whom Peretz has given rein to run the back of *TNR*'s book for thirty years, to nearly everyone's benefit (I say "nearly" because one is obliged to spill a drop for some of the writers reviewed there).

Peretz's legacy is his magazine. And so the best news the article brings is that Peretz's magazine will soon discontinue the worst thing about it—Peretz's blog.

## Vanity Fair

WINNER—COLUMNS
AND COMMENTARY

*Born in England in 1949 and educated at Oxford, Christopher Hitchens emigrated to the United States in 1981 and joined* Vanity Fair *as a contributing editor in 1992. These are the bare facts; behind them lay a stunningly rich career as a journalist and public intellectual. Hitchens was on a book tour for his memoir* Hitch-22 *when he discovered he had cancer of the esophagus, an episode described with characteristic wit in the first of the articles collected here, "Topic of Cancer." In a series of columns since then, Hitchens has gone on to describe his struggle not only with the disease but with its meaning to his friends and, well, enemies. "Both elegant and moving, these columns display insight and bravery," wrote the National Magazine Award judges. "Christopher Hitchens is the best writer in the worst of times, and we are grateful for him."* Vanity Fair *also won the National Magazine Award for Columns and Commentary in 2007 for work by Hitchens.*

Christopher Hitchens

# Topic of Cancer *and* Unanswerable Prayers *and* Miss Manners and the Big C

## Topic of Cancer

I have more than once in my time woken up feeling like death. But nothing prepared me for the early morning last June when I came to consciousness feeling as if I were actually shackled to my own corpse. The whole cave of my chest and thorax seemed to have been hollowed out and then refilled with slow-drying cement. I could faintly hear myself breathe but could not manage to inflate my lungs. My heart was beating either much too much or much too little. Any movement, however slight, required forethought and planning. It took strenuous effort for me to cross the room of my New York hotel and summon the emergency services. They arrived with great dispatch and behaved with immense courtesy and professionalism. I had the time to wonder why they needed so many boots and helmets and so much heavy backup equipment, but now that I view the scene in retrospect I see it as a very gentle and firm deportation, taking me from the country of the well across the stark frontier that marks off the land of malady. Within a few hours, having had to do quite a lot of emergency work on my heart and my lungs, the physicians at this sad border post had shown me a few other postcards from the interior and told me that my immediate next stop would have to be with an oncologist. Some kind of shadow was throwing itself across the negatives.

The previous evening, I had been launching my latest book at a successful event in New Haven. The night of the terrible morning, I was supposed to go on *The Daily Show* with Jon Stewart and then appear at a sold-out event at the 92nd Street Y, on the Upper East Side, in conversation with Salman Rushdie. My very short-lived campaign of denial took this form: I would not cancel these appearances or let down my friends or miss the chance of selling a stack of books. I managed to pull off both gigs without anyone noticing anything amiss, though I did vomit two times, with an extraordinary combination of accuracy, neatness, violence, and profusion, just before each show. This is what citizens of the sick country do while they are still hopelessly clinging to their old domicile.

The new land is quite welcoming in its way. Everybody smiles encouragingly and there appears to be absolutely no racism. A generally egalitarian spirit prevails, and those who run the place have obviously got where they are on merit and hard work. As against that, the humor is a touch feeble and repetitive, there seems to be almost no talk of sex, and the cuisine is the worst of any destination I have ever visited. The country has a language of its own—a lingua franca that manages to be both dull and difficult and that contains names like ondansetron, for antinausea medication—as well as some unsettling gestures that require a bit of getting used to. For example, an official met for the first time may abruptly sink his fingers into your neck. That's how I discovered that my cancer had spread to my lymph nodes and that one of these deformed beauties—located on my right clavicle, or collarbone—was big enough to be seen and felt. It's not at all good when your cancer is "palpable" from the outside. Especially when, as at this stage, they didn't even know where the primary source was. Carcinoma works cunningly from the inside out. Detection and treatment often work more slowly and gropingly, from the outside in. Many needles were sunk into my clavicle area—"Tissue is the issue" being a hot slogan in the local Tumorville tongue—and I was told the biopsy results might take a week.

Working back from the cancer-ridden squamous cells that these first results disclosed, it took rather longer than that to discover the disagreeable truth. The word "metastasized" was the one in the report that first caught my eye, and ear. The alien had colonized a bit of my lung as well as quite a bit of my lymph node. And its original base of operations was located—had been located for quite some time—in my esophagus. My father had died, and very swiftly, too, of cancer of the esophagus. He was seventy-nine. I am sixty-one. In whatever kind of a "race" life may be, I have very abruptly become a finalist.

· · ·

The notorious stage theory of Elisabeth Kübler-Ross, whereby one progresses from denial to rage through bargaining to depression and the eventual bliss of "acceptance," hasn't so far had much application in my case. In one way, I suppose, I have been "in denial" for some time, knowingly burning the candle at both ends and finding that it often gives a lovely light. But for precisely that reason, I can't see myself smiting my brow with shock or hear myself whining about how it's all so unfair: I have been taunting the Reaper into taking a free scythe in my direction and have now succumbed to something so predictable and banal that it bores even me. Rage would be beside the point for the same reason. Instead, I am badly oppressed by a gnawing sense of waste. I had real plans for my next decade and felt I'd worked hard enough to earn it. Will I really not live to see my children married? To watch the World Trade Center rise again? To read—if not indeed write—the obituaries of elderly villains like Henry Kissinger and Joseph Ratzinger? But I understand this sort of non-thinking for what it is: sentimentality and self-pity. Of course my book hit the best-seller list on the day that I received the grimmest of news bulletins, and for that matter the last flight I took as a healthy-feeling person (to a fine, big audience at the Chicago Book Fair) was the one that made me a million-miler on United Airlines, with a lifetime of free upgrades to look forward to. But irony is my business and I just can't see any ironies here: would it be less poignant to get cancer on the day that my memoirs were remaindered as a box-office turkey, or that I was bounced from a coach-class flight and left on the tarmac? To the dumb question "Why me?" the cosmos barely bothers to return the reply: Why not?

The *bargaining* stage, though. Maybe there's a loophole here. The oncology bargain is that, in return for at least the chance of a few more useful years, you agree to submit to chemotherapy and then, if you are lucky with that, to radiation or even surgery. So here's the wager: you stick around for a bit, but in return we are going to need some things from you. These things may include your taste buds, your ability to concentrate, your ability to digest, and the hair on your head. This certainly appears to be a reasonable trade. Unfortunately, it also involves confronting one of the most appealing clichés in our language. You've heard it all right. People don't have cancer: they are reported to be battling cancer. No well-wisher omits the combative image: You can beat this. It's even in obituaries for cancer losers, as if one might reasonably say of someone that they died after a long and brave struggle with mortality. You don't hear it about long-term sufferers from heart disease or kidney failure.

Myself, I love the imagery of struggle. I sometimes wish I were suffering in a good cause, or risking my life for the good of others, instead of just being a gravely endangered patient. Allow me to inform you, though, that when you sit in a room with a set of other finalists, and kindly people bring a huge transparent bag of poison and plug it into your arm, and you either read or don't read a book while the venom sack gradually empties itself into your system, the image of the ardent soldier or revolutionary is the very last one that will occur to you. You feel swamped with passivity and impotence: dissolving in powerlessness like a sugar lump in water.

. . .

It's quite something, this chemo-poison. It has caused me to lose about fourteen pounds, though without making me feel any lighter. It has cleared up a vicious rash on my shins that no doctor could ever name, let alone cure. (Some venom, to get rid of those furious red dots without a struggle.) Let it please be this mean and ruthless with the alien and its spreading dead-zone colonies. But as against that, the death-dealing stuff and life-preserving stuff have also made me strangely neuter. I was fairly reconciled to the loss of my hair, which began to come out in the shower in the first two weeks of treatment, and which I saved in a plastic bag so that it could help fill a floating dam in the Gulf of Mexico. But I wasn't quite prepared for the way that my razorblade would suddenly go slipping pointlessly down my face, meeting no stubble. Or for the way that my newly smooth upper lip would begin to look as if it had undergone electrolysis, causing me to look a bit too much like somebody's maiden auntie. (The chest hair that was once the toast of two continents hasn't yet wilted, but so much of it was shaved off for various hospital incisions that it's a rather patchy affair.) I feel upsettingly denatured. If Penélope Cruz were one of my nurses, I wouldn't even notice. In the war against Thanatos, if we must term it a war, the immediate loss of Eros is a huge initial sacrifice.

These are my first raw reactions to being stricken. I am quietly resolved to resist bodily as best I can, even if only passively, and

**260**
**Christopher Hitchens**

to seek the most advanced advice. My heart and blood pressure and many other registers are now strong again: indeed, it occurs to me that if I didn't have such a stout constitution I might have led a much healthier life thus far. Against me is the blind, emotionless alien, cheered on by some who have long wished me ill. But on the side of my continued life is a group of brilliant and selfless physicians plus an astonishing number of prayer groups. On both of these I hope to write next time if—as my father invariably said—I am spared.

# Unanswerable Prayers

When I described the tumor in my esophagus as a "blind, emotionless alien," I suppose that even I couldn't help awarding it some of the qualities of a living thing. This at least I know to be a mistake: an instance of the "pathetic fallacy" (angry cloud, proud mountain, presumptuous little Beaujolais) by which we ascribe animate qualities to inanimate phenomena. To exist, a cancer needs a living organism, but it cannot ever *become* a living organism. Its whole malice—there I go again—lies in the fact that the "best" it can do is to die with its host. Either that or its host will find the measures with which to extirpate and outlive it.

But, as I knew before I became ill, there are some people for whom this explanation is unsatisfying. To them, a rodent carcinoma really is a dedicated, conscious agent—a slow-acting suicide-murderer—on a consecrated mission from heaven. You haven't lived, if I can put it like this, until you have read contributions such as this on the websites of the faithful:

> Who else feels Christopher Hitchens getting terminal throat cancer [*sic*] was God's revenge for him using his voice to

blaspheme him? Atheists like to ignore FACTS. They like to act like everything is a "coincidence". Really? It's just a "coincidence" [that] out of any part of his body, Christopher Hitchens got cancer in the one part of his body he used for blasphemy? Yea, keep believing that Atheists. He's going to writhe in agony and pain and wither away to nothing and then die a horrible agonizing death, and THEN comes the real fun, when he's sent to HELLFIRE forever to be tortured and set afire.

There are numerous passages in holy scripture and religious tradition that for centuries made this kind of gloating into a mainstream belief. Long before it concerned me particularly I had understood the obvious objections. First, which mere primate is so damn sure that he can know the mind of god? Second, would this anonymous author want his views to be read by my unoffending children, who are also being given a hard time in their way, and by the same god? Third, why not a thunderbolt for yours truly, or something similarly awe-inspiring? The vengeful deity has a sadly depleted arsenal if all he can think of is exactly the cancer that my age and former "lifestyle" would suggest that I got. Fourth, why cancer at all? Almost all men get cancer of the prostate if they live long enough: it's an undignified thing but quite evenly distributed among saints and sinners, believers and unbelievers. If you maintain that god awards the appropriate cancers, you must also account for the numbers of infants who contract leukemia. Devout persons have died young and in pain. Bertrand Russell and Voltaire, by contrast, remained spry until the end, as many psychopathic criminals and tyrants have also done. These visitations, then, seem awfully random. While my so far uncancerous throat, let me rush to assure my Christian correspondent above, is not *at all* the only organ with which I have blasphemed . . . And even if my voice goes before I do, I shall continue to write polemics against religious delusions, at least until it's hello darkness my old friend. In which case, why not cancer of the brain? As a terrified, half-aware imbecile, I might even scream for a priest at the close of business, though I hereby state while I am still lucid that the entity thus humiliating itself would not in fact be "me." (Bear this in mind, in case of any later rumors or fabrications.)

.   .   .

The absorbing fact about being mortally sick is that you spend a good deal of time preparing yourself to die with some modicum of stoicism (and provision for loved ones), while being simultaneously and highly interested in the business of survival. This is a distinctly bizarre way of "living"—lawyers in the morning and doctors in the afternoon—and means that one has to exist even more than usual in a double frame of mind. The same is true, it seems, of those who pray for me. And most of these are just as "religious" as the chap who wants me to be tortured in the here and now—which I will be even if I eventually recover—and then tortured forever into the bargain if I *don't* recover or, presumably and ultimately, even if I do.

Of the astonishing and flattering number of people who wrote to me when I fell so ill, very few failed to say one of two things. Either they assured me that they wouldn't offend me by offering prayers or they tenderly insisted that they would pray anyway. Devotional websites consecrated special space to the question. (If you should read this in time, by all means keep in mind that September 20 has already been designated "Everybody Pray for Hitchens Day.") Pat Archbold, at the *National Catholic Register,* and Deacon Greg Kandra were among the Roman Catholics who thought me a worthy object of prayer. Rabbi David Wolpe, author of *Why Faith Matters* and the leader of a major congregation in Los Angeles, said the same. He has been a debating partner of mine, as have several Protestant evangelical conservatives like Pastor Douglas Wilson of the New St. Andrews College and Larry Taunton of the Fixed Point Foundation in Birmingham, Alabama. Both wrote to say that their assemblies were praying for me. And it was to them that it first occurred to me to write back, asking: Praying for what?

As with many of the Catholics who essentially pray for me to see the light as much as to get better, they were very honest. Salvation was the main point. "We are, to be sure, concerned for your health, too, but that is a very secondary consideration. 'For what shall it profit a man if he gains the whole world and forfeits his own soul?' [Matthew 16:26.]" That was Larry Taunton. Pastor Wilson responded that when he heard the news he prayed for three things: that I would fight off the disease, that I would make myself right with eternity, and that the process would bring the two of us back into contact. He couldn't resist adding rather puckishly that the third prayer had already been answered . . .

So these are some quite reputable Catholics, Jews, and Protestants who think that I might in some sense of the word be worth saving. The Muslim faction has been quieter. An Iranian friend has asked for prayer to be said for me at the grave of Omar Khayyám, supreme poet of Persian freethinkers. The YouTube video announcing the day of intercession for me is accompanied by the song "I Think I See the Light," performed by the same Cat Stevens who as "Yusuf Islam" once endorsed the hysterical Iranian theocratic call to murder my friend Salman Rushdie. (The banal lyrics of his pseudo-uplifting song, by the way, appear to be addressed to a chick.) And this apparent ecumenism has other contradictions, too. If I were to announce that I had suddenly converted to Catholicism, I know that Larry Taunton and Douglas Wilson would feel I had fallen into grievous error. On the other hand, if I were to join either of their Protestant evangelical groups, the followers of Rome would not think my soul was much safer than it is now, while a late-in-life decision to adhere to Judaism or Islam would inevitably lose me many prayers from both factions. I sympathize afresh with the mighty Voltaire, who, when badgered on his deathbed and urged to renounce the devil, murmured that this was no time to be making enemies.

The Danish physicist and Nobelist Niels Bohr once hung a horseshoe over his doorway. Appalled friends exclaimed that surely he didn't put any trust in such pathetic superstition. "No, I don't," he replied with composure, "but apparently it works whether you believe in it or not." That might be the safest conclusion. The most comprehensive investigation of the subject ever conducted—the "Study of the Therapeutic Effects of Intercessory Prayer," of 2006—could find no correlation at all between the number and regularity of prayers offered and the likelihood that the person being prayed for would have improved chances. But it did find a small but interesting *negative* correlation, in that some patients suffered slight additional woe when they failed to manifest any improvement. They felt that they had disappointed their devoted supporters. And morale is another unquantifiable factor in survival. I now understand this better than I did when I first read it. An enormous number of secular and atheist friends have told me encouraging and flattering things like: "If anyone can beat this, you can"; "Cancer has no chance against someone like you"; "We know you can vanquish this." On bad days, and even on better ones, such exhortations can have a vaguely depressing effect. If I check out, I'll be letting all these comrades down. A different secular problem also occurs to me: what if I pulled through and the pious faction contentedly claimed that their prayers had been answered? That would somehow be irritating.

·　　·　　·

I have saved the best of the faithful until the last. Dr. Francis Collins is one of the greatest living Americans. He is the man who brought the Human Genome Project to completion, ahead of time and under budget, and who now directs the National

Institutes of Health. In his work on the genetic origins of disorder, he helped decode the "misprints" that cause such calamities as cystic fibrosis and Huntington's disease. He is working now on the amazing healing properties that are latent in stem cells and in "targeted" gene-based treatments. This great humanitarian is also a devotee of the work of C. S. Lewis and in his book *The Language of God* has set out the case for making science compatible with faith. (This small volume contains an admirably terse chapter informing fundamentalists that the argument about evolution is over, mainly because there *is* no argument.) I know Francis, too, from various public and private debates over religion. He has been kind enough to visit me in his own time and to discuss all sorts of novel treatments, only recently even imaginable, that might apply to my case. And let me put it this way: he hasn't suggested prayer, and I in turn haven't teased him about *The Screwtape Letters*. So those who want me to die in agony are really praying that the efforts of our most selfless Christian physician be thwarted. Who is Dr. Collins to interfere with the divine design? By a similar twist, those who want me to burn in hell are also mocking those kind religious folk who do not find me unsalvageably evil. I leave these paradoxes to those, friends and enemies, who still venerate the supernatural.

Pursuing the prayer thread through the labyrinth of the web, I eventually found a bizarre "Place Bets" video. This invites potential punters to put money on whether I will repudiate my atheism and embrace religion by a certain date or continue to affirm unbelief and take the hellish consequences. This isn't, perhaps, as cheap or as nasty as it may sound. One of Christianity's most cerebral defenders, Blaise Pascal, reduced the essentials to a wager as far back as the seventeenth century. Put your faith in the almighty, he proposed, and you stand to gain everything. Decline the heavenly offer and you lose everything if the coin falls the other way. (Some philosophers also call this Pascal's Gambit.)

Ingenious though the full reasoning of his essay may be—he was one of the founders of probability theory—Pascal assumes both a cynical god and an abjectly opportunist human being. Suppose I ditch the principles I have held for a lifetime, in the hope of gaining favor at the last minute? I hope and trust that no serious person would be at all impressed by such a hucksterish choice. Meanwhile, the god who would reward cowardice and dishonesty and punish irreconcilable doubt is among the many gods in which (whom?) I do not believe. I don't mean to be churlish about any kind intentions, but when September 20 comes, please do not trouble deaf heaven with your bootless cries. Unless, of course, it makes *you* feel better.

# Miss Manners and the Big C

Ever since I was felled in mid-book tour this summer, I have adored and seized all chances to play catch-up and to keep as many engagements as I can. Debating and lecturing are part of the breath of life to me, and I take deep drafts whenever and wherever possible. I also truly enjoy the face time with you, dear reader, whether or not you bring a receipt for a shiny new copy of my memoirs. But here is what happened while I was waiting to sign copies at an event in Manhattan a few weeks ago. Picture, if you will, me sitting at my table, approached by a motherly-looking woman (a key constituent of my demographic):

SHE:    I was so sorry to hear you had been ill.

ME:    Thank you for saying so.

SHE:    A cousin of mine had cancer.

ME:    Oh, I *am* sorry to hear that.

SHE:    [*As the line of customers lengthens behind her.*] Yes, in his liver.

ME:      That's never good.

SHE:     But it went away, after the doctors had told him it was incurable.

ME:      Well, that's what we all want to hear.

SHE:     [*With those farther back in line now showing signs of impatience.*] Yes. But then it came back, *much* worse than before.

ME:      Oh, how dreadful.

SHE:     And then he died. It was agonizing. *Agonizing.* Seemed to take him forever.

ME:      [*Beginning to search for words.*] . . .

SHE:     Of course, he was a lifelong homosexual.

ME:      [*Not quite finding the words, and not wishing to sound stupid by echoing "of course."*] . . .

SHE:     And his whole immediate family disowned him. He died virtually alone.

ME:      Well, I hardly know what to . . .

SHE:     Anyway, I just wanted you to know that I understand *exactly* what you are going through.

This was a surprisingly exhausting encounter, without which I could easily have done. It made me wonder if perhaps there was room for a short handbook of cancer etiquette. This would apply to sufferers as well as to sympathizers. After all, I have hardly been reticent about my own malady. But nor do I walk around sporting a huge lapel button that reads: ASK ME ABOUT STAGE FOUR METASTASIZED ESOPHAGEAL CANCER, AND ONLY ABOUT THAT. In truth, if you can't bring me news about that and that alone, and about what happens when lymph nodes and lung may be involved, I am not all that interested or all that knowledgeable. One almost develops a kind of elitism about the uniqueness of one's own personal disorder. So, if your own first- or secondhand tale is about some other organs, you might want to consider telling it sparingly, or at least more selectively. This suggestion applies whether the story is intensely depressing and lowering to the spirit—see above—or whether it is intended to convey uplift and optimism: "My grandmother was diagnosed with terminal melanoma of the G-spot and they just about gave up on her. But she hung in there and took huge doses of chemotherapy and radiation at the same time, and the last postcard we had was from her at the top of Mount Everest." Once again, your narrative may fail to grip if you haven't taken any care to find out how well or badly your audience member is faring (or feeling).

•       •       •

It's normally agreed that the question "How are you?" doesn't put you on your oath to give a full or honest answer. So when asked these days, I tend to say something cryptic like, "A bit early to say." (If it's the wonderful staff at my oncology clinic who inquire, I sometimes go so far as to respond, "I seem to have cancer today.") Nobody wants to be told about the countless minor horrors and humiliations that become facts of "life" when your body turns from being a friend to being a foe: the boring switch from chronic constipation to its sudden dramatic opposite; the equally nasty double cross of feeling acute hunger while fearing even the scent of food; the absolute misery of gut-wringing nausea on an utterly empty stomach; or the pathetic discovery that hair loss extends to the disappearance of the follicles in your nostrils, and thus to the childish and irritating phenomenon of a permanently runny nose. Sorry, but you did ask . . . It's no fun to appreciate to the full the truth of the materialist proposition that I don't *have* a body, I *am* a body.

But it's not really possible to adopt a stance of "Don't ask, don't tell," either. Like its original, this is a prescription for hypocrisy and double standards. Friends and relatives, obviously, don't really have the option of not making kind inquiries. One way of trying to put them at their ease is to be as candid as possible and not to adopt any sort of euphemism or denial. So I get straight to the point and say what the odds are. The swiftest way of doing this is to note that the thing about Stage Four is that there is no such thing as Stage Five. Quite rightly, some people take me up on it. I recently had to accept that I wasn't going to be able to attend my niece's wedding, in my old hometown and former university in Oxford. This depressed me for more than one reason, and an especially close friend inquired, "Is it that you're afraid you'll never see England again?" As it happens he was exactly right to ask, and it had been precisely that which had been bothering me, but I was unreasonably shocked by his bluntness. I'll do the facing of hard facts, thanks. Don't you be doing it, too. And yet I had absolutely invited the question. Telling someone else, with deliberate realism, that once I'd had a few more scans and treatments I might be told by the doctors that things from now on could be mainly a matter of "management," I again had the wind knocked out of me when she said, "Yes, I suppose a time comes when you have to consider letting go." How true, and how crisp a summary of what I had just said myself. But again there was the unreasonable urge to have a kind of monopoly on, or a sort of veto over, what was actually sayable. Cancer victimhood contains a permanent temptation to be self-centered and even solipsistic.

.         •         •         •

So my proposed etiquette handbook would impose duties on me as well as upon those who say too much, or too little, in an attempt to cover the inevitable awkwardness in diplomatic relations between Tumortown and its neighbors. If you want an instance of exactly how not to be an envoy from the former, I would offer you both the book and the video of *The Last Lecture*. It would be in bad taste to say that this—a prerecorded farewell by the late professor Randy Pausch—had "gone viral" on the Internet, but so it has. It should bear its own health warning: so sugary that you may need an insulin shot to withstand it. Pausch used to work for Disney and it shows. He includes a whole section in defense of cliché, not omitting: "Other than that, Mrs. Lincoln, how was the play?" The words "kid" or "childhood" and "dream" are employed as if for the very first time. ("Anyone who uses 'childhood' and 'dream' in the same sentence usually gets my attention.") Pausch taught at Carnegie Mellon, but it's the *Dale* Carnegie note that he likes to strike. ("Brick walls are there for a reason . . . to give us a chance to show how badly we want something.") Of course, you don't have to read Pausch's book, but many students and colleagues did have to attend the lecture, at which Pausch did push-ups, showed home videos, mugged for the camera, and generally joshed his head off. It ought to be an offense to be excruciating and unfunny in circumstances where your audience is almost morally obliged to enthuse. This was as much an intrusion, in its way, as that of the relentless motherly persecutor with whom I began. As the populations of Tumortown and Wellville continue to swell and to "interact," there's a growing need for ground rules that prevent us from inflicting ourselves upon one another.

## The Paris Review

WINNER—ESSAYS AND CRITICISM

The Paris Review *was founded in 1953 by George Plimpton, Peter Matthiessen and H. L. Humes; an editorial statement in the first issue was written by William Styron. Yet despite this pedigree, the only National Magazine Award* The Paris Review *had ever won until this year was for Photojournalism, in 2007. But this was not the first National Magazine Award honoring the work of John Jeremiah Sullivan; in 2003, his story "Horseman, Pass By," won the Feature Writing award for* Harper's Magazine *(and also received the Eclipse Award for writing about thoroughbred racing, a likely first for an Ellie winner). Now the Southern editor of* The Paris Review, *Sullivan spent his twenty-first year living as "a kind of apprentice to a man named Andrew Lytle"—a legendarily talented novelist, essayist, and editor. Fifteen years later came this essay, of which the National Magazine Award judges wrote: "Reading it, you can taste the bourbon whiskey and smell the cedar used to build Mister Lytle's coffin."*

John Jeremiah Sullivan

# Mister Lytle:
# An Essay

When I was twenty years old, I became a kind of apprentice to a man named Andrew Lytle, whom pretty much no one apart from his negligibly less ancient sister, Polly, had addressed except as Mister Lytle in at least a decade. She called him Brother. Or *Brutha*—I don't suppose either of them had ever voiced a terminal *r*. His two grown daughters did call him Daddy. Certainly I never felt even the most obscure impulse to call him Andrew, or "old man," or any other familiarism, though he frequently gave me to know it would be all right if I were to call him *mon vieux*. He, for his part, called me boy, and beloved, and once, in a letter, "Breath of My Nostrils." He was about to turn ninety-two when I moved into his basement, and he had not yet quite reached ninety-three when they buried him the next winter, in a coffin I had helped to make—a cedar coffin, because it would smell good, he said. I wasn't that helpful. I sat up a couple of nights in a freezing, starkly lit workshop rubbing beeswax into the boards. The other, older men—we were four altogether—absorbedly sawed and planed. They chiseled dovetail joints. My experience in woodworking hadn't gone past feeding planks through a band saw for shop class, and there'd be no time to redo anything I might botch, so I followed instructions and with rags cut from an undershirt worked coats of wax into the cedar until its ashen whorls glowed purple, as if with remembered life.

The man overseeing this vigil was a luthier named Roehm whose house stood back in the woods on the edge of the plateau. He was about six and a half feet tall with floppy bangs and a deep, grizzled mustache. He wore huge glasses. I believe I have never seen a person more tense than Roehm was during those few days. The cedar was "green"—it hadn't been properly cured. He groaned that it wouldn't behave. On some level he must have resented the haste. Lytle had lain dying for weeks; he endured a series of disorienting pin strokes. By the end they were giving him less water than morphine. He kept saying, "Time to go home," which at first meant he wanted us to take him back to his house, his real house, that he was tired of the terrible simulacrum we'd smuggled him to, in his delirium. Later, as those fevers drew together into what seemed an unbearable clarity, like a blue flame behind the eyes, the phrase came to mean what one would assume.

He had a deathbed, in other words. He didn't go suddenly. Yet although his family and friends had known for years about his wish to lie in cedar, which required that a coffin be custom made, no one had so much as played with the question of who in those mountains could do such a thing or how much time the job would take. I don't hold it against them—against us—the avoidance of duty, owing as it did to fundamental incredulity. Lytle's whole existence had for so long been essentially posthumous, he'd never risk seeming so ridiculous as to go actually dying now. My grandfather had told me once that when *he'd* been at Sewanee, in the thirties, people had looked at Lytle as something of an old man, a full sixty years before I met him. And he nursed this impression, with his talk of coming "to live in the sense of eternity," and of the world he grew up in—Middle Tennessee at the crack of the twentieth century—having more in common with Europe in the Middle Ages than with the South he lived to see. All of his peers and enemies were dead. A middle daughter he had buried long before. His only wife had been dead for thirty-four years, and now Mister Lytle was dead, and we had no cedar coffin.

But someone knew Roehm, or knew about him; and it turned out Roehm knew Lytle's books; and when they told Roehm he'd have just a few days to finish the work, he set to, without hesitation and even with a certain impatience, as if he feared to displease some unforgiving master. I see him there in the little space, repeatedly microwaving Tupperware containers full of burnt black coffee and downing them like Coca-Colas. He loomed. He was so large there hardly seemed room for the rest of us, and already the coffin lid lay on sawhorses in the center of the floor, making us sidle along the walls. At least a couple of times a night Roehm, who was used to agonizing for months over tiny, delicate instruments, would suffer a collapse, would hunch on his stool and bury his face in his hands and bellow "It's all wrong!" into the mute of his palms. My friend Sanford and I stared on. But the fourth, smaller man, a person named Hal, who'd been staying upstairs with Lytle toward the end and acting as a nurse, he knew Roehm better—now that I think of it, Hal must have been the one to tell the family about him in the first place—and Hal would put his hands on Roehm's shoulders and whisper to him to be calm, remind him how everyone understood he'd been allowed too little time, that if he wanted we could take a break. Then Roehm would smoke. I remember he gripped each cigarette with two fingertips on top, snapping it in and out of his lips the way toughs in old movies do. Sanford and I sat outside in his truck with the heater on and drank vodka from a flask he'd brought, gazing on the shed with its small bright window, barely saying a word.

Weeks later he told me a story that Hal had told him, that at seven o'clock in the morning on the day of Lytle's funeral—which strangely Roehm did not attend—Hal woke to find Roehm sitting at the foot of his and his wife's bed, repeating the words "It works," apparently to himself. I never saw him again. The coffin was art. Hardly anyone got to see it. All through the service and down the street to the cemetery it wore a pall, and when people lined up at the graveside to take turns shoveling dirt back into the pit, the hexagonal lid—where inexplicably Roehm had found a spare hour to do scrollwork—grew invisible after just a few seconds.

.    .    .

There had been different boys living at Lytle's since not long after he lost his wife, maybe before—in any case it was a recognized if unofficial institution when I entered the college at seventeen. In former days these were mainly students whose writing showed promise, as judged by a certain well-loved, prematurely white-haired literature professor, himself a former protégé and all but a son during Lytle's long widowerhood. As years passed and Lytle declined, the arrangement came to be more about making sure someone was there all the time, someone to drive him and chop wood for him and hear him if he were to break a hip.

There were enough of us who saw it as a privilege, especially among the English majors. We were students at the University of the South, and Lytle was the South, the last Agrarian, the last of the famous "Twelve Southerners" behind *I'll Take My Stand*, a comrade to the Fugitive Poets, a friend since youth of Allen Tate and Robert Penn Warren; a mentor to Flannery O'Connor and James Dickey and Harry Crews and, as the editor of *The Sewanee Review* in the sixties, one of the first to publish Cormac McCarthy's fiction. Bear in mind that by the midnineties, when I knew him, the so-called Southern Renascence in letters had mostly dwindled to a tired professional regionalism. That Lytle hung on somehow, in however reduced a condition, represented a flaw in time, to be exploited.

Not everyone felt that way. I remember sitting on the floor one night with my freshman-year suitemate, a ninety-five-pound blond boy from Atlanta called Smitty who'd just spent a miserable four years at some private academy trying to convince the drama teacher to let them do a Beckett play. His best friend had been a boy they called Tweety Bird, whose voice resembled a tiny reed flute. When I met Smitty, I asked what music he liked, and he shot back, "*Trumpets.*" That night he went on about Lytle, what a grotesquerie and a fascist he was. "You know what Andrew Lytle said?" Smitty waggled his cigarette lighter. "Listen to this: 'Life is melodrama. Only art is real.'"

I nodded in anticipation.

"Don't you think that's *horrifying?*"

I didn't, though. Or I did and didn't care. Or I didn't know what I thought. I was under the tragic spell of the South, which you've either felt or haven't. In my case it was acute because, having grown up in Indiana with a Yankee father, a child exile from Kentucky roots of which I was overly proud, I'd long been aware of a nowhereness to my life. Others wouldn't have sensed it, wouldn't have minded. I felt it as a physical ache. Finally I was somewhere, there. The South . . . I loved it as only one who will always be outside it can. Merely to hear the word *Faulkner* at night brought gusty emotions. A few months after I'd arrived at the school, Shelby Foote came and read from his Civil War history. When he'd finished, a local geezer with long greasy white hair wearing a white suit with a cane stood up in the third row and asked if, in Foote's opinion, the South could have won, had such and such a general done such and such. Foote replied that the North had won "that war" with one hand behind its back. In the crowd there were gasps. It thrilled me that they cared. How could I help wondering about Lytle, out there beyond campus in his ancestral cabin, rocking before the blazing logs, drinking bourbon from heirloom silver cups and brooding on something Eudora Welty had said to him once. Whenever famous writers

came to visit the school they'd ask to see him. He was from another world. I tried to read his novels, but my mind just rico-
cheted; they seemed impenetrably mannered. Even so, I hoped
to be taken to meet him. One of my uncles had received such an
invitation, in the seventies, and told me how the experience
changed him, put him in touch with what's real.

The way it happened was so odd as to suggest either the involvement or the nonexistence of fate. I wasn't even a student at
the time. I'd dropped out after my sophomore year, essentially
. in order to preempt failing out, and was living in Ireland with a
friend, working in a restaurant and failing to save money. But
before my departure certain things had taken place. I'd become
friends with the man called Sanford, a puckish, unregenerate back-
to-nature person nearing fifty, who lived alone, off the electric
grid, on a nearby communal farm. His house was like something
Jefferson could have invented. Spring water flowed down from an
old dairy tank in a tower on top; the refrigerator had been ret-
rofitted to work with propane canisters that he salvaged from
trailers. He had first-generation solar panels on the roof, a dirt-
walled root cellar, a woodstove. He showered in a waterfall. We
had many memorable hallucinogenic times that did not help my
grades. Sanford needed very little money, but that he made doing therapeutic massage in town, and one of his clients was none
other than Andrew Lytle, who drove himself in once a week, in
his yacht-sized chocolate Eldorado, sometimes in the right lane,
sometimes the left, as he fancied. The cops all knew to follow him
but would do so at a distance, purely to ensure he was safe. Often
he arrived at Sanford's studio hours early, and anxiously waited
in the car. He loved the feeling of human hands on his flesh, he
said, and believed it was keeping him alive.

One day, during their session, Lytle mentioned that his current boy was about to be graduated. Sanford, who didn't know
yet how badly I'd blown it at the school, or that I was leaving, told
Lytle about me and gave him some stories I'd written. Or poems?

Doubtless dreadful stuff—but perhaps it "showed promise." Toward the end of summer airmail letters started to flash in under the door of our hilltop apartment in Cork, their envelopes, I remember, still faintly curled from having been rolled through the heavy typewriter. The first one was dated, "Now that I have come to live in the sense of eternity, I rarely know the correct date, and the weather informs me of the day's advance, but I believe it is late August," and went on to say, "I'm presuming you will live with me here."

That's how it happened, he just asked. Actually, he didn't even ask. The fact that he was ignoring the proper channels eventually caused some awkwardness with the school. But at the time, none of that mattered. I felt an exhilaration, the unsettling thrum of a great man's regard, and somewhere behind that the distant onrushing of fame. His letters came once, then twice a week. They were brilliantly senile, moving in and out of coherence and between tenses, between centuries. Often his typos, his poor eyesight, would produce the finest sentences, as when he wrote the affectingly commaless "This is how I protest absolutely futilely." He told me I was a writer but that I had no idea what I was doing. "This is where the older artist comes in." He wrote about the Muse, how she tests us when we're young. As our tone grew more intimate, his grew more urgent too. I must come back soon. Who knew how much longer he'd live? "No man can forestall or evade what lies in wait." There were things he wanted to pass on, things that had taken him, he said, "too long to learn." Now he'd been surprised to discover a burst of intensity left. He said not to worry about the school. "College is perhaps not the best preparation for a writer." I'd live in the basement, a guest. We'd see to our work.

It took me several months to make it back, and he grew annoyed. When I finally let myself in through the front door, he didn't get up from his chair. His form sagged so exaggeratedly into the sofa, it was as if thieves had crept through and stolen his bones and left him there. He gestured at the smoky stone fireplace with its enormous black andirons and said, "Boy, I'm sorry the wood's so poor. I had no idea I'd be alive in November." He watched as though paralyzed while I worked at building back up the fire. He spoke only to critique my form. The heavier logs at the back, to project the heat. Not too much flame. "Young men always make that mistake." He asked me to pour him some whiskey and announced flatly his intention to nap. He lay back and draped across his eyes the velvet bag the bottle had come tied in, and I sat across from him for half an hour, forty minutes. At first he talked in his sleep, then to me—the pivots of his turn to consciousness were undetectably slight, with frequent slippages. His speech was full of mutterings, warnings. The artist's life is strewn with traps. Beware "the machinations of the enemy."

"Mr. Lytle," I whispered, "who is the enemy?"

He sat up. His unfocused eyes were an icy blue. "Why, boy," he said, "the *bourgeoisie!*" Then he peered at me for a second as if he'd forgotten who I was. "Of course," he said. "You're only a baby."

I'd poured myself two bourbons during nap time and felt them somewhat. He lifted his own cup and said, "Confusion to the enemy." We drank.

•     •     •

It was idyllic, where he lived, on the grounds of an old Chautauqua called the Assembly, one of those rustic resorts—deliberately placed up north, or at a higher altitude—which began as escapes from the plagues of yellow fever that used to harrow the mid-Southern states. Lytle could remember coming there as a child. An old judge, they said, had transported the cabin entire up from a cove somewhere in the nineteenth century. You could still see the logs in the walls, although otherwise the house had been made rather elegant over the years. The porch went all the way around. It was usually silent, except for the wind in the pines. Besides guests, you never saw anyone. A summer place, except Lytle didn't leave.

He slept in a wide carved bed in a corner room. His life was an incessant whispery passage on plush beige slippers from bed to sideboard to seat by the fire, tracing that perimeter, marking each line with light plantings of his cane. He'd sing to himself. The Appalachian one that goes, "A haunt can't haunt a haunt, my good old man." Or songs that he'd picked up in Paris at my age or younger—"Sous les Ponts de Paris" and "Les Chevaliers de la Table Ronde." His French was superb, but his accent in English was best—that extinct mid-Southern, land-grant pioneer speech, with its tinges of the abandoned Celtic urban Northeast ("boyned" for burned) and its raw gentility.

From downstairs I could hear him move and knew where he was in the house at all times. My apartment had once been the kitchen—servants went up and down the back steps. The floor was all bare stone, and damp. And never really warm, until overnight it became unbearably humid. Cave crickets popped around as you tried to sleep, touching down with little clicks. Lots of mornings I woke with him standing over me, cane in one hand, coffee in the other, and he'd say, "Well, my lord, shall we rise and entreat Her Ladyship?" Her ladyship was the Muse. He had all manner of greetings.

For half a year we worked steadily, during his window of greatest coherence, late morning to early afternoon. We read Flaubert, Joyce, a little James, the more famous Russians, all the books he'd written about as an essayist. He tried to make me read Jung. He chopped at my stories till nothing was left but the endings, which he claimed to admire. A too-easy eloquence, was his overall diagnosis. I tried to apply his criticisms, but they were sophisticated to a degree my efforts couldn't repay. He was trying to show me how to solve problems I hadn't learned existed.

About once a day he'd say, "I may do a little writing yet, myself, if my mind holds." One morning I even heard from downstairs the slap-slap of the old electric. That day, while he napped, I slid into his room and pulled off the slipcover to see what he'd done, a single sentence of between thirty and forty words. A couple of them were hyphened out, with substitutions written above in ballpoint. The sentence stunned me. I'd come half-expecting to find an incoherent mess, and afraid that this would say something ominous about our whole experiment, my education, but the opposite confronted me. The sentence was perfect. In it, he described a memory from his childhood, of a group of people riding in an early automobile, and the driver lost control, and they veered through an open barn door, but by a glory of chance the barn was completely empty, and the doors on the other side stood wide open, too, so that the car passed straight through the barn and back out into the sunlight, by which time the passengers were already laughing and honking and waving their arms at the miracle of their own survival, and Lytle was somehow able, through his prose, to replicate this swift and almost alchemical transformation from horror to joy. I don't know why I didn't copy out the sentence—embarrassment at my own spying, I guess. He never wrote any more. But for me it was the key to the year I lived with him. What he could still do, in his weakness, I couldn't do. I started listening harder, even when he bored me.

His hair was sparse and mercury-silver. He wore a tweed jacket every day and, around his neck, a gold-handled toothpick hewn from a raccoon's sharpened bone-penis. I put his glasses onto my own face once and my hands, held just at arm's length, became big beige blobs. There was a thing on his forehead—a cyst, I assume, that had gotten out of control—it was about the size and shape of a bisected Ping-Pong ball. His doctor had offered to remove it several times, but Lytle treated it as a conversation piece. "Vanity has no claim on me," he said. He wore a gray fedora with a bluebird's feather in the band. The skin on his face was strangely young-seeming. Tight and translucent. But the rest of his body was extraterrestrial. Once a week I helped him bathe. God alone knew for how long the moles and things on his back had been left to evolve unseen. His skin was doughy. Not saggy or lumpy, not in that sense—he was hale—but fragile-feeling. He had no hair anywhere below. His toenails were of horn. After the bath he lay naked between fresh sheets, needing to feel completely dry before he dressed. All Lytles, he said, had nervous temperaments.

I found him exotic; it's probably accurate to say that I found him beautiful. The manner in which I related to him was essentially anthropological. Taking offense, for instance, to his more or less daily outbursts of racism, chauvinism, anti-Semitism, class snobbery, and what I can only describe as medieval nostalgia, seemed as absurd as debating these things with a caveman. Shut up and ask him what the cave art means. The self-service and even cynicism of that reasoning are not hard to dissect at a distance of years, but I can't pretend to regret it, or that I wish I had walked away.

There was something else, something less contemptible, a voice in my head that warned it would be unfair to lecture a man with faculties so diminished. I could never be sure what he was saying, as in stating, and what he was simply no longer able to keep from slipping out of his id and through his mouth. I used to walk by his wedding picture, which hung next to the cupboard—the high forehead, the square jaw, the jug ears—and think, as I passed it, "If you wanted to contend with him, you'd have to contend with *that* man." Otherwise it was cheating.

I came to love him. Not in the way he wanted, maybe, but not in a way that was stinting. *Mon vieux*. I was twenty and believed that nothing as strange was liable to happen to me again. I *was* a baby. One night we were up drinking late in the kitchen and I asked him if he thought there was any hope. Like that: "Is there any hope?" He answered me quite solemnly. He told me that in the hallways at Versailles, there hung a faint, ever-so-faint smell of human excrement, "because as the chambermaids hurried along a tiny bit would always splash from the pots." Many years later I realized that he was half-remembering a detail from the court of Louis XV, namely that the latrines were so few and so poorly placed at the palace, the marquesses used to steal away and relieve themselves on stairwells and behind the beautiful furniture, but that night I had no idea what he meant, and still don't entirely.

"Have I shown you my incense burner?" he asked.

"Your what?"

He shuffled out into the dining room and opened a locked glass cabinet door. He came back cradling a little three-legged pot and set it down gently on the chopping block between us. It was exquisitely painted and strewn with infinitesimal cracks. A figure of a dog-faced dragon lay coiled on the lid, protecting a green pearl. Lytle spun the object to a particular angle, where the face was darker, slightly orange-tinged. "If you'll look, the glaze is singed," he said. "From the blast, I presume, or the fires." He held it upside down. Its maker's mark was legible on the bottom, or would have been to one who read Japanese. "This pot," he said, "was recovered from the Hiroshima site." A classmate of his from Vanderbilt, one of the Fugitives, had gone on to become an officer in the Marine Corps and gave it to him after the war. "When I'm dead I want you to have it," he said.

I didn't bother refusing, just thanked him, since I knew he wouldn't remember in the morning, or, for that matter, in half an hour. But he did remember. He left it to me.

Ten years later in New York City my adopted stray cat Holly Kitty pushed it off a high shelf I didn't think she could reach, and it shattered. I sat up most of the night gluing the slivers back into place.

.        .        .

Lytle's dementia began to progress more quickly. I hope it's not cruel to note that at times the effects could be funny. He insisted on calling the K-Y Jelly we used to lubricate his colostomy tube *Kyé Jelly*. Finally he got confused on what it was for and appeared in my doorway one day with his toothbrush and a squeezed-out tube of the stuff. "Put *Kye* on the list, boy," he said. "We're out."

Evenings he'd mostly sit alone and rehash forty-year-old fights with dead literary enemies, performing both sides as though in a one-man play, at times yelling wildly, pounding his cane. Allen Tate, his brother turned nemesis, was by far the most frequent opponent, but it seemed in these rages that anyone he'd ever known could change into the serpent, fall prey to an obsession with power. Particularly disorienting was when the original version of the mock battle had been between him and me. Him and the Boy. Several times, in reality, we did clash. Stood face-to-face shouting. I called him a mean old bastard, something like that; he told me I'd betrayed my gift. Later, from downstairs, I heard him say to the Boy, "You think you're not a *slave*?"

There was a day when I came in from somewhere. Polly, his sister, was staying upstairs. I loved Miss Polly's visits—everyone did. She made rum cakes you could eat yourself to death on like a goldfish. There were homemade pickles and biscuits from scratch when she came. A tiny woman with glasses so thick they magnified her eyes, her knuckles were cubed with arthritis. Who knew what she thought, or if she thought, about all the nights she'd shared with her brother and his interesting artist friends. (Once, in a rented house somewhere, she'd been forced by sleeping arrangements to lie awake in bed all night between fat old Ford Madox Ford and his mistress.) She shook her head over how the iron skillet, which their family had been seasoning in slow ovens since the Depression, would suffer at my hands. I had trouble remembering not to put it through the dishwasher. Over meals, under the chandelier with the "saltcellar" and the "salad oil," as Lytle raved about the master I might become, if only I didn't fall into this, that, or the other hubristic snare, she'd simply grin and say, "Oh, Brutha, how *exciting*."

On the afternoon in question I was coming through the security gate, entering "the grounds," as cottagers called the Assembly, and Polly passed me going the opposite way in her minuscule blue car. There was instantly something off about the encounter, because she didn't stop completely—she rolled down the window and yelled at me, but continued to idle past, going at most twenty miles per hour (the speed limit in there was twelve, I think), as if she were waving from a parade float. "I'm on my way to the store," she said. "We need [*mumble*] . . ."

"What's that?"

"BUTTAH!"

I watched with a bad feeling as she receded in the mirror. Back at the cabin, Lytle was caning around on the front porch in a panic. He waved at me as I turned into the gravel patch where we parked. "She's drunk!" he barked. "Look at this bottle, beloved. Good God, it was full this morning!"

I tried to make him tell me what had happened, but he was too antsy. He wore pajamas, black slippers without socks, a gray tweed coat, and the fedora.

"Oh, I've angered her, beloved," he said. "I've angered her."

As we sped toward the gate, he gave me the story. It was as I suspected. The same argument came up every time Polly visited, though I'd never seen it escalate so. They had family in a distant town with whom she remained on decent terms, but Lytle insisted on shunning these people and thought his little sister should as well. It had to do with an old scandal about land, duplicity involving a will. A greedy uncle had tried to take away his father's farm. But these modern-day cousins, descendants of the rival party, they weren't pretending, as Lytle believed, not to understand why he wouldn't see them—I think they were genuinely confused. There'd been scenes. He'd stood in the doorway and denounced these people, in the highest rhetoric, "Seed of the usurper." They must have thought he was further gone mentally than he was, that when he uttered these curses he had in mind some carpetbagger from olden days, because the relatives just kept coming back, despite never having been allowed past the porch steps. Now Miss Polly had let them into the vestibule, nearly into the Court of the Muse. Lytle viewed this as the wildest betrayal. He'd been beastly toward them, when he rose from his nap, and Polly had fled. He himself seemed shaken to remember the things he'd said.

"Mister Lytle, what did you say?"

"I told the truth," he said passionately. "I recognized the moment, that's what I did." But in the defensive thrust of his jaw there quivered something like embarrassment.

He mentions this land dispute in his "family memoir," *A Wake for the Living*, his most readable and in many ways his best book. That's perhaps an idiosyncratic opinion. There are people who've read a lot more than I have who consider his novels lost classics. But it may be precisely because of the Faustian ego that thundered above his sense of himself as a novelist that he carried a lighter burden into the memoir, and this freedom thawed in his style some of the vivacity and spontaneity that otherwise you find only in the letters. There's a scene in which he describes the morning his grandmother was shot in the throat by a Union soldier in 1863. "Nobody ever knew who he was or why he did it," Lytle writes, "he mounted a horse and galloped out of town." To the end of her long life this woman wore a velvet ribbon at her neck, fastened with a golden pin. That's how close Lytle was to the Civil War. Close enough to reach up as a child, passing into sleep, and fondle the clasp of that pin. The eighteenth century was just another generation back from there, and so on, hand to hand. This happens, I suppose, this collapsing of time, when you make it as far as your nineties. When Lytle was born, the Wright Brothers had not yet achieved a working design. When he died, Voyager II was exiting the solar system. What do you do with the coexistence of those details in a lifetime's view? It weighed on him.

The incident with his grandmother is masterfully handled:

> She ran to her nurse. The bullet had barely missed the jugular vein. Blood darkened the apple she still held in her hand, and blood was in her shoe. The enemy in the street now invaded the privacy of the house. The curious entered and stared. They confiscated the air. . . . To the child's fevered gaze the long bayonets of the soldiers seemed to reach the ceiling, as they filed past her bed, staring out of boredom and curiosity.

Miss Polly passed us again. Apparently she'd changed her mind about the butter. We made a U-turn and trailed her to the cabin. Back inside they embraced. She buried her face in his coat, laughing and weeping. "Oh, sister," he said, "I'm such an old fool, god-*damn* it."

· · ·

I've wished at times that we had endured some meaningful falling-out. In truth he began to exasperate me in countless petty ways. He needed too much, feeding and washing and shaving and dressing, more than he could admit to and keep his pride. Anyone could sympathize, but I hadn't signed on to be his butler. One day I ran into the white-haired professor, who shared with me that Lytle had been complaining about my cooking.

Mainly, though, I'd fallen in love with a tall, nineteen-year-old half-Cuban girl from North Carolina, with freckles on her face and straight dark hair down her back. She was a class behind mine, or what would have been mine, at the school, and she could talk about books. On our second date she gave me her father's roughed-up copy of *Hunger*, the Knut Hamsun novel. I started to spend more time downstairs. Lytle became pitifully upset. When

I invited her in to meet him, he treated her coldly, made some vaguely insulting remark about "Latins," and at one point asked her if she understood a woman's role in an artist's life.

There came a wickedly cold night in deep winter when she and I lay asleep downstairs, wrapped up under a pile of old comforters on twin beds we'd pushed together. By now the whole triangle had grown so unpleasant that Lytle would start drinking earlier than usual on days when he spotted her car out back, and she no longer found him amusing or, for that matter, I suppose, harmless. My position was hideous.

She shook me awake and said, "He's trying to talk to you on the thing." We had this antiquated monitor system, the kind where you depress the big silver button to talk and let it off to hear. The man hadn't mastered an electrical device in his life. At breakfast one morning, when I'd made the mistake of leaving my computer upstairs after an all-nighter, he screamed at me for "bringing the enemy into this home, into a place of work." Yet he'd become a bona fide technician on the monitor system.

"He's calling you," she said. I lay still and listened. There was a crackling.

"*Beloved,*" he said, "*I hate to disturb you, in your slumbers, my lord. But I believe I might freeze to DEATH up here.*"

"Oh, my God," I said.

"*If you could just . . . lie beside me.*"

I looked at her. "What do I do?"

She turned away. "I wish you wouldn't go up there," she said.

"What if he dies?"

"You think he might?"

"I don't know. He's ninety-two, and he says he's freezing to death."

"*Beloved . . . ?*"

She sighed. "You should probably go up there."

He didn't speak as I slipped into his bed. He fell back asleep instantly. The sheets were heavy white linen and expensive. It seemed there were shadowy acres of snowy terrain between his limbs and mine. I floated off.

When I woke at dawn he was nibbling my ear and his right hand was on my genitals.

I sprang out of bed and began to hop around the room like I'd burned my finger, sputtering foul language. Lytle was already moaning in shame, fallen back in bed with his hand across his face like he'd just washed up somewhere, a piece of wrack. I should mention that he wore, as on every chill morning, a Wee Willie Winkie–style nightshirt and cap. "Forgive me, forgive me," he said.

"Jesus Christ, Mister Lytle."

"Oh, beloved . . ."

His having these desires wasn't the issue. I couldn't be that naïve. His tastes in that area were more or less an open secret. I don't know if he was gay or bisexual or pansexual or what. Those distinctions are clumsy terms in which to address the mysteries of sexuality. But on a few occasions he'd spoken about his wife in a manner that to me was movingly erotic, nothing like any self-identifying gay man I've ever heard talk about women and sex. Certainly Lytle had loved her, because it was clear how he missed her, Edna, his beautiful "squirrel-eyed gal from Memphis," whom he'd married when she was young, who was still young when she died of throat cancer.

Much more often, however, when the subject of sex came up, he would return to the idea of there having been a homoerotic side to the Agrarian movement itself. He told me that Allen Tate propositioned him once, "but I turned him down. I didn't like his smell. You see, smell is so important, beloved. To me he had the stale scent of a man who didn't take any exercise." This may or may not have been true, but it wasn't an isolated example. Later writers—including some with an interest in not playing up the issue—have noticed, for instance, Robert Penn Warren's more-than-platonic interest in Tate, when they were all at Vanderbilt together. One of the other Twelve Southerners, Stark Young—he's rarely mentioned—was openly gay. Lytle professed to have carried on, as a very young man, a happy, sporadic affair with the brother of another Fugitive poet, not a well-known person. At one point the two of them fantasized about living together, on a small farm. The man later disappeared and turned up murdered in Mexico. Warren mentions him in a poem that plays with the image of the closet.

The point—the reason I risk being seen to have "outed" a man who trusted me, and was vulnerable when he did—is that you can't fully understand that movement, which went on to influence American literature for decades, without understanding that certain of the men involved in it loved one another. Most "homosocially," of course, but a few homoerotically, and some homosexually. That's where part of the power originated that made those friendships so intense and caused the men to stay united almost all their lives, even after spats and changes of opinion, even after their Utopian hopes for the South had died. Together they produced from among them a number of good writers, and even a great one, in Warren, whom they can be seen to have lifted, as if on wing beats, to the heights for which he was destined.

Lytle himself would have beaten me with his cane and thrown me out for saying all of that. To him it was a matter for winking and nodding, frontier sexuality, fraternity brothers falling into bed with each other and not thinking much about it. Or else it was Hellenism, golden lads in the Court of the Muse. William Alexander Percy stuff. Whatever it was, I accepted it. I never showed displeasure when he wanted to sit and watch me chop wood, or when he asked me to quit showering every morning, so that he could smell me better. "I'm pert' near blind, boy," he said. "How will I find you in a fire?" Still, I'd taken for granted an understanding between us. I didn't expect him to grope me like a chambermaid.

I stayed away two nights, and then went back. When I reached the top of the steps and looked through the back-porch window, I saw him on the sofa lying asleep (or dead—I wondered every time). His hands were folded across his belly. One of them rose and hung quivering, an actor's wave; he was talking to himself. It turned out, when I cracked the door, he was talking to me.

"Beloved, now, we must forget this," he said. "I merely wanted to touch it a little. You see, I find it the most *interesting* part of the body."

Then he paused and said, "Yes," seeming to make a mental note that the phrase would do.

"I understand, you have the girl now," he continued. "Woman offers the things a man must have, home and children. And she's a lovely girl. I myself may not have made the proper choices, in that role . . ."

I closed the door and crept down to bed.

Not long after that, I moved out, both of us agreeing it was for the best. I re-enrolled at the school. They found someone else to live with him. It had become more of a medical situation by that point, at-home care. I drove out to see him every week, and I think he welcomed the visits, but things had changed. He knew how to adjust his formality by tenths of a degree, to let you know where you stood.

.     .     .

It may be gratuitous to remark of a ninety-two-year-old man that he began to die, but Lytle had been much alive for most of that year, fiercely so. There were some needless minor surgeries at one point, which set him back. It's funny how the living will help the dying along. One night he fell, right in front of me. He was standing in the middle room on a slippery carpet, and I was moving toward him to take a glass from his hand. The next instant he was flat on his back with a broken elbow that during the night bruised horribly, blackly. His eyes went from glossy to matte. Different people took turns staying over with him, upstairs, including the white-haired professor, whose loyalty had never wavered. I spent a couple of nights. I wasn't worried he'd try anything again. He was in a place of calm and—you could see it—preparation. His son-in-law told me he'd spoken my name the day before he died.

When the coffin was done, the men from the funeral home picked it up in a hearse. Late the same night someone called to say they'd finished embalming Lytle's body; it was in the chapel, and whenever Roehm was ready, he could come and fasten the lid. All of us who'd worked on it with him went, too. The mortician let us into a glowing side hallway off the cold ambulatory. With us was an old friend of Lytle's named Brush, who worked for the school administration, a low-built bouncy muscular man with boyish dark hair and a perpetual bowtie. He carried, as nonchalantly as he could, a bowling-ball bag, and in the bag an extremely excellent bottle of whiskey.

Brush took a deep breath, reached into the coffin, and jammed the bottle up into the crevice between Lytle's ribcage and his left arm. He quickly turned and said, "That way they won't hear it knocking around when we roll it out of the church."

Roehm had a massive electric drill in his hand. It seemed out of keeping with the artisanal methods that had gone into the rest of the job, but he'd run out of time making the cedar pegs. We stood over Lytle's body. Sanford was the first to kiss him. When everyone had, we lowered the lid onto the box, and Roehm screwed it down. Somebody wished the old man Godspeed. A eulogy that ran in the subsequent number of *The Sewanee Review* said that, with Lytle's death, "the Confederacy at last came to its end."

He appeared to me only once afterward, and that was two and a half years later, in Paris. It's not as if Paris is a city I know or have even visited more than a couple of times. He knew it well. I was coming up the stairs from the metro into the sunshine with the girl, whom I later married, on my left arm, when my senses became intensely alert to his presence about a foot and a half to my right. I couldn't look directly at him; I had to let him hang back in my peripheral vision, else he'd slip away; it was a bargain we made in silence. I could see enough to tell that he wasn't young but was maybe twenty years younger than when I'd known him, wearing the black-framed engineer's glasses he'd worn at just that time in his life, looking up and very serious, climbing the steps to the light, where I lost him.

## The Antioch Review

FINALIST—ESSAYS
AND CRITICISM

*After his father is killed—crushed between a motorcycle and the guardrail on a winding country road—William Giraldi searches out every piece of information about the accident. He travels to Pennsylvania to inspect the site of the accident, talks to those who were there, telephones the coroner for a description of the fatal injuries, interviews the mechanic who inspected the motorcycle after the crash, and finally sits astride the machine itself. "William Giraldi's essay clamps your attention with a viselike grip," wrote the National Magazine Award judges. "Almost unbearably emotional, it is as precisely engineered, flawless, gorgeous and unsparing as the motorcycle that killed his father." Giraldi teaches in the Arts and Sciences Writing Program at Boston University. His novel* Busy Monsters *was published in August 2011.* The Antioch Review *was also nominated for National Magazine Awards in 2010 for Uwe Timm's story "The Coat" and in 2009 for Maureen McCoy's essay "Vickie's Pour House: A Soldier's Peace."*

William Giraldi

# The Physics
# of Speed

I f I hadn't been so unhinged by my father's death, and if someone had asked me to participate in the laying to rest of his
body, I would have insisted that he be buried in his frayed
work clothes, in a pine coffin that my grandfather and uncles
had constructed with their own hands, using my father's own
tools. I would have vetoed the unspeakable business of embalming. Those sick clowns sewed a smile on his face. They no doubt
believe they honor death with all that prettification, but really
they mock it, turn it into a minstrel show, a spooky carnival.

What did they do with my father's blood after they drained it
from him? And what did they discuss as they pumped the fuming formaldehyde into his body? The Yankees? Descartes's laugh-
able proofs for the existence of God, or the universe as conceived
by Leibnitz, the harmonious result of a divinity's will? Desperate families like my own are to blame for the nasty, bewildering work of the mortician. They would rather have seen my father
made up like a life-size doll than confront the inevitability of
all flesh.

Loved ones like to say, "The funeral home was packed, standing room only. I had no idea how many people were touched by
so-and-so." Few, I think, are ushered out the way Jay Gatsby is:
in solitude, the world indifferent. At my father's viewing there was
a line from the casket, through the room, out the double doors,

down the hall, out the front door, around the building, and into the parking lot, which wasn't spacious enough to accommodate all the Buicks, Fords, and Cadillacs. I wasn't aware of this at the time because I was sitting in a stupor with my girlfriend and my family at the casket.

Earlier in the day my brother and I had asked my grandfather if it was acceptable to display a large photograph of my father and his motorcycle, a red and white Yamaha YZF R1, one of the fastest super-bikes in production. That was the first thing you saw upon entering the room: this photo of my father smiling behind the machine that killed him. My brother and I wanted it there because that machine was his talent. For years, as we were growing up, my father hadn't been able to afford such a bike. When he was finally able, he kept it under a special blanket in the garage, and shined it lovingly with new socks. When he and his friends went on riding trips he brought the bike inside the motel room with him. He modified it with the best accessories. In his black and red professional racing suit and gleaming black Shoei helmet, he looked like a demon.

But you should have seen us in front of the casket before the hundreds of viewers arrived: my entire family in a semicircle, overcome with moans, trying to hold each other up, gaping at my father and that sinister smile sewn on his face. The rouge and lipstick were perverse, even though the mortician, in her faux sympathetic voice, had told us before entering that "he looks great," as if he had just had a haircut. The texture of his skin was about what I had expected: plastic, like a Halloween mask. His fingers were sewn together, his eyelids sewn shut.

I remembered, as a teenager, my grandmother telling me that she had never, in all her years of being married to him, seen my grandfather cry. Many of us thought he was incapable of it. But now his giant frame shook with sobs when we left him alone at the casket, and I could only guess what he was thinking: that this mess was his fault because he had passed along his obsession with motorcycles to my father, had taught him to ride, and was the one person who had had the power to dissuade him from that obsession, to convince him that the dangers outweighed the pleasures. He never did because he knew he didn't have the right. No one had the right to ask him to stop riding, to forfeit his passion for speed. And so we couldn't save him.

.       .       .

In the following days I learned that absence takes up space, has mass, moves from room to room. Grief is much heavier than fear. Fear hung before me in anticipation, whereas the grief was planted like a sequoia in my stomach, its roots reaching far down into my legs for water, its branches reaching up through my arms and torso and neck, the poison from its fruit spilling into my cells.

Each terrible dawn stretched across the day and illuminated my father's absence.

Sometime soon after the funeral I told my grandmother that the worst lay behind us: the shock, the preparations, the viewing and burial. I didn't mean it, though; I knew the worst was ahead, would always be ahead. Not having my father as witness and counsel to my and my brother's lives, as grandfather to our children, as escort down the aisle for my sister, unleashed in me a monstrous sorrow, one that caused me to coil up in a corner and pound the carpet with my fist. But this was the anticipation of future regret, and I had quite enough perplexity and distress in the present: namely, the growing obsession with how my father crashed his cycle into that Pennsylvania guardrail.

Different stories had been filtering in from the half-dozen riding partners he was with that day, and some of the stories made little sense to me. My father had complained of brake problems at the gas station just prior to the crash; he planned to lag behind, let someone else lead. Yamaha had recently issued a recall on some portion of the R1's braking system; my father never changed the brakes, and so most of the guys were convinced that his brakes failed when he went into that turn, because an expert rider doesn't just crash into a guardrail for no reason. Two guys claimed they heard my father say, "I don't feel well," a sentence that was not in his vocabulary. Someone who sees the stoic endurance of pain as a sign of election does not complain of feeling unwell. Did he have a heart attack or heat stroke? Someone offered the idea that a deer might have bounced out in front of him, but not two minutes earlier a multitude of screaming engines sped down the road sounding like the goddamn apocalypse; no deer runs out into that unless it's deaf.

Supposedly there was a disgruntled old man in a pickup truck, not pleased by the earsplitting machines passing him illegally at a hundred miles an hour. Someone floated the absurd speculation that, because my father was taking it easy at the rear of the pack, this farmer ran him down into the guardrail. Even a five-year-old can tell you that it's not possible for a pickup truck to gain ground on a Yamaha R1. If my father had seen in his mirror an angry truck getting too close, all he would have had to do is downshift from third to second gear, crank the throttle, and in three seconds there would have been a football field between his back tire and the truck's front grille.

And there was something else nagging at me: my father had mounted a miniature digital camera to the anterior of the bike so he could study his riding style and make improvements for the following Sunday. But the camera was missing, and it took me a few days to discover that one of his riding partners had taken it before the police arrived on the scene. He knew the evidence would reveal many traffic illegalities. This information created a mass in my throat that would not dissolve: a person I didn't know was in possession of my father's camera, and on that camera was most probably the crash that killed him. I made angry phone calls until the camera was returned, but I didn't watch the footage.

No one witnessed my father hit the guardrail. The pack was pushing hard down the sinuous blacktop. The place he hit was a ninety-degree right turn just over a crest in the road. My uncle Tony told me this from experience: "He was on a road he didn't know, and he's trying to take it easy while the other guys are hauling ass ahead of him. He's afraid he'll get lost, won't be able to find his way back to the highway. It happens all the time. You get lost you're screwed. So he speeds up to try and catch them. There's that crown in the road, and the sharp right turn just beyond it. He had what's called a high-side. As soon as he saw the turn he locked up the back brake, which you never do unless you're going a hundred-and-five and need to stop fast. Mostly your brake work is done with the front brake. So as the back brake locks the bike doesn't want to stay up, it wants to go over, one way or the other. When your father felt the bike slipping under him to the right, he tried to save it. He didn't want to low-side; he was thinking about the bike. And when he straightened up to the left, the tires caught on the road and flung him like a slingshot over the bike, into the guardrail, headfirst. This all happened in two seconds or less. If he had let the bike slide from under him to the right, without trying to straighten up and save it, he would have gone feet-first into the side of the road and got up to walk away, no problem."

There was a crack in my father's helmet; my uncle had taken it from the hospital and washed an entire gallon of blood from it in the kitchen sink. It's difficult to crack a helmet; it told us that my father struck the guardrail with frightening force, causing three injuries, any one of which was fatal: a broken neck, a crushed throat, and massive brain trauma. When the pack realized he wasn't behind them they waited; when he didn't show they turned around and found him half beneath the guardrail, the bike half on top of him, blood streaming from his helmet and settling in a thick pool around his head and shoulders. The old man in the pickup truck was there, and a couple who lived in the house nearby, and some others who had stopped. Another rider claimed he heard my father say "Oh God," and saw him move his arm on top of his chest as he was being lifted into the ambulance.

.     .     .

A day or so after the burial the men of my family made the hour-and-fifteen-minute drive to the crash site, to the town of Springfield in Bucks County, Pennsylvania. My grandfather, unwilling or unable to see the site, opted to remain behind; so my two uncles, my cousin, my brother, and I left Jersey before nine in the morning on a day when the weather matched perfectly the day that saw my father's death. Before we left, my grandmother had given me a white wooden cross to pound into the soil near the spot where he died; I took it without protest. I couldn't decide how I felt about the name of the road he died on: Slifer Valley. It reminded me of Robert Lowell's words "a savage servility slides by on grease." The name suggested sinews and dips, reptilian, perilous. Eliminate the first and last letters and you are left with the word "life." How many winding miles did the two-lane, double-lined pavement cut through that beautiful, lush valley?

The spot was secluded, near a bubbling brook. Trees formed a canopy overhead and farmland lay in the distance. The road was serene; few cars passed. We parked off to the side. There was a smear from my father's helmet on the guardrail, and beneath it, soaked into the macadam, was a dark circle of his blood. The blood is not the life; the blood is the death. In the road I found pieces of the bike: white and red paint chips, small plastic shards, and a steel foot peg. Up the road about thirty yards, in the direction we had come, was the crest, and on the near side of it we saw where the two hideous skid marks began: they were each more than fifty feet in length, punctuated by a space of forty feet.

No one wanted to believe that the accident was my father's fault, but the long skid marks were evidence that the bike was traveling at an insane speed as it emerged over the crest—he must have seen that ninety-degree turn waiting like a grave. My grandmother, especially, was eager to blame someone or something: the brakes, his riding partners, the old man in the pickup truck. Anybody but my father. My grandfather, too, was convinced that my father wasn't speeding because there was relatively little damage to the bike. If my father had been doing a hundred miles an hour, he reasoned, the bike would have been demolished. It would take me a week or so to formulate my own theory as to why the bike suffered just a gouge in the gas tank.

The middle-aged couple from the nearby house came out to greet us. They hadn't seen the crash but went to my father's side soon afterward. The husband wore aviator glasses; he looked to be recovering from extensive plastic surgery. I have no memory of the wife.

We shook hands, introduced ourselves, and then the husband said, "I unbuckled the helmet strap and told him to hang on, that help was on the way."

"That means a lot to us," I said.

"Anybody would have done it. It's what a person does in a situation like that. What was his name?"

"William Giraldi," I said. "The third."

He looked at his wife, then back at us, and said, "Our son was the third William, as well. He was killed, five years ago, on April 7, just one month earlier than your father. Same day, though. Someone shot him in the head. Only thirty years old. We never found the killer. It's a funny thing, both of them William, dying on the same day."

My brother glanced at my cousin, my cousin glanced at me, and both my uncles didn't know where to look. They just nodded, maybe in agreement of some kind, or understanding. I couldn't see the husband's eyes behind his dark glasses, and for some reason it occurred to me that he might not have eyes at all, just two black holes in his face.

I said, "There was an old man here at the crash, right? An old fella in a pickup truck?"

"Yes," he said. "He wasn't happy. When the other guys arrived he kept screaming at them, saying, See what happens? See what you did? At one point he wanted to drag your father out from underneath the guardrail, get the bike off him, but I said not to. Said it was best to wait for the paramedics. He was very concerned, though. His hand was crippled, very strange. He unloosened your father's jacket to give him some more air. There were some others here, too. Everybody was very concerned about him."

I wanted to interview this couple, ask them specific questions about the details of that day, what they saw and how it seemed to them; but I couldn't do it just then. The husband gave me his telephone number and told me I could call him; we had this between us now, this bond, this affiliation of grief: his son, my father, both named William, both dead long before their time, dead on the same day, their deaths tinged with mystery, no completion, no comfort.

As my uncles, brother, and cousin pounded the wooden cross into the earth, I squatted at the guardrail, my father's presence all but palpable to me:

*What did you expect on the other side of that crest, at a speed I cannot guess or ever dare to approach, the foliage a brown and green blur on either side of you, this blacktop meander disappearing on the horizon? My days will be ravished by wonder, picturing these Pennsylvania paths of asphalt and your ferocious color cutting a gash through the countryside. Your death is black and red, bright white and chrome, all around me. Now my own life shrinks and grows on this road, at this unkind ninety-degree turn you didn't see until much too late, the guardrail curving around it like a metal net that does not work. Where are we now? How can our planet expend the energy to turn? I want to sink into this spot, this place that claimed you, to see for myself in hope of believing, of understanding. I can see you, lying here, life bleeding out your ears and nose, your blue eyes unblinking at the diminishing sky. Perhaps a lone thought survives long enough to let you know: this Sunday will never end, and the race is underway. The ruin in the wake belongs to me. Who will reverse the heart and allow our blood to run backward? How can I choose to live in the hypothesis of reverse? Dad, what did you do?*

Before we departed that day I tried to memorize everything about that road and its surroundings: the trees, the brook, the fields in the distance, the homes set back on acres of property. I don't know why I have no memory of the yellow sign before the crest that warns of the ninety-degree turn ahead, a posted speed limit of just 20 mph. Why didn't he see that sign? That day was the only time I've ever been there, although I've been tempted to return. The place, of course, is haunted.

· · ·

My brother and I had the dismal task of going through my father's van, sorting through the tools and papers. A hopeless chocolate fiend—a taste I've inherited—my father had littered the van with candy and cookie wrappers. We smiled at this. The letters I had written him over the years, and some of the photos I had mailed him—from Myrtle Beach and Boston—were stuffed into one of the overhead compartments. I wanted to save everything, every receipt and scrap of paper that showed his handwriting. Since my brother lived in Colorado we agreed that the van would go to me, and indeed I would drive it for the next two years. My brother wanted the tools, all the instruments my father had touched and built with.

There was still the hurtful business of going through his clothes and all the things he had packed in the basement of his town-house. I discovered that my father, like me, hoarded everything: cards and letters, photos and notebooks, knickknacks and pamphlets. I found letters my mother had written to him, and a letter she had written to me during our two-year estrangement when I was in high school. Her words revealed a frigid personality, a woman deluded by a grandiose sense of self. I shuddered when I read them.

And I remembered this: When I was fifteen, my first girlfriend broke up with me for another boy, and of course I was distraught, the first real sadness of my life. One afternoon, in the strong sunlight of our spacious kitchen, my father asked me what the hell was the matter, when I was going to snap out of it. Move on, he said, you're fifteen, these things happen every day. I went into my room, found the sappy love notes the girlfriend had written to me, and returned to show them to my father. "Here," I said, thrusting them at him. "Read these and maybe you'll understand."

He unfolded the pages and read the girl's ridiculous words of love and always. Very carefully he refolded the notes and said, "Come with me, I want to show you something." In our garage, in an old cedar chest, my father had stockpiled every note, letter, and card my mother had ever written to him, fifteen years' worth. He thrust his hand into the chest, yanked out a fistful of paper, and said, "It's all bullshit. It doesn't mean anything. Words, that's all. Empty, useless words. Your actions are what count in this world. What you do. A person's words aren't worth shit." It didn't make me feel any better at the time, but the significance of that gesture would follow me for years. I wish I could say that my father and I took the cedar chest into the back yard and set it ablaze, the two of us standing together staring at the fire, at all my mother's untrue words disappearing in black smoke.

.        .        .

My girlfriend, Adra, and I spent the summer of 2000 at my godfather's newly renovated house in suburban Maplewood, New Jersey. I had received some cash from my father's estate—blood money—so neither of us had to work for the time being. We resigned ourselves to a regimen of reading, walking into town to browse and shop, barbecuing on the grill, sunbathing in the back yard, and watching films. And I waited, day after day, for the collapse, for melancholy to come and clobber me hard about the head.

At night, as Adra and I lay in bed after making urgent love, I'd be tormented by visions of my father crashing into the guardrail. I'd play it repeatedly in my mind, trying to see it, trying to comprehend how it happened, the unkind laws of physics that made it possible. Gravity, velocity, trajectory, Newton with his pencil and pad. I began thinking about the absurd fragility of the human skull, how it cracks like an unboiled egg, how unprotected we are in this life, no sufficient armor to shield us, our flesh easily torn, our bones easily shattered, veins and arteries snapping under pressure. Rubber, steel, and macadam came to seem like the most ominous inventions. The human form is not fit for this world; a house is a more reliable structure, an automobile more resilient. I fell victim to magical thinking—I had a child's belief that I could somehow undo what happened, that I could buy back my father from who or what had taken him. The money he left my siblings and me must have been causing me guilt, because I wanted to trade that money for his life, and actually thought—however fleetingly—that if I could just find the right person I could hand over the money and walk out with my father.

When I received the death certificate I was stunned to learn that the coroner's name was Grim, Steven Grim. With a name like that he must have felt his profession had always been inevitable. To name a coroner Grim in a piece of fiction would be a bad idea, and yet reality delivers us these bad ideas and then leaves us to ponder them. In the section titled "Immediate Cause" he had written "MULTIPLE TRÁUMATIC INJURIES" in caps, and underneath it "MOTORCYCLE ACCIDENT." But I needed to know more than that. When I called Grim's office, his assistant, who had worked on my father, was gracious enough to fill me in. I quickly jotted down these notes as he spoke: fractured neck, intercranium damage, massive head injury, helmet pulled up on the neck when he hit the guardrail causing fractured larynx, fractured lower part of cranial vault, possible chest injury, knocked-over lung, air in the chest outside the lung.

I said, "Would it have been possible for him to talk? One of his buddies said he heard him talk."

"Not possible," he said.

"What about move his arm? Another said he saw him move his arm."

"Not possible."

"Do you think he suffered?"

"Not possible. Not with those head injuries. There was no suffering," he said, and I knew that he was not just placating me.

And then, for some reason, he told me this: "Once, when I was an EMT, years ago, we responded to a suicide on the train tracks. Guy got cut clean in half. A real mess. I took his bottom half, my partner took his upper half, and we loaded him in the ambulance. Then, on the way to the hospital, the guy woke up and started walking on his hands, trying to get to his bottom half. Imagine that, the guy walking on his hands, dragging his bloody waist on the floor, trying to put himself back together. That lasted about nine seconds."

"Christ," I said.

"That's not the worst of it," he said. "I once had a mother punch me in the face, pull her dead eight-year-old daughter off the table, and drag her down the hallway by her ankle, trying to get her home. Security had to tackle her into the wall."

Grim's assistant—that soldier of truth, he who had literally seen inside my father, that place in his head where his thoughts came from, and that place in his chest where his love was—left me with these stories: the dying who refuse to die even when they want to, the bereaved who refuse to bury their dead. And he left me with those cold nouns, larynx and cranial vault. They split like thin, sun-baked shale. Human evolution had no way of anticipating steel and speed, and so we are like graham crackers in the grip of an angry child. Our bodies, so perfectly adapted to the African savanna of one million years ago, are simply waiting to be shredded in civilization. Grim's assistant also solved for me the riddle of why the motorcycle wasn't demolished: my father's chest and lung injuries were caused by the bike itself. It didn't splinter into a hundred pieces because my father's body came between it and the guardrail.

I was still frantic for information even though I knew that having it wasn't exactly prudent. But the possibility that his brakes had failed would not stop pestering me. When I learned that the insurance company had sent the bike to a motorcycle repair shop to have the brakes inspected, I called a guy named Matt who had done the inspection.

I said, "There was a recall on some element of those brakes."

He said, "The recall was never done, your father didn't do it. But the brakes didn't fail. One is worn down to the metal but they wouldn't have locked up or failed to stop. In my opinion he was trying to save his rotor by applying the back brakes because it's three hundred dollars to replace the rotor. The one pad is about twenty miles from worn down to metal, but the recall Yamaha did was for a bad adhesion connection pad, and that wasn't the problem here. They're original R1 brakes, never changed, but they have a life of nine to twenty thousand miles. The brakes didn't fail."

I thanked him and he said, "Listen, if it means anything to you, I could tell your father was an expert, a serious racer, not one of those Sunday riders."

"How could you tell that?"

"From the tires. The tread is worn in such a way that shows me he rode this bike hard, seriously hard. They're worn in the same way as a professional superbike that races on a track at a hundred-and-ninety miles an hour. You should be proud of that," he said.

Proud, I thought. I should be proud of a hundred-and-ninety miles an hour, an absurd speed no human was ever meant to reach. It sounded wrong to me, and yet, against my weakened will, I was proud. And I remembered what a friend had said to me shortly after the funeral: "To die like that, to go out doing what you love, what you're passionate about, what you're good at—that's the only way to die. It's honorable." Of course I don't believe that; people were telling me what they thought I wanted to hear. There's nothing honorable about dying a violent death at forty-seven years old and leaving behind a score of family members whose lives are all ruined in some way. We don't live in Homer's warrior society where a man's brutal death on the sand of Ilium is an indication of courage, a guarantee of praise and immortality in song. Nevertheless, the pride I felt for my father's passion and skill could not be denied; it was a small solace among so much discontent.

• • •

I knew I would have to see the bike myself, and my uncle Nicky agreed to accompany me to the cycle shop in Pennsylvania where the bike had been inspected. I crept out of bed at dawn one morning, left Adra sleeping beneath the comforter, and met my uncle on the highway. For the hour it took us to reach the cycle shop, he told me stories about the lunatic days he had spent riding with my father, grandfather, and uncle Tony, how close they had all come to getting maimed or killed, and the day he had spent in jail after getting caught by state troopers. "But it was fun," he said. "It was so much fun. I miss it."

If I had expected an epiphany or even inches of understanding by seeing the bike, I was in for a disappointment. Inside the shop each new bike gleamed as if held by moonlight; I inhaled the strong scent of fresh rubber and polished chrome. They were beautiful, each of them screaming for speed, for divinity. I thought: *I have arrived to touch the beast, the red and white fire that laid my father on a gurney.* We met Matt, the guy I had spoken to on the phone, the one who told me I should be proud. He and the others at the shop looked at my uncle and me and solemnly nodded in respect: a comrade had fallen, and we were the comrade's family. That is not to be overlooked: these men on motorcycles reveled in the camaraderie, the bond; they were a band of primordial hunters out for the kill that would sustain them. It was, my uncle told me, half of the reason he had ridden, because it solidified this bond with other daring men, a private club that chose its members carefully. It was noble to be part of this thrill that was larger than each of them. Every Sunday the ride replaced God, a substituting savior.

We went out back to the bike waiting in the sunlight. The wound in the gas tank reminded me of a claw's quick swipe at doughy flesh. The left handlebar was slightly bent from impact with the road. Sitting on the bike I felt as if concrete had been poured in my gut. My uncle squatted to inspect the front brakes, and I tried to imagine what my father saw at such high speeds, how the world looked around him as he raced through it. What else could I do but put my hands on that machine and try to imagine? We had driven all this way so I could touch the bike for five short minutes.

I thought the bike should be ours again, if for nothing else than to touch it and remember, but my grandparents didn't want the reminder parked in their garage, and they were calling the shots now. We all deferred to my grandmother's feelings, since it was obvious that she had been utterly dismantled by my father's death. Looking at my grandparents, I knew that I had never before seen lives so thoroughly destroyed. They visited the cemetery every afternoon, rain or sun, and came back in tears. I thought they might start taking lawn chairs, and I remembered the story of how Edgar Allan Poe, inebriated and estranged from God, used to sleep overnight at the grave of his young adored wife.

I had been asked by my grandparents to come up with words for the headstone, and I struggled with this because I knew that they and the rest of my family wanted something obvious and maudlin, the kind of remembrance typically printed in newspapers and sympathy cards. I wished I could have chosen lines by Donne or Hopkins, but when your family is not open to literature, and when you know they will be visiting the grave every day for the rest of their lives, Donne or Hopkins will not do. They were too defeated to solve riddles, and so I decided on lines they could appreciate and I could tolerate without wincing: "In your absence we will become you, / the strength you were in flesh, / the love you are in spirit. / We will ride hard and build well, / and live this life for you / until the instant we are one again."

"Ride hard" and "build well" are my father's own words, general advice he liked to give whenever he was asked for some. He himself did both. If my grandmother saw hope of an afterlife in the last line it is because she sees hope of an afterlife everywhere she looks. This calamity has only strengthened her belief, which is not uncommon: she needs the risen Christ if she is ever to be reunited with my father. She cannot stomach the fact that he lies in the cold ground, that he simply no longer is.

When the police report finally arrived in my mailbox it confirmed for me what I already knew. Under "OPINION and CONCLUSION" the investigating officer had written: "While a recall exists for the front brakes of the involved motorcycle, there is no indication the defect in the front brakes contributed to this accident. The existence of lining on three of the four brake pads, although very thin, was sufficient to stop Unit #1 when driven at legal and prudent speeds. The statements of uninvolved witnesses and the length of the one-wheel skid mark both indicate excessive speed, well above the posted suggested speed for the curve of 20 mph. Operator of Unit #1 was solely in violation for failing to drive at a safe speed."

Solely. I was finished looking into my father's death.

.     .     .

One afternoon I saw a dozen cars parked in front of the house directly across the street from my godfather's. The men were dressed in black suits, the women in black dresses. The wife, a young mother of two small children, had just been killed in her car on a wet highway, her body crushed inside the mangled steel. I saw the husband, the now single father, standing on the walkway, greeting some, bidding farewell to others. On the lawn and in the driveway lay tricycles and plastic toys strewn about. And then, for a moment, he was alone there: a car had driven away; the new arrivals had gone inside. It was just the two of us on that wide, oak-lined street in an upscale suburban town, directly across from one another, our hands shoved into our pockets in the same fashion, both looking at the space between us. Neither of us waved, neither nodded. We were strangers, and I recognized no significance, no connection, nothing binding us. Just that empty space there.

**The Atlantic**

FINALIST—PROFILE WRITING

*Donald Gray Triplett, seventy-seven, lives alone in Forest, Mississippi. Now retired from working at the local bank, he plays golf, drives a ten-year-old coffee-colored Cadillac and still travels—to date, he has visited twenty-eight U.S. states and thirty-six foreign countries. Triplett is also the first person ever diagnosed with autism. In this extraordinarily well-crafted article, John Donvan and Caren Zucker not only profile Donald T, as he is known in the medical literature, but explore the implications of his story for the 500,000 autistic children who will soon reach adulthood and eventually face life without the care of their parents. " 'Autism's First Child' is an immensely satisfying profile," wrote the National Magazine Award judges, "and a case study for the future of people living with autism—the challenges, the treatments and the rich potential of their lives." John Donvan is a correspondent for the ABC program* Nightline; *Caren Zucker is a television producer and the mother of a teenager with autism.*

John Donvan and
Caren Zucker

# Autism's
# First Child

I n 1951, a Hungarian-born psychologist, mind reader, and hypnotist named Franz Polgar was booked for a single night's performance in a town called Forest, Mississippi, at the time a community of some 3,000 people and no hotel accommodations. Perhaps because of his social position—he went by Dr. Polgar, had appeared in *Life* magazine, and claimed (falsely) to have been Sigmund Freud's "medical hypnotist"—Polgar was lodged at the home of one of Forest's wealthiest and best-educated couples, who treated the esteemed mentalist as their personal guest.

Polgar's all-knowing, all-seeing act had been mesmerizing audiences in American towns large and small for several years. But that night it was his turn to be dazzled, when he met the couple's older son, Donald, who was then eighteen. Oddly distant, uninterested in conversation, and awkward in his movements, Donald nevertheless possessed a few advanced faculties of his own, including a flawless ability to name musical notes as they were played on a piano and a genius for multiplying numbers in his head. Polgar tossed out "eighty-seven times twenty-three," and Donald, with his eyes closed and not a hint of hesitation, correctly answered "2,001."

Indeed, Donald was something of a local legend. Even people in neighboring towns had heard of the Forest teenager who'd calculated the number of bricks in the facade of the high school—the very building in which Polgar would be performing—merely by glancing at it.

According to family lore, Polgar put on his show and then, after taking his final bows, approached his hosts with a proposal: that they let him bring Donald with him on the road, as part of his act.

Donald's parents were taken aback. "My mother," recalls Donald's brother, Oliver, "was not at all interested." For one, things were finally going well for Donald, after a difficult start in life. "She explained to [Polgar] that he was in school, he had to keep going to classes," Oliver says. He couldn't simply drop everything for a run at show business, especially not when he had college in his sights.

But there was also, whether they spoke this aloud to their guest or not, the sheer indignity of what Polgar was proposing. Donald's being odd, his parents could not undo; his being made an oddity of, they could, and would, prevent. The offer was politely but firmly declined.

What the all-knowing mentalist didn't know, however, was that Donald, the boy who missed the chance to share his limelight, already owned a place in history. His unusual gifts and deficits had been noted outside Mississippi, and an account of them had been published—one that was destined to be translated and reprinted all over the world, making his name far better known, in time, than Polgar's.

His first name, anyway.

Donald was the first child ever diagnosed with autism. Identified in the annals of autism as "Case 1 . . . Donald T," he is the initial subject described in a 1943 medical article that announced the discovery of a condition unlike "anything reported so far," the complex neurological ailment now most often called an autism spectrum disorder, or ASD. At the time, the condition was considered exceedingly rare, limited to Donald and ten other children—Cases 2 through 11—also cited in that first article.

That was sixty-seven years ago. Today, physicians, parents, and politicians regularly speak of an "epidemic" of autism. The rate of ASDs, which come in a range of forms and widely varying degrees of severity—hence spectrum—has been accelerating dramatically since the early 1990s, and some form of ASD is now estimated to affect 1 in every 110 American children. And nobody knows why.

There have always been theories about the cause of autism—many theories. In the earliest days, it was an article of faith among psychiatrists that autism was brought on by bad mothers, whose chilly behavior toward their children led the youngsters to withdraw into a safe but private world. In time, autism was recognized to have a biological basis. But this understanding, rather than producing clarity, instead unleashed a contentious debate about the exact mechanisms at work. Differing factions argue that the gluten in food causes autism; that the mercury used as a preservative in some vaccines can trigger autistic symptoms; and that the particular measles-mumps-rubella vaccine is to blame. Other schools of thought have portrayed autism as essentially an autoimmune response, or the result of a nutritional deficiency. The mainstream consensus today—that autism is a neurological condition probably resulting from one or more genetic abnormalities in combination with an environmental trigger—offers little more in the way of explanation: the number of genes and triggers that could be involved is so large that a definitive cause, much less a cure, is unlikely to be determined anytime soon. Even the notion that autism cases are on the rise is disputed to a degree, with some believing that the escalating diagnoses largely result from a greater awareness of what autism looks like.

There is no longer much dispute, however, about the broad outlines of what constitutes a case of autism. *The Diagnostic and Statistical Manual of Mental Disorders*—the so-called bible of psychiatry—draws a clear map of symptoms. And to a remarkable degree, these symptoms still align with those of one "Donald T," who was first examined at Johns Hopkins University, in Baltimore, in the 1930s, the same boy who would later amaze a mentalist and become renowned for counting bricks.

In subsequent years, the scientific literature updated Donald T.'s story a few times, a journal entry here or there, but about four decades ago, that narrative petered out. The later chapters in his life remained unwritten, leaving us with no detailed answer to the question *Whatever happened to Donald?*

There is an answer. Some of it we turned up in documents long overlooked in the archives of Johns Hopkins. But most of it we found by tracking down and spending time with Donald himself. His full name is Donald Gray Triplett. He's seventy-seven years old. And he's still in Forest, Mississippi. Playing golf.

•        •        •

The question that haunts every parent of a child with autism is *What will happen when I die?* This reflects a chronological inevitability: children with autism will grow up to become adults with autism, in most cases ultimately outliving the parents who provided their primary support.

Then what?

It's a question that has yet to grab society's attention, as the discussion of autism to date has skewed, understandably, toward its impact on childhood. But the stark fact is that an epidemic among children today means an epidemic among adults tomorrow. The statistics are dramatic: within a decade or so, more than 500,000 children diagnosed with autism will enter adulthood. Some of them will have the less severe variants—Asperger's syndrome or HFA, which stands for "high-functioning autism"—and may be able to live more independent and fulfilling lives. But even that subgroup will require some support, and the needs of those with lower-functioning varieties of autism will be profound and constant.

How we respond to those needs will be shaped in great measure by how we choose to view adults with autism. We can dissociate from them, regarding them as tragically broken persons, and hope we are humane enough to shoulder the burden of meeting their basic needs. This is the view that sees the disabled in general as wards of the community, morally and perhaps legally, and that, in the relatively recent past, often "solved" the "problem" of these disabled adults by warehousing them for life—literally in wards.

Alternatively, we can dispense with the layers of sorrow and interpret autism as but one more wrinkle in the fabric of humanity. Practically speaking, this does not mean pretending that adults with autism do not need help. But it does mean replacing pity toward them with ambition for them. The key to this view is a recognition that "they" are part of "us," so that those who don't have autism are actively rooting for those who do.

Donald Triplett, the first person cast in the story of autism, has spent time in the worlds shaped by each of these views.

·　　·　　·

Donald drives his car with a light, percussive rhythm. After pressing on the gas pedal for a second, he lets up briefly, and then presses back down again. *Down. Release. Down. Release.* The tempo doesn't vary. It's late afternoon, and Donald is guiding his coffee-colored 2000 Cadillac, in hardly perceptible surges and glides, south along Mississippi's route 80. Though his forward posture and two-fisted grip on the wheel are those of an old man, his face beams like a boy's. He wears the expression, at once relaxed and resolute, of a man who is doing precisely what he wants to be doing.

The day's agenda thus far has included morning coffee with friends, a long walk for exercise, a *Bonanza* rerun on TV, and now, at 4:30, this short drive down route 80 to get in some golf. "I noticed," he mentions, "you have a Lafayette County sticker on your car." He's broken a long silence with that comment, a reference to the registration decal on the rental we parked in his driveway. His words hang there for a moment, and then he adds: "That means it comes from Lafayette County." That's all. Nodding to himself, Donald goes silent again, his focus returning to the road ahead or tuned to some inner monologue. Given his tendency to close his eyes for long moments when he speaks, this is probably the safest choice.

He parks just short of the front steps of the Forest Country Club, an establishment without pretensions. The one-story red-brick clubhouse fronts onto a well-tended, mostly flat course carved out of the woods. Membership is one hundred dollars per family per month, and a round of eighteen holes costs twenty dollars on a weekday. On any given day, the roster of players on the fairways includes lawyers and mechanics, bankers and truckers, salesmen and farmers—and Donald. Actually, Donald is there every day, weather permitting. And almost every day, he golfs alone.

Not everyone who plays here realizes that "DT"—as he's known around the club—has autism. But his quirks are hard to miss as he makes his way to the first tee, well within sight of members who take the shade in armchairs under the club's columned portico. A small man in khaki shorts and a green knit shirt, with a pink-camouflage bucket hat pulled down tight over his ears, Donald strides to the tee with the distinctive gait that is often a tip-off for autism—his arms out from his sides in the shape of a large capital A, his steps just slightly mechanical, his head and shoulders bobbing left-right-left in the rocking movement of a metronome.

The fact is that Donald's not a bad golfer: tee shots mostly on the fairway, passable short game, can nail a six-foot putt. His swing, however, is an unfolding pantomime, a ritual of gestures he seems compelled to repeat with almost every shot—especially when he really wants the ball to travel.

He licks the fingers of his right hand, and then his left. Squaring himself to the ball, he raises his club skyward, until it's straight up over his head, as if he were hoisting a banner. Sometimes he holds his arms up there for a long moment. Then he brings the club head back to earth, stopping not far from the ball, before taking it back up. He goes through a series of these backswings, picking up speed with each iteration until, stiff-legged, he inches forward to get his head over the ball. With one final stroke, he commits to contact. *Crack!* It's gone, and Donald, bouncing up and down at the knees, peers down the fairway to see the result. As a swing, it's the opposite of fluid. But it's Donald's own. And he never whiffs it.

Some days, Donald has no choice but to partner with other golfers, when the country club, honoring golf's traditions as a social game, reserves the entire course for a membership "scramble." In a scramble, golfers are randomly assigned to teams, which compete for lowest group score by picking the ball in the best position and having everyone on the team play from that spot. During one recent scramble, Donald made the rounds with Lori and Elk and Kenneth and Mary, all of whom seemed to be at least three or four decades younger than he was. But Donald held his own competitively, with his shots often enough the ones used. He also kicked in a passable amount of friendly banter, which was returned in the same spirit, though Donald's patter tended to get repetitive: "Way to hit that ball, Kenneth!" "Way to hit that ball, Lori!" "Way to hit that ball, Elk!" At times he would entertain variations, marrying his partners' names with words from his own private vocabulary: "Hey, Elkins the Elk!" "Hey, Mary Cherry!" "Okay, thank you, Kenneth the Senneth!"

Most of the time, however, Donald remained silent. This is in keeping with the decorum of the game, of course. But Donald appears comfortable with silence and, in a larger sense, content with the life he's leading, which resembles—with the car and the coffee and the golf and the TV—a retirement community's brochure version of how to live out the golden years. Donald has freedom, independence, and good health. All in all, life has turned out well for autism's first child.

·     ·     ·

Donald was institutionalized when he was only three years old. Records in the archives at Johns Hopkins quote the family doctor in Mississippi suggesting that the Tripletts had "overstimulated the child." Donald's refusal as a toddler to feed himself, combined with other problem behaviors his parents could not handle, prompted the doctor's recommendation for "a change of environment." In August 1937, Donald entered a state-run facility fifty miles from his home, in a town then actually called Sanatorium, Mississippi.

The large building where he was housed served what today seems an odd function: preemptive isolation for children thought to be at risk of catching tuberculosis. The place wasn't designed or operated with a child like Donald in mind, and, according to a medical evaluator, his response upon arrival was dramatic: he "faded away physically."

At the time, institutionalization was the default option for severe mental illness, which even his mother believed was at the root of Donald's behavior: she described him in one despairing letter as her "hopelessly insane child." Being in an institution, however, didn't help. "It seems," his Johns Hopkins evaluator later wrote, "he had there his worst phase." With parental visits limited to twice a month, his predisposition to avoid contact with people broadened to everything else—toys, food, music, movement—to the point where daily he "sat motionless, paying no attention to anything."

He had not been diagnosed correctly, of course, because the correct diagnosis did not yet exist. Very likely he was not alone in that sense, and there were other children with autism, in other wards in other states, similarly misdiagnosed—perhaps as "feeble-minded," in the medical parlance of the day, or more likely, because of the strong but isolated intelligence skills many could demonstrate, as having schizophrenia.

Donald's parents came for him in August of 1938. By then, at the end of a year of institutionalization, Donald was eating again, and his health had returned. Though he now "played among the other children," his observers noted, he did so "without taking part in their occupations." The facility's director nonetheless told Donald's parents that the boy was "getting along nicely," and tried to talk them out of removing their son. He actually requested that they "let him alone."

But they held their ground, and took Donald home with them. Later, when they asked the director to provide them with a written assessment of Donald's time there, he could scarcely be bothered. His remarks on Donald's full year under his care covered less than half a page. The boy's problem, he concluded, was probably "some glandular disease."

Donald, about to turn five years old, was back where he had started.

&bull; &bull; &bull;

Dr. Peter Gerhardt waves a credit card in his right hand, animated—as he often is—about the point he's trying to make. This time, it's a trick that he guarantees makes it impossible to swipe the card the wrong way. "You can slide it this way, or like this, or stick it in like this"—he jabs straight into the air in front of him, as if into a bank machine—"and if you keep your thumb in this position on the card, you will always swipe it the correct way."

Closer examination clarifies: the card he is holding is a Visa, and his right thumb completely covers the blue-on-white logo in the lower right corner, the sweet spot that makes the trick work. Keep your thumb there, Gerhardt pronounces, and the magnetic stripe will always line up properly, regardless of the type of card reader.

Gerhardt's demonstration isn't intended merely for news-you-can-use convenience. Rather, he's explaining how using a bank card fits into the bigger picture that has defined his career since he embarked on his doctorate in educational psychology at Rutgers in the early 1980s: the struggle people with autism face to be accepted into a world occupied by "the rest of us."

The truth is that we often deny to adults with autism the kind of empathy and support we make readily available to children with the condition—or, for that matter, to people with white canes at crosswalks. We underestimate their capabilities, reveal our discomfort in their company, and display impatience when they inconvenience us. The people standing in the back of a long supermarket checkout line aren't always going to say or do the nice thing when some odd-looking man in front is holding the whole place up because he can't figure out the credit-card swipe. It's in that moment, Gerhardt says, that the thumb-on-the-logo trick is a matter of "social survival." If the man with autism can navigate this situation successfully—and, just as important, be seen doing so—Gerhardt argues that our collective acceptance of people with autism in "our" spaces will tick up a notch. If the man fails, it will go the other way.

Gerhardt, who is a former president of the Virginia-based Organization for Autism Research and is now developing a program focused on adolescence to adulthood at the respected McCarton School in New York, is considered among the top experts in the country working with adults who have autism. But he jokes that this is chiefly because he's never faced much competition. "I have an entire career," he says, "based on people not wanting my job." Child development is the hot area in autism research; working with adults, Gerhardt says, "is not a career move." Adults present greater challenges: they are big enough to do real violence in the event of a tantrum; they are fully capable of sexual desires and all that those imply; and they're bored by many of the activities that can distract and entertain children with autism. "People want to treat these adults like little kids in big bodies," Gerhardt says. "They can't. They're adults." As such, he argues, they're equipped, as much as any of us, with the recognizable adult aspiration of wanting to "experience life."

"It's having friends," Gerhardt explains. "It's having interesting work. It's having something you want. It's all the things the rest of us value, once given an opportunity."

Gerhardt wants priority given to teaching the kinds of skills adults with autism need in order to survive independently: keeping track of money, asking for directions and then following them, wearing clean clothes, navigating public transport, recognizing a dangerous person, and—of extreme difficulty for most—looking a job interviewer in the eye. Gerhardt disputes the doubts he hears even within his profession about encouraging adults with autism to aspire to independence. "What's the worst thing that can happen?" he asks. "You know—he's at the supermarket and he drops some eggs, or somebody thinks he's a little weird. I would rather he be there alone, and only getting nine out of ten items he came shopping for, than need me there with him to get all ten. That's a much better way to live."

This leads to the question of *where* they will live. As it is, 85 percent of adults with autism still live with parents, siblings, or other relatives. But what happens when that is no longer an option? Large-scale warehousing is gone—and good riddance, most say. An obvious alternative is residential arrangements offering multiple spaces to people with autism, who can share support services under one roof in a setting that really is a home. At present, however, given both start-up costs and resistance from neighbors, the number of spaces in such homes is limited, and landing a spot can be extremely difficult: nationally, more than 88,000 adults are already on waiting lists.

All of which leads to an unsettling answer for those parents asking what happens, after they die, to their children with autism. We don't really know.

.    .    .

Most likely, Donald's name would never have entered the medical literature had his parents not had both the ambition to seek out the best help for him and the resources to pay for it. Mary Triplett had been born into the McCravey family, financiers who had founded and still controlled the Bank of Forest. Uncommonly for a woman at that time, particularly in that milieu, she had a college degree. After a doomed romance with a local cotton farmer's son, whom her family forbade her to marry—he later went on to renown as six-term segregationist U.S. Senator James "Big Jim" Eastland—she instead married the former mayor's son, an attorney named Oliver Triplett Jr. With a degree from Yale Law School and a private practice located directly opposite the county courthouse, Oliver would later hold the position of Forest town attorney and would be admitted to the bar of the Supreme Court of the United States. He was an intense man who had suffered two nervous breakdowns and who could get so lost in his thoughts that he'd return from walks in town with no recollection of having seen anyone or anything along the way. But as a lawyer, he was considered brilliant, and when he proposed to Mary, her family apparently raised no objections.

Their first son, Donald, was born in September 1933. A brother came along nearly five years later, while Donald was in Sanatorium. Also named Oliver, the baby stayed behind with his grandparents in Forest when, in October 1938, the rest of the family boarded a Pullman car in Meridian, Mississippi, headed for

Baltimore. Donald's parents had secured him a consultation with the nation's top child psychiatrist at the time, a Johns Hopkins professor named Dr. Leo Kanner.

Kanner (pronounced "Connor") had written the book, literally, on child psychiatry. Aptly titled *Child Psychiatry,* this definitive 1935 work immediately became the standard medical-school text and was reprinted through 1972. No doubt Kanner's stature was enhanced by his pedigree—he was an Austrian Jew with a medical degree from the University of Berlin—while his nearly impenetrable accent perfectly fit the image Americans had in mind when they used the word *psychiatrist.*

Kanner would always seem slightly perplexed by the intensity of the letter he had received from Donald's father in advance of their meeting. Before departing Mississippi, Oliver had retreated to his law office and dictated a detailed medical and psychological history covering the first five years of his elder son's life. Typed up by his secretary and sent ahead to Kanner, it came to thirty-three pages. Many times over the years, Kanner would refer to the letter's "obsessive detail."

Excerpts from Oliver's letter—the outpourings of a layman but also a parent—now hold a unique place in the canon of autism studies. Cited for decades and translated into several languages, Oliver's observations were the first detailed listing of symptoms that are now instantly recognizable to anyone who knows autism. It is not too much to say that the agreed-upon diagnosis of autism—the one being applied today to define an epidemic—was modeled, at least in part, on Donald's symptoms as described by his father.

Their little boy, Oliver wrote, had almost never cried to be with his mother. He appeared to have withdrawn "into his shell," to "live within himself," to be "perfectly oblivious to everything about him." Entirely uninterested in human beings—including his parents, for whom he displayed "no apparent affection"—he nevertheless had several obsessions, including "a mania for spinning blocks and pans and other round objects." He was fascinated with numbers, musical notes, pictures of U.S. presidents, and the letters of the alphabet, which he enjoyed reciting in reverse order.

Physically awkward, he also had intense dislikes: milk, swings, tricycles—"almost a horror of them"—and any change in routine or interruption of his internal thought processes: "When interfered with he has temper tantrums, during which he is destructive." Generally nonresponsive when his name was called—he seemed not to have heard—he instead had "to be picked up and carried or led wherever he ought to go." When asked a question, if he answered at all, he generally kept his response to one word, and then only if it derived from something he had memorized. Certain words and phrases captivated him, and he would loop them aloud endlessly: *trumpet vine, business, chrysanthemum.*

At the same time, Donald exhibited some prodigious, if isolated, mental skills. By the age of two, he could recite the Twenty-third Psalm ("Yea though I walk through the valley of the shadow of death . . .") and knew twenty-five questions and answers from the Presbyterian catechism by heart. And the random humming he engaged in while spinning blocks turned out not to be quite so random after all. Rather, he always picked three notes that, if played simultaneously on a keyboard, would blend into a perfect chord. Alone in thought, Donald gave the impression of a quite intelligent little boy, working through some sort of problem. "He appears to be always thinking and thinking," his father wrote. He was, in a heartrendingly comprehensive phrase, "happiest when left alone."

When Kanner finally met Donald, he confirmed all this, and more. Donald entered the room, Kanner later recalled, and headed straight for the blocks and toys, "without paying the least attention to the persons present." Kanner had a trick up his sleeve that today would draw disapproval: he pricked Donald with a pin. The result was revealing. Donald didn't like it—it hurt—but he didn't like Kanner any less for doing it. To Kanner, it seemed that he could not attach the pain to the person who'd inflicted it. Throughout the visit, in fact, Donald remained completely indifferent to Kanner, as uninterested in him as in "the desk, the bookshelf, or the filing cabinet."

The surviving medical records of that initial visit contain a notation preceded by a question mark: *schizophrenia*. It was one of the few diagnoses that came even close to making sense, because it was clear that Donald was essentially an intelligent child, as a person exhibiting schizophrenia might easily be. But nothing in his behavior suggested that Donald experienced the hallucinations typical of schizophrenia. He wasn't seeing things that weren't there, even if he was ignoring the people who were.

Kanner kept Donald under observation for two weeks, and then the Tripletts returned to Mississippi—without answers. Kanner simply had no idea how to diagnose the child. He would later write to Mary Triplett, who had begun sending frequent updates on Donald: "Nobody realizes more than I do myself that at no time have you or your husband been given a clear-cut and unequivocal . . . diagnostic term." It was dawning on him, he wrote, that he was seeing "for the first time a condition which has not hitherto been described by psychiatric or any other literature."

He wrote those lines to Mary in a letter dated September 1942, almost four years after he'd first seen Donald. The family had made three follow-up visits to Baltimore, all equally inconclusive. Perhaps hoping to allay her frustration, Kanner added that he was beginning to see a picture emerge. "I have now accumulated," he wrote, "a series of eight other cases which are very much like Don's." He hadn't gone public with this, he noted, because he needed "time for longer observation."

He had, however, been working on a name for this new condition. Pulling together the distinctive symptoms exhibited by Donald and the eight other children—their lack of interest in people, their fascination with objects, their need for sameness, their keenness to be left alone—he wrote Mary: "If there is any name to be applied to the condition of Don and those other children, I have found it best to speak of it as 'autistic disturbance of affective contact.'"

Kanner did not coin the term *autistic*. It was already in use in psychiatry, not as the name of a syndrome but as an observational term describing the way some patients with schizophrenia withdrew from contact with those around them. Like the word *feverish*, it described a symptom, not an illness. But now Kanner was using it to pinpoint and label a complex set of behaviors that together constituted a single, never-before-recognized diagnosis: autism. (As it happens, another Austrian, Hans Asperger, was working at the same time in Vienna with children who shared some similar characteristics, and independently applied the identical word— *autistic*—to the behaviors he was seeing; his paper on the subject would come out a year after Kanner's but remained largely unknown until it was translated into English in the early 1990s.)

Kanner published his findings in 1943, in a journal called *The Nervous Child*. Since writing to Mary the previous year, he had added two more cases to this total: eleven children, eleven histories. But he started the story with Donald.

·     ·     ·

For all the progress that Donald has made in the decades since— the driving, the golfing—conversation is an art that continues to elude him. He initiates on occasion, but his purpose is generally to elicit a piece of information he needs ("What time is lunch?") or to make a passing observation (his comment about the sticker on our car). A regular chat, the casual back-and-forth of kicking around an idea, is something he has never experienced.

When asked questions—even questions that invite some elaboration—he responds in a terse, one-way manner, like a man working his way through a questionnaire.

### Topic: Donald's sense of achievement at being able to multiply in his head

"Donald, how does it make you feel that it just comes out of your head?"

"It just comes out."

"Does it make you feel good?"

"Oh yes, oh yes."

"Can you describe it?"

"No, I can't describe it."

### Topic: Donald's memory of meeting the mentalist Franz Polgar

"Donald, do you remember Franz Polgar?"

"Yes, I do remember Franz Polgar."

[Silence.]

"When did he come?"

"Actually he came twice. He came in 1950 and 1951."

[Another long lapse.]

"Who was he?"

"He was a hypnotist."

"Can you tell me what he was like? Was he an old man?"

"He was probably 55 years old. And he'd be 110 if he were living."

As is clear from these exchanges, Donald's thinking likes to go to numbers—even when, as in this case, his arithmetic appears faulty—to dates and calculations and constants that order the world concretely and do not require interpretation. He even has a habit of assigning numbers to people he encounters, a sort of internal indexing system. An old acquaintance named Buddy Lovett, who resides one town over, in Morton, Mississippi, told us that Donald had assigned him the number 333 sometime in the late 1950s. Though he had not seen Donald for several years, he urged, with a hint of mischief, "Next time you see him, go ahead: ask him what my number is."

Indeed, the next day Donald nailed Lovett's number almost before hearing the end of the question. We ran this test several times, presenting the names of people all over Forest who had told us of being "numbered" over the years. Donald recalled every one, without hang or hiccup, though he can't explain the underlying system. The numbers just come to him, he says, and then stay forever.

Likewise, those who receive a Donald Number seem to remember it for the rest of their lives. An indelible distinction, a recognition they'll never have to share—it may feel akin to an honor.

That is almost certainly not what Donald intends. Honor is one of those concepts—an abstraction arbitrating between the ideal and the actual—unlikely to come easily to someone like Donald, who is far more comfortable in a world ordered by established facts, by what *literally is*. This is why it is generally believed that people with autism have difficulty lying, or appreciating a joke. Although Donald obviously enjoys pondering lists of people, places, and things, he does not engage easily with implication, mood, or emotion.

### Topic: The death of his mother, Mary Triplett, who took care of Donald for fifty-two years

"Donald, when did your mother die?"

"It was 1985. May 1985."

"Do you remember where you were?"

"I was at the bank. Her doctor had said it was just a matter of time . . . and I got the word saying that she had passed away with congestive heart failure."

"Do you remember how you felt?"

"It was rather expected. I wasn't really downhearted or weeping or anything like that."

"Were you not downhearted because . . . ?"

"I just don't react. Different people react differently to situations like that."

Asked whether he missed his mother, he replied—questionnaire again—"Yes, I miss her." He said he also misses his father, whose death in a 1980 car accident he described in a similarly matter-of-fact manner. He recalls that his dad's accident was a shock and, again, that he didn't cry.

.        .        .

Peter Gerhardt tells the story of his friend Tony, who was fifty-five years old when he got a crash course in the condolence hug. Tony, diagnosed with autism as an adult, had lived all his life under the same roof as his mother. Then she died.

The funeral marked the first time in his life that Tony had been placed in the category of "the bereaved," and, as he mingled among the other funeral goers, he learned that people in his position must be prepared to accept some intense and lingering hugs. He handled it fine, observing how his brother was responding to the same sorts of approaches and comprehending that the people doing this were trying to help him not feel sad. Then he went home, hugged his neighbor, and nearly got arrested.

It was the day after the funeral, and the elderly woman who lived next door—not a close family friend, but someone kindly observing the custom of bringing meals when there's been a death—came to his door with food she'd prepared. Tony thanked her, and she offered condolences.

According to Peter Gerhardt, what happened next is a textbook example of the kind of misunderstanding that bedevils people with autism. "Tony thought, *Well, she offered condolences. I'm supposed to hug her.* So he went to hug her." Gerhardt notes that the woman undoubtedly sent off strong social signals that she did not want to be embraced. But Tony failed to pick up on them: "He hugged her, probably somewhat awkwardly—a little too long, a little too hard, a little too low—because she went home and called the police [reporting] a sexual assault by the man next door."

To Gerhardt, this serves as a parable for interactions between people who have autism and those who don't: neither party did anything wrong, but neither knew enough to get it right. Tony, a man bright enough to have earned a college degree, simply lacked the instinctive experience—the *teachable* experience, Gerhardt contends—to tell whether or not a person wants a hug. He was sufficiently self-aware to understand that he was missing vital cues, but he had no idea what they were. He later explained to Gerhardt: "The rules keep changing on me. Every time I think I learn a new rule, you change it on me."

The answer to this problem, Gerhardt argues, is the right kind of education for the many Tonys out there. At present, he contends, schooling for children with high-functioning levels of autism overemphasizes traditional academic achievement—trying to learn French or the state capitals—at the expense of what someone like Tony really needs, a set of social skills that keep him from making mistakes such as hugging his neighbor the wrong way. These skills—like knowing how to swipe a Visa card—are not generally taught to kids with autism. And once they become adults, the teaching, in all too many cases, stops completely. In general, state-funded education ends the day a person with autism turns twenty-one. Beyond that, there are no legal mandates, and there is very little funding. "It's like giving someone a wheelchair on a one-month rental," Gerhardt says, "and at the end of the month, they have to give it back, and walk."

But there was another side to the equation in the hug incident: the neighbor's lack of education on the character of autism. Had she been more aware of Tony's condition and what it might occasionally entail, she might not have felt so threatened. At the very least, had she understood the situation, she could have simply told Tony that she'd like him to let go, rather than hoping he'd read social cues that were invisible to him.

As it was, the whole situation was quickly defused: Tony's brother arrived and offered both the neighbor and the police an explanation of Tony's disability, and she declined to press charges. But, as Gerhardt notes, a little more information on both sides might have prevented this misunderstanding in the first place.

.    .    .

Donald lives alone now, in the house where his parents raised him. Enshrined in honeysuckle and shaded by several old oaks, a few minutes' walk from Forest's faded business district, the house needs some paint and repairs. Several of its rooms—including the dining and living rooms, where his parents welcomed visitors— are dark and musty with disuse. Donald rarely enters that part of the house. The kitchen, bathroom, and bedroom are home enough for him.

Except for once a month, that is, when he walks out the front door and leaves town.

Perhaps the most remarkable aspect of Donald's life is that he grew up to be an avid traveler. He has been to Germany, Tunisia, Hungary, Dubai, Spain, Portugal, France, Bulgaria, and Colombia—some thirty-six foreign countries and twenty-eight U.S. states in all, including Egypt three times, Istanbul five times, and Hawaii seventeen. He's notched one African safari, several cruises, and innumerable PGA tournaments.

It's not wanderlust exactly. Most times, he sets six days as his maximum time away, and maintains no contact afterward with people he meets along the way. He makes it a mission to get his own snapshots of places he's already seen in pictures and assembles them into albums when he gets home. Then he gets to work planning his next foray, calling the airlines himself for domestic travel, and relying on a travel agent in Jackson when he's going overseas. He is, in all likelihood, the best-traveled man in Forest, Mississippi.

This is the same man whose favorite pastimes, as a boy, were spinning objects, spinning himself, and rolling nonsense words around in his mouth. At the time, he seemed destined for a cramped, barren adulthood—possibly lived out behind the windows of a state institution. Instead, he learned to golf, to drive, and to circumnavigate the globe—skills he first developed at the respective ages of twenty-three, twenty-seven, and thirty-six. In adulthood, Donald continued to branch out.

Autism is a highly individualized condition. The amount of room the brain makes available for growth and adaptation differs, often dramatically, from one person to the next. One can't presume that duplicating Donald's circumstances for others with autism would have the effect of duplicating his results.

Still, it's clear that Donald reached his potential thanks, in large part, to the world he occupied—the world of Forest, Mississippi—and how it decided to respond to the odd child in its midst. Peter Gerhardt speaks of the importance of any community's "acceptance" of those who have autism. In Forest, it appears, Donald was showered with acceptance, starting with the mother who defied experts to bring him back home and continuing on to classmates from his childhood and golfing partners today. Donald's neighbors not only shrug off his oddities but openly admire his strengths—while taking a protective stance with any outsider whose intentions toward Donald may not have been sufficiently spelled out. On three occasions, while talking with townspeople who know Donald, we were advised, in strikingly similar language each time: "If what you're doing hurts Don, I know where to find you." We took the point: in Forest, Donald is "one of us."

For a time, Donald's care was literally shifted out into the community. Kanner believed that finding him a living situation in a more rural setting would be conducive to his development.

So in 1942, the year he turned nine, Donald went to live with the Lewises, a farming couple who lived about ten miles from town. His parents saw him frequently in this four-year period, and Kanner himself once traveled to Mississippi to observe the arrangement. He later said he was "amazed at the wisdom of the couple who took care of him." The Lewises, who were childless, put Donald to work and made him useful. "They managed to give him [suitable] goals," Kanner wrote in a later report.

> They made him use his preoccupation with measurements by having him dig a well and report on its depth. . . . When he kept counting rows of corn over and over, they had him count the rows while plowing them. On my visit, he plowed six long rows; it was remarkable how well he handled the horse and plow and turned the horse around.

Kanner's final observation on this visit speaks volumes about how Donald was perceived: "He attended a country school where his peculiarities were accepted and where he made good scholastic progress."

Likewise, during high school, when Donald was again living back home with his parents, it appears his ways were mostly taken in stride. Janelle Brown, who was a few classes behind Donald (and the recipient of Donald Number 1,487), remembers that although he was teased a few times, he was generally regarded as a student who was enviably intelligent, even "brilliant"—again a legacy of his famous multiplication skills and brick-counting act. She recalls his sitting with a notebook and filling page after page with numbers, and her impression, as well as that of others, that they were seeing evidence of a superior mind at work.

It's clear in all this that with the passage of time, Donald's focus gradually turned outward. He increasingly came to terms with how his world was shaped, at the same time that his world was adjusting to him.

By 1957, he was a fraternity brother—Lambda Chi Alpha—at Millsaps College in Jackson, Mississippi, majoring in French and performing in the men's a cappella choir. (The choir director, we were told by one member, never used a pitch pipe, because he took any note he needed directly from Donald.)

The Reverend Brister Ware, of the First Presbyterian Church in Jackson, was a fraternity brother and roommate of Donald's. "He was a dear friend," Ware says, recalling that he tried in various ways to give Donald a hand up socially, though "it was challenging to integrate him." While training to be a water-safety instructor, he set out to teach Donald how to swim, "but the coordination was not so good for him." Undaunted, Ware set another goal: "I thought I would try to open up his personality," by introducing Donald to what was then a cool verbal affectation making the rounds, a way to pronounce the word *yes* as "yeeeeeeees." Ware's encouragements—to "put a little emotion and feeling and savoir faire into it"—again proved futile.

Ware was clearly rooting for his classmate, as were, he says, the other members of the fraternity. "I knew he was a little bit strange," he admits. "But he's genuine . . . I feel so lucky to have had him as a friend"—a friend, by the way, who gave Ware a number: 569.

Throughout Donald's youth, it helped, no doubt, that the Tripletts had money—the money to get Leo Kanner's attention in Baltimore, the funds to pay room and board at the Lewises' farm. As the town's bankers, they also had status, which may have discouraged the sort of cruelty that can come to people like Donald. One insightful resident of Forest put it this way: "In a small southern town, if you're odd and poor, you're crazy; if you're odd and rich, all you are is a little eccentric." When Donald was grown, the family bank employed him as a teller, and an irrevocable trust fund established by his family pays his bills to this day. The fund, according to his younger brother, Oliver, was designed with controls that ensure, as he put it, "some gal wouldn't be able to talk Don into marrying her and then abscond." In fact, Donald has never expressed any interest in girlfriends, nor has he had one.

But he has his brother—they dine together every Sunday, along with Oliver's wife—and he has a community that has always accepted him, since long before people in town had heard the word *autism*. Tranquility, familiarity, stability, and security—if we were talking about healing, these would create an ideal environment. Forest provided all of them for Donald, who didn't need to heal. He needed only to grow, and that he did, spectacularly. In one of her later letters to Leo Kanner, Mary Triplett reported: "He has taken his place in society very well, so much better than we ever hoped for." There were still difficulties, of course—she confessed to the psychiatrist, by this time a friend, "I wish I knew what his inner feelings really are"—but her fears of having borne a "hopelessly insane child" were long past. By the time she died, Donald had grown into manhood, learning more about the world and his place in it than she could ever have imagined in those early years.

But he never could count bricks. This, it turns out, is a myth.

Donald explained how it had come about only after we'd been talking for some time. It had begun with a chance encounter more than sixty years ago outside his father's law office, where some fellow high-school students, aware of his reputation as a math whiz, challenged him to count the bricks in the county courthouse across the street. Maybe they were picking on him a little; maybe they were just seeking entertainment. Regardless, Donald says he glanced quickly at the building and tossed out a large number at random. Apparently the other kids bought it on the spot, because the story would be told and retold over the years, with the setting eventually shifting from courthouse to school building—a captivating local legend never, apparently, fact-checked.

A common presumption is that people with autism are not good at telling fibs or spinning yarns, that they are too literal-minded to invent facts that don't align with established reality. On one level, the story of Donald and the bricks demonstrates again the risks inherent in such pigeonholing. But on another level, it reveals something unexpected about Donald in particular. At the time of that episode, he was a teenager, barely a decade removed from the near-total social disconnect that had defined his early childhood. By adolescence, however, it seems he'd already begun working at connecting with people, and had grasped that his math skills were something that others admired.

We know that because we finally asked him directly why he'd pulled that number out of the air all those years ago. He closed his eyes to answer, and then surprised us a final time. Speaking as abruptly as ever, and with the usual absence of detail, he said simply, and perhaps obviously, "I just wanted for those boys to think well of me."

## GQ

FINALIST—FEATURE
WRITING

*"The Suicide Catcher" is two
stories woven seamlessly
together. It is a profile of
Mr. Chen, who, without official
sanction, patrols the four-mile-
long Nanjing Yangtze Bridge to
prevent his countrymen from
leaping—"turning languid flips or
dropping straight as a pin"—into
the river 130 feet below. But it is
also a meditation on the terrifying,
desperate act of suicide. Both
stories are set against the backdrop
of a nation in ferment—a place
where 200,000 people kill
themselves each year. Many readers
know Michael Paterniti from his
book* Driving Mr. Albert: A Trip
Across America With Einstein's
Brain, *which began as a National
Magazine Award–winning feature
story for* Harper's Magazine.
*Since that story was published
in 1997, Paterniti's work has
been nominated six more times
for National Magazine Awards.
Of this* GQ *piece, the National
Magazine Award judges wrote:
" 'The Suicide Catcher" is elegantly
constructed and, even during the
dramatic climax in which Paterniti
accidentally becomes part of the
story, keeps its cool."*

Michael Paterniti

# The Suicide Catcher

T he bridge rose up and away from the city's northwest quadrant, spanning the great Yangtze River. And yet, from the on-ramp where the taxi let me off that Saturday morning, it seemed more like a figment of the imagination, a ghostly ironwork extrusion vanishing in the monsoon murk, stretching to some otherworld. It was disorienting to look at, that latticed half-bridge leaving off in midair, like some sort of surrealist painting. It gave off a foreboding aura, too, untethered and floating, and yet it couldn't have been more earthbound—and massive. Later I'd find out it was made from 500,000 tons of cement and 1 million tons of steel. Four miles long, with four lanes of car traffic on the upper deck and twin railroad tracks on the lower, it transferred thousands of people and goods to and from the city every day. But now the clouds clamped down, and a sharp scent of sulfur and putrid fish wafted on a dank puff of air. Rain slithered from the sky. There, before my eyes, the bridge shimmered and disappeared, as if it had never been visible in the first place.

Its formal name was the Nanjing Yangtze River Bridge, and it served one other purpose for the masses: At least once a week, someone jumped to his or her death here, but a total was hard to come by, in part because the Chinese authorities refused to count those who missed the river, the ones who'd leapt and had the misfortune of landing in the trees along the riverbank, or on the concrete apron beneath the bridge, or who were found impressed in the earth like mud angels, two feet from rushing water. Perhaps such strict bookkeeping came in response to the fact that China already posts the highest sheer numbers, about 200,000 "reported" suicide cases a year, constituting a fifth of all the world's suicides. For a long time, the Communist government simply ignored the problem, hoping it would go away, or maybe thinking in the most Darwinian terms of suicide as its own method of population control. One recent case highlighted just how the Chinese bureaucracy tended to deal with prevention. In the southern city of Guangzhou, workers had been ordered to smear butter over a steel bridge popular with jumpers, in order to make it too slippery to climb. "We tried employing guards at both ends," said a government official, "and we put up special fences and notices asking people not to commit suicide here. None of it worked—and so now we have put butter over the bridge, and it has worked very well."

In Nanjing, the bridge remained butterless, even as the city spit out its victims. Nanjing was now just another one of your typical 6-million-person Chinese metropolises, one of the famous "Three Furnaces" of China because of its unremitting summer heat. Daytime temperatures regularly topped ninety degrees here—due to hot air being trapped by the mountains at the lower end of the Yangtze River valley . . . and, oh yeah, because all the trees had been chopped down—and the sun rarely shone. Meanwhile, the city continued to explode in the noonday of the country's hungry expansion. The past was being abandoned at an astonishing rate, the new skyscrapers and apartment buildings replacing the old neighborhoods. Everything—and everyone—was disposable. Schisms formed. The bridge loomed. Loss led to despair, which, in turn, led to Mr. Chen.

•     •     •

I'd come through thirteen time zones just to see him. Once free of the taxi, I began trudging, a quarter mile or so, the bridge trembling under the weight of its traffic, piled with noisy green taxis and rackety buses, some without side panels or mufflers. Unlike the suspended wonder of Brooklyn or the quixotic *ponts* of Paris, this couldn't have been mistaken for anything but stolid Communist bulwark: at its apex, the bridge was about 130 feet above the water; was built with two twenty-story "forts," spaced one mile apart, that from a distance had the appearance of huge torches; and contained 200 inlaid reliefs that included such exhortations as OUR COUNTRY IS LED BY THE WORKING CLASS and LONG LIVE THE UNITY OF THE PEOPLE. A brochure claimed that the bridge was both the first of its kind designed solely by Chinese engineers and also "ideal for bird-watching." People teemed in both directions. Umbrellas unfurled, poked, and were ripped from their rigging, leaving sharp spiders dangling overhead. As I registered the passersby—their eyes fixed downward—everyone seemed a candidate for jumping, marching in that mournful parade.

He was close now. I could tell by the banners and messages—some were flags, some were just scraps of paper—that fluttered earnestly from the bridge. VALUE LIFE EVERY DAY, read one. LIFE IS PRECIOUS, declared another. His cell-phone number was emblazoned everywhere, including little graffitied stamps he'd left on the sidewalk, ones I tried to decipher beneath the blur of so many passing feet. And then Mr. Chen came into view, conspicuous for being the only still point in that sea of motion . . . and the only one sporting a pair of clunky binoculars, the only one watching the watchers of the river.

He stood at full attention at the South Tower. Perched off one side of the tower was a concrete platform surrounded by Plexiglas, a capsule of sorts where yawning sentries did their own dubious monitoring of the bridge through a mounted spyglass, as if conducting a sociological study at a great remove. The sentries looked like kids, while Mr. Chen, who stood out front on the sidewalk, among the people, looked every bit of his forty years. He had a paunch, blackened teeth, and the raspy cough of an avid smoker, and he never stopped watching, even when he allowed himself a cigarette, smoking a cheap brand named after the city itself. He wore a baseball cap with a brim that poked out like an oversize duck's bill, like the Cyrano of duck bills, the crown of which read THEY SPY ON YOU.

Six years earlier, working as a functionary for a transportation company, Mr. Chen had read a story about the bridge in the paper, about bodies raining to their end. Soon after, he quietly took his post at the South Tower. Ever since then, when not working his job, he'd been up on the bridge, pulling would-be's from the railing. According to a blog he kept, he'd saved 174 jumpers—and in the process had been hailed as one of China's great Good Samaritans. Of those he saved, some small number met near the bridge every year around Christmas to celebrate their new lives and ostensibly to offer their thanks. As part of the ceremony, they calculated their new ages from the date of their salvation. In this born-again world, no one was older than six.

Back home I'd stumbled on Mr. Chen's blog one day, reading it in jumbled Google translation, and became riveted by his blow-by-blow of life on the bridge. There'd been the husband and wife who'd jumped hand in hand. There'd been the man dressed in black, floating there on the water's surface as a boat tried to reach him, until the current finally sucked him away. Another fellow had been pulled off the railing, back onto the bridge, and in the fight that ensued—one during which Mr. Chen had to enlist the help of others—the man had bitten his tongue in half (good God!) and nearly bled to death on the sidewalk, leaving Mr. Chen covered in blood.

Mr. Chen's blog entries were sometimes their own desperate pleas: *Lovelorn girls of Henan, where are you?* read one. But more often they were a subdued, pointillistic chronicle of the day's dark news: . . . *middle-aged man jumped off bridge where the body fell to the flower bed: died on the spot. . . . Speaking in northern accent, man gave me a cigarette, said: Alas! Wives and children. . . . A woman in the southeast fort jumped in riverbed, dead on spot. . . . Next to statue at southwest fort, man died jumping to concrete, one leg thrown from body, only blackened blood left behind. Meaningless life!*

And yet standing sentry among the hordes, Mr. Chen seemed a bit comical, or his mission seemed the ultimate act of absurdity. How could he possibly pick out the suicidal on a four-mile-long bridge? Were they marked somehow, glowing only for him? As no one seemed to pay him any attention, he was forced to take himself twice as seriously. And he was so engrossed in the Kabuki of his work that it occurred to me how easy a mark he might make for a practical joker tying shoelaces together. Had his heroics only been a figment of his imagination? Was he as unstable somehow as his jumpers? And was he serious with those binoculars, especially with visibility reduced to fifty yards or so in the murk? When I introduced myself, he waved me off. "Not now," he said gruffly. "I'm working."

Then his binoculars shot up to his eyes, sheltered by the bill of his cap, and he fumbled with the focus knob while gazing deep into the masses, searching, it would seem, for that fleeting infrared flare of despair, for the moment when he'd be called into action, ready for his hero moment.

●        ●        ●

One's reasons for being on the bridge belonged to the mysterious underworld in all of us, but to choose to die so publicly, so dramatically—turning languid flips or dropping straight as a pin—was something I couldn't quite understand. After all the humiliation one suffered, all the monotonies and losses, the erasures and disintegrations, after being constantly consumed by society, was it a small reclamation of the self? And what would it feel like to fly, to prove you could? The mere glimmer seemed almost too dangerous to consider. If you let it in, is that when you started to feel the pull of this other force? Could it be stopped?

There were the Stoics, who justified suicide, and the Christians, who condemned it. There was the honorable seppuku of samurai, and the cowardly cyanide of Nazis. And there were suicide's other famous practitioners: Virginia Woolf, entering the River Ouse with a heavy stone in her pocket; Walter Benjamin, overdosing on morphine in a hotel room in Spain in the belief that he was about to be turned over to the Nazis; Sylvia Plath, turning on the gas . . . and then, later, her son, too. Meriwether Lewis shot himself in the chest; Kurt Cobain, in the head. There were Spanish matadors and Congolese pygmies. Auntie Em from The *Wizard of Oz* and Tattoo from *Fantasy Island*. William James, the great humanist philosopher who, tilting dangerously close to self-annihilation, wrote his father, "Thoughts of the pistol, the dagger, and the bowl began to usurp an unduly large part of my attention," and later proclaimed, "I take it that no man is educated who has never dallied with the thought of suicide."

Those on the bridge weren't dallying anymore. They'd come, one after the other, to jump, their lives reduced to this single sliver. Beneath the hum and blare of traffic came that insidious sucking sound. How could just one man stop it?

·　　·　　·

Mr. Chen appeared to have a very strict routine on the bridge, no matter if it was snowing, blowing, or broiling heat. He stood at full attention at the South Tower, where a large percentage of his encounters came within the first one hundred meters past the fort, in that area of the bridge that spanned from the riverbank to the river itself. "In so much pain," he would tell me, "they jump the second they think they're over the mother river. And a lot of them miss the water."

His routine called for maintaining his station for about forty minutes out of every hour—then he fired up his moped, an unconvincing contraption on the verge of breakdown, and putted off down the sidewalk, weaving between walkers, a little like John Wayne astride a miniature Shetland pony. These were his rounds, up and down the bridge, motoring out one mile to the North Tower and then turning back. If he sniffed trouble out there, he might linger—in some cases might be gone hours—but today he reappeared a short time later, stitching deftly through the crowd, then kickstanding his Rocinante and resuming his same exact position, his same exact suspicious disposition, his same exact focused gruffness beneath the bill of his cap. He wore a collared shirt and dark slacks. Though he was stout, with plump hands, he held himself like a much bigger person. Like two of himself.

The sky roiled and spit, as if we were lost inside some potion. Again, the scent of diesel and fish. After fifteen minutes or so, I had a splitting headache, and yet Mr. Chen stood nearly stock-still, unfazed, scanning the crowd with binoculars. His life was a grand monotony, but in his stillness and stasis, the possibility for calamity existed in every moment, and that's what kept him coiled and at the ready.

Mr. Chen would later describe a recurring nightmare that went like this: Someone was up on the railing, and he was sprinting as fast as he could to save the jumper. Over and over, he would arrive too late, as the body pushed from the railing to the hungry ghost below. He said that he'd been visited on the bridge by a foreign psychiatrist who asked him if he might draw a picture of whatever came to mind. So he did: of a large mountain disappearing up into the clouds, which the psychiatrist interpreted as Mr. Chen trying to carry the weight of the weightless sky. Or something like that. Mr. Chen was fuzzy on the details and didn't have much time for this nonsense. The encounter smudged into the same colorlessness of every other colorless moment in the colorless flow of time on the bridge.

The rain had let off and the fog shifted a little, though the weekend traffic had worsened—the city dwellers heading out to the country, the country dwellers heading into the city. I meandered out on the bridge for a moment, away from the tower and the armed sentries and Mr. Chen, who didn't seem to care a whit about me unless I planned to jump. As I gazed downriver, in the easterly direction of Shanghai, a shipyard with an enormous crane appeared in the near distance while a temple loomed with its wooden pagoda on a hill. Skimming the river's brown, roiling surface came a steady, dirgelike stream of barges loaded with lumber, coal, containers, and sand. The view into its muddy waters was not for the faint of heart. There was one of two ways to die from here: on impact with the water's surface, which at sixty-five miles per hour is like hitting concrete, the shattering of bone and internal organs, the instant blackout and massive bleeding, the general pancaking and dismemberment of the body—or by drowning, by somehow surviving the impact and waking underwater, swept away in the current, unable to muster a frog kick given the various possible combinations of broken pelvis/femur/back/jaw, etc. Below, the waters eddied and swirled, etching a secret language on the surface. When a train passed, the whole bridge seemed to buckle and sway, causing me to clutch the railing.

One of Mr. Chen's blog entries was simply entitled "Girl's Tears." It told the tale of a girl from the country who'd come to the bridge, not far from this spot here, to end her life. It started with the observation that tears shed by girls were like tears of angels "that come from disappointment—or was it regret?" This was a runaway, said Mr. Chen, and she stood "tummy railing," looking down at the water, despondent. When Mr. Chen approached, he gave her three options: (1) leave the bridge, (2) call emergency services for help, or (3) let Mr. Chen take her to his house, where she could live for a time with him, his wife, and their daughter. Mr. Chen took her phone and called her belligerent boyfriend, and as he spoke to him, she climbed the railing to jump. He seized her hand; she pulled away, climbing higher on the railing, teetering for a second there. He tore her from the railing, but as the police arrived, she ran into traffic, then tried to disappear in the crowd. The police apprehended her and took her away. It was over just like that. One second he could feel her breath on him; the next she was gone, and Mr. Chen, tough as he was, claimed to have burst into tears.

"Next day called number," he wrote on his blog. "Always unanswered."

The reason Mr. Chen was in the business of saving lives now was that, as a boy, he'd always gone unanswered. There is a saying in Chinese he used, that he never possessed "mother's shoes." With those words, he threw back an oversize shot of a potent grain alcohol. "Getting drunk loosens the tongue," he declared empirically, then refilled our teacups as we sat together in a tight, crowded restaurant near the bridge. He clinked them in a toast and tossed another mini-bucketful into the back of his throat, where, according to my simultaneous research, everything caught fire and napalmed down the gullet to the stomach, where, in turn, it flickered and tasered a while, like rotgut lava. We had left the bridge for lunch, and he had insisted that I drink with him. Sensing we might be in the midst of a transitional relationship moment, I joined him in the first few rounds but then thought better of it—there was no doubt this guy was going to drink me under the table—and eased off. He laughed when I did, a disparaging laugh, wondering aloud at what kind of American I was.

Our party now included my translator, Susan—who was born in Nanjing but raised in the United States—and a wordless man who had suddenly appeared, ostensibly a close friend of Mr. Chen's, called Mr. Shi. We'd arrived at this "family restaurant" sometime after noon, after we'd all left the bridge together, Mr. Chen on his moped and the three of us on foot, taking endless flights of stairs down through the South Tower to the ground, where Mr. Chen was waiting to ferry us, one by one, on the back of his moped to the restaurant. I didn't know where to put my hands, so I grabbed the bulk of his shoulders.

We sat down to filmy glasses of beer and a clear, unmarked bottle of grain alcohol, and saucers of peppers and tripe, tofu soup, noodles, and fish stew. Mr. Chen and Mr. Shi began smoking Nanjings until we were wreathed in smoke. Overhead a fan lopped away off-kilter, on the verge of unscrewing itself from the ceiling. The walls of the restaurant were sepia colored, plastered with old posters, Buddha sharing the wall with a liquor ad. The hissing sound of the wok—onions and chicken and squirming mung beans—agitated beneath the clatter of plates and the gruff, rising voices of men (there were no families here, only workmen) huddled at the eight or so tables, heads sluicing with liquor, too.

Mr. Chen explicated his opening statement. See, in the old times, before "the Communist liberation," a great deal of pride was connected to these homemade textiles, for both parent and child. The shoes and socks were a declaration of individual love in a country obsessed with the self-effacing collective. His own mother had always been an erratic presence, but after his parents split when he was eight, she disappeared for the better part of a decade—and so, too, did his "mother's love," as he put it. That's when he went to live with his grandmother, in a village outside the city. Widowed at eighteen, his grandmother served an important function in the village: She was a peacemaker and therapist of sorts, if utterly unschooled. It was from her that Mr. Chen had learned the fine art of persuasion. It was from the incompleteness of his own family that he'd built this not-so-secret life as the defender of broken humanity. And the weight of the task had become its own burden.

"I've aged terribly in my six years on the bridge," he said, again clinking teacups with Mr. Shi. "To age!" He drank and then admitted that he had a lot of gray hair, due to the weather and stress—stress on the bridge, stress at work, stress at home. He caught me gazing at the thick, black, spiky forest matting his head. "I've been dyeing it for years," he said.

He sat back, removed his glasses, rubbed his eyes with the backs of his hands. He poured another glass, this time hesitating before drinking, and spoke again as he stabbed a piece of tripe, then began to chew. On the bridge, he said, there were three types of jumpers, and they had to be dealt with either by force or finesse, by blunt words or wraithlike verbiage fashioned into a lasso. Mostly they came peaceably, but sometimes it was a donnybrook. The first category included the mentally unstable or clinically insane. In the frenzy of letting go, these were the ones who might take you with them, grasping onto anyone as some proxy for "mother's love." So—Mr. Chen would charge them like a dangerous man himself, wrestling, punching, kicking, doing whatever was necessary. "I'm very confident in my physical strength," he said. "Since I have no psychological training, my job is to get that person off the bridge as quickly as possible." Whereupon he might take him or her to "the station," which, as it turned out, was an in-patient psych ward at the highly reputed Nanjing University, one of the few places in the city where the suicidal could receive professional care and treatment.

The second category was the emotionally fragile, the wilted flower, the person who had lost someone—a husband, a child, a wife, a parent—or suffered from some sort of abuse and saw no way to go on. If the potential jumper was a woman, Mr. Chen's strategy was to try to bring her to tears, for that often broke the tension, and once emotion poured forth, he might grab for her hand and huddle her away. Men, by contrast, were both simpler and trickier. You forked one of two ways. Either you told him bluntly that you were about to punch him in the nose if he didn't step away from the railing, or you did the exact opposite: You approached in a nonthreatening, even companionable, manner, offering a cigarette to the figure lingering too long by the railing, and from there steered him to a place like this restaurant, where together you could drink grain alcohol and really talk, something that wasn't so easy in a culture that still held fast to a Confucian ethic of stoicism.

The final category, he said, included the ones who "failed really hard, or too often." Usually men, these would-be jumpers had often lost a great deal of money and weren't feeling so wonderful about themselves anymore, especially when their failures were thrown into relief by those riding on the heady high seas of the new China, driving fancy cars, wearing designer clothes, smoking expensive American cigarettes. Mr. Chen then pointed to Mr. Shi and said, "He was one of those."

Mr. Shi, a thin man of thinning hair, blinked laconically through the smoke. Though the stage was set for him to unspool his tale, he showed no interest in taking up the story. "Later," barked Mr. Chen. It was strange, and not a little confusing, how gruff he could be while making himself, and those around him, so vulnerable. When more plates of food arrived, he shoveled beans and noodles, fish and broccoli onto his plate, then lit upon it all as if it were prey, gobbling and drinking, then gobbling some more.

I regarded him once more in this dim light. He was unabashed in his mannerisms, a man who seemed to live so fully inside this hexed world of suicide that he had little time for polish or polite chitchat or getting-to-know-you. When I asked if he had heard of the famous Hollywood film *It's a Wonderful Life*, in which Jimmy Stewart plans to end his life on a bridge until an angel named Clarence saves him, he cut me off by shaking his head. No; he didn't care about movies or my attempts to draw fatuous parallels. Nor were we kindred spirits: Simply showing up did not confer membership to the club. He barely bothered to look at me when responding to my questions.

In turn, I soon found myself growing anxious there in that restaurant—very anxious—watching Mr. Chen and Mr. Shi drain glass after glass. My mind suddenly seized upon the notion that this was a Saturday, the busiest day on the bridge, and here we sat. However absurd it had felt to be standing on a four-mile bridge, thronged by thousands, trying to pick out jumpers, I felt a sudden onrush of dread at not being there at all, as if the welfare of all humanity depended on our vigilance. Part of it had to do with the effect of the grain alcohol. And part of it was fatigue—the result of all those time zones to get here. In that loud, hot space, I felt simultaneously this desire to stand and leave and yet to lay my head down and rest. The irrefutable truth was that nothing—neither butter nor Mr. Chen—would dissuade the jumpers from coming: So what was the point of being here at all?

That was the question that occurred to me now in that mung-bean-and-hooch restaurant, that hole-in-the-wall, listening to the guttural rebukes of Mr. Chen: What was I doing here at all, in a place where people came to kill themselves, 7,000 miles from my home and family? This wasn't an assignment that had been given to me. I'd chosen it. I'd come as if there were some message for me here, some fragment to justify, or obliterate, that slow bloom of doubt. But now I could feel the pressure under the soles of my feet: The bridge ran under me, too.

·　　·　　·

If you dig deep enough into the past, every family has its suicide. My maternal grandmother had told me the story of a relative, dating from the nineteenth century: a young woman fresh from Ireland, a Catholic who'd married a Protestant. She was isolated, living with her husband's family in upstate New York, in the region known as the North Country, and her life became a slow torment from which there seemed to be no escape, even after bearing a child. Her beliefs were pilloried and belittled. She slowly unraveled. One day she put rocks in her pocket and stepped into a cistern, where she drowned.

But such events didn't just belong to the past—or to some mythic country, either. From my own suburban hometown, I remembered a sweet, shy kid, roughly my age, who seemed incapable of any sort of demonstrativeness, who drove himself to the Adirondacks in winter, purchased a coil of rope along the way, found a sturdy tree, and hanged himself. I had nightmares about that boy, shagged in ice until his father found him and cut him down.

And the neighbor down the street, found in the bathtub . . . And the kid who ran his motorcycle into a tree, an accident but for the note left behind saying that's exactly what he intended to do . . . And so on. Even in suburbia, suicide had seemed like its own opaque parable, the never-happened, glossed-over secret.

I came upon the story of a boy, a British art student named Christian Drane, who'd photographed suicide spots in England for a school project—including a bridge in Bristol, where he was approached by a stranger who wondered if he was all right—and then hanged himself in the Polygon woods of Southampton. No one could believe it. He'd made everyone laugh. He had a tattoo on his arm, representing his family. Afterward, his girlfriend told an inquest that Christian was the happiest person she knew, "cheeky, spontaneous, excitable." He whisked her to Paris for her birthday, wrapped her in "fairy lights" and took her portrait. He posted other photos from his project online: other bridges, subway stations, and Beachy Head, the chalk cliffs of Eastbourne, the most famous of English suicide spots. Each bore the moniker "Close Your Eyes and Say Goodbye."

The photograph of Christian that accompanied many of the news stories showed a boy with mussed-up hair and pierced ears with black plugs, looking impishly askance at the camera. Had the pretense of the project emboldened him, or was "the project" merely his eventual suicide? His final note, which no one claimed to understand, read: "To mum and anybody who cares. I have done something I can never forgive myself for. I am a bad person. I am sorry."

· · ·

The Yangtze ever beckoned. And its pull was finally felt at the family restaurant by Mr. Chen, who abruptly stood, grunted a little, walked out the front door like a superhero summoned by dog whistle, then fired up his moped and went swerving off, his THEY SPY ON YOU double-bill back on his head, binoculars dangling around his neck. Left in his wake, we—Susan the translator, Mr. Shi, and I—straggled back to the bridge in a slow-motion amble. It felt good to be in the open air again, somehow cleansing after all the smoke and noise.

Bent like a harp, Mr. Shi was the kind of gentle man you instantly wanted to protect, to shield from life's bullies or from the falling monsoon rain that now switched on again. It seemed to pain him to have to speak. He was too slight for his somewhat dirty slacks and pale blue dress shirt—and carried himself with so little swagger he seemed resigned to the fact that he interested no one. Except *I* was interested. I wanted to know what Mr. Chen had meant when he'd identified Mr. Shi as one who'd failed really hard. Mr. Shi squinted at me as he lit a cigarette and then started to speak, hesitated, and started again. He said that several years back, his daughter had been diagnosed with leukemia. He'd borrowed money for her treatment and had fallen tens of thousands in debt, even making the desperate blunder of engaging with a local loan shark.

When he went to the bridge on that fateful day, he loitered by the railing long enough for Mr. Chen to lock in on him through his binoculars, and then this man was suddenly standing next to him, saying, "Brother, it's not worth it." After a while, Mr. Chen got

Mr. Shi to smoke a cigarette and coaxed him off the bridge, down to the family restaurant to drink and talk, whereupon Mr. Shi's entire story poured forth. Mr. Chen listened closely, trying to understand as best as possible Mr. Shi's predicament, and then began to formulate a plan. Mr. Chen would speak with the loan shark and all the other vengeful parties in the matter. He'd negotiate a truce, a repayment plan, a job search. He insisted that Mr. Shi meet him the following day, at his workplace, at the transportation company, where he often welcomed the weekend's forlorn and misfit to his desk, a recurring gesture that had left his bosses exasperated and threatening to fire him. He'd given Mr. Shi hope and friendship (though details of the repayment plan were murky), and Mr. Shi had found a way to begin life anew.

In this moment of sheepish intimacy—Mr. Shi had a habit of making eye contact, then looking away as if embarrassed—he reminded me of something Mr. Chen had said: "The people I'm saving are very, very kind. They don't want to hurt anyone, so the only way they can vent is by hurting themselves. In that moment when they are deciding between life and death, they are much simpler, more innocent in their thoughts. They almost become blank, a white sheet."

In a way, Mr. Shi was human pathos writ large; in another, he was the smidgen of hope that caused the caesura before jumping. It struck me as odd, however, that it required a moment like this, walking with him now, to realize that while the deeper, more ancient brain was at all times in dialogue with death, and while that dialogue asserted itself into one's conscious mind from time to time, the frontal lobe was a powerful combatant in self-denial. No matter what declivities I'd found in my own life, I'd always thought of suicide as something occurring over a divide, in the land of irrevocable people, when evidence suggested again and again—sweet Mr. Shi, right here in front of me!—that wasn't the case at all.

We climbed the South Tower stairwell back to the bridge and found Mr. Chen again, standing sentry, and he proffered us a slight if somewhat cool nod. He seemed so alone, standing there; even his wife and daughter knew little of his life on the bridge. They didn't know he'd once been stabbed in the leg; they didn't know the emotional storms he'd weathered on those days when he lost a jumper. ("I want to give them a clean piece of land," he said, using a turn of phrase. "I don't want them worrying.") Now the rain galloped harder; a sea of umbrellas popped open, moving south to north and north to south. Then, as quickly, the rain stopped, and a low-lying monster cloud filled with a muggy kind of light and a crowding heat blanketed everything. One wondered if there'd ever been blue sky in Nanjing. Below, the barges glided downriver in the same stream that carried fallen trees and clumps of earth in the direction of distant Shanghai. While Mr. Chen scoured the crowd, Mr. Shi crouched under the shelter of the fort and lit a cigarette. Cars and trucks and taxis came and went, honking horns, the taste of fuel and smog thick in the air.

Another reporter appeared on the bridge. Young and wearing a flouncy miniskirt and white high heels, she held a device that looked to be the size of a pen, which acted both as her tape recorder and camera. It seemed like secret-agent stuff, but she announced herself to be a student from Shanghai, here to do a big exposé on suicide. Softened a bit by alcohol and the spectral vision of youth itself, Mr. Chen intermittently answered her questions, allowing that the hours between ten A.M. and four P.M. were the most likely for attempts and that his method on the bridge boiled down to intuition. "I'm looking for their spirit as much as their expression and posture," he said. Then he made a grand show of getting on his moped, kicking it to life, and put-putting off on patrol, John Wayne again on his Shetland pony.

We both stood watching him go, the young woman and I, until he disappeared behind tatters of sky-fog that had come loose. In his absence, I was buffeted again by a wave of ennui, this crescendoing sense of uselessness. But then the young student reporter turned to me, beaming with bright eyes, and blurted in broken English, "What angel is he!"

.    .    .

There are always two countercurrents running through the brain of someone contemplating suicide, much like the currents working at odds in the river itself: the desire to escape and the dim hope of being saved. The mind, having fixated on suicide as an option, might take signs of encouragement in everything: cloud formations or rough seas or a random conversation. In the failure of the mailman to arrive. Or the store sold out of a particular brand of cereal. As the mind vacuum-seals itself to its singular course of action and as the body moves in concert—as suction takes hold and begins to claim its molecules—the only solution to the inevitable chain of unfolding events, the only possibility at being saved, is an intervention of some sort, a random occurrence or gesture. The hand on the shoulder. Then, the mind that has held so long and fast to the body's undoing might shift, and unburden, and de-aggregate, in some cases, almost instantly. Recidivism rates for those mulling suicide are low for all but the severely depressed. Help someone focus step by step across the bridge and he'll be less inclined to ever return.

In my reading, I kept coming back to William James, brother of Henry, journeying across the European continent in 1867, his despair at feeling a failure, the pull of ending it all. In his Norfolk coat, bright shirts, and flowing ties—"His clothes looked as if they had come freshly pressed from the cleaners," a contemporary once said, "and his mind seemed to have blown in on a storm"—he decamped to Berlin, and took the baths at Teplice, in what was then Bohemia. Later, plagued by intense back pain that had migrated to his neck, he took the hypnotic drug chloral hydrate as a sleep aid and tried electric-shock therapy, which failed to provide relief. In his deepest depression, he felt he'd arrived at a terminus. And yet he withstood the urge of self-annihilation, never again contemplating suicide. A friend of his, a woman named Minny, who helped encourage him through his troubled time (then died herself at a young age), reminded him in a letter of the proposition ever at work: "Of course the question will always remain, What is one's true life—& we must each try & solve it for ourselves."

·     ·     ·

Now, in the country that brought the world 20 percent of its annual suicide victims, I stood awaiting Mr. Chen's return while breathing in the particulates and invisible lead chips of progress. Time came to a very still point in the late afternoon, and I ambled out onto the bridge with Susan, the translator, realizing that whatever vision of Mr. Chen's heroism had brought me here in the first place, it was folly to think I'd actually ever see him save someone.

Susan was telling me about a family acquaintance who, years back, had jumped from the bridge in winter (most suicides here occurred in the fall and spring). Bundled in many layers against the elements, she had gone to the bridge in distress, climbed the railing, and leapt. One hundred and thirty feet down, at the speed of sixty-five miles an hour, she had hit the river, but if it was the angle or the specifics of her swaddling, if it was will or fate, she had lived, survived not just the fall but also the currents and hypothermia and, most of all, the killer flotsam. Every once in a while, for whatever reason, someone was chosen—but what I wanted to know was this: Having returned from the river, was she happy now, had she found in the aftermath her true life, solved the thing that had first gone missing in her? Susan considered the question. "I think happy enough," she said, "but who knows?"

Just then a man lurched past us, a flash of green. We paid him no mind, really, until he was about twenty steps beyond us, out where the bridge first met water. He stopped, put both hands on the railing, and threw a leg up. The green man's body rose, and now he was hooking his ankle on the top bar, then levering himself from vertical to horizontal until he lay on top of the railing. People streamed by, apparently unaware, staring down. Now the green man began to push his way over the railing, at which point I knew that I was not dreaming and that he was going to kill himself. I shouted, and then burst toward him, sprinting past Mr. Chen's posters and flags.

The green man began shifting to the other side, listing as if on the curl of a wave, half of him letting go into space. Reaching him, I reflexively planted a foot against the concrete base of the railing, latched an arm up and over, then wrenched his body as hard as I could while I pushed back from the railing. Just like that, his body, which was as limp and resigned as if he'd been filled with sawdust, came tumbling back into the real world, where he assumed the full proportions of his humanness again. He had a very tan face and rough hands. He reeked of alcohol. Even before we'd hit the ground, he'd blurted something in Chinese, and then repeated it as I held him in a tight bear hug, readying for a struggle that never came.

"I'm just joking," he implored. He had the supplicant, bedraggled demeanor of a man at loose ends. "I'm okay, thank you . . ."

Shocked back into the world of the living, the green man didn't wait for the question; he just began talking, in a fit of logomania. "The reason I tried to kill myself," he blurted, "is because my father was in the army . . ."

His story seemed disjointed, and more so because Susan was trying to do three things at once—translate, call Mr. Chen, who was not answering, and figure out how to get the attention of Mr. Shi, who was stationed back at the fort, casually smoking cigarettes. A crowd began to gather, an airless huddle. The man went on. "My father is ninety and very sick. We lost his documents in a fire, and we have no money to care for him. The government needs proof that he was in the army, but we are a family of soldiers. I was one, too . . ."

Mr. Chen had said that people become innocent again on the bridge. They become simple and open in a way that they never otherwise were in real life. And here I was, bear-hugging a man in green coveralls named Fan Ping, trying to crush some spirit inside him that had opted to, in Mr. Chen's words, "dive downward." He was talking to me earnestly, though I didn't understand a word. He was a child, needing someone to understand. His eyes swelled, and two streams of water released over his smooth, rounded cheeks. I don't know, but it didn't seem like crying exactly. It was like something done less out of grief than reflex. With my arms around him, hands chained, I could feel his heart thudding into mine. His breath of stale spirits filled my lungs. When I looked down, my shoes were his, two terribly dirty, scuffed sheaths of cheap, disintegrating leather. We could barely stand as we swayed together.

Fan Ping said that he was thirty-seven years old and that his mother had died three years earlier. He worked for a gas station, Sinopec, and made $400 a month. He was one of those known as a *guang gun*, or "bare branch," unmarried, a victim of demographics in a country where 20 million men went without wives. "What am I supposed to do now?" he said.

The crowd of onlookers registered their concern and curiosity. Some in the back were laughing, unsure of what indeed was transpiring or just made nervous by it. I had an irrational flash of hating those people in the back, of wanting to lash out, but all that really mattered was keeping my body between Fan Ping and the railing, in case he made another lunge. Eventually Mr. Chen appeared and dismounted from his moped. On cue, the crowd parted while Mr. Chen stepped forward, invested with the power and understanding of all the nuances at play here. Fan Ping started his story again—*army . . . sick father . . . dead mother . . . gas station . . . so sorry to try to kill self*—and Mr. Chen asked me to let go of the man, something I wasn't at all inclined to do. Then he pulled out a camera and took Fan Ping's picture, which seemed, at best, like an odd way to begin and, at worst, like a major violation of the man's privacy. Then, glaring straight at Fan Ping, who stood slumped and dirty, with bloodshot eyes, Mr. Chen spoke.

"I should punch you in the face," Mr. Chen said. "You call yourself a family man. . . . A son . . . Chinese? If your father hadn't been in the army, and if you didn't try to kill yourself just now, I'd punch you. You're not thinking—or are you just shirking your responsibility? I really would like to punch you now. Hand over your ID . . ."

Fan Ping seemed utterly flummoxed, reaching into his pocket and fishing out his identification card. Mr. Chen made a show of studying it, then derisively handed it back—was this a diversion, part of a new therapeutic method?—and in the same brusque tone asked what in the world was he thinking, coming up here like this? Fan Ping replied that he wasn't thinking at all; he just didn't have the money necessary to care for his father—and that his life boiled down to this vast, sorrowful futility.

Mr. Chen sized him up again, with a withering look. I could see part of Fan Ping's blue sock poking through the worn leather of his shoe. "Yes," said Mr. Chen dismissively. "We all have our troubles."

•     •     •

Watching Mr. Chen face off with Fan Ping in that gray late afternoon was like watching twin sons of different mothers: They were both short and stout. Mr. Chen asked Fan Ping where he lived. A country village outside the city. Mr. Chen asked how he'd gotten to the bridge. By foot, from his job. The conversation went on like this for some time while slowly Mr. Chen's tone shifted from outrage and aggression to a more familiar, fraternal concern, even sweetness. "I promise you that there's nothing we can't fix," he said, "but first we have to get you off this bridge." Then later: "I'm here to help you." In his dishevelment, Fan Ping didn't seem capable of movement, as perhaps he hadn't entirely given up on the idea that had brought him here in the first place. And Mr. Chen intuited this. He moved in closer and clasped his hand, a special shake, a locking of pinkies that meant brotherhood, then didn't let go, dragging Fan Ping to the fort and a bus stop there while the crowd followed. He arranged for Fan Ping to meet him at his office first thing Monday morning. He wrote the address on a scrap of paper and stuffed it into Fan Ping's pocket. He punched the digits of Fan Ping's cell-phone number into his own.

"You promise you'll be there," Mr. Chen said.

"I will," said Fan Ping.

"Unless you try to jump off the bridge between now and then," Mr. Chen deadpanned. It wasn't quite a joke, but Fan Ping laughed, as did several in the crowd looking for some sort of release—and then Mr. Chen made it all okay by laughing, too.

Meanwhile, the student reporter from Shanghai grabbed me, tottering on high heels, and asked if she might conduct an interview. Not waiting for an answer, she began peppering me with questions, compensating for my lack of Chinese with her almost-English: "Do American engage in this so-called suicide event?" . . . "From bridges is always the favorite, no?" . . . "Does American— you—have fixes for problem?" . . . "Do you also enjoy *Sex and the City*?"

I couldn't even pretend. My hands, which rarely shake, were shaking. And I floated from my body, watching Mr. Chen and Fan Ping walk ahead, watched—from some high, hovering angle—as Mr. Chen placed the man on a bus and Fan Ping squished down the aisle in his disintegrating shoes and took his place by the window, looking straight ahead. The bus gurgled, backfired, then lurched forward, gone in a plume of gray smoke. That's when some part of me came tumbling back down to myself. I turned and strode back out on the bridge to the spot where

Fan Ping had readied to die. I came to the railing, peered down once more to the dark, roiling waters, and felt as if I might regurgitate my lunch noodles.

There would have been no way to survive that fall. And for some reason, standing there, I felt a sharp pang of loss, though no one had been lost. I felt I'd been a step too late, though I'd been one step ahead. It wasn't Fan Ping I was thinking about; it was all the other lives—within me and disparate from me—that had been lost. Yanking Fan Ping from the railing hadn't offered a stay of any kind; instead, it brought death nearer. Mr. Chen wasn't a caricature but a bearer of so much imminent grief. I was bound to him by a feeling Mr. Chen had elucidated for me in one of our talks, a feeling of standing in a spot like this on the bridge, after an incident like this, hovering between heaven and earth, "heart hanging in air."

•    •    •

Back at home, the months passed, and so the day-to-day reasserted itself. And yet sometimes, randomly, Mr. Chen appeared in my mind, standing guard at his station at the South Tower, scanning the crowd. And on those few occasions when I found myself describing what happened on the bridge to friends, I could hear my voice retelling the story of Fan Ping, and it sounded preposterous, even delusional. It sounded as if I might be a man of comical self-importance or full of conspiracies, the sort who wears a hat that reads THEY SPY ON YOU. Soon I stopped mentioning it altogether. After Fan Ping pulled away on the bus that day, I had joked with Mr. Chen about catching up to him on the big scoreboard of lives saved.

"It's 174 to 1," I told him. "Watch your back."

He smirked dismissively and said: "You're only given a half point for that one."

As it turned out he was right again. He already knew what I'd later find out. That is, if I'd ever imagined saving someone from a bridge, it probably would have been a fantasy bathed in altruistic light, in which I . . . SAVED . . . A . . . HUMAN . . . LIFE! But then it slowly dawned on me: I'd tried to stop Fan Ping merely so I wouldn't have to live with the memory of having watched him fall. My worry now was that he would somehow succeed in trying again.

So I contact Mr. Chen. He tells me that on the Monday morning after Fan Ping tried to kill himself—the morning that the two men were supposed to meet at his office—Mr. Chen arrived at work and his boss promptly fired him. He left the office building immediately and went to his station at the bridge, not so much because he was despondent but because that was where he felt he belonged. All the while, he dialed Fan Ping's number over and over again, but the phone was out of order. And remained that way, all these months later.

There's nothing to do now, says Mr. Chen, but wait for him to come back. Rest assured, he'll stop Fan Ping. Even as he's recently saved a father, and a few students, and a woman with a psychiatric problem. He knows what Fan Ping looks like. In broiling heat and blowing monsoon, he's out there, ever vigilant, waiting in his double duck-bill, scanning the crowd for Fan Ping—and all the others, too, who might possess thoughts of a glorious demise. He assures me he'll be waiting for them all—and you and me, as well—binoculars trained on our murky faces, our eyes sucked downward, trying to read the glimmer off the surface of the river below.

The only question remains: Can he reach us in time?

## Texas Monthly

FINALIST—PUBLIC
INTEREST

*Arrested at the age of twenty-six and convicted of murder in 1984, Anthony Graves spent eighteen years behind bars—twelve of them on death row—for a crime he did not commit. Pamela Colloff, a senior editor at* Texas Monthly, *drew on more than 10,000 pages of police reports and court records to write "Innocence Lost," her 14,000-word account of Graves's arrest, trial and imprisonment. The story spurred a reinvestigation of the case that ended, just one month after the publication of "Innocence Lost," with Graves's release from prison. "Innocence Found" recounts the events that led to Graves' exoneration. "Read 'Innocence Lost,'" wrote the National Magazine Award judges, "and try not to shake with rage. Read 'Innocence Found' and rejoice that not even venality and incompetence can withstand the truth."* Texas Monthly *was also nominated for the National Magazine Award for Public Interest in 2001 for Colloff's story "They Haven't Got a Prayer," about the struggle over school prayer in Santa Fe, Texas.*

Pamela Colloff

# Innocence Lost *and* Innocence Found

## Innocence Lost

### I.

A few hours before dawn on a sticky summer night in Somerville, a one-stoplight town ninety miles northwest of Houston, police chief Jewel Fisher noticed the faint smell of burning wood. Fisher was following up on a late-night prowler call east of the main drag, in the predominantly black neighborhood that runs alongside the railroad tracks. Turning down the town's darkened streets, he suddenly caught sight of a house on fire and realized that he was looking at the home of forty-five-year-old Bobbie Davis, a supervisor at the Brenham State School. Flames climbed the walls and skittered along the roof of the one-story brick structure, casting a murky orange glow. The windows had already been smashed in by several neighbors, who had screamed the names of the children they feared were trapped inside, pleading for them to wake up. Fisher quickly radioed for help, but when volunteer firefighters arrived, they discovered the bodies of Bobbie, her teenage daughter, and her four grandchildren inside. Each person had been brutally attacked and left to die in the blaze.

Word of the killings, which took place on August 18, 1992, traveled quickly through Somerville. The tragedy had no precedent; it was—and eighteen years later remains—the most infamous crime in Burleson County history. "Many in the neighborhood remarked that this was the kind of thing that you expected to happen somewhere else, not in Somerville," read a front-page article in the *Burleson County Citizen-Tribune*. Bobbie had been bludgeoned and stabbed. Her sixteen-year-old daughter, Nicole Davis, a popular senior and top athlete at Somerville High School, had been bludgeoned, stabbed, and shot. Bobbie's grandchildren—nine-year-old Denitra, six-year-old Brittany, five-year-old Lea'Erin, and four-year-old Jason—had been knifed to death. (Bobbie's daughter Lisa was mother to the oldest and youngest children; Bobbie's son, Keith, was father to the two middle girls.) All told, the victims had been stabbed sixty-six times. Even the youngest member of the Davis family, who stood three and a half feet tall, had been shown no mercy. Jason, who investigators would later determine had cowered behind a pillow, was stabbed a dozen times. His body had been doused in gasoline before the house was set on fire.

After daybreak, neighbors gathered to survey the ruins of the Davis home, and TV news crews from Houston came by helicopter, circling overhead. Two Texas Rangers arrived that morning, and two more later joined them, but they had few early leads. There were no obvious suspects and hardly any clues; the fire had ravaged the crime scene, and the killer—or killers—had left behind no witnesses. A night clerk at the Somerville Stop & Shop, Mildred Bracewell, came forward to say that two black men with a gas can had purchased gasoline shortly before the time of the murders. A hypnotist employed by the Department of Public Safety elicited a more precise description from her of one of the men, and a forensic artist sketched a composite drawing of the suspect. Still, there were no arrests.

Four days after the murders, the Rangers got their first break. Five hundred mourners—nearly one third of Somerville—turned out for the funeral, which was held in the local high school gymnasium. Among them was Jason Davis's absentee father, a twenty-six-year-old prison guard named Robert Carter, whose bizarre appearance that day drew stares. His left hand, neck, and ears were heavily bandaged, as was most of the left side of his face. When Bobbie's sister-in-law approached him at the cemetery to inquire about his injuries, Carter's wife, Cookie, quickly answered for him. "His lawn mower exploded on him," she said. Carter added without explanation, "I was burned with gasoline." His conversation with his deceased son's mother, Lisa Davis, was no less strange. Lisa had suffered an unimaginable loss; that day, she would bury two children, as well as her mother, sister, and two nieces. (That her own life had been spared was a quirk of fate; had she not traded shifts with a coworker at the Brenham State School, she would have been at the Davis home on the night of the murders.) As Carter reached to embrace her, she took a step back, startled by what she saw. "What happened?" she asked, studying his face. Abruptly, Carter turned around and walked away.

After the funeral, the Rangers paid Carter a visit at his home in Brenham, fifteen miles south of Somerville. "I figured y'all would be over here to talk to me because of the bandages," he told them. The Rangers had learned from Lisa that she had recently filed a paternity suit against Carter, a first step in obtaining child support. Carter had been served with papers just four days before the killings. Ranger Ray Coffman, the case's lead investigator, read Carter his Miranda rights and asked him to come in for questioning.

That afternoon, at the DPS station in Brenham, Carter sat down with the four veteran Rangers assigned to the case: Coffman, Jim Miller, George Turner, and their supervisor, Earl Pearson. The Rangers were skeptical that one person could have brandished the three weapons used in the murders—a gun, a knife, and a hammer—and had surmised early on that the Davis family had been killed by as many as three assailants. Carter was grilled by the Rangers, but he remained steadfast in his insistence that he knew nothing about the killings. He had burned himself, he told them, while setting fire to some weeds in his yard. By evening, he and the Rangers had reached an impasse, and he agreed to take a polygraph exam. Three of the investigators—Coffman, Miller, and Turner—drove him to Houston, where the test could be administered by a licensed polygraph examiner. He failed it sometime after eleven P.M.

The Rangers continued to interrogate him until well past midnight. After several hours, they wore down Carter's resistance, and he finally agreed to make a statement about the crime. At 2:53 A.M., Ranger Coffman turned on the tape recorder, and Carter began to talk. He had been present at the Davis home on the night of the murders, he allowed, but it was another man—his wife's first cousin, Anthony Graves—who was to blame. As he began, he stumbled over the killer's name, once calling him Kenneth. Later he corrected himself: "I said Kenneth. It wasn't Kenneth. I'm sorry. Anthony."

Carter told the Rangers that he had driven Graves to the Davis home after one o'clock in the morning. Graves, he said, had asked him if he knew any women, and the only prospect who had come to Carter's mind was sixteen-year-old Nicole. He had dropped Graves—who was, by Carter's own admission, a stranger to the Davis family—off at the front door while he stayed in the car. He did not say exactly how Graves had gotten inside. As he waited for Graves to return, Carter said, he heard someone shouting, and then screams. Alarmed, he let himself in to look around. To his horror, he said, he had walked in on a killing spree. "There was blood everywhere," Carter said. "He was going from room to room." Carter maintained that he helplessly looked on while Graves single-handedly murdered the Davis family. "I had no part in it," he insisted, though he had already accurately described the precise locations where many of the victims had been killed.

Afterward, he said, Graves had retrieved a gas can from the storage room, poured gasoline throughout the house, and set it ablaze, scorching him in the process. Remarkably, he expressed no anger toward the man who, by his own telling, had just murdered his son. After the rampage, he said, he drove Graves back to Brenham and dropped him off at Graves's sister's apartment.

During the tape-recorded conversation, the Rangers never stopped to ask Carter fundamental questions that could have determined whether Graves was actually present at the scene of the crime. They never pushed Carter to explain why he would have taken a man who was looking for sex to a house full of sleeping children. Or why Graves would have brutally murdered six people he did not know. They never questioned him about the improbable logistics of the crime he had just described. (How had Graves managed to find a gas can inside the storage room of a house he had never visited?) Nor did they press Carter to admit his own role in the killings. (Wouldn't Bobbie Davis, whose body was found nearest the front door—where investigators had determined there was no sign of forced entry—have been more likely to let in Carter, the father of her grandchild, than a stranger who had turned up at her house in the middle of the night?) Even after Carter divulged that he had burned his own clothes upon returning home, Ranger Coffman continued to focus on his accomplice, twice prompting Carter to say that he wanted to help investigators find his son's killer.

Although Carter's statement was badly flawed, the Rangers had gotten what they wanted: an admission from Carter that he was at the scene of the crime and the name of an accomplice. The possibility that he had falsely named Graves to shift the attention away from himself was never fully explored and would haunt the case during its long and meandering path through the court system over the next eighteen years. "I hope that you don't use this to lock me up," Carter said when he was done, his face still partially obscured by bandages.

What evidence the Rangers were able to find later that day pointed exclusively to Carter himself. A cartridge box in his closet held the same type of copper-coated bullets that had been used to kill Nicole. The .22-caliber pistol that he usually kept above his bed was missing. The Pontiac Sunbird that he had admitted driving to the Davis home was gone; he had traded it in at a Houston car dealership two days after the killings. And yet even as his story fell apart, the Rangers continued to pursue their case against Graves. Two warrants were issued hours after Carter made his statement: one for Carter, who was immediately arrested, the other for Graves. There was no physical evidence that tied Graves to the crime and no discernible motive—only the word of the crime's prime suspect.

Graves, who had moved back to Brenham from Austin that spring after getting laid off from an assembly line job at Dell, was picked up before noon at his mother's apartment and brought to the Brenham police station in handcuffs. In the station's booking room, a surveillance camera captured the half hour that passed as the twenty-six-year-old—who was never told why he was being detained—waited, bewildered. He repeatedly asked an officer who busied himself with paperwork what he was being held for, but he was informed that he would have to wait until a magistrate arrived to read him the charges. Graves turned his attention to another officer, who he hoped would be more forthcoming, but the man feigned ignorance. "You don't know neither?" Graves said, sighing. "I wish somebody would tell me what's going on." When the justice of the peace finally appeared, Graves jumped to his feet, eager for information.

"You're Anthony Charles Graves?" asked the justice of the peace, glancing up from the warrant that she held before her. She was flanked by two police officers.

"Yes, ma'am," he said.

"Anthony, this is going to be your warning of rights," she said. Her delivery was matter-of-fact: "You're charged with the offense of capital murder."

"*Who?*" he said, dumbfounded. He stared back at her blankly.

"An affidavit charging you for this offense has been filed in court," she continued. As she read him his Miranda rights, he watched her in disbelief. "At this time, no bond has been set," she said. "Do you understand what I've told you, Anthony?"

Graves held up his hands in protest. "Capital *murder?*" he said, incredulous. "Me? Wh-wh-who murdered? I mean—"

A man wearing a white Western hat interrupted him. "You'll have a chance to talk to the officers who are actually working the case," he said.

"This is a *big* mistake," Graves said, his voice rising. "Capital *murder?*" Dubious, he turned to the police officer who had brought him down to the station. "This is a joke," he said, breaking into a grin, as if he were suddenly on to the elaborate prank that he seemed certain was being played on him. "Somebody's messing with me, right?" The officer, who did not smile back, ordered him to have a seat.

Graves studied the copy of the arrest warrant that the judge had handed to him, trying to make sense of it. He repeated the words "capital murder" eighteen times, enunciating each syllable as if doing so would help him better grasp their meaning. "This is a big mistake," he repeated. "This has got to be straightened out *today.*" Finally, before he was led down the hall to talk to the Rangers, he slapped the side of his head and cried out, "Am I dreaming?"


## II.

Roy Allen Rueter was listening to the radio at Magnetic Instruments, a Brenham machine shop, when he heard the news that Graves had been charged with six counts of capital murder. Graves had worked for Rueter for three years before moving to Austin to work at Dell, and he had played third base for the company softball team, the Magnetic Instruments Outlaws. Though the two men outwardly had little in common—Rueter, who is white, hailed from a prominent local family; Graves, who is black, was raised in Brenham's federal housing projects—they had become close friends. After Outlaws games, they would talk late into the night about softball and women, and Graves had counseled the twice-divorced Rueter on matters of the heart. "He could always lift you up out of your own self-indulgent misery," Rueter said. "He had a big, deep laugh and a lot of charm. Everyone liked Anthony, especially women." Rueter later proposed to a former classmate of Graves's, to whom he has been married for the past nineteen years, and he credits Graves, who offered encouragement and counsel during their courtship, for bringing them together. When they got married, Graves was in the wedding party.

The news on the radio deeply affected Rueter. "I knew—everyone who knew Anthony knew—it had to be a mistake," he said. "I could never imagine him raising his hand to any woman or child, much less doing what he was accused of doing. It was inconceivable." Rueter called the best lawyer he could think of, Houston defense attorney Dick DeGuerin, and asked him to take on the case. The veteran trial lawyer agreed to represent Graves at his upcoming bond hearing, where the state would have to prove that it had enough evidence to hold Graves. DeGuerin's expertise did not come cheap; his fee for the hearing and a preliminary investigation was $10,000. Without hesitation, Rueter wrote him a check. "I figured it would take a few days to get straightened out, and then Anthony would come home," he said. "I kept thinking, 'Christ, how did Anthony's name get mixed up in this?'"

While Rueter's father gave his son a job in the family business and bankrolled his favorite diversion—the Outlaws—Graves's father had been an ephemeral presence in his son's life. Graves's childhood in Brenham, the home of Blue Bell Ice Cream, did not unfold in the pastoral small town of the creamery's television commercials, which are heavy on mom-and-apple-pie nostalgia. He was born to a single mother, Doris Graves, just after her seventeenth birthday and raised in the dreary projects on Parkview Street. His father, Arthur Curry, was a musician and an inveterate womanizer who worked for the Santa Fe Railroad. "He lived with us for a while, and then he'd wander, and then he'd come back," Doris told me with a shrug. "He was the man of my dreams, the love of my life—blah, blah, blah. That's the way the story goes." They married when Graves was two and had four more children together, but Curry's visits grew more infrequent. In his absence, Graves became the man of the house, making sure that his brothers and sisters did their homework, ate dinner, and went to bed while Doris worked the two to ten P.M. shift at the Brenham State School. Graves succeeded in keeping out of trouble, except when it came to girls. When he was fourteen, he told Doris tearfully that he had gotten a girl pregnant. "He said, 'Mama, don't you think it's time you taught me about the birds and the bees?'" she recalled. "And I said, 'Looks like you've already been stung.'"

Graves was a handsome kid with a dazzling smile, and he was popular with his peers. The 1980 Brenham High School yearbook, *The Brenhamite*, features photo after photo of him as a smooth-faced freshman, beaming beside his teammates. He played football and basketball, and he ran track, but it was baseball that he excelled at. His sophomore year, he was devastated to learn that he had been cut from the varsity team to make room for seniors. Rather than be relegated to junior varsity, he moved in with his paternal grandfather in Austin and enrolled in Westlake High School, an elite, virtually all-white school with a championship baseball team.

Former coach Howard Bushong, who led Westlake to state titles in 1980 and 1984, remembered him as a likable kid with a good arm and serious potential. "I was excited to have his caliber of talent in our program," he said. But Graves's chance to prove himself—and to perhaps cinch a college scholarship or advance to the minor leagues, as Westlake's best players often did—was short-lived. His grandfather handed him off to his father, who was living in Austin but who would disappear for days on end, leaving him stranded without food or a way to get to school. Halfway through the semester, his father left for good. Doris picked up her son and brought him back to Brenham.

When Graves returned, he was held back because he had not finished his semester at Westlake. His loose-limbed confidence was gone; rather than throw himself back into baseball, he sat out the next season. He dropped out of school his senior year after another girlfriend informed him that she too was pregnant. Interest from a major league scout, who had approached him about playing in the minors, fizzled once he quit the team. Graves was seventeen, with two children—a three-year-old son and a newborn—to support. He went to work at Blue Bell, loading trucks, and got a job in a factory that made metal clothes hangers. The following year, 1983, his father was shot and killed by a romantic rival in Houston. In the wake of his father's death, Graves briefly moved to California, where he worked as a security guard. When he returned to Texas, he got into the first real trouble he had ever been in; at twenty-one, he was arrested during a Brenham Against Drugs sweep. After he learned that prosecutors were seeking a fifteen-year sentence, he agreed to plead guilty to selling a small amount of pot and cocaine. He served 120 days in a minimum-security prison in Sugar Land.

After his stint in Sugar Land, Graves put his life in order and went to work as a machine operator at Magnetic Instruments, making oil field equipment. He got along with the other men in the shop, and he helped the Outlaws maintain a winning record on the softball field. During his three years with the company, there was only one incident that had left Rueter shaking his head. One morning, when Graves was working on little sleep, a coworker swiped two doughnuts that Graves had set aside for breakfast. Graves sucker-punched him, breaking his nose, and when the man lunged for him, Graves ran to his toolbox and pulled a paring knife. A coworker immediately stepped in and defused the situation. No police report was filed, and neither man lost his job; they were both sent home for a week without pay. Later, though, the confrontation would be used to cast Graves, who had no prior history of violence, as someone who was capable of an act as brutal as the Davis murders.

.　　.　　.

Graves's whereabouts at the time of the murders could be confirmed by at least three people, all of whom placed him at his mother's apartment in Brenham. His nineteen-year-old brother, Arthur, and his sister Deitrich, who was twenty-one, remembered him coming home shortly before midnight with his girlfriend, Yolanda Mathis. According to Graves's brother, sister, and girlfriend, it had been a typical night at home. Graves and Mathis had eaten fast food from Jack in the Box and stayed up talking, while Arthur had carried on a marathon phone conversation with a female friend. At about two A.M., the couple had lain down on a pallet on the living room floor. (Graves, who was out of work, was staying at the apartment temporarily.) Arthur recalled getting off the phone at about three A.M. Before turning in for the night, he had checked to see if the front door was locked. The apartment was cramped, and in order to reach the door, he had needed to step over Graves and Mathis. "Anthony got annoyed," Arthur told me. "He said, 'Man, what are you doing? Turn out the light!'" By then, the crime—which had gotten under way sometime after one A.M., according to Carter's statement—was done. Somerville's chief of police had reported the fire at roughly 2:56 a.m.

According to Dick DeGuerin, their story was corroborated by someone he interviewed in the course of his investigation, someone who had no allegiances to Graves: the middle-aged white woman who had been on the other end of the line with Arthur. She and Arthur, a soft-spoken gospel singer who played the organ at New Hope Baptist Church, often talked late into the night, and sometimes he sang her love songs. On the evening of the murders, he had serenaded her with Johnny Mathis standards. When Graves caught him crooning "Misty" into the phone, he had ribbed his little brother mercilessly. The woman, who could overhear Graves mocking his brother in the background, had come to Arthur's defense, and Arthur had passed the phone so that she could have a word with Graves herself. "She could verify that he had been home when the crime was being committed, but she was reluctant to get involved because she was white," DeGuerin said. "She was concerned that it would look funny that she had been on a long telephone call with Arthur in the middle of the night. But she did candidly tell me that Arthur had a beautiful voice and that Graves had gotten on the phone while Arthur was singing to her. She said that if she had to testify, she would." (The woman, who has denied ever speaking to DeGuerin, did not respond to interview requests for this story.)

Ranger Coffman's fifty-one-page report makes no mention of the white woman—or of Arthur, Deitrich, Mathis, or the Jack in the Box employee who vividly remembered Graves's visit to the drive-through window, down to the precise details of the order he placed. In fact, little of the report concerns Graves at all; Carter is its focus. So cursory was the Rangers' investigation into Graves that they never bothered to search his mother's apartment, where he was arrested. (Some items of clothing and his aunt's car, which he had been driving, were processed by the DPS crime lab, but nothing was discovered that connected him to the crime scene.) Had the Rangers spoken to more people who knew Graves, they would have learned that while he and Carter had indeed met before, through Cookie, they were not friendly; they traveled in different circles and knew each other only in passing. An introvert, Carter worked the night shift at a prison in Navasota and was considered a bit "off" by people who knew him. He had little in common with the easygoing, gregarious Graves.

When the Rangers questioned Graves after his arrest, they pressed him to tell them about the killings, but Graves insisted that he had no idea what they were talking about. When they told him that "Robert" had fingered him as the killer, he was unable to place his accuser. (Days later Graves would tell a grand jury that if Robert Carter had indeed implicated him in the Davis murders, "he needs psychiatric evaluation.") He agreed to take a polygraph exam, and like Carter, he was driven to Houston. That evening, Graves—who had not eaten since the previous night and was rattled after more than seven hours in police custody—failed the test. Polygraphs are not admissible in court because of their unreliability, but they can help determine the direction of an investigation. Again the Rangers demanded that he tell them everything he knew about the murders, urging him to give Carter up. Exhausted, Graves broke down in tears, reiterating that he had no knowledge of the crime. When he did not confess to the killings, he was taken to jail.

Three days later, when Carter testified before a grand jury, he recanted the story he had told the Rangers, saying that he had been pressured to name an accomplice. (Exactly what had transpired during the hours leading up to Carter's tape-recorded statement to the Rangers is unknown; no audio or video recording was made of his interrogation, and the Rangers declined to be interviewed for this article.) "I said 'Anthony Graves' off of the top of my head," he insisted. "They told me they would cut me a deal, that I could walk if I give up a name, if I give up a story, and that's what I did." His attempt to clear Graves would have been more credible had he not claimed that he too knew nothing about the crime.

With Carter waffling, the Rangers' case against Graves rested on Mildred Bracewell, the convenience store clerk who had undergone hypnosis to help the investigation. After Graves's arrest, Bracewell had picked him out of a photo lineup and a subsequent live lineup. (Her husband, who had also been at the Stop &

Shop that night, could not.) Bracewell was never able to identify Carter, and her selection of Graves was problematic; he did not fit her original description or resemble the composite drawing that had been sketched from her hypnotically recalled memories. Bracewell had originally told investigators that the man was tall, with an oblong face, and clean shaven. Graves was five feet seven, moonfaced, and had a mustache.

At the bond hearing that October, more witnesses turned up to bolster the state's case. Graves had been put in a cell directly opposite Carter's at the county jail, and a sheriff's deputy and a jailer took the stand to say that they had separately overheard him admit his guilt to Carter. "Yeah, I did it, and don't say a thing about it," the jailer, Shawn Eldridge, remembered him saying. The sheriff's deputy, Ronnie Beal, recalled, "I heard Mr. Graves state to Mr. Carter that he had done the job for him and to keep his damn mouth shut." DeGuerin tore apart the witnesses' credibility, getting Beal to admit that he had not yet met either inmate when he heard them talking through the intercom, casting his identification of their voices into doubt. And Eldridge was forced to acknowledge that on the night in question, he did not write down what he had heard; in fact, he had waited eight days before making a statement to law enforcement officers about Graves's purported confession, a long time to withhold critical information in a high-profile murder case.

Ranger Coffman told the court that there were other witnesses who had heard Graves's remarks, but they were not called to testify. Before stepping down from the stand, the Ranger added that he had seen "what appeared to be blood" on a pair of Graves's shoes, a claim that was not substantiated when the results later came back from the crime lab.

But, DeGuerin warned Graves, no matter how flimsy the evidence against him, the judge was not likely to dismiss such a high-profile case. In the end, Graves—whose arrest had been heralded on the front page of the local newspaper—was denied bond. He would have to remain in the county jail for the next two years, until his case went to trial. After the bond hearing, DeGuerin withdrew as Graves's attorney. According to Rueter, DeGuerin had informed him that taking the case to trial would run between $150,000 and $200,000, an amount that Rueter had balked at. "Had I known then what I know now, I would have tried to find a way to pay the whole damn thing," Rueter told me, his eyes watering. "I mean, how do you put a price on a human life?"

## III.

The case that the Rangers handed off to the Burleson County district attorney's office was hardly a slam dunk. "I think in many ways the Graves case was the most difficult case that I tried," said Charles Sebesta, who served as the district attorney of Burleson and Washington counties for twenty-five years. "But at the same time, the cupboard wasn't bare when it came to evidence. We were comfortable with the evidence." Sebesta—who is lanky and genteel but who enjoyed a reputation during his long tenure as chief prosecutor as a bare-knuckle courtroom adversary— faced enormous pressure not only to win a conviction against Graves but also to secure a death sentence. Somerville mayor Tanya Roush captured the community's anger over the killings when she told the *Austin American Statesman* that some residents did not think putting Graves and Carter on trial was worth the trouble. "They're saying, 'Bring back the hangin' tree, and save the taxpayers' money,'" she said.

In Graves's case, the prosecution's star witness had recanted, and four Rangers had been unable to turn up a plausible motive or any physical evidence that tied Graves to the crime. Still, the district attorney's office pressed ahead, trying to build a case from the few prospective witnesses it had. Prosecutors also charged another person as an active participant in the Davis murders: Carter's wife, Cookie. Her indictment stemmed from her unpersuasive testimony before the grand jury, in which she had insisted that Carter had been home with her all evening on the night of the murders. She had also sworn that she had seen no burns on his face when she had left for work the next morning. Investigators had learned that at a health clinic, she had directed a nurse to bandage her husband's wounds in such a way that he would not look too conspicuous at a funeral they were obligated to attend. Most significantly, Cookie had a bitter rivalry with a member of the Davis family. Both she and Lisa had sons with Carter, born just eight months apart. According to Carter, the paternity suit had capped a tumultuous few years, during which he and Lisa had carried on an affair. Shortly before the murders, Cookie had given him an ultimatum, demanding that he choose between her and Lisa.

Neither the Rangers nor the prosecution seems to have seriously considered the notion that Carter might have named Graves in order to deflect attention from his wife. Nor was another theory fully explored: that Carter, as he would insist after his own trial, was actually telling the truth when he claimed to have had no accomplice. The district attorney had a clear vision of what had happened on the night of August 18, 1992. "There were three weapons, and there were three active participants in the crime: Graves, Cookie, and Carter," Sebesta told me. "As far as culpability, we know that Graves was the worst one. He had the knife. He was going room to room killing the children. Carter told us that."

Despite his belief that all three people had executed the crime, the only case that Sebesta could easily make was the one against Carter. The evidence against him—particularly the bullets that tied him to Nicole's murder—was substantial, and in February 1994 a jury in the Central Texas town of Bastrop, where the trial was moved on a change of venue, found him guilty of capital murder and sentenced him to death. As Graves's trial date drew near, Sebesta negotiated a deal with Carter's appellate attorney: If Carter testified against Graves, the state would allow him to plea to a life sentence if his conviction were reversed on appeal. The chances of a reversal were slim, but Carter was inclined to placate the district attorney, given that his wife was under indictment, and he agreed to help the prosecution when Graves went to trial. Even so, Sebesta was not convinced that he would testify. "Our agreement with Carter was extremely tentative," he said.

The prosecution caught a lucky break that August, one month before jury selection began, when Ranger Coffman and an investigator with the district attorney's office spotted Rueter shaking hands with Graves at a pretrial hearing. The investigators took Rueter aside to ask him a few questions. Despite a wild goose chase that Carter had led them on, the murder weapons had never been discovered, and they were eager to know if Graves had ever owned a knife. "I told them that I'd given Anthony a souvenir knife, but it was a piece of shit that wouldn't hardly stay together," Rueter said. "I'd bought two at the same time and kept one for myself. Mine was so flimsy that I had to keep a rubber band wrapped around it so it would stay shut." Rueter readily agreed to hand over his knife for testing, certain that nothing would come of it. "I'm around metal all day, and I knew that thing couldn't kill a rabbit," he said. "I figured they would test it and that would be the end of that." Rueter's switchblade, however, would become a powerful tool in the hands of the prosecution.

"We were going forward with the case even without the knife," Sebesta told me. "But the knife evidence was a godsend."

•          •          •

When *The State of Texas v. Anthony Charles Graves* got under way on October 20, 1994, it was clear that the case would likely be won or lost on Carter's testimony. But even on the eve of his scheduled court appearance—with opening statements having already been made—prosecutors were not certain that their most important witness would actually take the stand or what he planned to say if he did. Carter's most recent telling of the murders, which he had recounted to Ranger Coffman weeks earlier, implicated Graves and a shadowy third figure named "Red," whom he described as "a fellow from Elgin" who had "red hair . . . gold in his mouth, red complexion." (Carter would later say that Jamaican drug dealers were to blame.) The night before he was scheduled to testify, the prosecution team visited him in the Brazoria County jail, in Angleton, a small town about an hour's drive south of Houston, where the proceedings had been moved, at the defense's request, in hope of finding an impartial jury.

At the outset of the meeting, Carter did not regale his visitors with another fantastical story. Instead, he made a simple declaration, one that could have altered Graves's fate if Carter had waited to announce it on the witness stand the following morning. "I did it all myself, Mr. Sebesta," he blurted out. "I did it all myself."

The district attorney was unconvinced. "I gave no credence to it, because it didn't happen," Sebesta told me. "Six people were killed. There were multiple stab wounds, and some of the victims were hit over the head with a hammer. One of them was shot five times. We talked about it for a few minutes, and finally I said, 'I'm tired of this. We're wasting our time.'"

Sebesta quickly shifted the focus of the conversation to Carter's wife. In fact, it was the subject of Cookie, not Graves, that occupied the rest of the evening. For the next two hours, Sebesta grilled Carter about Cookie and what role she might have played in the killings. As the night wore on and Carter continued to insist on his wife's innocence, a polygraph examiner was brought in to question him about her involvement. He concluded that Carter showed signs of deception when he answered no to two questions: "Was Cookie with you at the time of the murders?" and "Was Red actually Cookie?" When Carter was informed that he had failed the test, he began to weep.

According to Sebesta, he then confessed that Cookie had taken part in the killings, claiming that she was the one who had wielded the hammer. (Carter added that he had shot Nicole, while Graves stabbed the remaining victims.) Assistant prosecutor Bill Torrey would later write: "This examination, which concluded about 10:30 p.m., was instrumental in 'breaking' down Carter's resistance and facilitating his testimony; testimony which, in post-verdict interviews with jurors, was absolutely essential in their minds, toward corroborating a largely circumstantial case."

The next morning, as the time neared for Carter to take the stand, he had cold feet. At 7:30 A.M., when the district attorney met with him again, "he basically said that he wasn't going to testify, period," Sebesta recalled. "He said, 'I can't give her up.' " Finally, shortly after 9 a.m., following several reminders from the bailiff that Judge Harold Towslee was waiting for them, Sebesta approached Carter with a deal: If he agreed to take the stand, prosecutors would not ask him about Cookie. Carter at last relented. He would testify against Graves.

Before Carter raised his right hand to be sworn in, Sebesta informed the court of the prosecution's agreement with the witness: Carter would testify as long as he was not questioned about his wife's possible involvement in the murders. The district attorney made no mention of the fact that Carter had claimed, less than twenty-four hours earlier, to have committed the crime by himself, though prosecutors are required by law to hand over any exculpatory evidence to the defense, whether they believe its veracity or not. Sebesta would later claim—when the issue came to light during Graves's appeals—that he was "ninety-nine percent" certain he had told Graves's lead attorney, Calvin Garvie, of Carter's declaration when they bumped into each other in the hallway that morning. Garvie remembers things differently. "He obviously didn't tell me that," he explained to me. "That conversation never took place." Had Sebesta informed him of such a crucial admission, he said, "You can be sure that I would have asked Carter about that on cross-examination."

Graves, who sat behind the defense table in a borrowed suit, his expression stoic after two years behind bars, was elated to learn that Carter was testifying. "There's no way this man can sit in front of me and tell a lie like this," he told Garvie. But when Carter took the stand, he told the jury exactly what prosecutors had hoped for, recounting in a slow, deliberate voice how the two men had gone to the Davis home on the night of the crime. Carter took responsibility for only Nicole's death; Graves, he testified, had wielded the knife. (He never mentioned who had bludgeoned the victims with a hammer.) In this version of the story, Carter added a new flourish: Graves had taken part in the murders because he was enraged that Bobbie Davis had received a promotion that he felt his mother, who was also a supervisor at the Brenham State School, deserved. And to explain away his grand jury testimony, in which he had declared Graves's innocence, he stated that he had done so out of fear; one day at the county jail, he said, his and Graves's cells had both been left open, and Graves had threatened and choked him. Jailers had apparently forgotten to lock the cells that held the two highest-profile murder suspects in the county's history.

The defense had not been certain until that morning that Carter would testify, and Garvie's cross-examination was brief and superficial. Garvie, who had never handled a death penalty case before, told me that he was hamstrung by what he and his court-appointed co-counsel, Lydia Clay-Jackson, did not know: They were unaware not only of Carter's last-minute recantation but also of his statement naming Red as a third assailant, which was not provided to them until later in the trial, when Ranger Coffman took the stand. In addition, the defense attorneys had chosen to pursue an unusual trial strategy: Even though the deal that prosecutors had struck with Carter did not prevent the defense from questioning Carter about his wife, Garvie elected not to. He and Clay-Jackson thought that the indictment against Cookie, like the indictment against Graves, was unfounded, given the lack of evidence against her. They also believed that one of their strongest witnesses was Cookie's sixteen-year-old daughter, Tremetra Ray, who could tell the jury that Graves had never called the Carter residence shortly before the murders to ask Carter if their plans were "still on," as Carter had testified. But Tremetra also maintained that her mother was home on the night of the murders. And so Garvie never questioned Carter about the deal he had made with prosecutors, or asked him who had swung the hammer that night, or pressured him to explain what Cookie's role—if any—might have been.

Before Carter was shackled and transported back to death row, Sebesta posed a seemingly harmless question on redirect examination. "With the exception of the time you went to the grand jury and denied any involvement, all the different stories that you have told have all involved Anthony Graves, have they not?" he asked.

In fact, both the district attorney and his witness knew otherwise; as recently as the previous evening, Carter had said that he had acted alone. But Carter agreed. "They have," he said.

Sebesta summoned a procession of prosecution witnesses to the stand, but Mildred Bracewell, the hypnotized store clerk, was not among them. Carter had changed his story since making his original statement to the Rangers, testifying that he had purchased gasoline *before* picking up Graves and driving to Somerville; his new account made Bracewell's eyewitness identification all but impossible. In her absence, the district attorney focused instead on the "knife evidence." Rueter's switchblade—state exhibit #192—was shown to the jury, and Rueter was called to testify that he had given Graves a virtually identical knife. Travis County medical examiner Robert Bayardo, who delivered a detailed account of the victims' stab wounds, stated that the blade, or a knife just like it, could have been the murder weapon. Yet under cross-examination, he also conceded that its dimensions were "very common." To buttress his testimony, Sebesta called

Ranger Coffman to the stand. With his resolute gaze, the lawman was the picture of unimpeachable authority. As he held state exhibit #192 in his hands, it was easy to forget that Rueter's switchblade was not the actual murder weapon but a stand-in with no connection to the crime.

The Ranger described how, on a visit to the medical examiner's office, he had observed Bayardo insert the switchblade into puncture wounds found on two of the victims' skulls. (A forensics expert would later conclude during Graves's appeals that Bayardo's techniques were not only unscientific and inaccurate but also likely damaging to the evidence—a claim that the former medical examiner denies. "The knife went in and out without any force, without damaging the bone," he told me.) When the coroner slid the knife into the skulls, the Ranger told the jury, "it fit like a glove."

The two original witnesses from the jail—Ronnie Beal and Shawn Eldridge—were called to testify, as were two more men: inmate John Bullard, who had been arrested for forgery, and a local rancher named John Robertson. Bullard claimed to have heard Graves ask Carter, "Did you tell them everything?" and observed the two inmates using hand signals after they realized that the intercom was on. (Bullard also admitted that he had been on three different psychotropic medications at the time.) Robertson, who told the jury that he had stopped by the jail to drop off dinner for a friend, stated that he had overheard Graves say, "We f—ed up big-time," and assure Carter that any incriminating evidence had been disposed of. Like Beal and Eldridge, he professed to have listened to the two men over the jail intercom. But in aggressive cross-examination of all four men, Clay-Jackson was able to establish that the intercom worked only intermittently and that the jail, which was not air-conditioned, had been noisy that August night, with a fan whirring and a TV blaring in the background. She scored her best point of the trial when she had Eldridge, the jailer, look over his log from the night in question, which included detailed notations ("Served supper"; "Med. to Bullard") but no mention of Graves's supposed confession.

After the state rested, the defense called Robert Bux, the deputy chief medical examiner for Bexar County, who testified that the fatal injuries could have been caused by "any single-edged knife." Wanda Lattimore, a supervisor at the Brenham State School, disproved the motive that Carter had provided for Graves when she told the jury that Graves's mother had never expressed any interest in the position to which Bobbie Davis had been promoted. But the defense's best effort to establish Graves's innocence—proving that he was home at the time of the crime— fell short, handicapped by the fact that the white woman whom Arthur had sung to on the phone refused to testify. ("She cried and told me that her parents would disown her if they ever knew about her relationship with me," Arthur said, still thunderstruck at the memory.) Arthur told the jury in no uncertain terms that his brother had been at home that night, but his sister Deitrich was never called to corroborate his testimony. That task fell to Graves's girlfriend, Yolanda Mathis. Shortly before Mathis took the stand, while jurors were outside the courtroom, Sebesta sprang a trap.

"Judge, when they call Yolanda Mathis, we would ask, outside the presence of the jury, that the court warn her of her rights," the district attorney announced. "She is a suspect in these murders, and it is quite possible, at some point in the future, she might be indicted."

Never before, in the more than two years that had passed since the killings, had Mathis been identified as a suspect. (When I pressed Sebesta about this, he said, "There was some thought that she could've been a fourth person in the vehicle," although nothing in the Ranger reports or the trial record supports such a charge. In hindsight, he added, "I don't think she was involved.") Garvie could have requested that Judge Towslee stop the proceedings and hold a hearing, at which point Sebesta would have been obligated to show the court what proof he had to substantiate his claim. But Garvie never called his bluff. ("I thought he would fight for my son because he was of color too," said Doris, who had retained Garvie by cashing in her life savings. "But he let Sebesta intimidate him.") Ethically, Garvie told me, he felt bound to warn Mathis, who had no attorney, that she had been named as a possible suspect. When he and Clay-Jackson informed her that she could face indictment for the murders, she became hysterical. Terrified, she refused to testify.

Mathis's absence left a gaping hole in the defense's case that went unexplained to the jury. Making matters worse, the witness whom Graves's attorneys had pinned their hopes on, Tremetra Ray, strained credulity when she testified that both her mother *and* stepfather, Robert Carter, had been home all evening on the night of the murders. Before the state rested at the close of the five-day trial, Sebesta underscored the fact that the switchblade Rueter had given Graves was never recovered, emphasizing that Graves had denied owning a knife when he had testified before the grand jury. "We have a co-defendant who has placed Anthony Graves at the scene," Sebesta told the jury. "He has placed a knife in his hand." In the end, though jurors knew about Carter's deal with prosecutors, they chose to believe his account of the night of August 18, 1992. After more than twelve hours of deliberation, they found Graves guilty of capital murder.

"Five children and a grandmother had been brutally murdered, and because of that, I think the burden on the state to prove its case beyond a reasonable doubt was somewhat less than it should have been," Garvie told me. During the trial's emotional penalty phase, a death sentence seemed all but a foregone conclusion. After Graves's workplace fight was offered as proof of his propensity for violence, the jury listened as the anguished members of the Davis family cataloged their grief. "There are some crimes that are so violent, that are so horrendous, that there is but one decision that you as a jury can make," Sebesta advised jurors at the conclusion of his closing argument. "Pick up the photographs of those six people and you'll know what to do." The jury—whose foreman was the panel's lone black member—took less than two hours to assess a punishment. Anthony Graves was sentenced to death.

## IV.

Four years later, on January 14, 1998, Carter penned a remarkable letter to his high school English teacher, Marilyn Adkinson, and her husband, Howard, a pastor, both of whom had visited him on death row. "I'm not sure how to begin this letter, but with God's help, of course, 'I can do all things' (Phil. 4:13)," wrote Carter, who had undergone a dramatic jailhouse conversion since Graves's trial. In careful handwriting that filled three pages, he confessed to the Adkinsons that he had falsely testified against Graves to protect his wife—"she is totally innocent"—and, by extension, their son, Ryan. "The D.A. and law enforcement believe she was involved, so I lied on an innocent man to keep my family safe," he wrote. "I even told the D.A. this before I testify against Graves, but he didn't want to hear it."

Both Carter and Graves had been sent to the Ellis Unit, in Huntsville, where they separately lived out their days amid the more than four hundred condemned men awaiting their execution dates. After their convictions, charges against Cookie were dropped due to a lack of evidence. During his time on death row, Graves maintained a near-spotless disciplinary record. (He was cited once for possessing what was deemed to be contraband: some green peppers that he had swiped from the food cart.) Carter, meanwhile, diligently read the Bible, making detailed notations in the margins. As his execution date approached, he spoke of Graves's innocence to more than half a dozen people, including his appellate attorneys and at least two death row inmates: Alvin Kelly, who was executed in 2008, and Kerry Max

Cook, who had been sentenced to death for the 1977 murder of a Tyler woman. (During his fourth trial, in 1999, Cook pleaded no contest in exchange for his freedom. DNA evidence later showed that semen at the crime scene belonged to another man.) Of hearing Carter's confession, Cook would write in his memoir, "As I looked deeply into the face of Robert Carter, I knew—just as I knew my own innocence—I had witnessed the truth."

Carter also penned letters to the Davis family, declaring that Graves had no knowledge of the crime. To Lisa, he wrote, "I just don't want [an] innocent person to die for something they don't know anything about." To Kenneth Porter, the father of Lisa's other murdered child (the "Kenneth" he would later suggest had been on his mind when he gave his initial statement to the Rangers), he wrote, "I am the only one responsible . . . I also know that I have lied in the past about this and I can certainly understand you and the rest for not wanting to believe me now." Hopeful that he could correct the record, he reached out to Graves's state habeas counsel, Patrick McCann. "He asked me to come to Huntsville because he had important information to tell me," McCann said.

Carter had contacted McCann at a critically important time in Graves's appeals. The Texas Court of Criminal Appeals had reviewed his case, and in 1997 it upheld his conviction. The court—which in the late nineties overturned 3 percent of capital convictions, the lowest reversal rate of any state in the nation—had rejected the argument that there was insufficient evidence at trial to corroborate Carter's testimony. McCann had been appointed to handle the next phase of Graves's appeals: filing a state writ of habeas corpus. In the long and byzantine path that a case follows through the courts after a defendant is handed a death sentence, the writ ushers in the most important stage, in which new and exculpatory evidence can be introduced. But the time frame when such evidence may be brought before the court is finite; in Texas, death row inmates are usually limited to a single state habeas appeal—and only during this habeas phase may new facts be introduced. McCann hurried to Huntsville to meet with Carter, who he hoped would admit that his testimony at Graves's trial had been perjured. As a court reporter took notes, Carter gave McCann a deposition in which he claimed sole responsibility for the crime.

There was just one problem: Carter's attorney, Bill Whitehurst, had already barred McCann from speaking to his client. "We could not have our client going out and giving depositions, talking about how guilty he was, at the same time that we were presenting a federal writ of habeas corpus, trying to get him a new trial," Whitehurst explained. "It was obvious that McCann believed in his client's innocence and wanted to do everything he could to help him, and I respect that. But I also had an obligation to my client, which I took very seriously." In going around Whitehurst, McCann—who was less than three years out of law school— had also failed to notify the district attorney's office of his plans to take a deposition from Carter. It was a fatal error: Because he had deprived prosecutors of the chance to cross-examine Carter, the deposition was rendered inadmissible. McCann's only remaining opportunity to get Carter on the record was to subpoena him to appear at a 1998 evidentiary hearing that Judge Towslee had granted on several issues raised in the writ. But Whitehurst, a past president of the State Bar, warned the young lawyer that Carter would plead the Fifth if he were subpoenaed. Rather than risk his case on a notoriously unreliable witness, McCann did not call him. The court would never hear Carter's recantations.

Thirteen days before Carter's execution, in the spring of 2000, after all of his appeals had been exhausted, Graves's counsel was granted the opportunity to question Carter under oath. Attending the death row deposition were Sebesta and Graves's new appellate lawyers: veteran capital defender Roy Greenwood and former state district judge Jay Burnett. (McCann, a navy reservist, had been called to active duty in Bosnia.) As he sat before the assembled attorneys in his starched prison whites, Carter stated in a low, flat voice that he alone had murdered the Davis family. Without betraying any emotion, he said that he had set out for Somerville on the night of August 18, 1992, with the intention of killing his son. He did not attempt to justify himself or explain whether or not he had anticipated that five other people would be present at the Davis home that night. (Nicole, Brittany, and Lea'Erin had returned the previous day after spending the summer in Houston.) Yet he did describe in specific and chilling detail how he had carried out the crime. First, he said, he had stabbed Bobbie to death after knocking her unconscious with a hammer. As for how he had overpowered the remaining victims single-handedly, Carter was nonchalant. "They were asleep," he said.

Under cross-examination from Sebesta, Carter grew animated, pushing back as the district attorney once again questioned him about Cookie. "I told you personally, just like I told Ranger Coffman that day when you came to that jail," Carter said. "I told you, just like I told my brother, 'It was all me,' but you said you didn't want to hear it."

"We said we wanted the truth, didn't we, Robert?" asked Sebesta. "Isn't that what we told you? 'We want the truth'?"

"I'm talking about the day at the jail," Carter countered. "You said that you didn't want to hear that coming out of me."

"I don't recall that," Sebesta said.

On May 31, 2000, the day that Carter was set to die, his family gathered in Huntsville. He read the Bible, visited with his mother, and ate his final meal: a double cheeseburger and fries. At 6:02 P.M., he was led to the execution chamber, where he was strapped to the gurney. After two IVs were inserted into his arms, the warden asked if he had any last words. "I'm sorry for all the pain I've caused your family," Carter said, turning toward the six grieving relatives of Bobbie Davis who had gathered as witnesses. "It was me and me alone. Anthony Graves had nothing to do with it. I lied on him in court." Carter looked to his own family, who stood on the other side of the execution chamber, behind Plexiglas, but Cookie was not there. She had become distraught that morning and returned to Brenham. "I am ready to go home and be with my Lord," Carter said, shutting his eyes. As the lethal dose of chemicals flowed into his veins, he coughed, then uttered a soft groan. He was pronounced dead at 6:20 P.M.

· · ·

Death row inmates who maintain that they have been wrongly convicted are at the mercy of not only the judiciary—where capital appeals typically take more than a decade to move through both the state and federal courts—but also of reporters, law professors, journalism professors, and student volunteers, who may or may not choose to look into their claims of innocence. Often an inmate's last hope is to capture the attention of an organization like the University of Houston Law Center's Texas Innocence Network, an ad hoc organization of professors and law students that researches such claims. (Court-appointed appellate attorneys who lack the resources to fully investigate capital cases are usually grateful for the help.) The Innocence Network—which works in conjunction with the journalism department at Houston's University of St. Thomas—first learned about Graves from his attorneys; David Dow, the network's director, suggested to a journalism professor at St. Thomas named Nicole Cásarez that her students look into the case.

"We started with nothing," remembered Cásarez, a former Vinson & Elkins associate with short brown hair and a concerned, precise manner. "Four or five students and I drove to Austin in the fall of 2002, and we read the trial transcript, sitting around Roy Greenwood's dining room table, taking handwritten notes. From there, we asked ourselves, 'Who do we need to talk to?'" She and her students next traveled to Brenham, where they met two of Graves's alibi witnesses, Arthur and Deitrich Curry. Cásarez and her students found the siblings to be credible, but it was their interview with Yolanda Mathis that left a profound impression. "Yolanda confirmed that she had been with Anthony all night, but she also explained that they had not been in a big, serious relationship," Cásarez said. "She had been one of many women in Anthony's life. That was important, because she did not have the motivation that a brother or sister might have to cover for him. She told us, 'Why would I still say I was with him that night if it weren't true? I'm married. I'm a mother. Why would I want to protect a child murderer?'" The conversation was a turning point for Cásarez. "Until then, all we knew was that Yolanda had been called and didn't testify," she said. "Hearing her story, seeing how thin the evidence had been at trial, I began to feel very uncomfortable with this case."

At the time, Graves's prospects looked bleak. In 2000 the Texas Court of Criminal Appeals had denied his writ of habeas corpus—in essence, concluding that he had received a fair trial. Afterward, his lawyers filed a motion asking the court to grant him another habeas appeal, arguing that he should be granted such an opportunity because his first habeas attorney had been incompetent. (McCann's failure to subpoena Carter, they reasoned, was proof of ineffective assistance of counsel.) The court agreed to consider the claim, but in January 2002, a six-to-three majority ruled against Graves once again. Writing for the majority, Judge Cathy Cochran stated that a defendant was guaranteed the right to a qualified court-appointed attorney but not necessarily to one who performed well. Judge Tom Price penned a stinging dissent, noting that it was the Court of Criminal Appeals that had appointed McCann to Graves's case in the first place. "'Competent counsel' ought to require more than a human being with a law license and a pulse," he observed. With that, Graves's state appeals were done. His last resort would be the federal courts, which would not be able to take into account Carter's recantations.

"If it wasn't in the state record, the federal court couldn't consider it," Cásarez explained.

But if his federal appeals were successful, there was always the chance—however unlikely—that he would be granted a retrial, in which any new or exculpatory evidence that had been discovered would likely be admissible. So Cásarez and her students forged ahead, interviewing upward of one hundred people over the next few years. "We got in touch with anyone who might know anything about the case," Cásarez said. They tried, fruitlessly, to convince the white woman whom Arthur had serenaded on the night of the murders to speak with them, but she refused. "She had denied knowing Arthur, so I made Xerox copies of cards she had sent him and a note she had written on the back of one of her deposit slips and forwarded them to her," Cásarez said. "A man's life was on the line."

They succeeded in getting Carter's older brother, Hezekiah, who had dodged them several times before, to finally agree to an interview when they visited him at his house in Clay, near Somerville. Hezekiah explained that he had traveled all the way to Angleton—a nearly three-hour drive—on the eve of his brother's testimony in Graves's trial at the behest of the district attorney, who had arranged to pay for his expenses and a hotel room. "Mr. Sebesta told me that Robert was having reservations about testifying," he wrote in a sworn affidavit. "I agreed to come down to Angleton and talk to Robert." Hezekiah stated that before taking the stand, his brother had been "troubled, uncomfortable and scared."

Cásarez's students also met with John Bullard, the heavily medicated jailhouse snitch, who, they learned, was under the mistaken impression that his testimony had helped Graves. Bullard, whose cell had been near Graves's, explained that he had only heard the man proclaim his innocence. Cásarez interviewed jailer Wayne Meads, who had been on duty at the county jail on the same night that Beal, Eldridge, and Robertson claimed to have overheard Graves admit to taking part in the killings. Meads told Cásarez that he had overheard nothing unusual on the intercom that night. "If I had heard either Carter or Graves confess, it would be something I would never forget," he said. Casting more doubt on the reliability of the jailhouse testimony was a revelation about Robertson. Acting on a tip, one of Cásarez's students, Sarah Clarke Menendez (who would later go on to graduate from Harvard Law School), sifted through records at the Burleson County courthouse and found that Robertson had been under indictment at the time that he reported Graves's alleged statements to investigators. The charges against him, for cruelty to horses, were never pursued.

One of the most revelatory moments in Cásarez's investigation came when she visited Marilyn Adkinson, Carter's high school English teacher. Adkinson had never observed any signs of trouble in Carter when he was younger, she told Cásarez—in fact, he had no criminal record before the killings—but she mentioned something that she had found curious. Carter had held on to a book that she had assigned his class years before, Theodore Dreiser's *An American Tragedy*. He had never gotten around to reading it until he was on death row. When he finished it, Adkinson explained to Cásarez, he had told her, "This is my life."

The novel, which served as the inspiration for the 1951 film *A Place in the Sun*, tells the story of a young man from humble origins who is torn between two women: a wealthy woman, whom he hopes to wed, and a poor woman, with whom he shares a secret relationship. The poor woman gets pregnant and threatens to reveal their affair unless he marries her. Afterward, he takes her on a boat ride, and when their rowboat capsizes, he hangs back as she struggles to keep her head above water. Ignoring her pleas for help, he watches her drown. The parallels to Carter's life were not exact—neither woman in his life was wealthy by any measure—but the story gave Cásarez insight into the psyche of a man who had, by his own admission, felt enough rage to kill his own illegitimate child.

At the conclusion of *An American Tragedy*, the protagonist is caught, arrested, tried, and sentenced to death. Before he is executed, he becomes a Christian. "Marilyn told me that Robert really identified with this character," said Cásarez. "He told her, 'If I had read this book in high school, maybe all of this would never have happened.'"

·   ·   ·

From the viewpoint of the federal courts, the most important development in Graves's case would turn out to be a casual remark that Sebesta himself made to a television producer after Carter's execution. In 2000, during George W. Bush's first run for the White House, Geraldo Rivera came to Texas to make an hour-long NBC special, *Deadly Justice*, about capital punishment. Although Graves's case had received scant media attention in the eight years since his arrest, the show's producers interviewed him at the urging of Kerry Max Cook, whose own case was highlighted in the documentary. Sebesta agreed to talk to producers as well. While the cameras were rolling, the district attorney admitted—for the first time—that Carter had told him, before taking the stand at Graves's trial, that he had acted alone. "He did tell us that," Sebesta said. "'Oh, I did it myself. I did it.' He did tell us that."

The documentary, which painted Graves's case in broad strokes, did not seize upon the singular importance of the district attorney's admission. "If Sebesta had not said what he said, there's a fair chance that Anthony would have been executed by now," Greenwood told me. "His statement allowed us to raise a Brady claim for the first time, and that was the only winner we had." *Brady v. Maryland*, a landmark 1963 Supreme Court ruling, requires prosecutors to turn over any exculpatory evidence to the defense. Failing to do so is a "Brady violation," or a breach of a defendant's constitutional rights—a claim that Greenwood could raise before the federal courts.

"This was the ultimate in Brady material," Greenwood said. "It was a one-witness case, and the witness recanted! And it was not divulged to the defense." That fact—that in the midst of Graves's trial, Carter had told the district attorney that he had acted alone—did not come to the attention of Graves's lawyers until the deposition Carter gave shortly before his death. "Having Carter say it didn't matter," explained Cásarez. "What mattered was having Sebesta admit it, which he did, on camera. Otherwise, it would have just been Carter's word against Sebesta's."

Even with such a powerful argument in hand, it would take several years before Graves's claim was considered by a federal court in any substantive way. The Fifth Circuit Court of Appeals began reviewing his case in 2003 after a lower court had denied relief, and the following year, it granted an evidentiary hearing. At issue was Carter's statement to Sebesta that he had acted alone, as well as a second comment that the district attorney claimed Carter had made on the eve of his testimony at Graves's trial: "Yes, Cookie was there; yes, Cookie had the hammer." (Sebesta did not mention this until 1998, during a hearing in Graves's first habeas appeal; Carter consistently denied ever implicating his wife in the crime.) The evidentiary hearing, which took place in federal district court in Galveston, included testimony from Sebesta and Graves's two trial lawyers. U.S. magistrate judge John Froeschner, who presided over the hearing, found as fact that Sebesta did not reveal to the defense Carter's statement that he committed the murders alone. But he denied Graves's Brady claim, saying that Carter's comments would not have altered the outcome of the trial; a jury, he reasoned, would still have decided to convict him. U.S. district judge Samuel Kent delivered a ruling that upheld Judge Froeschner's findings the following year.

Dispirited, Greenwood asked Cásarez if she would begin drafting Graves's clemency petition to the Board of Pardons and

Paroles. (In 2005 Cásarez reactivated her law license so that she could join Graves's legal team.) "It was the end of the road," Cásarez said. "The Supreme Court was not going to take the case. If Anthony didn't get his conviction reversed by the Fifth Circuit, it was done, dead, over."

Greenwood appealed the decision to the Fifth Circuit, and on March 3, 2006, a three-judge panel handed down a stunning rebuke to the lower courts. In a unanimous opinion, the panel held that the state's case had hinged on Carter's perjured testimony. Had Graves's attorneys known of Carter's statements to the district attorney, wrote circuit judge W. Eugene Davis, "the defense's approach could have been much different . . . and probably highly effective." The court reserved particular criticism for Sebesta for having prompted two witnesses to say on the stand that Carter had never wavered, other than in his grand jury testimony, in identifying Graves as the killer. (Sebesta had done this not only with Carter but with Ranger Coffman as well.) Wrote Davis, "Perhaps even more egregious than District Attorney Sebesta's failure to disclose Carter's most recent statement is his deliberate trial tactic of eliciting testimony from Carter and the chief investigating officer, Ranger Coffman, that the D.A. knew was false."

With the stroke of a pen, Graves's conviction was overturned. The ruling did not make any determination as to his actual innocence or guilt. But by finding that his conviction had been improperly obtained, the court paved the way for a new trial.

Students began arriving in Cásarez's office late that afternoon. "We read the opinion out loud, and we were cheering," she said. "We were so relieved that finally someone saw the case the way we did." Amid the jubilation, she and her students puzzled over how to convey the news to Graves. "Death row inmates can't get phone calls, but I knew that he sometimes listened to *The Prison Show*," Cásarez said. "So we called KPFT, and I explained what had happened, and they agreed to call me at eight o'clock that night and give me one or two minutes on the air. My students and I wrote a short statement. I had to practice reading it without crying, because every time I read it, I would start crying. Anthony wasn't listening to *The Prison Show* that night, but someone else on death row heard the show and gave a note to one of the guards to take to him. The note said, 'Hey bro, just heard your conviction's been overturned. Congratulations. Guess you'll be getting out of here at last.' "

## V.

On September 6, 2006, Graves walked off of death row. But there was no celebration beyond the floodlights and the coils of concertina wire, no crush of television reporters shouting questions, no tearful embrace with his mother, whom he had been allowed to touch just once during his fourteen years of incarceration. Instead, Graves walked out of his six-by-ten-foot concrete cell and into the arms of Burleson County sheriff's deputies, who transported him back to the county jail in Caldwell, where he would await retrial. The Fifth Circuit's ruling had not exonerated him, and he still faced the original criminal charges that had been filed against him in 1992. In the eyes of Burleson County, he remained a murderer, and a child killer at that. Judge Towslee's successor—his daughter, Judge Reva Towslee-Corbett—set his bail at $1 million.

The Burleson County district attorney's office, which Sebesta left in 2000, could have dismissed the charges against Graves. A federal court had thoroughly discredited the testimony that had put him on death row, and the man who had admitted to the killings had already been executed. Still, many people—most notably the surviving members of the Davis family—believed in Graves's guilt and were not persuaded by Carter's eleventh-hour recantations. Days after Graves's conviction was overturned, Bobbie Davis's niece, Anitra Davis, told the *Houston Chronicle*, "We are still waiting for justice." The county moved forward with plans to retry Graves, and in early 2007 it appointed former Navarro County district attorney Patrick Batchelor as special prosecutor. (The Burleson County district attorney's office recused itself from the case after Judge Towslee-Corbett ruled that an assistant district attorney, who had helped prosecute Graves thirteen years earlier, could not take part in the new trial.) A skilled adversary, Batchelor had previously won the capital conviction of a Corsicana man accused of a 1991 triple murder, Cameron Todd Willingham, who later became the subject of national debate when updated forensic science called his 2004 execution into question.

In February 2007 Batchelor announced that he would be seeking the death penalty against Graves. The defense suffered another setback that July, when Judge Towslee-Corbett handed down a startling decision: Carter's original trial testimony would be admissible at Graves's retrial. The judge reasoned that Graves's constitutional right to "confront the witness"—that is, to question or challenge his accuser—had already been satisfied when Carter was subject to cross-examination in 1994. Attorneys with the Lubbock-based Innocence Project of Texas, which had taken on Graves's case pro bono after Greenwood retired, filed a motion with the trial court arguing that any retrial in which Carter's testimony could be read to a jury would simply be a replay of Graves's original, flawed trial, a situation that amounted to double jeopardy. Judge Towslee-Corbett denied the claim, as did the Tenth Court of Appeals, in Waco, where the attorneys appealed her decision. Last year, the Court of Criminal Appeals declined to take up the case, allowing Judge Towslee-Corbett's ruling to stand.

Graves's retrial is now set to begin in February. As if his path through the legal system had not been protracted enough, the retrial has been beset by delays, including months in which parts of the victims' skulls and other key exhibits have gone missing. (The evidence was later discovered in an old jail cell that had been welded shut.) Batchelor, who stepped down from the case for health reasons in late 2009, has been replaced by special prosecutor Kelly Siegler, a former Harris County assistant district attorney who has sent no fewer than nineteen defendants to death row. Siegler, who declined to comment on this case before trial, is known for her flamboyance and ability to make the horror of a crime viscerally real for a jury. She once famously re-created a murder by pretending to stab another attorney with the actual murder weapon while straddling him on a blood-stained mattress.

Representing Graves will be veteran capital defender Katherine Scardino and her co-counsel, Jimmy Phillips Jr. Assisting the trial lawyers as third chair will be Cásarez, who can quote the trial record from memory. In 1997 Scardino won the first acquittal for a Harris County capital murder defendant in twenty-three years. She still does not know whether Judge Towslee-Corbett, in admitting Carter's testimony into evidence, will also allow in his letters, statements, and deposition recanting his accusations against Graves. "It would be an injustice if Robert Carter's last statement is not heard by this jury," Scardino told me. "Even the strongest disbeliever has to stop and take note that he proclaimed Anthony's innocence from the gurney."

Meanwhile, the former district attorney remains as convinced of Graves's guilt as he was sixteen years ago, at his trial. Sebesta believes that Carter's change of heart was nothing more than a last-ditch effort to protect his wife. "I think Carter was afraid that Graves would make a deal with us after he was executed and give up Cookie in exchange for a life sentence," he said.

As we sat and talked one afternoon in Caldwell, Sebesta explained that he had known Carter's family all of his life. The Sebestas hailed from Snook, in southeastern Burleson County, and the Carters lived just down the road, in Clay. "He was a heck of a basketball player," said Sebesta of the man he sent to death row. The young man he remembered was "a little wimp," not someone who was capable of cold-blooded murder. "He was the instigator, but he wasn't the primary actor in this thing," he said. "As far as complicity goes, I think it was Graves, Cookie, and then Carter." It was the streetwise Graves, he held, who had wanted to "straighten things out" with Bobbie Davis. In his view, Graves, who throughout the trial had "stared straight ahead with steel-looking eyes," was utterly, morally debased. Sebesta said he had received "bits and pieces of information" that Graves and Cookie were kissing cousins, a charge he had insinuated to the jury at Graves's trial.

Still stung by the Fifth Circuit's ruling, Sebesta told me that he had taken a polygraph exam, which he publicized in advance to local media, to prove that he had disclosed Carter's statements to Garvie. After the first test was inconclusive, Sebesta took a second polygraph, using a different test structure, which he passed. ("In the opinion of this examiner, you have been completely truthful," read the polygraph report that Sebesta provided to me.) Indeed, the former prosecutor has gone to extraordinary lengths to clear his name. Last year, he paid for space in the Caldwell and Brenham newspapers to publish a 5,000-word letter in which he vigorously defended himself. "When I get backed in a corner, I come out fighting," he told me. The seventy-year-old former prosecutor seemed keenly aware of his legacy. "We did not withhold evidence," he said, his blue eyes insistent. "I couldn't sleep at night if I would've done something like that."

•     •     •

For the past four years, as Graves has awaited trial, he has been confined to the Burleson County jail, a colorless, low-slung building by the side of Texas Highway 36, in Caldwell. Unlike his last stay at the jail, Graves, who is now forty-five, is not housed side by side with other inmates; given the nature of the crime for which he stands accused, the county has relegated him to solitary confinement, citing concerns about his safety. Besides brief exchanges with the guards and phone calls that are limited to fifteen minutes, his only human interaction takes place on Wednesdays and Sundays, when he is allowed a twenty-minute visit by family and friends. He cannot touch his visitors; they talk by phone, separated by a sheet of Plexiglas.

One day in June, I was escorted into a windowless, concrete room inside the jail, where Graves and I were permitted to sit face-to-face to discuss his case. A jailer led him in, and after his hands were unshackled, he took a seat across the table from me. The photos I had seen of him were taken when he was still a young man, but Graves is now a grandfather, and he has settled into middle age. His face was soft and round, his body thicker beneath his black-and-white-striped uniform.

As we talked, his story came tumbling out: of the Rangers, who were certain he was guilty, no matter what he said to the contrary; of the lineup, in which a woman he had never seen before had fingered him as the killer; of his trial, in which he listened to witnesses testify that he had confessed in jail to his guilt; of the souvenir knife, which the prosecution had held up as the murder weapon; of the man whose accusations against him could never be taken back, even after a dying declaration attesting to his innocence. We had been allotted two hours for our visit, but it was not enough. A jailer signaled that our time was up. Graves gave me an apologetic nod as he rose to go. "Maybe the sheriff will let you come back," he said.

The sheriff, however, was not amenable to another media visit. And so I sent Graves a long list of questions, and in letters that followed, he described his time on death row, where his cell had afforded an unnerving view whenever a condemned man went to meet his fate. "Unfortunately for me, I could look out the window of my cage and see the officers placing the inmate in the van to be taken to the Walls Unit, to be executed," he wrote. He explained his agony at being convicted of the Davis killings. "Never in a million years could I have imagined my life like this . . . to end up defending allegations that I'm somehow capable of killing women and children," he explained. He drew a detailed drawing of his cell at the county jail, where a TV serves as his lifeline to the outside world. He signed off one letter, "Do you think Elena Kagan will be confirmed to the Supreme Court? Her hearing began today."

In hopes of continuing our conversation in person, I returned to see Graves one Wednesday afternoon during visiting hours, when the jail's reception area was crowded with women and children. Our time was limited to twenty minutes, so I kept my questions simple. I asked if we could talk more about his life now.

"I've missed so much," Graves said. "My children are all grown. I have grandkids I've never touched." His voice broke. "I've been alive for the past eighteen years, but I haven't *lived*," he said.

He had already told me that he was not a particularly religious person, so I asked what sustained him.

"Knowing I'm innocent," he replied. "I'm not just going to lay down my life for something I didn't do."

Eventually I got to the question I had been wanting to ask. I was curious how he remembered the world that he had left behind when he was twenty-six years old. "If you ever get out of here—" I began.

"*When* I get out," he interrupted. "When."

"When you get out, what do you want to do first?" I ventured.

"Hug my mother and my children," he said. "Take a bath. Eat some ribs off the barbecue pit, or a hamburger with real lettuce and tomatoes and onions." He closed his eyes for a moment, as if savoring a memory he had secreted away. "Take my shoes off and touch the grass," he said. "Or just open a door. Open a door so I can walk outside."

# Innocence Found

The 6,640th day of Anthony Graves's incarceration—October 27, 2010—began like any other. He awoke at five o'clock in the morning to the sound of the food cart rattling down the hall of the Burleson County jail, where a guard slid his breakfast tray through a slot in his cell door. At seven o'clock, the overhead fluorescent lights came on, illuminating the windowless cell where he had lived in solitary confinement for the past four years. Graves turned on the TV, switching it to the local morning newscast. The forty-five-year-old inmate compulsively watched the news, trying to keep up-to-date on a world he had left behind when a newcomer named Bill Clinton was running for president. When it came time for his allotted hour of exercise, a guard escorted him to an empty concrete room, where he walked briskly in circles. He could glimpse the sky through four small windows above him that were covered in chicken wire. Every so often, when the wind kicked up outside, he could feel the breeze against his skin.

Eighteen years earlier, Graves had been arrested and charged with the most notorious crime in Burleson County history: the brutal slayings on August 18, 1992, of a well-liked Somerville woman named Bobbie Davis, her daughter, and her four grandchildren, each of whom had been stabbed multiple times before their home was set ablaze. The crime's prime suspect, Robert Carter—a man whom Graves had known only in passing—had fingered Graves as the killer. Although at least three people could place Graves at his mother's apartment at the time of the crime and no physical evidence linked him to the scene, he was charged with capital murder. With the help of Carter's testimony, he was convicted in 1994 and sentenced to death. Graves would likely have been executed if not for a pivotal admission by the case's lead prosecutor, district attorney Charles Sebesta, who let slip that Carter had, in fact, confessed to having committed the murders by himself. (Carter was executed in 2000.) That disclosure led a federal court to overturn Graves's conviction in 2006, after finding that Carter's statements had been withheld from the defense. Yet the ruling did not strike down the original charges of capital murder, so Graves was moved from death row to the Burleson County jail, in the Central Texas town of Caldwell, to await retrial; he was housed in solitary confinement because of concerns about his safety. At his new trial, slated to begin on February 14, 2011, prosecutors again planned to seek the death penalty.

After recreation time, Graves sat down to write a letter, in which he shared his certainty that special prosecutor Kelly Siegler would persuade a jury to find him guilty. The former Harris County assistant district attorney had sent nineteen men to death row and was known for securing convictions in old, difficult cases that were often based on circumstantial evidence. "She has a win-at-all-costs reputation," Graves noted in his careful handwriting. "She'll throw mud against the wall and see what sticks."

Graves's letter was a response to a note I had sent him several days earlier. We had corresponded for four months while I worked on an article for *Texas Monthly* that detailed the lack of evidence tying him to the Davis murders ("Innocence Lost," October 2010), and we had continued the conversation in the weeks that followed. He knew that in mid-September—two days after the story was published—Siegler had requested a sit-down meeting with his attorneys. At that meeting, she had startled his defense team by acknowledging that she had serious reservations about the state's case. She went on to say that they should not spend too much time on trial preparation but should give her a month to talk to various witnesses to ensure that she had not missed any key information. Siegler asked that they allow anyone who had been hesitant to talk in the past to meet with her and her investigator. If she found that there was insufficient evidence, she said, she would recommend that charges be dismissed.

Lead defense attorney Katherine Scardino was dubious; she had faced down Siegler before, and she suspected this was a tactical move, meant to delay her and her co-counsel from preparing for trial. Nicole Cásarez—a lawyer and journalism professor who had devoted the past eight years to investigating Graves's case— worried that Siegler was trying to pump them for information that she could later exploit. Graves, too, was skeptical. "She's interested in winning, not truth-seeking," he wrote.

Graves never finished the letter. He was interrupted shortly after four o'clock, when the jail supervisor appeared outside his cell. Without explanation, the jailer unlocked the cell door and ordered Graves to follow him. Graves was allowed to walk without handcuffs. Bewildered, he was led to an interrogation room, where he saw that Cásarez and her co-counsel Jimmy Phillips Jr. were waiting. He was surprised, since they rarely visited unannounced.

Cásarez took his hands in hers and stared at him intently. "Remember you telling me that God is good?" she began. Years earlier, he had told her a story about how, on the day he learned that his conviction had been overturned, he had wanted to scream and shout, but he was mindful of being surrounded by men who still had execution dates. So instead he had looked up to the ceiling of his cell and said simply, "God is good."

Graves nodded, studying her face for a clue as to what was going on.

"God *is* good," Cásarez said, struggling to maintain her composure. "All charges have been dropped."

He looked at her, dumbfounded.

"You're free," she said more emphatically. "You're going home."

"Are you playing with me?" he whispered.

Cásarez shook her head. "It's over," she said. "It's finally over."

On the table beside her was a dismissal order from the court filed at 3:57 P.M. that stated, "We have found no credible evidence which inculpates this defendant." The decision to drop all charges had come so suddenly that the defense team had only learned the news earlier that afternoon. As Graves leaned against Cásarez, he broke down.

They stood together and cried for a long time. "Hey," Cásarez said finally, smiling at the irony of what she was about to suggest. "Let's get out of here."

Graves hurriedly changed into the only clothes he owned: a gray blazer, button-down shirt, and navy-blue slacks that his attorneys had bought him for court appearances. He packed his life's possessions—a toothbrush, toothpaste, a tin of hair grease, a stack of letters, and legal papers related to his case—into a single cardboard box and an onion sack. As he walked out of the jail's sally port and into the parking lot, he took in the moment. Except for a lone TV crew that had been tipped off to his release, no one was waiting to greet him. His own family did not yet know that charges had been dropped; Cásarez had not trusted that he would be let go until she was handed the judge's dismissal order moments before she saw him. Except for the sound of the occasional car passing by on Texas Highway 21, there was only silence. Graves stood in the late-afternoon sunshine. "Eighteen years," he said.

•     •     •

The next morning, at the courthouse in Brenham—where Graves's retrial was to have been held—Burleson County district attorney Bill Parham told reporters at a hastily organized press conference that he was "absolutely convinced" of Graves's innocence. Parham, who was elected DA in 2008, made clear that he did not decide to drop charges because too many witnesses had died over the years or because key exhibits had become degraded or because memories had faded. After a thorough reexamination of the case, he and the three people who flanked him that morning— Siegler; the district attorney's investigator, Otto Hanak; and Texas Ranger Andres de la Garza—had all come to the same conclusion. "There's not a single thing that says Anthony Graves was involved in this case," Parham said. "There is *nothing*." When Siegler's turn came to address reporters, she placed the blame for Graves's wrongful conviction squarely on former DA Charles Sebesta. "It's a prosecutor's responsibility to never fabricate evidence or manipulate witnesses or take advantage of victims," she said. "And unfortunately, what happened in this case is all of those things." Graves's trial, she said, had been "a travesty."

To anyone familiar with Graves's odyssey through the criminal justice system, the prosecution's about-face was a staggering reversal. During Sebesta's twenty-five-year tenure as district attorney— at one time he oversaw four contiguous counties between Houston and Austin—he was arguably the region's most powerful figure, and he had relentlessly pursued Graves, even though the case, as he had once conceded, "was not a slam dunk." When Graves's conviction was reversed, Sebesta had staked his legacy on the case. He took two polygraph exams in an attempt to prove that he had disclosed exculpatory evidence to the defense, and he spent thousands of dollars to run full-page ads in two local newspapers that detailed why, in his estimation, Graves was a murderer. Siegler's withering assessment that morning ("Charles Sebesta handled this case in a way that would best be described as a criminal justice system's nightmare") reframed the narrative: It was Sebesta, not Graves, who had done wrong. Her reputation as a fierce advocate of victims' families made her unequivocal statements to reporters all the more credible; she could hardly be considered soft on crime or apt to be sympathetic to a man she had any reason to believe had actually stabbed four children to death.

That Siegler—known for having been one of the most aggressive prosecutors in Harris County, which has sent more people to the death chamber than any other county in the nation—had backed away from a capital murder case had the entire Houston defense bar talking. And so on a brisk November morning one week after the press conference, I visited her at her well-appointed Memorial home to find out what, exactly, had happened. Scattered across her dining room table, where we sat and talked, were yellow legal pads filled with her voluminous notes on the case. "I got sworn in as special prosecutor in February 2010, and I brought nineteen banker's boxes full of documents home from Brenham to read," she told me. (Most rural counties rely on special prosecutors to try death penalty cases because of their complexity; prior to Siegler, the case had been handled by special prosecutor Patrick Batchelor and lawyers at the attorney general's office.) As she had sifted through nearly two decades' worth of court papers—a task that took her six weeks—she had become increasingly puzzled. The Texas Rangers' reports, she noted, focused almost exclusively on Carter. And their investigation had not uncovered any discernible motive for Graves.

"Common sense tells you that a person doesn't stab babies unless he's really mad about something, and Graves didn't know the Davises," she said. "It didn't make sense." She was particularly struck by the absence of physical evidence. "Why wasn't Graves burned too?" she said, referring to Carter's extensive injuries. "If he stabbed six people, why didn't he have any cuts or marks? Why was there no blood on his clothes or in his car?" Siegler told me she had still been operating under the assumption that Graves was guilty, but she knew that she would need new information— such as a piece of evidence that could undergo DNA testing—to make her case.

For more than three hours that morning, Siegler led me through the transcript of *The State of Texas v. Anthony Charles Graves*, pointing out where she was troubled by Sebesta's tactics. "This is from a pretrial hearing on July 22, 1994," she said, ticking off the volume and page number in the court record. Dressed casually in jeans, the forty-eight-year-old career prosecutor, who was narrowly defeated in 2008 for Harris County DA, delivered her comments with the same focused intensity of a good trial lawyer during closing arguments. "Sebesta says, 'We want to put the court on notice that there is a strong indication that this defendant, Anthony Graves, may have been involved in the yogurt shop murders in Austin, Texas,'" she said, arching her eyebrows in incredulity. "Sebesta is accusing him of participating in another capital murder—and with what evidence?" she said. (No one else has ever suggested that Graves had anything to do with the infamous 1991 quadruple homicide.)

Later, she pointed to a moment during the trial when Sebesta announced outside the presence of the jury that Graves's girlfriend, Yolanda Mathis—the defense's most important alibi witness—had become a suspect herself. The Rangers who originally investigated the case told Siegler that, in fact, Mathis had never been a suspect. Still, Sebesta asked the judge to warn Mathis of her rights before she took the stand. "If someone needs to be warned of their rights in a criminal trial, they can't be called to testify," Siegler explained. "Sebesta knew what a good witness she was—he had heard her grand jury testimony—and he didn't want the jury hearing what she had to say." His gamble worked: Yolanda, who became hysterical, left the courthouse. "Then he had the nerve in final arguments to say, 'Where's Yolanda?'" said Siegler. "And the jury never knew why she didn't show up."

Siegler's concerns mounted, she told me, as she realized that the trial strategy she had initially counted on was doomed. "My plan had been to find enough evidence to indict Theresa Carter again, and then flip her," she said, referring to Robert Carter's wife, Cookie, who had been charged in the Davis murders and held in the county jail but never brought to trial. "But the more I read, the more I realized that we didn't have anything on Theresa Carter. I couldn't figure out how she'd been indicted."

Siegler made a lengthy list on legal pad paper—her "to-dos," as she called them—of everyone who needed to be interviewed, from former cell mates of Graves's to people who had not been contacted since the 1992 investigation. She wanted to see what information shook out, if any, that she might be able to take to trial. In the process, she would need to conduct a wholesale re-investigation of the case. That Graves was in fact innocent did not sink in until later. "My thinking went from 'We're going to get this ready for trial' to 'Whoa, this is going to be hard to get ready for trial' to 'Okay, can we even go to trial?'" she said.

In April, Siegler had to shift her focus to another death penalty case she was handling for Burleson County. The Myron Douglas Phillips case, which was slated to go to trial in July, would occupy the rest of her spring and summer. When she saw Parham and Hanak at a pretrial hearing, she warned them of what she had found. "Guys, I've read everything on Graves, and we have big problems," she said.

．　　　．　　　．

On September 27 Siegler sat down with Graves's attorneys for their extraordinary face-to-face meeting. During the wide-ranging discussion, which spanned two hours, Siegler focused her attention on Cásarez, asking her detailed questions about her research: What was the name of the polygraph examiner who had administered a test to Carter on the eve of his testimony at Graves's trial? Exactly when did the Jack in the Box clerk see Graves on the night of the crime? Had she ever spoken with Cookie's cell mate? Initially, Siegler told me, she had discounted Cásarez and her undergraduate journalism students at the University of St. Thomas, in Houston. "I thought they were exaggerating the facts because they were rabid anti–death penalty people who had an agenda," she said. "But we wouldn't have gotten to this point if not for their work. As we did our investigation, we found that they were dead-on. Every aspect of the case fell apart when it was critically examined."

Over the course of the next month, Siegler and Hanak, a former Texas Ranger with an understated, deliberative manner, interviewed upward of sixty people. "Our approach was not 'Let's go over your previous statements real quick and then we'll let you know when to show up in court,'" Siegler told me. "It was 'We've got some concerns about this case, so we're approaching it with fresh eyes. Tell us what you've never said before. Let's start at the beginning.'"

That shift in tone yielded important new information. They spoke with all of Graves's alibi witnesses—something the Rangers who initially investigated the case had never done—and found them to be credible. One was Graves's sister Deitrich Curry, who told them that shortly before her brother's trial, she had been visited by two investigators who had warned her that if she left the county to travel to Angleton, where the trial had been moved, she would be arrested on outstanding traffic warrants. (Graves's defense attorneys, who made critical errors at trial, never called her to testify.) Parham, who was receiving frequent updates on the progress of the investigation, was deeply troubled when he heard Curry's story. "When you look at what happened to both her and Yolanda, you start to see a pattern of witness intimidation," he said.

In early October, Siegler met with retired Texas Ranger Ray Coffman, who had led the investigation that resulted in Graves's arrest. "He told me things that he had probably never told anyone before, which helped us get to today," she said. Coffman recounted a conversation with Sebesta, which he had never forgotten, that had taken place just before a grand jury was to begin examining what Cookie's role might have been in the murders. The retired Ranger said he had asked Sebesta, "How are you going to get an indictment on her when we don't have any evidence?"

As Coffman told it, Sebesta had gestured with one hand, as if rolling dice, then boasted, "I'm going to play me a little Tennessee gambler today."

Cookie's former attorney, Rob Neal, lent credence to the notion that Sebesta had pursued an indictment against Cookie with no solid evidence. (Neither Neal nor Coffman would comment for this story.) According to Seigler, Neal said that Sebesta had made a surprising disclosure in the fall of 1992, not long after Cookie was charged with the Davis murders: He told Neal that he had no actual intention of prosecuting her. In fact, Neal told Siegler, shortly before Cookie's probable cause hearing—at which Sebesta would have been required to disclose the evidence he had against her—she was released on a $50,000 personal bond, just eight weeks after being indicted. "She was charged with murdering six people and she was allowed to go home?" Siegler said to me, shaking her head in disbelief. The significance of Neal's and Coffman's disclosures was enormous, since the implicit threat of Cookie's prosecution had been instrumental in getting a reluctant Carter to finally agree to testify against Graves. (Carter penned a letter four years after the trial in which he claimed to have falsely testified against Graves in order to protect his wife, who was "totally innocent," he wrote. "The DA and law enforcement believe she was involved, so I lied on an innocent man to keep my family safe.") "Neal thought she had been indicted so that Sebesta would have leverage against Carter," Siegler told me.

When I later contacted Sebesta, he strenuously defended his prosecution of Graves. He did not deny the "Tennessee gambler" story, explaining, "Every time a prosecutor walks into the courtroom and selects a jury, he is literally rolling the dice." Nor did he deny having the conversation with Neal. However, he insisted that the exchange had taken place in 1994, after both Carter and Graves had gone to trial, when he realized that neither man would testify against Cookie. "I did tell Rob Neal that I had no intention of going to trial *at that particular time*," he e-mailed me. "That's when we made the decision to release her on bond." He could not explain why Cookie had been released two years earlier, long before either man went to trial.

As their investigation continued, Siegler and Hanak invited the former district attorney to come down to his old office one afternoon to discuss the case. "I asked him, 'How exactly did you indict Cookie?' and he said, 'Well, there was evidence,'" Siegler recalled. "So I pressed him. I said, 'Charles, *what* evidence?' And the only thing he could come up with was that curling iron burn." (At the time of her arrest, Cookie had a small mark above her left elbow that she attributed to a curling iron.) The burn had not been photographed or documented during the original investigation, and in Siegler's opinion, it was hardly enough to warrant capital murder charges. As she summarized the problems she had encountered with the case, she told Sebesta that one of the prosecution's star witnesses, ex-jailer Shawn Eldridge, could no longer be counted on to say that he had overheard Graves saying, "I did it." (Eldridge admitted that he was not sure whose voice he had heard over the jail intercom.) "I told Sebesta that if the case ever went to trial, he would be called as a witness and he would have to answer some difficult questions," she said. Sebesta—a voluble man who usually enjoyed holding forth on the Graves case—was visibly subdued that day. "His hands were shaking," Siegler said. "He wasn't the same person that had been described to me. I almost felt sorry for him."

Hanak continued to work his way through the to-do list, approaching friends, acquaintances, and relatives of Graves's who had seen him in the hours leading up to, and following, the crime. Many had not been taken seriously by previous investigators, or had never been interviewed at all, and were wary of his intentions. But Hanak was patient, sitting on sagging front porches and lawn chairs and making conversation until they agreed to talk. All of them placed Graves in Brenham, sixteen miles away from the scene of the murders. They recalled an untroubled young man who had driven to the Jack in the Box for a hamburger with his girlfriend, gone to bed, and then dropped his aunt off at work the next morning. The portrait that emerged was hardly that of a man consumed with homicidal rage.

"About halfway into this investigation, I had a sickening feeling," Hanak told me the week after Graves's release, as we discussed the case at the district attorney's office in Brenham. He explained that he had begun his career in law enforcement in 1978, at the age of eighteen, as a prison guard, walking the halls of death row. "I never would have believed that an innocent man could end up there," he said. "Never. Not until I worked this case." He pulled out the legal pad he had carried with him during his investigation and flipped to a page on which he had scribbled two headings: "Evidence" and "Witnesses." Below the headings, the page was empty. "I kept trying to fill in the blanks, but there was nothing there," he said.

By late October, Siegler and her team—including Ranger de la Garza, who assisted Hanak in the final days of the investigation—had come to a consensus. "I can't pinpoint the exact day, but our thinking evolved from 'We have insufficient evidence to go to trial' to 'This is an innocent man,'" she told me. Helping them make their final determination was seeing the switchblade that the original prosecution had argued was the twin of the knife that had been used to inflict sixty-six stab wounds. (The actual murder weapon was never recovered.) "When the AG's office handed it over to us, Otto and I looked at each other, because the knife had no hilt," Siegler told me. "Now, think about this for a minute. If you're using a knife that has no hilt and you're thrusting it into skulls and bone—with that many victims, that many times—at some point your hand is going to slip and get cut." Parham summed up their outlook at that stage of the investigation: "We realized the prosecution's entire case came down to 'Carter said Graves did it, and by the way, here are some gruesome crime scene photographs.'"

On October 26 the prosecution team drove to Cypress, out-side Houston, to tell the Davis family that they planned to drop all charges. Although Siegler had laid the groundwork two weeks earlier, when she told Bobbie Davis's sister and three surviving children that she was not certain the case could go to trial, the conversation that night quickly devolved into a heated argument, with one member of the extended family accusing her of being unwilling to try the case because she was afraid to lose. For nearly three hours, she, Parham, and Hanak shared their find-ings, but a few of the nearly two dozen Davis relatives who were present remained unconvinced.

"It's hard to stop believing something you've believed for eighteen years," said Keith Davis, who lost his mother, sister, six-year-old daughter Brittany, and five-year-old daughter Lea'Erin. When I met with him, one week after Graves's release, he was slowly coming to accept that the man whose execution he had fought for had, in fact, been wrongfully convicted. "You have to understand—there were so many things we didn't know," he said. "We were outside the courtroom when we saw Yolanda Mathis leave. We didn't know Sebesta had threatened her. He told us she didn't testify because her story wasn't true." Sebesta also told them, Davis said, that Graves might have been involved in the yogurt shop murders.

"We're mad. I'm not going to lie," he continued matter-of-factly. "This could have ended ten years ago, when Carter was ex-ecuted. We've had to relive this every day since then. I've seen Graves hundreds of times in court, and every time, I thought I was looking at the man who murdered my children."

•     •     •

Thirteen days after Graves walked out of the Burleson County jail, I visited him at his brother's apartment, on a leafy, shaded street dotted with genteel old homes south of Brenham's main square. I had talked to him briefly at the defense's press conference, held the day after his release in Houston, where more than fifty reporters and cameramen had squeezed into Katherine Scardino's office to listen to what he had to say. Under the glare of the television lights, he had been remarkably poised. ("I never hesitated," he explained of his decision in 2008 to turn down a life sentence in exchange for a guilty plea. "I said, 'You either free me or kill me, but I'm standing on what's right.'") Still, it was a shock to see him that afternoon standing at the front door. My last visit to the apartment had been in June, to interview his brother Arthur Curry, back when Graves was still facing the possibility of another death sentence. Now he was home, dressed in a Dallas Cowboys T-shirt and jeans, a brand-new cell phone in his pocket. Gone were the handcuffs, the isolation, the fear of never being believed. It was a beautiful autumn day; a breeze rustled the oak trees above him, and he was free to go wherever he pleased. "Crazy, I know," he said, breaking into a grin as I walked up the driveway and shook my head in amazement. "It's crazy."

He had just finished making himself a breakfast of sausage, grits, and eggs over easy: the second meal he had cooked in eighteen years. As we sat and talked in Arthur's living room, he told me about his new life. "I'm a vagabond," he said, explaining that he was living out of a suitcase, moving back and forth between his brother's place, Cásarez's house in Houston, and his sister's home in Pflugerville, north of Austin. He had no car, no job, and only a few hundred dollars to his name. His first order of business was to get a new driver's license, "so I can prove who I am," he said. Once he had his ID and some spending money, he wanted to visit the Northeast, where he planned to move. "I have a friend in Boston who wants to help me get my life together," he said. Although he hoped to seek compensation from the state—in theory, he is entitled to $1.4 million under the Tim Cole Act, a state law that grants ex-inmates $80,000 for each year they were wrongfully incarcerated—his odds of actually receiving money looked slim. The wording of the court order that resulted in his release referred only to the lack of evidence against him, not his "actual innocence," a legal standard that must be met to receive compensation. The state comptroller's office will likely render a decision by early 2011.

As we sat and talked, Graves seemed no different than when I had met him at the Burleson County jail—calm, self-possessed, and extraordinarily normal considering everything he had been through. But there were signs that his reentry had not been easy. I noticed that the blinds in the living room were half-drawn and the TV was tuned to the news, as if he were trying to approximate, in some small way, his previous surroundings. "I'm still adjusting," he said. "I was by myself for so long that it's hard to be around too many people right now." Even visiting the grocery store or being at a large family gathering was overwhelming. Sleeping had been difficult, he explained, because he had become accustomed to the thin plastic mattress that covered his steel bunk at the county jail, where he had balled up his clothes into a makeshift pillow. "The first night I was out, I tossed and turned because I was on a real bed with all these pillows and a ceiling fan to keep me cool. My body wasn't used to that kind of comfort."

The previous night, he said, he had invited his sons over to watch football, and they had shared a beer together. His three boys—who were twelve, eight, and seven years old at the time of his arrest—were now grown men with families of their own. "Anthony is thirty, Terrance is twenty-seven, and Alex is twenty-six," he said, gesturing toward family photos from which he was conspicuously absent. "I missed their ball games, the births of their children, all the big moments in their lives. So we can't pick up where we left off. I don't feel comfortable coming in and trying to play the role of dad. I'm just trying to be a good friend."

I asked him about Sebesta's comments to the *Brenham Banner-Press* a day after his release, in which the former district attorney—in a front-page story titled "Sebesta Sticking to Original Claim: Guilty"—said he remained certain that Graves had taken part in the Davis murders. To make his point, Sebesta disclosed that Graves had failed a 2008 polygraph exam. Polygraphs are not admissible in court because of their unreliability, but Graves explained to me that he had agreed to take one because he was confident it would clear him—and because special prosecutor Patrick Batchelor had promised to drop all charges if he passed the test. (Batchelor is best known for his prosecution of Cameron Todd Willingham, whose 2004 execution has come under scrutiny as new forensic science techniques have since called his guilt into question.)

Graves vividly remembered the day when he was driven to Dallas for the polygraph. The examiner, he recalled, spent seven hours with him before actually administering the test. "He would make small talk with me for a few minutes, walk out of the room, stay gone for about thirty minutes or an hour, then come back in and ask me another couple questions," he told me. "This started at nine o'clock in the morning, and he didn't give me the test until four o'clock that afternoon. That whole time, I'm sitting there waiting to take a test that could give me back my freedom. So by the time four o'clock rolled around, I was no calm, cool, collected person." In hindsight, he said, he was cynical about the purpose of the polygraph. "When they told me I had failed, I knew it was a game, just another game," he said. As for Sebesta's publicizing it, Graves shook his head and smiled. "I think he's on a sinking ship by himself," he said. "To be honest with you, Charles Sebesta is the last thing on my mind right now."

To listen to him that morning was to marvel at the fact that he had survived eighteen years of "hell," as he succinctly described it, with his dignity, integrity, and mental health intact. He was hopeful about the future, not bitter about the past. But personally, as an observer, I couldn't help but feel angry. As we talked, I shared with him what had been nagging at me ever since Siegler had publicly denounced Sebesta. To anyone familiar with Graves's case, the notion that just one person was at fault for the wrong that had been done to him was too simple a story line. The truth, I thought, was much worse. Absent from Siegler's critique was any mention of Ranger Coffman, whose flawed investigation had led to Graves's arrest. (Rick Ojeda, an ex–FBI agent who was hired by the defense to reexamine the case, told me it was "by far the sloppiest, and most blatantly biased, investigation I've seen in twenty-two years of law enforcement.") Also overlooked were the appellate judges who rubber-stamped his conviction for twelve years; his new trial judge, Reva Towslee-Corbett, who ruled that Carter's perjured testimony could be entered into evidence and read to the jury at his retrial; Batchelor, who pursued a death sentence even though he had so little solid evidence that he offered to dismiss all charges if Graves passed a polygraph; and assistant attorney general Lance Kutnick, who relied on junk science (a "scent lineup" conducted by now disgraced dog handler Keith Pikett) to try and build a case against him.

The reinvestigation had left me with more questions than answers, I told Graves. Why had Batchelor and Kutnick, who jointly handled the case for three years, not examined the evidence with the rigor that Siegler had? Why had Coffman—who went on to serve as the chief of the Texas Rangers until his retirement, in 2009—not spoken up after Cookie's indictment? Why had Coffman given conflicting accounts under oath as recently as 2007 regarding whether or not Carter had told him that he had acted alone?

Graves smiled as I grew more and more animated, citing problems with his case that I wished Siegler had delved into more deeply. He, by contrast, seemed remarkably at peace. And so I had to ask him: How was he not consumed with anger? "I'll get angry if people don't take what happened to me seriously enough to push for change," he said. "I want prosecutors to be held accountable. But I've given too many years, and too much of my energy, to being angry, and I won't let negativity defeat me. The people who did this to me, they have to look at themselves in the mirror. But me, I have to live."

## Virginia Quarterly Review

WINNER—FICTION

Fiction was once a mainstay of magazines, even mass-market titles. In fact, the first National Magazine Award for Fiction was won by Redbook in 1970. Since then, the number of consumer magazines that publish fiction has dwindled. Fortunately, fiction continues to find a home in literary magazines, many of them, like Virginia Quarterly Review, associated with colleges and universities. The circulation of VQR is only 5,000, but the magazine regularly rewards its readers with award-winning stories both in print and online. In recent years, VQR has received National Magazine Award nominations in categories ranging from Photojournalism and Single-Topic Issue to News Reporting and Multimedia Package and has won five Ellies, including the award for General Excellence in 2006. According to the VQR editors, "Minor Watt" is "precisely the kind of complex, witty and linguistically dense fiction" they seek. As for the National Magazine Award judges, they "roundly agreed that this story is a true original—one that delivers in every respect."

Paul Theroux

# Minor Watt

Minor Watt, the real-estate developer and art collector, was seated at the Jacobean dining table with the fat baluster legs that served as his desk, waiting for his wife—soon to be ex-wife—to arrive. He had been thinking of himself, but the graceful Chinese vase with a tall flared neck, resting on the antique table, made him reflect that, as with so many things he owned—perhaps all of them—he was able to discern its inner meaning in its subtle underglaze, the circumstances of his acquiring it, its price of course, its provenance, all the hands that had touched it and yet left it undamaged, its relation to his own life, its secret history, its human dimension, almost as though this pale porcelain with the tracery of a red peony scroll was human flesh. And then after this flicker of distraction he thought of himself again.

How people said, "You're the calmest man in the world."

He always replied, "As I made more money my jokes got funnier," and when they laughed, he added, "and I got better looking."

"You're amazing," they said, with a glance at his collection—the Noland painting, "Lunar Whirl," on the wall behind him, the objects glinting on side tables and shelves and in the glass cabinet. Was that a human skull?

"And my collection got more valuable."

"One of a kind," they said.

The only gift anyone can make to a much wealthier person is an extravagant compliment, often expressing the opposite of what the poorer person feels, yet inevitably with a grain of truth and a stammer of ambiguity. The visible fact of his wealth, Minor Watt knew—his collection like a set of trophies—made these people at times incoherent and yet obvious. Instead of "He has this great thing," they thought, "I don't have this great thing."

He lifted his gaze to the works arrayed in his office, a sampling of his areas of collecting, the Noland, a Khmer head of Vishnu in stone, a Chola bronze Shiva Nataraj, an old Dan mask with red everted lips, and a squat Luba fetish figure bristling with rusty nails, a greenish celadon salver propped on a stand, a massive Marquesan u'u club with small skull-shaped bas-reliefs for eyes, and beside it like an echo an Asmat skull. More human skulls were ranged on a backlit shelf. Among collectors of tribal art, skulls constituted a silent trade, and they were an early and lasting passion with Minor Watt: New Guinea ancestor skulls with cowries lodged in the eye sockets and others over-modeled with clay and painted like masks, some of them shiny from use as head rests, like large chestnuts, the same rich color; Kenyah skulls from Sarawak scratched with scrimshaw lizards on the cranial dome, smoke-dark Ifugao enemy skulls side by side on a smoky plank, Tibetan skulls and skull cups, chased in silver, and more, all of them saturated with mana.

No one said "one of a kind" with surprise. Minor Watt had grown prosperous in the roofing business in New York, city of flat roofs. "A flat roof is designed to leak," he said, and his familiarity with the bones of these buildings led him to speculate successfully in real estate. From the age of thirty or so, Minor Watt had had everything he'd ever wanted, every dollar, every woman, every serious business deal, every artifact—his eye fell upon a standing bodhisattva, a mustached Maitreya, from Gandhara, carved in schist, second century, Kushan period, clutching a plump vial that contained the elixir of immortality. A duplex on Park Avenue, a house by the sea in Connecticut, with a set of buildings that served as his personal museum. A loving wife— where was she?

His art works were not for warehousing but for display— showing them was his incentive for collecting. He'd loved taking his wife to the opera, Inca gold glittering at her throat. Even more than the joy that drove his collecting passion was the knowledge that in buying a rare object he had prevented someone else from owning it. Another pleasure was his certainty that, even as he was examining a piece, its value was rising, no matter what the stock market was doing. He had bought a small Bacon in London—a head of George Dyer. Over the years its value had increased two hundred fold. Those human skulls: even if similar ones could be found, which was doubtful, they'd cost twenty times what he'd paid.

One of the paradoxes of the people who praised these objects was that in most cases they had no idea what they were looking at. At first, Minor Watt's pride made this almost a sorrow to him; and then, out of snobbery, such ignorant remarks delighted him. "I love this African stuff," someone would say, smiling at a fierce-faced Timor house post. The Gandharan piece from the Swat Valley was taken to be Greek. "Byzantine," an art historian said of an eighteenth-century Lalibela painting of the Ethiopian saint Gabbra Menfes Queddus. His old cartoonish reverse-glass paintings done by itinerant Chinese artists in Gujarat baffled all viewers. "Indonesia? Bali?" A bulb-headed Fijian throwing a club known as an *ulu* was assumed to be a Zulu knobkerrie: and no one ever noticed that the ivory inserts on its sides were human molars, its five victims.

And which of them would know that this Chinese vase was Ming? Minor Watt and his wife had bought it together after much discussion in Shanghai; they'd just finished a Yangtze cruise in 1980 and had hand-carried it back to the States. The vase, treasured, as all these objects were, like members of their family, had accompanied them through six changes of address. As though demanding custody, she'd included it as part of the divorce settlement. Had she noticed it glowing in the display cabinet on her previous visit, when she came with her lawyer?

He heard his intercom buzz, and then his secretary's voice, "Your wife is here."

Already it was an odd word, since they'd agreed to the divorce months before and had now signed most of the papers. In mentally moving her out of his life he was reminded of his mood when he sent a piece to be auctioned, how he had no feeling for it; even though it still had monetary value, it was dumb and mummified, and, the thing having lost all meaning and hope, he smiled as he let it slip away.

He had wondered which woman would show up—the angry woman, the sad woman, the wild-eyed woman, the over-sensitive woman, the rejected one, the triumphant one, the sulker, the smirker, the old friend.

She was none of these when she entered the room. She looked thinner—all the fury was gone, leaving her pinched, the anger wrung out of her. Such corrosive emotion was unsustainable over so many months: she looked cured of an illness, weaker, subdued, much paler. The fighting had ended, and now like people who knew each other far too well, they were rueful with disillusionment, meeting merely to observe a few formalities, wishing they were strangers.

"Hello, Minor." She spoke in the spongy voice of languor and abandonment; her eyes were drawn to the vase.

She was here to pick up the valuable old keepsake and then go. She had been reluctant to come. He had told her it was too fragile to risk mailing, but this was turning into a formal ritual of farewell. He would pass her this lovely vase and she'd carry it away in its cushioned box, the Chinese purpose-built padded coffin with the sliding lid and the rope-like handle—carry it as they had done more than twenty years ago in what had been one of their many treasure hunts, but an important one: he'd also been an early investor in the Chinese economic miracle.

"Sunny." Her name was Sonia.

She sat down in the antique Savonarola-style chair, in the same knees-together posture he'd seen so many times, but this was perhaps the last time—not perhaps. It was all at an end, a true breakup: no more wifehood for her—she'd probably never remarry and forfeit the alimony. He smiled thinking of his rich pretense of complaining about money, knowing in his heart that money never mattered, because there was always money; but such a vase as this was, even as the philistines guessed, one of a kind. It was promised to Sonia, and yet he could not see beyond the finality of this handover to any future for himself.

She hadn't been a trophy wife: he had loved her; she had been part of his great luck and his achievement and he had educated her in appreciating his vast art collection. Now she knew what a Scythian chariot finial was; and she knew why this Ming vase was precious for its copper-red underglaze; so fragile and yet unmarked. Knowing his collection this well she was the only person who truly knew him.

"I can't stay long."

Saying this, still looking at the vase, she seemed as though she had moved on, and had the unimpressed body-snatched look of a woman who was perhaps newly involved with another man.

"I understand. I've got things to do. I'm still in business, in spite of what's happening." Not until he spoke did he realize he was resentful. He went on, "You expected to see me ruined?" She wasn't listening. So he said, "I hate these people who are complaining about the economy. They created the downturn. I did too. That's why I saw it coming. Only a fool thinks it's straight North forever. I'd love to find a way to show them how foolish they've been." She didn't react. He leaned toward her. "It wasn't straight North with us. It's South now."

Her eyes were dark and unperforated.

He said, "So here it is."

"It's beautiful," she said. "Thanks."

She meant, *Thanks for agreeing to give it to me*—because she knew its value. It had symbolized that long-ago trip, the best phase of their marriage; as well as the taste that she had acquired from him; her insight into his personality.

But she didn't know that he had already surrendered it; that he was merely going through the motions. He didn't care about it anymore. He was surprised that she had agreed to this meeting, which was trouble for her, since she'd gotten the Connecticut house in the settlement, but had put it up for sale and now lived elsewhere—she refused to give him her address. Yet the thought of her being inconvenienced gave him some satisfaction.

"I know just what I'm going to do with it. I have the perfect place for it."

This annoyed him. It meant that she had a house or an apartment that she loved—a shelf in that place; perhaps someone to admire it with her. *I found it in Shanghai, when China was just opening up.* He resented her certainty, the way it seemed to represent a part of her future that she'd already begun to live, without him. He was wrong about her seeming as though she were weakened after an illness; she was strengthened in her recovery.

"I've got the old box for you to carry it in." He tapped the lid.

The pale cedar box was still crusted with the red wax seal from the antique dealer in Shanghai, the folded export permit, a tissue-flimsy certificate, marked with chops and stiff at one corner with glued-on stamps. The box was as venerable as the vase, though Sonia didn't seem to think so. It held as many memories, perhaps more, for being unregarded, plainer and more durable.

All this time he had been sitting behind the great carved dining table that was his desk, talking across his blotter as though to an employee. He got up and walked to the front of it, avoiding Sonia's side, circling, so that he stood apart, facing the vase.

"If you're pressed for time—you've a place for it, huh?—you might as well take it away."

He leaned, he reached, and lifted it, then turned to her. Startled by his sudden offer, she raised both her hands to receive it, a mother's gesture, to bring it to her body, and cradle it like a baby. With a sudden warp of nausea in his throat he let it drop and before she could grasp, it plunged in a blurred column of its own pale light. As it smashed, she clawed the empty air with feral fingers and a second later put her futile hands to her face.

"Sorry," he said, softly, the word no more than a breath in the aftermath of the smash.

She let out a sharp cry, as though she'd seen a precious creature die. Even in the worst moments of their marriage he had never seen that look of loss on her face, an expression of pain amounting to agony. But the exaggerated expression seemed comic, as terror sometimes does to a bystander. He surprised himself by laughing—and because it was involuntary, like the reaction to a wisecrack, it was full-throated, a great guffaw, a joyous snort-honk of gusto that was like a sound of health.

Hearing him she began to cry, bobbing her head with sobs, and when he stepped nearer to comfort her, he lowered his foot onto the broken pieces, rocking his shoe, grinding them smaller, like a big jaw masticating nuts. Any hope that the fragments could be glued back together ended with the heavy molar-crunch of that footfall.

She did not say another word. When she left—he could see in her posture, in her shoulders, the angle of her neck and heady— she was a different and defeated woman.

He said sorry again, and it was like the eloquence of the richest satire. The exhilaration was still rattling in his throat. He had not thought he was capable of such an elaborate undoing of the ritual. He shouted again across his office as the door shut. "Sorry!"

"An accident," he murmured, after she'd gone. But was it? People said, "There are no accidents." They would have added, "It was an unconscious wish to break the vase and upset Sonia."

And she had been—devastated. He had not realized how passionately she must have craved it until the thing broke and her face fell; until she left the office, moving stiffly, wounded, her posture altered, one shoulder higher than the other. She would not have looked more punished if he had physically assaulted her, beaten her head against a wall. Yet—for the sake of melodrama, he lifted his hands in a slow sacramental way—he had not laid a finger on her.

It was one thing to withhold an irreplaceable piece, or to sell it; it was another thing entirely to destroy it. Fascinated to think that the vase—such a live presence moments ago—no longer existed, he felt a thrill that very nearly undid the ache of incompleteness he'd sensed in himself that morning, the vase on his desk, knowing that Sonia was on her way. In the past, the nearest he'd come to this feeling was in a casino, stacks of chips piled in front of him, the roulette wheel spinning, Sonia round-shouldered behind him, horrified that he might lose it all. But he hadn't cared—he was giddy at the prospect of losing. The thrill was visceral, an access of strength, a physical lift, an intimation of perverse power that drained from him when he won. In defiance, he put all his winnings on one number and he was so exultant when he lost he could recall each witnessing slack-jawed face at the table.

The memory of Sonia and the vase was most of all a memory of her fear: how scared she looked, wild-eyed in terror as the thing fell, and not just by the shattering of the vase, but by his laughter—the insult of it—and she had hurried away, as though from a murderer. The act undid everything she knew about him: it made him a stranger to her. He was well aware of being self-taught and inarticulate, yet this smash showed virtuosity.

"The Ming vase," he later told friends. "It got T-boned. By me."
He smiled at their shocked silence. People at the periphery
could be possessive of someone else's treasures, as though these
things were aspects of the friendship. Did they think he was so
rich that he would hand them over?

These memories buoyed him through the rest of the divorce,
the last of the paperwork, the depositions, all the signatures, the
summing up, the attorney's fees. Whenever he became glum—
wondering *What next?*—he summoned up the moment in his
office when the vase slipped from his fingers, the finality of its
breaking, the shoe crunch, and the look of loss on her face.

Minor Watt had a collector's caressing habit when alone, of
padding around his apartment in slippers, picking up the smaller
objects in his collection, holding them to the light and turning
them slowly, as you are forbidden to do in museums. He savored
the details that made them unique, the subtle flourishes, not
only the texture carved into an elephant tusk but the buttery hue
of old ivory, the tiny human stick figure like a petroglyph in-
cised into the shaft of a Tongan war club, the scarification represented on the cheeks of a Chokwe *pwo* mask, the gecko gouged
into the dome of a Kenyah skull, the diamond in the forehead of a
small seated silver-cast Buddha. Leonard Baskin sometimes wrote
a note in pen strokes on a watercolor in his elegant hand. Minor
Watt owned three such Baskins—three different notes. No two
Francis Bacons were alike; many seemed provisional and splashed.
Minor Watt's *Study for a Head of George Dyer* was over-painted in
one corner, streaked in another, rubbed with the dust from Bacon's
studio. The painting was not large, but all Bacons were valuable,
almost absurdly so. Some collectors kept them in vaults, with albums of Krugerrands and taped blocks of hundred dollar bills.

He'd been eating. He rose from the table and lifted the *Study
for a Head of George Dyer* from the wall and propped it against
the silver Victorian wine cooler, near his plate of meat. Imitating
the George Dyer pout, he braced and gripped his steak knife and
raked it, two swipes; then held it on his lap. He marveled at the

sight of his own knees through the slashes he'd made—the real world framed by the rags of the painting. He poked at the long slashes. Hearing him grunt, his servant Manolo opened the dining-room door. "You okay, boss?"

But Minor Watt's feeling was muted. He'd wished someone had seen him, as Sonia had—not Manolo, who had no idea, but a true witness, even better a connoisseur.

He called a friend, Doug Redman, who owned several Bacons, but prints, the limited-edition signed lithographs. Redman had often remarked on this painting.

Redman came over that same night, because Minor Watt had said, "It's about my Bacon. I want you to see it."

Minor Watt was sitting before his fireplace when Redman entered the room. At first he did not believe that the slashed painting in his lap was the *Head of George Dyer*. The profile was familiar, the frame unmistakable.

Minor Watt said, "It's the Bacon. You know it's the Bacon."

"But what fuckwit damaged it?"

"I did!" Minor Watt cried out, giddy from hearing his own shrieky voice. The man leaned closer and looked pained, seeing that it was the Bacon. Minor Watt threw it into the fire and at once the canvas caught and flames rushed over it, making a black hole in the slower burning frame.

Redman groaned and made as if to snatch at it, but the canvas was just smut and soot.

"What's wrong with you?" he said in a tentative voice, too fearful to be angry, as though dealing with a crazy man who might run at him.

He'd expected this art collector's shock, but Redman's terror made Minor Watt even happier.

"Gone!" Minor Watt said, and Redman stepped back. "Totaled!"

"How can you do a thing like that, especially in this economy?"

"Your objection is that I'm wasting money—not destroying a work of art. You're the fuckwit—you don't deserve to live."

Redman talked—word got around; but no one asked Minor Watt straight out if he had destroyed the painting. To several of them Minor Watt said, "By the way, I fried the Bacon."

Having a witness gave the destruction a greater meaning, and made it all the more satisfying. But the problem was to find someone who knew enough about such an eclectic collection. Most of the idiots had no idea. It was no good smashing something in private. Someone else had to know; someone had to care. Who better than the painter himself? The Noland target painting was an early one from 1965. Minor Watt invited Kenneth Noland to his house, and encouraged the softly smiling white-haired man to admire his own painting. "One of my favorites," the old man said. And then, with Noland watching, Minor Watt stepped close and shot an arrow into the bull's-eye. Before the startled No-land could protest, Minor Watt threw down his bow and swiped at the painting with a dagger.

"Whoa," Noland said, staggering a little and raising his hands to protect his face, as though he expected to be assaulted. And then, cursing, he hurried from the room.

"It was like wasting one of his children," Minor Watt told Noland's dealer, because the dealer had once asked to buy back the painting.

The dealer said, "I don't think anyone has ever done what you've done."

"People used to tell me that all the time," Minor Watt said, "but for once I think you're right."

He owned a set of crockery that had been used at Vailima by Robert Louis Stevenson, a dinner service for eight. He invited seven friends; Manolo served a gourmet meal; Minor Watt told the story of the plates, how they had been brought by old Mrs. Stevenson, visiting from Edinburgh ("They'd been in the family for years"); explained the monogram; called attention to the gilded rims. Over dinner the talk was of selling valuables and budgeting. "We're selling our plane." "We've auctioned our Stella." "We've put Palm Beach on the market."

When the meal was over, he asked the diners to carry the plates onto the upper deck of his penthouse. He stacked them and, fascinated by the oddity of the pile of plates resting on a rail, a pillar of bone china, the diners watched him push them over the edge onto the tiled terrace below.

As a woman screamed, Minor Watt said, "Now we don't have to wash them."

That look of joy meant he had to be insane, probably dangerous—they were afraid. They would never forget this, he knew. And he saw how they sidled away, made excuses to leave.

About fifteen minutes later, one of them, the Irby Wilders, came back.

"Minor—you okay?"

"Never better. You?"

Irby's mouth was shut tight, his eyes narrowed, like a man on the deck of a ship in a gale. He said, "I'm wondering where the bottom is."

"It's down there," Minor Watt said, pointing to the smashed plates.

He knew this disillusioned investor thought he was crazed by the recession. But "Never better" was exactly how he felt. He was strengthened by the dropping of the irreplaceable plates.

.　　.　　.

Minor Watt did not say the word, though he knew the feeling that preceded this act of violence. It was disgust. Disgust had made him drop the Ming vase. What was the origin of his disgust? He did not know; it wasn't money, but it was related to wealth, a kind of fatness. Many people he knew were embarrassing themselves in their economies. Now they believed him when he said, "None of that for me." He was well aware that by ridding himself of these rare objects all the sourness in him was gone; and he had an appetite again.

He saw the point of murder now, and not simple homicide, but cannibalism. He'd found the cabinet of skulls an aesthetic satisfaction, like a rare ossuary. He'd never understood the pleasure of eating the bodies of these men, or emptying these skulls of the brain and spooning it into a bowl and gorging on this gray jelly. Now he appreciated the magnificence of eating flesh, the great appetite, the ritual devouring. The destruction of the vase and the plates and paintings—pieces as unique as any man—was not vandalism. It was enrichment, a source of power. He was eating art.

Two couples, dinner guests at the plate drop, the Diamonds and the DeSilvas, called separately, expressing concern—pretending to sympathize. "You must be under a lot of pressure"—and they suggested to Minor Watt that if there were any other items in his collection that he wanted to get rid of they would be glad to accept them. He'd smashed the plates, therefore—their reasoning went—he didn't care about them, and would probably hand over a precious object for nothing or very little.

"But I do care," Minor Watt said, after he'd hung up. "That's why I did it."

*You do something spontaneously, perhaps accidentally, with no thought of the consequences,* he thought, *and sometimes you're surprised at what you've provoked.* His roofing career leading to real estate had proven that. Smashing china was a revelation, and a cure.

The Diamonds said they had always been very fond of Minor Watt's Tang celadon bowl, smuggled out of Cambodia, perhaps stolen from the National Art Museum in Phnom Penh. The man who'd sold it to him had remarked on its solidity, how this thick piece of pottery had survived through twelve centuries.

"That piece could take a direct hit."

Minor Watt had always smiled, and felt small and somewhat in awe, remembering those words. He invited the Diamonds for tea. He called attention to the jade-colored glaze, the inimitable crackle, and allowed them to salivate at the prospect of the gift—they were actually swallowing, gulping in anticipation. Then he asked them to put on protective goggles—"You'll see it better." Humoring him—he was insane, wasn't he?—they put them on and Minor Watt took a hammer to the bowl and, with his tongue clamped in his teeth, pounded the celadon to dust. The DeSilvas had hinted on the phone of their liking for an Edward Lear water-color of the Nile depicting Kasr el-Saidi among some riverside palms. These people, too, pleased to be invited for tea, let their covetous gaze wander over the painting.

"The color is brighter without the glass," Minor Watt said, and removed the painting from its frame. He served tea and, after filling their cups, dribbled the pot of hot tea over the water-color, as the man held his sobbing wife.

Minor Watt said, "Sorry," as mockery, but he thought: *Of course I know what I'm doing.* Power over works of art that he owned; but also power over these people. He had the power to terrorize them, too, without ever touching them.

Each thing he destroyed strengthened him; each person he terrified through his destruction made him someone to be feared. It had never been his intention; it was all a revelation. Money had no meaning anymore. He'd amassed his art collection believing it would inspire respect—and it had, to a degree; and it had inspired envy, too. The assumption in New York was that he would eventually give the collection to a museum. To these people, and perhaps to a museum, these objects represented wealth—the absurd bias toward money. Even a museum would not regard them as collectors' items, one of a kind. These days the museum would sell them, to stay afloat, and Minor Watt would be forgotten. It disgusted him to think that transformed into money they were replaceable. The collector's conceit was always that he or she was a temporary custodian.

"No, I am the owner—the last owner!" Minor Watt said.

Destroying them meant that he was the equal of the person who made them—more than that, he was more powerful. He wiped these rare things from the face of the Earth, leaving only a memory in which he mattered; and a memory was the more evocative, even mystical, for its vagueness. After centuries of use and veneration, of being handled and crated and resold, catalogued, photographed, admired, the small thin-rimmed jade bowl balanced on Minor Watt's fingers, in his lovely kitchen, before the blinking eyes of the museum curator, was tipped into a blender. And before the man could react, Minor Watt clapped the lid on and poked the button labeled *Liquefy.*

More ingenious in devising ways to destroy these works of art, each one appropriate to the object, his intention was to make the destruction as memorable as the object itself.

He had some supporters, all of them art students, video artists, creators of installations, one who worked with decaying food, another with human blood, who interpreted Minor Watt's destruction as a form of art, a kind of ritual theater, performance art. They sent him letters. They praised him for turning his back on art history to create something new.

"You are a total hero," one of them said—a pretty purple-haired woman, very thin, black fingernails, neck tattoo, torn black clothes, big boots.

Her praise alarmed him, though her look kept him watching. She had come with a group to his uptown office. He had agreed to meet them in the foyer, his security people in attendance.

"You got a Rauschenberg?" a man in the group asked: spiky hair, mascara, the same boots.

"An early one," Minor Watt said. "Birds, animals."

"Wipe it! Whack it! Know what Rauschenberg did? Bought a DeKooning drawing and erased it. Erased it! Exhibited it as his own work. It's in a museum. Is that radical?"

"You're way beyond that, man. You're like a whole new movement—iconoclasm."

He smiled and sent them away. Iconoclasm was nothing new. The word had been in use for five centuries. Minor Watt continued destroying because destruction gave him a greater appetite for shattering a whole lovely thing, the breaking of each piece meant the breaking of a barrier that admitted him to a region of cold ferocity. The act of destruction had nothing to do with art. He laughed at the students who claimed his destruction as a form of conceptual art. No, he went on breaking his collection because—he felt sure—he had entered a realm of self-indulgence he'd never guessed at before. He was gluttonous for more. He was not an artist, he was a child smashing a doll, and he was also a ruler punishing a province, a tyrant carrying out a massacre. He did it with a smile, and knew that the great destroyers were smilers—destruction was proof of wealth.

He went on smiling and never uttered the simple truth that he had discovered: *No matter how outrageous my assault on art, no one can stop me.*

He still bought art. And at auctions, when he saw how passionately someone wanted to acquire something, he wagged a finger and outbid them. Later, he contrived ways to show these people that he'd destroyed the thing they had craved. Other bidders hated to see him enter a sale, but he could not be banned—and he knew that the auctioneers were secretly pleased that he was bidding, because he bid without limit.

Who could prevent him from destroying a thing he owned? He jeered at his critics. "You'd think I was committing murder!" It was worse than murder for some of these people. And these were the same people who'd stood by, indifferent to the cruelty of the Taliban rule in Afghanistan: stoning women to death for adultery, hacking the hands from thieves, and after Friday prayers, the beheadings. And who cared? But when the Taliban dynamited the ninth century standing Buddhas in Bamiyan these same people howled in pain, demanding military action, the overthrow of the Taliban, the siege of Kabul—and it had happened!

But Minor Watt now understood the Taliban, and their earlier incarnation, the White Huns of the fifth century who'd taken their axes and maces to the Buddhas and stupas of Gandhara, not far from Bamiyan. What lay behind these furious acts of purification was a demonstration of will. Never had these destroyers seemed stronger, fiercer, less sentimental, more resolute, more intent in their mission: inaccessible, unappeasable, figures of pure horror and domination. It was certain that invaders or rulers who would dynamite a beautiful work of art placed even lower value on human life, because art works were one of a kind, and people were pretty much the same. Even those people whom Minor Watt knew seemed to feel this way.

So vandalizing his art works, he was regarded as worse than a crank. He was a homicidal maniac.

He told people he knew, who objected, that he might have stopped had the reaction against him not been so strong. He wondered if what he said was the truth, because the reaction—the sense of outrage, the condemnation—energized him. What right did they have to say, "How dare you"?

Though it was unimaginable to the art collectors and connoisseurs, the destruction became easier for him. "Why am I doing it, why am I so effective and precise? Because I am a connoisseur!"

How fragile, how insubstantial these objects were. A Japanese woodblock print was made of rice paper. Even his greatest Utamaro hardly raised a flame before the astonished and insulted eyes of Mr. Harada, and it left a mere smudge of ash. The value of a cricket cage was its lid, a deeply carved cookie of ivory that could be pinched apart; and the gourd was easily crumbled. In a gesture of strangulation he broke these things in his hands, and to be certain that they wouldn't be reassembled he stamped his shoe on them, grinding them with his sole. He slashed paintings, he crushed porcelain, he hammered silver pots flat.

And he required witnesses—the effort was almost wasted without someone watching, especially someone who cared, who would report it.

These witnesses believed they could persuade him not to destroy the thing. They tried (as they saw it) to talk him off the ledge. "Think of the implications of what you're doing." He thought of the implications. They were his motives. Their concern only made him more intent on finishing the job.

Minor Watt never raised his voice; he was not angry. His calm way in this destruction unnerved anyone who watched him, as though he were about to stick a knife in their eye. There were always plenty of willing witnesses these days, since their hope was that at the last minute he'd have a change of heart; but the witnesses themselves gave him conviction.

Something else that animated him was the desire to destroy each thing differently. "I could simply set my house on fire" he told one collector. "I could stack everything I owned onto a pile and set it alight. But that would be meaningless."

And he wanted to add that a massacre can mean less than a single execution.

"So what you're doing has a meaning?" Doug Redman had asked.

"Yes, I think so. The experience of seeing a lovely thing leave the world forever. The drama of extinction, so to speak. It's a death."

He was not, he said, the first person to destroy works of art. The Vandals had given the world a word by doing it. The Chinese emperor, Ch'in Shi-huang, had burned every book in his kingdom in the year 213 BCE. Spanish conquistadors had stolen golden ornaments from the Inca people and hammered them into crucifixes. In the Second World War, bombing raids by Germans had targeted specific churches and museums, not only to demoralize the British but to demonstrate German might. Baron Gustav Braun von Sturm said, "We shall go out and bomb every building marked with three stars in the Baedeker Guide." The devastating raids on Britain called the Baedeker Blitz leveled thousands of ancient buildings, their contents—paintings, furniture, silver—reduced to ashes. Most of the Old Master paintings stolen by Irish terrorists in the 1970s from English houses and museums had never been found and had probably been kicked to bits or sold for guns.

Compared to this, trashing a Francis Bacon was negligible. Bacon himself regularly destroyed paintings he'd done that didn't suit him, and laughed when the critics howled. The destruction had not diminished him; it had made him loom larger.

But though the historical precedent for the destruction of artwork was ancient, the novelty that Minor Watt introduced was using his own art collection, piece by piece; and, while it seemed a form of insanity, it was both unprecedented and lawful.

He felt no remorse—far from it. He was suffused with an unexpected sense of power, greater than anything he'd felt in acquiring the works. He knew the joy of a winning bid, the cry of "Sold!" The arrival of the wooden crate, the dismantling, the revealing of the painting, the urn, the skull, the statue, the goblet. But destroying any of these things gave him the intense pleasure that could only be compared with devouring something rare—eating an endangered species, the feeling the Chinese had when feasting on a bear paw or a moose nose or the liver of a tiger.

He envisioned no end to it. He had enough money to go on buying art. The disgusted foretaste of destroying a thing he saw in a salesroom or a catalogue filled him with an urgency to buy it.

The discouraged Bennett Hembergs said, "It's not yours—art belongs to the world. We are merely the preservers, keeping these pieces for future generations."

"I disagree," Minor Watt said in his quiet way. "I am disproving that. By destroying them I am making them mine."

He did not say (though he implied it) that it was his intention that no one would ever see them again. No one would bear witness to them. Knowing they were irreplaceable, he did his best to prevent anyone from photographing them whole.

"You're like a murderer—a rapist who kills his victims!"

He laughed—the tyrant laugh. "You don't know what murder is!" These were things that belonged to him. "No one can prevent me from destroying my own property, providing I do it in safety."

The great pity, in Minor Watt's mind, was that he was the true connoisseur; that he had studied these pieces with such care that no one saw as deeply into them as he did. "What a loss," they said; but they didn't know the half of it. The witnesses, the gallery owners, the collectors, were not ignorant, but neither did they fully understand the works—their historical importance, even their monetary value.

Art critics condemned him—his name became a euphemism for gratuitous violation. He was denounced and vilified. Yet he gloried in the abuse. It proved how successful he'd been: he wanted his efforts to be known. And, by the way, it showed how wealthy he was—the word potlatch was used. He'd made the money-men afraid; he made them look small and mean.

Not everyone howled. Some women were attracted to him for these acts of destruction. Unstable women, on the whole; too eager; excited by the danger of being so close to the fires that scorched his paintings, the dazzle of the knife blades, the clubs that smashed the pots. They were like the panting people who chased fire engines or joined window-breaking mobs, or wrote letters to serial killers, falling in love with them, marrying them on Death Row. The women were perhaps destructive themselves and had lived by ruining other people—but not on this scale. The ingenuity of Minor Watt shredding his paintings, smashing his porcelain, crushing the decorated skulls, microwaving his majolica, roasting his Polynesian clubs in the fireplace, had not occurred to them—they didn't own any works of art. He avoided these women. What did they know?

And at the parties he attended he was treated as notorious. Stab a Stella and people flee—or hang around, transfixed. He stopped going to parties. "Charisma vampires," he said; they sapped his energy.

What alarmed the art world was that Minor Watt had the means to replace these works. He showed up at auctions—the other bidders glared at him; and when he was successful, gloom descended on the salesroom, for it was known that the piece he'd bought—painting, book, pot, sculpture, dueling pistol, helmet, whatever—would be shattered to bits; if it happened to be a rare South Indian bronze it would be blow-torched into a sorry lump of unrecognizable metal. Ownership to Minor Watt meant oblivion.

Some art works cried out to be destroyed. Certain statues, certain paintings, the carvings that collectors referred to as "exquisite." They seemed defiant, and not just the delicate ones but the robust images too. The broad black strokes in a wall-sized Rothko seemed to stare at Minor Watt and say, "Kick me."

Had these works of art been people he would have been arrested, convicted of murder and imprisoned. And yet what he did was regarded by most people who knew of it as worse than murder. Yet he was almost delirious in his innocence, free to slash paintings and shatter gold Mayan ornaments, and all the rest, because the objects belonged to him.

Furious people visited him, to vent their feelings. Even a policeman: "Your neighbors are complaining . . . smoke . . . noise."

He laughed: "What noise?" Even stepped on, a Meissen shepherdess made less noise than someone chewing corn flakes.

"Your neighbors said they heard gunshots."

"Yes. I blew holes in a Jasper Johns. It seemed created to be shot at. Then I burned it. I have a permit to carry a gun."

"I'll need to write it up. It was a painting?"

"It was a target."

The sound of the gunshots had rippled through him and swelled him with a sense of power. He felt bigger, stronger, more visible; his name was on people's lips. He was better known, more famous as a destroyer of artworks than he'd ever been as a collector—and that was another motivator, the conceits of the other collectors, the presumption, the calculation. He laughed when one of them said, "A piece just like that sold at auction for a million-two." In the past they had ignored him, taken him for a philistine. What philistine? His eye was unerring in choosing the greatest works to destroy—the best went first, then the less-good works. In this way he proved that he had taste. Had he been a philistine he would not have discriminated. But he was a connoisseur; and he brought all his connoisseurship to his destruction.

Some dealers—not many—avoided him; some auction houses tried publicly to bar him from sales. But because of the money he was willing to pay, in a period when business had never been worse, he was discreetly welcomed, usually after hours, in the galleries and studios. And he was willing to pay more than anyone else. He didn't haggle. If he saw a thing he liked he bought it without hesitating.

He grew to love the twitch of greedy anticipation in the moist eyes of the art dealer on his entering the gallery; the subtle hints that a certain object might be worthy of his attention—not the best piece in the place, but always the most expensive.

This afternoon the dealer was Tony Faris. He had an early Hopper. He called to his assistant Mara to prop the painting on an easel.

Buyers and collectors said, "Can you make me a price?" or "What's the best you can do?"

Minor Watt smiled at Faris and said, "How much?"

The price was named. He studied Faris's mouth uttering the big number, the dry lips, the licking tongue, the jerking head.

"I'll write you a check," he said. Then, because Faris had hesitated, and Mara had glanced at her boss, said, "How do you want me to pay for it?"

He loved the way Faris said, "Cash is good."

"Send it to me—pack it well."

Faris knew he was sending the piece to its doom. They all did. Collaborators!

"I know you'll be happy with it."

Happy, yes, because if it were not such great quality he would not have bought it; would not trouble himself to slash it, burn it, pour acid over it, melt it, batter it with a hammer.

The assistant, Mara, brought the Hopper to him in a taxi. He invited her up to his apartment and led her through part of his collection, his usual challenge, daring her to identify them.

"Naga," she said correctly of a red beaded necklace in a framed box. "Reverse glass painting—Hanuman," and "Mughal khanjar—real jewels in the hilt." She seemed reverential, even moved by the objects. "And that is a dah," she said, of a silver dagger.

"You know what you're looking at."

"Many of these things have a practical use." She was glancing from the Marquesan club to the Dan mask to a Zulu headrest. "Not art objects, but useful tools," she said. "To you, they are emblems of power."

He lifted the Marquesan *u'u* and wondered if he should smash it.

"The language of things," she said.

He knew why they were so willing to consign these artworks to oblivion. The money he paid was one incentive, but there was a larger issue: the scarcer the work, the rarer the masterpiece in any area, the greater the demand, the higher the price. A finite number of Hoppers existed. Minor Watt's oil Hopper had painted in Rockland, Maine, in the summer of 1926—moored fishing boats, a clutter of drooping telephone wires, the serene old culture, the ugly tilted crosstrees. Hopper had spent less than three months in Rockland. He'd done fewer than a dozen paintings. The destruction of this painting increased the value of all the rest of them; Faris probably had kept a better one for himself.

The Noland prices rose on the news that he'd wrecked two early targets. He pounded his Gandharan Maitreya figure, a "Buddha of the future" into fragments and the market for these strangely Hellenic Central Asian sculptures became buoyant.

He had never collected coins, inros, netsukes, perfume bottles; apart from a few pieces he'd given Sonia, jewelry left him cold. And what sort of spectacle would they make on a bonfire, or in a crucible—a sparklet, a fizz, a bad smell. Even melted, the heaviest earrings—West African or Indian—would amount to no more than a twisted nugget of gold. He craved a visible triumph, a blaze, a marble statue reduced to powder, to be sneezed into nothingness.

The painter Tristram Cowley invited him to his studio, and Minor Watt sat while Cowley showed him his latest work. Minor Watt admired the detail, made comments. He knew what these painters wanted him to do—buy a picture, not the best one. They held back. Minor Watt was patient. He chatted, waiting until the better pictures were slid out and leaned against the wall. Cowley's pieces were based on x-rays. Minor Watt chose *Compound Fracture*.

"You know where to send it."

Cowley knew what would happen to *Compound Fracture*. And he knew what would happen to his reputation, to the value of his work: it would be a breakthrough.

But such a painter was not the best witness to the destruction. Critics were excellent—they grieved. And the most knowledgeable critics were the best. They were able to appreciate the worth of the pieces; they could put a price tag on them, but few of them could afford to buy them, and so they were truly shocked to see Minor Watt slash them to rags.

After a nighttime visit to the New York studio of another painter, Minor Watt was walking to the corner to find a taxi when he was set upon and pushed to the sidewalk by two men.

At that moment, a police cruiser happened to drift past, interrupting the assault—though the two attackers slipped between the buildings and got away.

"You okay? They get anything?"

"I'm fine. I have my wallet. My watch." Patting himself, Minor Watt was gladdened that he felt no pain.

"I guess we got here just in time. Lucky. They could have done some damage."

Minor Watt smiled at that notion—that they might have broken his bones. Maybe they were men who objected to what he was doing? Or maybe they were thugs, looking for trouble.

It happened again—this time a gunshot fired into his car that was parked in a public lot. He was not in the car, but the bullet through the windshield entered at the level of his head. That was a message—not a random act of violence, but an attempted murder. He lost count of the people who would be glad to see him dead. Sonia would smile and tell people what a bastard he was— and never mention how they had loved each other. He bought a bulletproof car and hired a bodyguard, and, secure, he was gleeful, thinking that there were people who were so outraged by the destruction of his artworks that they were prepared to kill him.

The phone rang in his bulletproof car, a woman. "This is Mara, from the Tony Faris gallery. Mr. Faris would like to speak with you."

"Put him on," Minor Watt said.

"Right away—but I just wanted to say that I read about that trouble you had and I'm really sorry."

"Thanks for noticing. You're Mara?"

"You remember."

" 'The language of things.' I liked that."

Then Faris was on the line, saying, "Are you all right?"

Other people called—dealers, galleries, auctioneers, painters, sculptors. In almost every case, they were people who wished to sell him work; all of them well aware of his plans for the piece: the knife, the hammer, the acid bath, the crucible, the bonfire, the oven.

Sonia called. She sounded terrified, and her anxious questions told him that she was afraid he might hurt her.

The mugging and the gunshot, and his protective measures took so much of his time that for three weeks or more he did not destroy anything. In this period of reflection he realized that he would never run out of works to destroy. He felt a twinge of inhibition. Faris's sale of the Edward Hopper gave him his first intimation. Even if he concentrated on, say, Chola bronzes—a niche of Indian art—he'd only find at most a dozen masterpieces. Museums and die-hard collectors had the rest, which would be the more valuable for his destruction of the others.

And so he stopped and pondered what to do next. This pause proved accidentally helpful. He saw that he was regarded as a dominant force in the art world, almost as though his destruction was a form of art criticism, causing fear and gratitude. His spell of doing nothing created suspense. He liked the idea that he was spreading alarm by not lifting a finger; that he'd become a symbol of intimidation.

*I have not drawn blood*, he thought, *not one drop. I have not hurt a single person physically. I have not put a hand on anyone. I have never raised my voice. I have not cursed, nor shown anger, nor damaged anyone else's property.*

The paradox he saw in the partial destruction of his collection was that he had helped to stimulate the art market and inflate some prices. This was a drawback, if not a defeat. In his period of inaction and watchfulness, his phone warbled all the time—dealers chattering to do business—and he was tempted. But he knew their motives. He was being used. Perhaps this was to be expected, but he saw it as a diminution of his power. He despised them, but he began to doubt himself for having set a wayward impulse loose.

Escaping his apartment, leaving his phone behind, he walked the New York streets in dark glasses and loitered in the open spaces where other anonymous people were idling—Central Park, Union Square, Battery Park. He strolled, sensing that he was being watched, possibly followed; the shutter click of someone ducking out of view whenever he turned. Maybe one of those demented art students?

Sitting on a bench one day in Central Park, near the zoo, he became aware that it was trembling beneath him—the slats, even a gentle rocking of the frame. At the far end of the bench a young woman sat with her face in her hands, her shoulders heaving. She might have been crooning a lullaby softly to herself; but she was sobbing.

At first, Minor Watt turned away and prepared to go. What made him linger was the suspicion that the woman would think, in his abrupt departure, that he was rejecting her—and that might make her feel even worse.

Seemingly grief-stricken, she turned her smeared face to him and said, "I'm so sorry."

Now it was too late for him to leave. Nodding at her with a look of consolation he saw that she was beautiful. Her misery made her fragile and pretty, her sorrow creasing her features with complexity.

"You're Mister Watt," she said.

He was not surprised: he felt that the world knew him, even in his dark glasses and his oblique outings.

Looking closer, he recognized her as the woman from the gallery—Faris's assistant—where he'd bought the Hopper he'd destroyed. The language of things.

What he'd first noticed about her—her Asiatic pallor, the porcelain smoothness of her skin—was more emphatic, probably because of her weeping. She had the ageless look of someone who'd been kept in a darkened room her whole life: the luminous delicacy of her face, her small shoulders, her slender hands.

In contrast was the fullness of her breasts, which seemed to have a personality of their own—she leaned, and they seemed to swing for him. Why had he not noticed her beauty before?

"I know you," he said.

"Mara," she said.

"How about a cup of coffee?"

At the nearby outdoor cafe, she told him she was being evicted for not paying her rent. And the reason she had no money was that Faris had laid her off after Minor Watt had stopped buying pictures. "No one's buying art these days."

In this period, Minor Watt felt responsible for much that was happening in the world of business, and in the city generally. He sensed that he had influenced great shifts of money, not just in the art market but all over, because art was linked to so many areas of the economy. His destruction had made art an even more valuable commodity.

"I used to destroy my artwork," he said. " You know I'm famous for that. I sometimes think that it was my wish to be an ascetic."

"No," Mara said, and got his attention—no one ever disagreed with him. She went on, "Ascetics are driven by pride, the desire to be like gods. You are different from anyone else."

He stared at the pretty lips that had said this. He thought of installing Mara in his apartment—he had plenty of room. But he said, "How much are we talking about?"

Mara mentioned a round figure. It was nothing to him, yet with facial expressions and movements of his head he made his habitual show of puzzling over the amount.

He always carried a quantity of ready cash, in case he might see a piece he wanted to buy; and dealers almost swooned when they saw real money. He picked out the amount she had named from his wallet, and folded it, pushing it across the table, the way he might ante up in a poker game.

Palming the money, Mara began to cry again, and then dabbing her eyes she wrote something on a napkin and put it into his hand. And, as though overcome by his kindness, she hurried away, without another word.

He saw that a telephone number had been stabbed into the limp napkin. But he didn't call her. Almost a week went by; and she called him, asking him whether he wished to visit her.

"Because you're responsible for my being here," she said. "I make good coffee."

Had she forgotten saying that? When he visited her she opened a bottle of wine and poured him a glass.

"How have you been doing?"

"You know this economy better than I do. I've sent out a million applications."

He knew she meant: *I don't have any work.*

"I know the art galleries are hurting."

"You did them a huge favor," she said. "But my background is finance."

She was a banker, reduced to flunkying for Tony Faris. To make it easier for her, he said, "How much do you need?"

She mentioned a figure, raised it by a third, smiled sadly. She said, "I'll pay you back with my first paycheck."

She took the money and made it disappear in her pale hand. She was beautiful, perhaps the more so for looking submissive, with her slightly tangled hair, wearing her best dress. She had a dancer's legs—slender and yet strong, like her fingers, and her head was small and well shaped on her long neck.

As he was reflecting on her doll-like beauty—thinking *Chinese? Cambodian?*—she said, "The first time I saw you with Faris in the gallery I knew you were powerful—the way you carried yourself. I knew you by reputation. I hadn't realized how young and handsome you were."

"Very kind of you," Minor Watt said. "Made my day."

And as he got up to leave, Mara said, "You don't have to rush off."

He said, "I'm tempted to stay."

But he kissed her lightly and left, wondering at this turn of events.

Then it was he who called her, and met her again at the cafe in the park; he offered her more money, and she took it without mentioning that she'd pay him back. This happened two more times. It seemed that his giving her money kept her from finding a job, though at the third meeting she said she was still sending out applications.

"Anyone interested?"

"Sporadically," she said, and held his hand, tugging. She told him about her family, from Mizoram in Assam, all Baptists, yet with an ancient pedigree. Her full name was Mara Lai Pawl. That was how she'd known the Naga necklace and the khanjjar and the silver dah. But she was alone here; she had not found another Mizo in New York. Minor Watt thought, *Imagine!*

"Meet me tomorrow," he said, and specified a store on Madison Avenue.

He took her to buy jewelry; he helped her pick out some shoes. She selected some clothes, he sat while she tried them on, and he thought how she was like a small daughter saying, "How do you like my new dress, Daddy?" He paid for the clothes.

Walking away from the last store—Barney's—around the corner to the Pierre for a drink, he said, "You should have a boyfriend, pretty girl like you."

"Fired him," she said. "Besides, I have you."

He did not reply, just kept walking, and he could see that she was thrown. He said, "Would you do something for me?"

Mara didn't hesitate. She said, "Anything."

He let her move into an empty apartment in one of the buildings he owned that was visible from where he lived. Using binoculars he could sometimes see her at her window. He began to live for these glimpses, Mara flashing past, or lingering to look out, not knowing that she was being caressed by his gaze.

Minor Watt went on visiting in the oblique way of a wealthy and secretive friend. He sat and held her in a scrutinizing way, thinking: *What is it about her that makes her lovely?* The only way to possess her was not to love her, but to support her, to satisfy her with money—and yet to keep her a little hungry and apart. He knew that feeling—the poor might be content with the little they have, but the rich always want more. Sonia had always resisted; her defiance subdued him, and he loved her, but he had never truly possessed her.

By the second month Mara in her acceptance became entirely dependent on him.

"I saw Faris the other day," he said. "He told me I was ruthless."

"He doesn't know anything. You're really very compassionate."

"You think so?"

She had a beautiful smile. "Oh, yes."

She didn't know him. He was a stranger, as featureless as a bank, which was all he was to her, a source of light and money; her sole support.

But with the connoisseurship he'd acquired over many years, he knew her well. She was as familiar to him as any object he'd studied, and like those objects she was an empty vessel, self-regarding, inward looking, even smug and needing to be held, like all the art he'd ever owned. But that didn't matter. She was also one of a kind, exotic for being a Mizo, lovely in her own way, perhaps lovelier, more delicate and fragile, more breakable than any piece that had ever passed through his hands; and she belonged to him.

What Minor Watt imagined happening, and what he rehearsed in his mind, was that on the anniversary of Sonia leaving him, the beginning of the stock-market slide, he would take out the dah that Mara had once recognized and named, he would carry it to the apartment that she occupied, and he would confront her, gripping the foot-long dagger by its silver hilt. And then, as before, when facing Sonia with the rare vase, he would hope for inspiration. Perhaps nothing would happen. Perhaps in dramatic finality he would lift his hand and slash Mara's throat and watch her bleed to death on the carpet from Khotan. And he would say to all the people who condemned him, "Now do you see?"

What actually happened was that he visited the apartment, the dah tucked inside his jacket. Mara smiled when she let him in, but she also seemed to notice that his posture was odd. He was slightly canted to one side, favoring a crease in his jacket.

Minor Watt touched her, smoothing her pale slender neck with his fingers, a characteristic gesture.

Then he said, "I'm not going to hurt you."

Mara stepped back, with widened eyes, moving her lips, as though translating what he had just said into her own language, and terrified by it. Surprised by her reaction—why wasn't she reassured?—Minor Watt slipped his hand beneath his jacket and located the knife. But Mara was quicker; she moved on him with an old-fashioned slap, an efficient Asiatic chop, and the knife clattered to the hardwood floor. She dived at it and with a sweeping gesture grasped the handle, shook off its scabbard and poked the blade at him. Flapping his hands in distress, Minor Watt shrieked—his own voice scared him: she had cut him, she had drawn blood. No one had ever injured him. Fearing for his life, he grew small, as Mara loomed. In that moment she ceased to be ornamental. She was a horror to him—as though one of his pieces of art had come alive; turning into tribeswoman, suddenly feline, with blazing eyes, she pointed the dagger at him.

Minor Watt was murmuring as though in prayer, pleading for his life, as Mara said, "This is a Burmese dah, but we have similar knives in Mizoram. Some are well made. Most of them are tools," she went on, examining the blade, "instruments for cutting—for killing." Now she held it to his anguished face. "They are not trophies. Not art—but useful objects. Now I think you know that."

Minor Watt backed away, looking at the ugly thing in her hand, reminding her that he had been kind to her.

"Here's what I want you to do for me," Mara said.

"Anything," he said.

"Remove all your clothes," she said.

"Please."

Without raising her voice, Mara repeated her request. And he obeyed, undressing slowly, and finally stepping out of his boxer shorts, one hand cupped for the sake of modesty at his groin, the other raised to protect his face, at the level of the blade.

Begging her now, he was gabbling, and Mara's look of disgust convinced him that she meant to kill him. She made as if to slash him, but only nicked his chin. Even so, he howled at the sight of the blood that dripped on his pale belly.

She prodded again, moving him with the blade into the elevator and to the ground floor, then let him run. And—grateful, eager—he fled from the apartment, out of the building, naked, his hands and body smeared, absurd, from touching his wounds; and on the busy street, a laughingstock, a hilarious news item in these anxious times.

## Poetry

FINALIST—GENERAL
EXCELLENCE, LITERARY,
POLITICAL, AND
PROFESSIONAL MAGAZINES

*"Poetry is news that stays news."* That's Ezra Pound, and even if you don't agree, there's no denying that Joel Brouwer's "Lines from the Reports of the Investigative Committees" is, to use another cliché, ripped from the headlines. A poem that's also a news story—about the offshore oil spill, the largest in our history, that resulted from the April 2010 explosion and sinking of the Deepwater Horizon—"Lines from the Reports of the Investigative Committees" is an example of the work to be found in Poetry. Founded in 1912, Poetry has a rich history—contributors have included Yeats, Eliot, and, yes, Pound—but in recent years the magazine has gotten new attention, including the 2011 National Magazine Award for General Excellence for Literary, Political, and Professional Magazines. As the National Magazine Award judges said: "Poetry presents new verse, smart, thoughtful criticism and beautifully written essays. The magazine succeeds in proving that poetry is both vital to contemporary life and brimming with vitality."

Joel Brouwer

# Lines from the Reports of the Investigative Committees

The Department of the Interior and Department of Home-
land Security announced a joint enquiry into the explosion
and sinking of the Transocean Deepwater Horizon on
April 22. The US House of Representatives Committee on
Energy and Commerce Subcommittee on Oversight and
Investigations and Senate Committee on Energy and Natural
Resources have also announced investigations.

Last week BP launched its own investigation into the
incident and has an investigation team at work in Houston,
Texas.

—bp.com, April 28, 2010


Beneath three thousand feet, the sea is wholly dark.
The shuttle feeds hydraulics to the blind shear ram
and represents a single failure point for disconnect.
Recommendation: Declare selected points on earth
invisible. Affected communities have been provided
with limited quantities of powdered milk
and other staples. Many questions remain. Some
close their eyes under water instinctively.
Imagination can create a sense of peril where

no real peril exists. Safety equipment tests
were necessarily imaginary; mechanisms in question
were wholly inaccessible. A journalist sinking
into the mud was told to toss his camera
to a colleague and hold extremely still. In this
sense, we are our own prisoners. Investigators
have salt in their hair and sand in their teeth.
The hotel pool is empty. Yet questions remain.
Barbeque billboards depict grinning pigs in aprons
and toques. Cleanup crews recover thousands
of plastic milk jugs from the shallows. Do these
images appeal to the death drive? Care should be
taken to ensure the highest possible reliability
from that valve. Thousands in affected communities
have been evicted and live in tents. Demonstrators
have prevented investigators from accessing
hotel stairwells. 1900: Rudolf Diesel
demonstrates an engine fueled by peanut oil
at the Paris World's Fair. The Vietnamese owner
of Bad Bob's BBQ Buffet tells a journalist
she last drank powdered milk in a refugee camp
"a thousand years ago." Items available only
in limited quantities are found in Appendix C.
Cleanup crews have stacked thousands of drums
of dispersant in hotel parking lots. Dominant
failure combinations for well control suggest
additional safety mechanism diversity
and redundancy provide additional reliability.
Bank of America will offer limited foreclosure
deferments in affected communities. Thousands
of years ago, a pronghorn ram slipped beneath
the surface of a tar pit, jerking its snout
for air. Recommendation: Live at inaccessible
elevations. Recommendation: Close your eyes.

Recommendation: Prevent access to the invisible.
Engineering reports noted required safety
mechanisms were unlikely to function yet were
required for safety's sake. If the committee
may offer an analogy, a blind surgeon is dangerous,
an imaginary surgeon harmless. Still, questions
remain. BP's 2010 Q1 replacement cost profit
was $5,598 million, compared with $2,387 million
a year ago, an increase of 135%. Unlimited
quantities of peanuts are available. However,
care must be taken to ensure continued high
reliability of the shuttle valve, since it is
extremely critical to the overall disconnect
operation. Phenomena not meant to be accessed
or imagined are found in Appendix E. Cleanup crews
are sometimes idled for lack of fuel. 1913: Diesel
found dead, drowned under suspicious circumstances.
The investigators' hotel toilets won't flush.
Midas turned everything he touched to gold.
In this sense, seabirds cloaked in oil are rich.
Cleanup crews live in tents and are provided
with limited quantities of barbeque and wear
white canvas jumpsuits like prisoners on furlough.
If the committee may offer an analogy, the death
drive resides at wholly dark depths of imagination
and fuel issues from a wound we've opened there.

## Los Angeles

WINNER—FEATURE WRITING

You cannot bargain with lady death. But you can rely on this story to tell you what'll happen to you after she comes to get you. With unforgiving detail, Ben Ehrenreich traces your journey with death: the transport service that'll get you to the mortuary on time; the county coroner's office (where garden shears are the great equalizer); the freelance pathologist whose white Hummer is emblazoned with his phone number, 1-800-AUTOPSY; the embalmer who'll Superglue your lips shut; the crematorium that specializes in the incineration of the well fed. Finally you visit the largest cemetery in North America. Somebody shovels dirt on top of you. Somebody else tamps it down. You're done. As the National Magazine Award judges said, "This is a cleverly constructed, unexpectedly witty examination of the death industry, brazenly written in the second person." A novelist and essayist, Ben Ehrenreich is a contributing editor at Los Angeles, which also won the 2011 National Magazine Award for General Excellence.

Ben Ehrenreich

# The End

You've made some bargains.

We all have. Maybe you allow yourself a single Tommy's burger every six months. Maybe you've given up meat altogether, or red meat anyway, most of the time. Maybe you're serious about this and you've given up all refined grains and any processed anything; the extra buck a pound to buy organic seems a reasonable sacrifice. You've given up booze, cigarettes, pills, cocaine, sex with strangers. You tell yourself you don't miss them. You wear sunscreen and eat flaxseeds. You go to the gym on breezy Sundays when you'd rather lie around. You go to yoga classes even though the chanting makes you want the world to end. You sold your motorcycle years ago. You cross at the light and look both ways.

No matter how many sacrifices you make to Lady Death, no matter how rich the offerings you lay before her altar, she will know where to find you. When she comes, she will hold you tight, and she will never let you go. Don't be frightened. She takes us all.

Even here in Los Angeles, in the glow of so much newness, she takes 60,000 of us each year.[1] That's 164 each day. Imagine them all lying side by side, napping forever without a snore. The

---

1. She's not likely to run out soon. Another 150,000 of us are born each year.

sun goes down and rises again, and 164 more are sleeping beside them, resting cheeks on shoulders, ears on arms. One day you will join their still parade. Chances are good—about one in four in L.A. County—that death will grab you by the heart. Coronary disease is by far our leading cause of mortality, as it is in the rest of the country. L.A.'s specific inequities, though, travel as deeply through death as they do through life. In this and other ways, death maps life. If you're an African American or a Latino male and you die before seventy-five, you're more likely to die of homicide than any other cause. The same goes if you're of any race or either gender and you live in South L.A. If you're white or live west of La Cienega and it's not your ticker that gets you, it will most likely be an overdose, or a car crash, or lung cancer,[2] or your own hand—murder is not even in the running.

Whoever you are and wherever you live, you will go. You will not be you anymore. Not exactly. You will be a corpse, a cadaver, a decedent, a "loved one." You will be remains. The death industry employs more euphemisms than politicians do.[3] Someone will find what's left of you. A child, spouse, or parent. A nurse or passerby. Whoever it is will call for help. At home, at work, or in the street, he or she will dial 911. In a hospital, hospice, or nursing home, someone will call your doctor, who will check one last time for vital signs, declare you dead, and fill out the proper forms. A nurse will remove your clothes and close your eyes. (Not just for modesty's sake: Rigor mortis hits the eyelids fast.) He or she will tie a tag bearing your name, which you can no longer speak, onto one of your toes, cover you with a plastic shroud, and wheel you to an elevator and thence to the morgue. In most hospitals it is in the basement. You will be rolled from

2. Smog makes for great sunsets, but it doesn't make us special. Lung cancer is the most common form of cancer nationwide.
3. The novelist Evelyn Waugh had his fun with this: "Normal disposal is by inhumement, entombment, inurnment or immurement, but many people just lately prefer insarcophagusment."

the gurney into a refrigerated drawer. The door will close behind you. It will be dark and cold, but you won't care.

## Power Words

So here you are, dead and alone. Chances are you didn't want this, but your wishes were ignored. Whatever happens to the part of you that you recognize as somehow quintessentially you (call it soul, self, spirit, spark), the other part isn't finished yet— the fleshly part, the limbs and guts that ached and pleased you in so many ways, the meaty bits that you vainly or grudgingly dragged around for all those years. That piece is still of interest to the bureaucrats. It is still a potential source of profit. In your absence its journey is just beginning.

The path forks before it. Which way it goes will be determined by the cause of your demise. All the state wants is a death certificate: Think of it as a letter from your doctor excusing you from paying income tax forever. The county, though, wants to know why you died and if there might be a reason to push the cops and the courts and the jails into motion. The coroner holds the key to all that machinery. The key itself is what you once called you. If you have not been under the care of a physician for six months, if you die during surgery or as a result of injuries sustained in an accident or an assault (self-inflicted or otherwise), or if there's any suspicion that your death might be something other than "natural," your next stop will be the Los Angeles County Department of Coroner—which is, assistant chief coroner Ed Winter[4] tells me more than once, the busiest such department in the country.

It investigates 18,000 deaths a year, dispatching thirty-six investigators[5] to the far edges of its jurisdiction—from Lancaster to Long Beach and West Covina to Catalina Island, from oil

4. Lakshmanan Sathyavagiswaran is the chief coroner.
5. This includes two who specialize in the deaths of infants.

tankers and cruise ships anchored off the coast to jets on the runway at LAX. One of those investigators will come to you. He or she (let's go with she, because more often these days the investigators are women) will search your pockets for ID. If you are at home, she will nose around for medical records. She will interview relatives, witnesses to your final moments, and the police at the scene. She will photograph and examine you. You've seen this part on TV. When she has finished, she and a driver will load you into the rear of a white county van and take you on one last drive down one last freeway, through one last Sig-Alert, off that final off-ramp onto Mission Road. At the corner of Marengo they will pull into a driveway at the side of an elegant old brick building. They will open the back of the van, roll you out, and take you inside, where you will wait quietly in the coroner's fridge until one of twenty-five overburdened pathologists is ready to examine you.

Winter, a sixty-one-year-old goateed ex-cop with a cranky sort of charm, squints and counts the day's cases on his computer monitor. It's 9:30 in the morning. "Since eight o'clock, I've gotten one, two, three, four, five more," he says. "Got an undetermined, a child. Got an accident, sixty-three-year-old male. Another accident: unknown male Caucasian, thirty to forty, found unresponsive by passerby at a construction site. And an unknown male found floating in the ocean dressed in T-shirt and jeans, Pacific Coast Highway." He stops reading and looks up. "We're frigging always busy."

It's not just the dead. The telephone rings, and it's a reporter. He has questions about Brittany Murphy's husband.[6] Winter puts the call on speakerphone and rolls his eyes. When Winter and I first met a few weeks earlier, he pushed a sheet of paper across his desk. It was an inventory of celebrity deaths the

6. If you missed it: Actress Murphy was found dead (pneumonia, anemia, and drug intoxication) in the home she shared with her screenwriter husband, Simon Monjack, who was found dead there five months later (pneumonia and heart disease).

coroner's office had investigated during the previous year. Michael Jackson's name was listed twice.

In the lobby Winter introduces me to Lieutenant David Smith, a genial, dapper man of forty-six with a white handlebar mustache, who supervises the department's identification and notification division. Right now Smith's mind is on other things. "Part of the issue I'm dealing with here," he tells me in the elevator, "is extremely overweight bodies that have to be cremated." By state law, if nobody picks you up after thirty days, you will be incinerated.[7] In bureaucratese this is called "county disposition," or "county dispo" for short. Smith located a private crematorium willing to kindle his uncollected dead, but it wouldn't take bodies over 350 pounds. He found a mortuary in Orange County that wanted seven bucks for every pound over 350, but even it topped off at 400 pounds. "I had one the other day who was 710 pounds," Smith says. The problem seems to have been solved: Odd Fellows Cemetery in Boyle Heights specializes in the incineration of the truly obese and charges a flat rate of one dollar a pound.

Again, death maps life. County budgets are tight, and more families can't afford funerals. L.A. County will charge your next of kin $352 to pick up your ashes (cremains, if you prefer), which is about what Forest Lawn wants just to chauffeur you from your deathbed to its oven door. So more families than ever have to settle for the grim anonymity of "county dispo."

Smith's main responsibility is to identify you and notify your family that you have died. If the investigator sent out to the scene was unable to make a positive ID, you are for the moment a John or Jane Doe. These categories, Smith says, are further subdivided into "soft Does" and "hard Does." You are a soft Doe if you were found locked in your own apartment, for instance, and the investigator is pretty sure you are you—but you are too decomposed for anyone to be certain. Your fingers are too far gone to yield prints,

---

7. It's an issue of space; cremation reduces you to the size of a shoe box.

but Smith's people[8] should be able to confirm your identity through dental records or X rays. You are a hard Doe if you were discovered in an alley or in the trunk of a car and you didn't have your wallet and there was no one around who knew that you were you. Then the only real options are fingerprint databases and DNA, and the latter is likely to be on record only if you've been convicted of a felony.

Once they've pinned a name on you, Smith and two other investigators will start looking for your family. If they turn up an address, they'll send a letter out. If they find a phone number, they'll call. "We notified somebody through MySpace one time," Smith says. The phone calls can be tricky. Some people laugh on hearing the news. Some are apathetic. Some start screaming. "If the phone just drops, we call 911," Smith says. "We don't want another case." Sometimes the next of kin are in denial. "You have to use the power words: 'They're dead.'"

Your family might demand to come in and see you one last time. This generally means they can't afford a funeral and want a chance to say good-bye. County rules forbid them from viewing you in the flesh, so the best Smith can do is show them a photo. "I'm good with Photoshop," he says, "so if the face looks really bad, I'll try to remove as much blood as possible, take the bullet out of the head. Decomposed bodies I can't do much with."

If your family members really miss you, Smith says, they will talk to your photo as if you could hear them. Sometimes they will pet it, as if you could still feel their fingers on your face.

## All the King's Horses

If you become a coroner's case, you have a decent shot at being eviscerated within a few days of your death: Pathologists employed

---

8. Actually, it's just one person: the tall guy in the corner cubicle whose job it is to identify every unnamed corpse in the 4,000 square miles of L.A. County.

by the coroner perform about 7,800 autopsies a year, though many of those are partial autopsies, in which the examiner inspects only the specific organs that catch his or her interest. In the 1960s, autopsies were performed on more than half the patients who exited the hospital through the morgue. That number has since fallen to less than 10 percent. Insurance companies loathe spending money on the living and are even stingier with the dead. This has opened up a market niche large enough for Vidal Herrera to park his Hummer in. Perhaps you've seen it. It's white and emblazoned on both sides with the name of his company: 1-800-AUTOPSY.

Herrera is fifty-eight and stocky, with a trim white beard and a round, lively face. The guys in the neighborhood call him "Muerto." Today, standing in the courtyard of his Valley Boulevard compound in El Sereno, he is wearing a T-shirt that says WHAT HAPPENS IN THE MORGUE STAYS IN THE MORGUE. In addition to performing complete autopsies for $3,000 a pop and harvesting and transporting donated organs, Herrera rents mortuary equipment to the studios for film and TV shoots and has a side business producing custom "coffin couches"—cut-down caskets transformed into sofas. He shows me one in silver and black with a Raiders logo embroidered on a cushion.

Despite his nickname, Herrera's vivacity is uncontainable. He takes me to his office and tells me about his years with the coroner's department, where he worked as a morgue attendant, a photographer, an autopsy assistant, and finally for five years as an investigator. He talks about a woman in Compton eaten by her cats, about the time he retrieved a "floater" from a drainage canal in Lomita and his clothes filled with maggots, and about his last day on the job in 1984, when he ruptured three disks in his spine trying to lift an obese pastry chef who had shot herself. "She reminded me of a gorilla," he says, and recounts his subsequent struggles with depression and the revelation that he suffered from post–traumatic stress disorder. Until a psychiatrist told him otherwise, he says, he had thought that his recurring nightmares of mutilated corpses were normal. On one wall of his office, among Halloween props and Grateful Dead posters, is a framed caricature of Herrera grinning in black surgical scrubs. A speech bubble above his head reads "A chance to slash is a chance for cash."

If your survivors have suspicions about the cause of your death and can afford to put their minds at ease, they can call Herrera or one of his eager competitors. If they do, you will end up like the sixty-year-old woman now lying naked on Herrera's stainless-steel autopsy table. She is short and overweight and hasn't breathed in five days. Her arms and lower legs are tanned a yellowish brown, but her belly, breasts, and thighs are a startling white because all of her blood has drained to her back. Her toenails are still crimson with polish. Herrera dons blue latex gloves and a long, black rubber butcher's apron for the occasion, but he's there only to watch. His autopsy assistant, Sean Sadler, will do the honors, along with a pathologist who asks me not to use his name. I will call him Dr. Gray.

Sadler begins with a Y-incision. Using a scalpel, he slices down from each shoulder to the sternum and from there to just above the black snare of hair beneath her navel. The patient does not flinch, not even when Sadler peels back the skin of her chest with a retractor, causing her breasts to loll on her biceps. He cuts through her ribs with pruning shears, pausing to observe the softness of her bones—osteoporosis, he suggests—and the fractures left by whoever had attempted CPR. He trims away the heavy yellow fat around her heart, slices through the arteries and veins, and hands the once vital organ to Dr. Gray, who weighs and dissects it on a plastic cutting board. The lungs come out next. Sadler works the scalpel under the patient's chin to loosen the organs of her neck: the thyroid and parathyroid glands, the esophagus and trachea. He goes organ by organ, handing each to Dr. Gray, who slices and studies them, then drops a sliver of each into a jar of diluted formaldehyde. He traps another sliver in a plastic cassette for the toxicologist and tosses what is left into the "gut bucket"—a small, wheeled trash can at his feet.

In the end, when her torso has been reduced to what is called a "canoe," and her skullcap rocks on the table beside her right shoulder, and a single drop of blood-brown water hangs like a tear beneath her eye, Dr. Gray decides it was her heart that killed her, although she also had pneumonia and a terrible back injury—four inches of spine swollen and saturated with blood—that must have kept her in constant and excruciating pain. He shows me her butterflied heart. The two halves of her mitral valve don't quite match, which means more to him than it does to me.

If it were you instead of her, you would not recognize yourself. The yellowy red mess inside of you would seem to have little to do with even your most intimate understanding of yourself. You would be startled by the pleasant purplish hue of your liver, the graceful drape of your small intestines, the stubborn white ball of your skull. The smells you release would surprise you, as would the awful groaning crack your spine makes when Sadler pries the vertebrae apart to get at the tender cord. But since the worst indignity—your death—has already occurred, do you think you'd really mind?

## A Happy Life

If your death is sufficiently unremarkable that the coroner has no designs on your remains, you will likely avoid the invasive curiosity of the county and go straight to the funeral parlor that will handle what are politely called "the arrangements." If the funeral director has the staff on hand, he will send a man with a van to fetch you, but chances are good that he will subcontract the task to someone like Angelo Patrick.

Patrick runs Patco Transportation Services. When I meet him at a Denny's in Hollywood, he is wearing a black suit and tie and a flawlessly white shirt with two golden pens protruding from the pocket. There is a somber intensity to him that is barely disguised by the softness of his voice or the formality of his speech and bearing. Patrick grew up in South Carolina and earned a degree in biology, but in 1971, there were not many jobs in the sciences for a black man in the South. Two years later he moved to L.A. and enrolled in mortuary school.

In the decades since Patrick graduated, the "death care" business, once known as the "dismal trade," has changed sharply. Beginning in the late 1980s, the industry underwent a massive consolidation. Racing to corner the market before baby boomers started dying off, a few giant firms—the largest of them being Houston-based Services Corporation International—began buying up hundreds of independent mortuaries and cemeteries. Usually the conglomerate kept the individual locations' original names but combined their operations—and jacked up prices.[9] The traditionally American send-off—a viewing at the funeral home, followed by services at the church and a motorcade to the cemetery—gave way to the corporate all-in-one. The big cemeteries now have mortuaries, chapels, and even florists on-site, which cuts out the old side industries. So-called first-call services like Patco are among the few subsidiary contractors that have survived the shift.

Technically, Patrick's job is fairly simple. The mortuary calls him and tells him where you are. He drives to the address, knocks on the door, rolls you into a sheet, ties off the ends, hoists you onto a gurney, wheels you to the van, drops you at the mortuary, and waits for his next call. "There's never any funny stuff," he says. "The dead, they don't say anything."

His work, however, does have its complications. First, there is "decomp." Patrick can tell it will be an issue before he even parks, when he sees the police officers standing at the far end of the sidewalk smoking cigars to cover the smell. Aside from the odors,

9. This will be familiar to fans of *Six Feet Under*.

there are fluids to deal with and parts of you that stain his clothes. Stairs can be a problem. You don't get any lighter when you die. If you're a pack rat or a hoarder, you will make Patrick's task still more difficult. You might have too much junk around for him to wheel you out, which means he'll have to carry you. Sometimes he can't find the dead for all the trash that crowds their homes.

Then there are the living. Patrick remembers one large tattooed fellow who did not want to part with his mother's remains. "He had just come out of prison. He didn't want Mom to be dead yet. It took six guys, his uncles, to hold him down on the floor while I took the body and ran—literally ran." Another man threatened Patrick with a hammer after Patrick had covered his wife's face. "She's going to suffocate," the man said. Patrick uncovered it.

"You get them in the bathtub, on the toilet, in the bed, in the backyard. Everywhere people go, we pick them up," says Patrick, leaning over his eggs and grits, which he does not touch. "From the littlest person to the most important person. Musicians, Indian chiefs, whoever. I pick them up."

Patrick was raised a Baptist. When he was twelve, he watched his father die of a heart attack and found he could no longer believe in the God who had taken his father from him. He married an observant Jehovah's Witness and became one, too. Religion, he says, "offered the possibility that I might one day see my father again." His work has eroded that faith. Patrick is sixty now and no longer married, and he doesn't bother himself with God. "When people die, I don't know where they go, just like I don't know where we come from," he says. "I see a lady die at 115. I see babies die at three months—I can hold the baby in my hand. I see kids die at three, four years old. I see teenagers, rich people, poor people, white people, black people. Everybody dies."

The only ones that disturb him, he says, are the lonely ones, the ones he finds decomposing in their living rooms, surrounded by empty bottles with the television still on. He remembers a woman he found lying on her kitchen floor. She had been there for two weeks even though her daughter lived just four doors down.[10]

Patrick smiles a tight, sad smile. "It's like the Epicurean philosophers say, 'Eat, drink, and be merry, for tomorrow we die.' There's a lot of truth to that. How much of your life are you willing to be unhappy? How much of your life are you willing to give up? What is a happy life?"

## Euphoria

Los Angeles holds a special place in the history of death. Until relatively recently, Europeans "were as familiar with the dead as they were familiarized with the idea of their own death," writes the French historian Philippe Ariès. They painted decomposing cadavers in manuscripts and carved them on church walls. Starting in the high Middle Ages, though, Ariès argues, Western attitudes began to change: "Death, so omnipresent in the past that it was familiar, would be effaced . . . would become shameful and forbidden." By the middle of the twentieth century, the British anthropologist Geoffrey Gorer was writing about "the pornography of death," observing that "natural processes of corruption and decay have become disgusting"—just as sex had been rendered obscene by the Victorians. The dead had become an affront to the living.[11]

Neither Gorer nor Ariès knew quite what to make of the United States, which in many ways followed the general Western trend, banishing decay from polite conversation. At the same

10. Almost everyone else in the death industry says it's children's bodies that they have a hard time with. Dead children present challenges that are not only existential. It's very hard to make kids look "natural" says Isis Huckins, who supervises hair, cosmetics, and "casketing" at Rose Hills, "because they don't wear makeup."

11. The Gorer and Ariès books are shelved in an obscure corner of the Central Library, wedged between the books on sex and drinking.

time, Americans ritualize death in a manner extraordinary to Europeans. Until a few years ago, even a basic working-class American funeral—from the open-casket display of the chemically preserved and cosmetically improved decedent to the long, slow procession of cars to the graveside—matched a level of pomp reserved across the Atlantic only for the most celebrated dead.

Southern California, home to the theme-park necropolis Forest Lawn, came to represent the apotheosis of America's disturbingly "euphoric" approach to mortality, to borrow Ariès's term. Angelenos not only failed to tastefully ignore death, they did everything they could to render it sunny, cheerful, lifelike. To Evelyn Waugh, who parodied Forest Lawn in his 1948 novel *The Loved One*, such vulgarity was symptomatic of the "endless infancy" of West Coast culture. To the journalist Jessica Mitford, the "American way of death" was a crude product of capitalist manipulation. We had elaborate funerals because the funeral industry was able to charge us more for them; Forest Lawn's kitsch was just a sophisticated strategy for lubricating the checkbooks of the grieved.

No aspect of American funereal ritual has been more consistently alarming to foreign observers than embalming, which is practiced nowhere else in the world with the near universality that it achieved in North America. Mitford characterized embalming as expensive quackery, a recently revived pagan practice without roots in the Judeo-Christian tradition. The funeral industry's insistence on its hygienic necessity, she argued, lacked any scientific or medical foundation. Waugh was better humored about the practice, if no less horrified at the notion of being, as he put it, "pickled in formaldehyde and painted like a whore, / Shrimp-pink incorruptible, not lost or gone before."

To Kenneth Schenk, however, embalming is an art, perhaps soon to be lost. Schenk could not be more different from Mr. Joyboy, Waugh's priggish, pink-eyed chief embalmer. "Through the whole sex-drugs-and-rock-and-roll era I was known as the rebel embalmer," he says with more than a hint of pride. Schenk is a trade embalmer, which means he freelances for the few remaining independent mortuaries. He is seventy, and his hair stops well short of his collar, but back before it turned its current lustrous white, he wore it to the middle of his back. He came to L.A. from Florida in 1960 and did his apprenticeship with the legendary Jack Lowry, who famously embalmed Jean Harlow and who, Schenk says, "mixed his own fluids at Pierce Bros. down in the basement."

In those days L.A. still had a "Mortuary Row"—a string of grand funeral homes with high-ceilinged lobbies and marble staircases stretching along Washington Boulevard. Sitting in a booth at the Pantry downtown, Schenk waxes nostalgic about that now invisible geography, long since sliced in half by the Harbor Freeway and transformed into a jumble of repair shops and warehouses. Spearing a bite of coleslaw with Russian dressing, he tells me exactly what he will do to you if you fall into his able, practiced hands.

You will be there waiting for him when he arrives in the mortuary's prep room.[12] He will put on a paper gown and latex gloves. He will wash you and position your limbs. He'll insert small, nubbed plastic disks beneath your eyelids to make sure that they stay shut. He will suture your lips closed, and if they don't stay shut, he will Superglue them.

When he's ready, Schenk will select his fluids, taking into account the time that has passed since your death (the longer it has been, the stronger the chemicals), the cause of your death (some medications interact poorly with embalming fluid), and the color

---

12. State law limits access to prep rooms. One funeral director lets me peek into a small white-tiled room, in the middle of which stand two porcelain tables. Canvas straps hang from the ceiling. Beside the door is a gurney bearing a tiny old woman in a flower-print blouse. Her face is covered with a towel.

of your skin ("Formaldehyde," he says, "will turn a white person a nice shade of green"). He will choose a spot for his incision, usually the carotid or femoral artery. He will lift the artery with a steel hook and insert a plastic injection tube attached to an embalming machine. Another tube will go into the corresponding vein. Schenk will turn on the machine, adjusting for pressure and flow, and it will pump preservative fluid in through your arteries, pushing your blood out through your veins, into the sink, and down the drain.

The process lasts about an hour, depending on your size and the condition of your circulatory system.[13] Then Schenk will poke a pointed, hollow instrument called a trocar through your abdominal wall. It will act as a sort of siphon, sucking gases and liquids from your intestines, stomach, bladder, heart, and lungs. "It's not for the weak of heart," Schenk says. Once you've been sufficiently cleaned out, he will inject more embalming fluid directly into your organs.

If you've been autopsied, all this will take a little longer and cost a little more. "Basically the arterial system is gone," Schenk says, so he will have to inject fluid directly into each of your limbs and both sides of your brain. Then he will sew you up "nice and tight." All that's left is makeup, hairstyling, perhaps a touch of the "restorative arts" if disease or injuries have damaged your features. An eyelid, a nose, even an ear can be sculpted out of beeswax.

Not long ago Schenk got a call from a mortuary offering him a job everyone else had refused. "It was a gal that had been murdered and put in the trunk of a car and not found for 12 days, and it was the heat of the summer." Schenk demurred, but the funeral director persisted. "Miracles can be done," Schenk says. "We preserved this gal and made her viewable. The family was almost ecstatic."

13. Schenk prefers Japanese clients: "Something about eating all that rice and raw fish keeps their arterial systems in good shape."

Once, he says, "during the hippie era," he embalmed a fallen rock climber whose long hair, matted with blood, had been shaved and stuffed into a bag. Schenk washed out the blood and painstakingly laid the hair out to dry. One at a time, he matched the strands by length, texture, and curl and, as patient as his silent client, reconstructed the climber's coiffure. "It takes a guy that has an artist's eye," says Schenk, beaming. "Not everyone can do it."

## 1,550 Degrees

Maybe you're not fond of worms or maybe you're claustrophobic. Perhaps you've read Jim Crace's novel *Being Dead*, which lovingly chronicles the decomposition of a murdered couple, or the chapter in Mary Roach's *Stiff* about the stages of decay, from elementary autolysis to full-blown putrefaction (when you become "soup"). Maybe your imagination suffices to make you prefer quick, purifying flame. Or perhaps you'd just rather be portable: No one stays put for long these days, and urns pack more easily than caskets. Maybe you're Buddhist and believe the flames will help you cast aside the now useless shell of this life so that you can move unencumbered to the next. Or perhaps the thought of being scattered to the breeze feels more like freedom than any other image of eternal rest you can conjure.

Whatever your reasons, you wouldn't be alone. According to a funeral industry data tracker, inaptly named Vital Statistic Analyses, more than half of Californians were cremated in 2009. In Greater Los Angeles cremations have gone up 40 percent over the past five years. The trend is recent: In 1970, fewer than 5 percent of Americans met that final flame.[14] Philippe Ariès calls incineration "a manifestation of enlightenment, of modernity" and sug-

---

14. Cremation was not permitted for Catholics until 1963. Leonard and Lawrence, who manages Mount Sinai Memorial, says even "Jews have discovered cremation," although it is anathema under Jewish law.

gests that, as "the most radical means of getting rid of the body and of forgetting it, of nullifying it," cremation is the method best suited to the abstraction and uprootedness of modern life.

It is also a lot cheaper. A bare-bones cremation at downtown's Armstrong Family Malloy-Mitten mortuary will set your survivors back $665, less than a third of the cost of the lowest-end burial plot at Forest Lawn (not counting casket, vault, memorial plaque, embalming fees, burial charges, and carnation boutonnieres). If you're not afraid of fire and you choose to go that way—or someone chooses for you—your mortuary will likely dispatch you to a crematorium. Few mortuaries cremate their own, and few crematoriums deal directly with consumers. An employee of a transport service like Angelo Patrick's will drop you off at the crematory door, fill out the requisite paperwork, and depart confident that you will be much easier to carry when he returns to pick you up. Specifically, you will fit in a five by seven by ten-inch box, and you will weigh between three and ten pounds. "I call that radical weight reduction," says Aida Bobadilla, who manages Odd Fellows Cemetery in Boyle Heights, the same Odd Fellows that David Smith at the coroner's office contracts with for the fiery disposal of the morbidly obese.

The process is simple. "It's very much like you're cooking," Bobadilla says. A pale, slender woman with dark eyes and a sudden, flashing laugh, she is sixty-three but easily could pass for fifty. Sitting on the couch in the lobby, she looks me up and down. "You, three hours," she says. "Me, three hours." Heavier folks take longer. Lieutenant Smith's 710-pounder took six hours. They are also more complicated to burn. Fat produces a great deal of heat,[15] which means that someone has to be there standing by to regulate the chamber's temperature.

---

15. Think of grilling: The coals flare up more beneath sausages than fish. Fatty tissue produces twenty times as much heat as lean muscle.

State law requires that you be combusted in a container, which might be a cardboard box or a hand-buffed walnut casket with mattress springs and quilted velvet lining. Once it has burned away, you will, too. "We direct the flame toward the torso," Bobadilla says, "and the flames feather out to the extremities." If for any reason you roll to one side or otherwise attempt to flee the flames, a technician may open the door to the retort, as the cremation chamber is called, and nudge you into place with a pole. The retort will rise to 1,550 degrees Fahrenheit, hot enough to turn most of you to vapor. "The skin melts, the skin bubbles, and then it's gone."

And the smell? I ask Bobadilla if her neighbors complain about the scent of singed hair and roasting meat. She assures me that the temperature is too high for anyone to notice anything. At most, "you may smell like paper burning," she says, and that's probably just the casket going up. Cremation chambers are designed to capture any unseemly emissions. The only way to tell that someone's cooking, she says, is to search the sky above the smokestacks for wavy lines of heat.

When all of you has burned that can be burned, the technician will turn off the gas and rake out what little is left: charred and brittle fragments of bone—sometimes a femur or a piece of skull will be recognizable. He or she will collect these shards of you in a metal pan, allow them to cool, then pass a magnet over them to catch any metal intermingled with you: eyeglass frames, fillings, buttons, zippers, the cotter pins, springs, and hinges from your casket.[16] Bobadilla once found a gold fingernail.

You are at this point officially cremains. In a large industrial blender you will be processed into powder. Your relatives will not want to find chunks. You will then be poured into a gusseted plastic pouch, which will be sealed and placed inside a "tempo-

---

16. Pacemakers must be removed; they tend to explode.

rary plastic urn"—i.e., a box—wrapped in brown paper, and meticulously labeled inside and out. The mortuary will send someone to get you, and you, more portable than ever, will have a lot of options.

You can stay in your plastic urn and go straight to the back of the closet. You can express your personality until the end of time in an urn shaped like a golf bag, or an angel, or a duck. You can doze in a locket on a loved one's neck. You can rest eternally in the Buddhist Columbarium atop the highest peak in Rose Hills Cemetery, commanding a view (if only you still had eyes!) of the entire L.A. basin, from Catalina to Mount Baldy and beyond. You can be scattered at sea to commune with the fish. You can be packed in fireworks and rocketed into the heavens. But you cannot be scattered on the infield at Dodger Stadium, or the outfield, or anywhere in Disneyland at all—do not even ask.

Odd Fellows is also a cemetery, so Bobadilla walks me outside to show me the Civil War graves and tell me about the ghosts—not just the ones that she sometimes spots flitting around the office but the one she's only heard about: the Phantom Lowrider. People arriving for funerals have told her they've seen it in their rearview mirrors. Some say it's white, others black. No one can describe the driver's face. When they turn to look, Bobadilla says, "there's nothing there."

I walk around and don't see any ghosts. There's a funeral going on to my right, a family gathered around a grave. They've hired mariachis. Right now they're singing "Amor Eterno," and the tune is so perfectly sad that the air above the graveyard seems to expand a little. I circle past the mourners and back to the gates until I see it—a low chimney of beige brick just behind the lobby where Bobadilla and I had been sitting. She was right. There is no smoke, but the palm trees and the eucalyptus on the far side of the smokestack are shivering and slipping, as if the sky itself has lost all confidence and allowed the atmosphere to sag.

## The Moment You've Been Waiting For

Then there are the holes. If you feel sometimes that the surface streets are just that, *surface*, that the concrete and asphalt crust of the city is hiding something big beneath our feet, you are right. In 2003, construction workers digging a drainage canal for the Playa Vista condo complex unearthed the bones of 396 Gabrieliño-Tongva Indians at the edge of the Ballona wetlands. The site is now a soccer field. Two years later on the other side of town, crews working on the Eastside extension of the Metro Gold Line found the remains of 174 people, most of them Chinese laborers, just south of Evergreen Cemetery. Some of the graves dated to the 1880s. At that time, and for decades to come, Chinese could not be buried alongside white Angelenos and were consigned to a potter's field outside the cemetery grounds. They have since been moved into the cemetery proper and rest on the other side of a low chain-link fence from the current potter's field.

If no one else will, you can count on the county to put you in a hole. Once officials have given up finding someone to take you off their hands, you will be cremated, says Estella Inouye of the county's Decedent Affairs Division. You will be stored for three years and then buried, along with everyone else who died that year, in a mass grave behind the county crematorium. This December, Inouye expects to inter the unclaimed remnants of at least 1,700 people who died in 2007. It will be crowded down there, but everyone will have at least a little privacy: The ashes stay in their urns. "I don't have the staff to be scattering," Inouye says.

If you are lucky, you will be neither so poor nor so alone in death that you will end up in the county's care, which means that you might find a plot on the other side of the fence at Evergreen, beneath the brown grass with the dead elite of yesteryear: the Lankershims and the Van Nuyses, the Rimpaus, Hollenbecks, and Breeds. It is peaceful there. Birds glide from tree to tree. Families sit in the shade on folding chairs, sharing a meal six feet above someone dear. Traffic is a distant oceanic hum.

Cemeteries are quieter and most of them are greener than the cities of the living that surround them, but these cities of the dead are not so different otherwise. They are, for instance, just as segregated. At Evergreen you'll find an outlying Armenian neighborhood, sprawling Mexican sections (someone has spelled out the words "*te amo*" in small stones at the foot of a new grave), an inner circle of shiny headstones engraved in Japanese, and an early stratum of dead whites with streets named after them.

Evergreen is unusual in that it never banned the burial of African Americans. The same cannot be said of the original Forest Lawn in Glendale, where the giant wrought-iron gates for decades refused entrance to blacks, Jews, and Chinese—even after they had been reduced to permanent passivity. Today all paying guests are welcome. At Forest Lawn, though, the apparent democracy imposed by the lack of headstones—everyone gets the same bronze marker flush with the grass, which makes mowing that much easier—hides a rigid real estate hierarchy that reflects L.A.'s own, from lumpen, lowland subdivisions to gated hilltop mansions. Anyone can stroll through the Courts of Remembrance or the Wee Kirk o' the Heather (satirized by Waugh as the "Wee Kirk o'Auld Lang Syne") or meditate beneath the stained-glass replica of Da Vinci's *The Last Supper*, but if you want to visit the elect who rest in the Garden of Honor,[17] a sign on the locked gate says you will need a "golden key of memory, given to each [plot] owner at time of purchase." Jim Wilke, park vice president of Glendale Forest Lawn, will not tell me how much such a plot might cost, except that it reaches "into the six figures."

17. It's down the ridge from the Court of Freedom, with its bronze George Washington, engraved Casey Stengel quote, and giant mosaic of John Trumbull's *The Declaration of Independence*.

It was not Forest Lawn's ill-concealed class structure that Waugh and Mitford found so distasteful but the cemetery's brash modernity and autocratic cheer.[18] Forest Lawn was designed to be "as unlike other cemeteries as sunshine is unlike darkness," declared founder Hubert Eaton ("The Builder") in his "Builder's Creed," which begins with his assertion that "I believe in a happy eternal life" and goes on to banish every symbol of judgment or even grief from its architecture.

The mantle of necrological innovation, however, has been passed. When Tyler Cassity bought Hollywood Forever cemetery in 1998, one of the goals, says longtime friend and executive vice president Jay Boileau, "was to revolutionize memorialization." Technology, Boileau and Cassity believed, could transform funeral practices that hadn't changed significantly in millennia. Ultimately they hoped to do away with the material side of death, preserving just a shred of DNA and a digitally archived memorial to the departed: uploaded interviews, documents, photos, music. "We pretty quickly realized that rituals have meaning to people," says the forty-year-old Boileau, who with his shaggy hair, jeans, and untucked shirt looks more like a graphic designer than a cemetery executive. "People want to come to the cemetery, they want a headstone, they want to have a funeral."

Boileau now keeps busy curating Hollywood Forever's cultural programs, bringing concerts and screenings to the mausoleum lawns, letting the living party where the esteemed dead—Cecil B. De Mille, Rudolph Valentino, Douglas Fairbanks, Dee Dee Ramone—sleep. His ambitions, though, have not shrunk. When I ask what he wants done with his own remains, Boileau hesitates, then answers that he has hoped for a while to establish an ossuary at Hollywood Forever. "I've offered my skull to adorn the door," he says. "Why not, right?"

18. In other words, it was its Americanness that they disliked.

Cassity, in the meantime, has been pushing innovation in a different direction, toward "green burial"—no embalming, no casket, no headstone, native grasses instead of fertilized fields of sod. In 2004, he bought Fernwood Cemetery in Marin County as a pastoral, live-oak-and-eucalyptus yin to Hollywood Forever's glamorous urban yang. The trend is spreading. Joshua Tree Memorial Park, the only cemetery offering green burial in Southern California, boasts hand-dug graves. So far it has only done two green burials—one in a wicker coffin, the other in a shroud.

Chances are that you will spend eternity in something more substantial, a repository somewhere between a $195 fiberboard #1650 Alternative Container and the $25,000 polished bronze Promethean.[19] Chances are also good that your burial will be more corporate and industrial than breezily bucolic. Dave Worker takes me through the routine at Whittier's Rose Hills Memorial Park and Mortuary, the largest cemetery in North America and possibly the world, where he is the park superintendent. "We average thirty a day, six days a week," Worker says. Much of his job is logistical: dispatching crews and plotting traffic, making sure that processions do not collide, that tractors don't block the lanes for hearses. Wearing black jeans and a striped shirt, his gray hair slicked neatly back, Worker, who is 46, looks more casual-Friday than Quasimodo-Gothic. He sends his grave diggers to Dale Carnegie seminars to sharpen their communication skills.

Two days before your funeral one of Worker's workers will locate your plot and paint a perfect forty-by-ninety-six-inch rectangle around your hole-to-be. Another will come by later with a sod-peeling machine and roll the rectangle of grass into three tidy cylinders. Next comes the dig team. No unnecessary

19. "They have two shifts, eight-hour shifts, and they polish it continually for two weeks," a funeral director says. "It's like looking at a mirror."

back pain here: Worker's crew will use a backhoe to scoop out six and a half feet of earth. It won't take more than twenty minutes. On the day of the event a setup crew will install a "vault-lowering device," into which they will place the bottom half of your vault.[20] They will then cloak the border of the hole with artificial turf, unfold a few chairs, and erect a canopy to shelter your guests from sun or rain.

Now it's your cue, the moment you've been waiting for. You make your entrance. Your pallbearers roll your casket from the hearse and shoulder you up and over to the grave. They set you down in the vault so that your casket creates "a sort of visual focal piece" for the ceremony, as Worker puts it. Somebody says something. Somebody cries. Probably they pray. You can't hear anything. Your lid is closed, and you're dead. Somebody turns a crank and lowers you slowly into the ground. Somebody removes the straps and the lowering device. The show is over. Your mourners embrace. They exchange tissues and comforting words. They leave you there in your box at the bottom of your hole.

Don't despair. Worker's crew has not forgotten you. With a special dolly they lower the lid of the vault over your casket. They seal you in with tape. The backhoe returns. Somebody shovels the dirt on top of you while someone else tamps it down around the edges of the vault. They roll out the sod. They water it. They collect the flowers, the canopy, the chairs. They work steadily. They have other graves to dig and other graves to fill. They leave you there. You're done.

---

20. The vault is the concrete box in which your box, like a Russian doll, will lie. Most cemeteries require you to buy one on the pretext that it keeps the ground from settling.

## *Mother Jones*

FINALIST—FEATURE
WRITING

*In 2006, the young journalist Mac McClelland traveled to Southeast Asia, where she befriended a group of Karen activists who were working, often at great risk, to document the genocidal campaign being waged against their people by the military government in Burma. Four years later, McClelland returned to complete the reporting for this story, which blends memories of murder and oppression with moments of near-comedy, as the Karen for the first time encounter MySpace and modern American sexual politics. "A coming-of-age story blooms within Mac McClelland's harrowing account," said the National Magazine Award judges. "Casual exchanges make the characters real; brutal details make their agony palpable." McClelland was working as a copy editor at* Mother Jones *when she began writing this story; she now covers human-rights issues for the magazine and writes a blog,* The Rights Stuff, *for the MoJo website. The story formed the basis for McClelland's book* For Us Surrender Is Out of the Question: A Story From Burma's Never-Ending War.

Mac McClelland

# For Us Surrender Is Out of the Question

"**D**o you want a cigarette?" I ask Htan Dah, holding up a pack of Thai-issue Marlboros. We are sitting on opposite sides of a rectangular table, talking over the spread: three bottles of vodka, two cartons of orange juice, plates of sugared citrus slices, nearly empty bottles of beer and bowls of fried pork, sweet corn waffles, pad thai, a chocolate cake. We share the benches with two guys each, and half a dozen others hover.

The men are all in their twenties. Most of them are solid and strong and hunky; their faces shine because they're drunk, and it's July. They could be mistaken for former frat boys unwinding after another tedious workday.

Except that they're stateless. They are penniless. They speak three or four languages apiece. Two of them had to bribe their way out of Thai police custody yesterday, again, because they're on the wrong side of the border between this country and the landmine-studded mountains of their own. Htan Dah's silky chin-length hair slips toward his eyes as he leans forward. My Marlboros are adorned with a legally mandated photographic deterrent, a guy blowing smoke in a baby's face, but it doesn't deter Htan Dah. Nor is he deterred by the fact that he doesn't smoke. Tonight, he is flushed with heat and booze and the virility and extreme hilarity of his comrades. Tonight, as always, he is celebrating the fact that he's still alive. He takes a cigarette. "Never say no," he says, and winks at me.

. . .

I'd arrived at Mae Sot a few weeks before. This city in western central Thailand is a major hub for people, teak, gems, and other goods that enter the country illegally from Burma. The place is rife with smugglers, dealers, undocumented immigrants, and slaves. My bus arrived in the late afternoon. I wasn't connected to any aid or charity organization—I'd just happened on a website of a group that said it was promoting democracy in the Texas-size military dictatorship of Burma, and eventually volunteered, via e-mail, to help its activists living in Thailand learn English. (As I was to discover, the particulars of their mission were far more dangerous, and illegal, so I'll refer to them as Burma Action.)

At the station, I was met by The Guy, whose name wasn't The Guy, but whose actual name I didn't catch when he mumbled it twice and then just shook his head and laughed when I asked him to repeat it one more time. After a brief ride in a three-wheeled tuk-tuk, we arrived at a gold-detailed black gate that stood heavy sentry at the road. Behind it stood Burma Action's local HQ, a big but run-down house, two stories of worn wood and dirty concrete with a balcony on the left, cement garage on the right. The Guy gave me a quick tour. The "kitchen" had a sink and some dishes; cooking took place out in the dining room/garage. He took a few steps farther. "Bathroom." He gestured into a cement-walled room through an oversize wooden door. There was a squat toilet set into the floor, and in lieu of toilet paper a shallow well with a little plastic bowl floating on top. There was also, running the length of the left wall, a giant waist-high cement trough filled with water and dead mosquitoes.

"What's that?" I asked.

"A bath."

I looked at it, jet-lagged. "How does it work?" I asked.

He exhaled hard through his nose, a whispery snort. "Like this," he said, pantomiming filling a bowl with water and dumping it over his head. "Are you hungry?"

I asked The Guy what was in the soup he offered me.

"I don't know the word in English," he said. "Leaves?"

Close. Twigs, actually. The Guy pulled a stump of wood up next to me at the table, and watched me chew through the sautéed woody stems.

"So, where are you from?" I asked.

"Me?"

I nodded.

"I am kuh-REN. Everybody here, we are all kuh-REN."

Oh, man. It was starting to come together now.

When I'd landed in Bangkok, a Burma Action employee had picked me up at the airport to make sure I found the bus station and the right eight-hour bus north. She was tiny and Thai and heavily accented, and repeatedly told me during our cab ride that everyone I was about to be working with was Korean. It seemed sort of weird that a bunch of Koreans would move to Thailand together to work for peace in Burma, but I thought that was nice, I guessed, and even wrote in my journal, relievedly, "Koreans tend to have excellent English skills."

When I'd arrived at the Mae Sot bus station, The Guy had asked if I was his new volunteer.

"Yes," I'd said. "You're not Korean."

I'd done my homework before leaving the States. I had read about the Karen. But I'd only seen the word written down, and had assumed that it sounded like the name of my parents' blond divorced friend. I didn't know how it was pronounced any more than most Westerners would've been certain how to say "Darfur" ten years ago.

•       •       •

When I turned the corner from the kitchen into the large living room, four pairs of dark eyes looked up from a small TV screen. I smiled, but The Guy, leaning against the wall with his arms folded, didn't make any introductions, so I sat on the marble floor among the legs of the white plastic chairs the guys were sitting in, quiet amid the rise and fall of their soft tonal syllables, deep, bubbling, like slow oil over stones. The TV blared Thai. Mosquitoes sauntered in through the screenless windows, possible hosts to malaria, dengue fever, Japanese encephalitis. I'd no natural resistance to the latter two, and I'd opted against taking the sickening drugs for the former. Not wanting to be the white girl who ran upstairs to hide under a mosquito net at dusk, I watched the guys laughing and talking, like a partygoer who didn't know anyone. I pulled my air mattress out of my bag and started blowing it up. I got bit. I scratched. I shifted my sit bones on the shiny tile. Finally, I stood up.

"I'm going to bed," I told The Guy.

He nodded, and looked at me for a second. It was 7:30. "Are you okay?" he asked. I'd just taken twenty-seven hours of planes and automobiles. I'd glanced at the phrases "Forced marriage" and "Human trafficking" on a piece of paper taped to the wall behind the computers in the adjacent room. I said that I was fine and headed upstairs. I dropped my air mattress under the big blue mosquito net and lay down. I had no real idea who these people were, or what they did here, or even what I was supposed to do here. I appeared to have my work, whatever it was, cut out for me, since The Guy (real name: The Blay) seemed to be among the few who spoke English. My digestive system had its work cut out for it, too, since these guys apparently ate sticks. Lying there, listening to my housemates laugh and holler downstairs, I comforted myself with the thought that these Karen seemed nice. I couldn't have guessed then, drifting to sleep to the sound of their amiable chatter, that every last one of them was a terrorist.

•  •  •

Imagine, for a moment, that Texas had managed to secede from the union and that you live there, in the sovereign Republic of Texas. Imagine that shortly after independence, a cadre of old, paranoid, greedy men who believed in a superior military caste took over your newly autonomous nation in a coup. Your beloved president, who had big dreams of prosperity and Texan unity, whom you believed in, was shot, and now the army runs your country. It has direct or indirect control over all the businesses. It spends 0.3 percent of GDP on health care and uses your oil and natural gas money to buy weapons that Russia, Pakistan, and North Korea have been happy to provide. It sends your rice and beans to India and China while your countrymen starve. There is no free press, and gatherings of more than five people are illegal. If you are arrested, a trial, much less legal representation, is not guaranteed. In the event of interrogation, be prepared to crouch like you're riding a motorbike for hours or be hung from the ceiling and spun around and around and around, or burned with cigarettes, or beaten with a rubber rod. They might put you in a ditch with a dead body for six days, lock you in a room with wild, sharp-beaked birds, or make you stand to your neck in a cesspool full of maggots that climb into your nose and ears and mouth. If you do manage to stay out of the prisons, where activists and dissidents have been rotting for decades, you will be broke and starving. Your children have a 10 percent chance of dying before they reach their fifth birthday, and a 32 percent chance they'll be devastatingly malnourished if they're still alive. What's more, you and 50 million countrymen are trapped inside your 268,000-square-mile Orwellian nightmare with some 350,000 soldiers. They can snatch people—maybe your kid—off the street and make them join the army. They can grab you as you're going out to buy eggs and make you work construction on a new government building or road—long, hard hours under the grueling sun for days or weeks without pay—during which you'll have to scavenge for food. You'll do all this at gunpoint, and any break will be rewarded with a pistol-whipping. Your life is roughly equivalent to a modern-day Burmese person's.

Now imagine that you belong to a distinct group, Dallasites or something, that never wanted to be part of the Republic in the first place, that wanted to either remain part of the United States, which had treated you just fine, or, failing that, become your own free state within the Republic of Texas, since you already had your own infrastructure and culture. Some Dallasites have, wisely or unwisely, taken up arms to battle the Texas military government, and in retaliation whole squads of that huge army have, for decades, been dedicated to terrorizing your city. You and your fellow Dallasites are regularly conscripted into slavery, made to walk in front of the army to set off land mines that they— and your own insurgents—have planted, or carry hundred-pound loads of weaponry while being severely beaten until you're crippled or die. If you're so enslaved, you might accompany the soldiers as they march into your friends' neighborhoods and set them on fire, watch them shoot at fleeing inhabitants as they run, capturing any stragglers. If you're one of those stragglers and you're a woman, or a girl five or older, prepare to be raped, most likely gang-raped, and there's easily a one-in-four chance you'll then be killed, possibly by being shot, possibly through your vagina, possibly after having your breasts hacked off. If you're a man, maybe you'll be hung by your wrists and burned alive. Maybe a soldier will drown you by filling a plastic bag with water and tying it over your head, or stretch you between two trees and use you as a hammock, or cut off your nose, pull out your eyes, and then stab you in both ears before killing you, or string you up by your shoulders and club you now and again for two weeks, or heat up slivers of bamboo and push them into your urethra, or tie a tight rope between your dick and your neck for a while before setting your genitals on fire, or whatever else hateful, armed men and underage boys might dream up when they have orders to torment and nothing else to do. And though you've been sure for decades that the United States can't possibly let this continue, it has invested in your country's oil and will not under any circumstances cross China, which is your country's staunch UN defender and economic ally, so you really need to accept that America is decidedly not coming to save you. Nobody is.

Now your life is pretty much equivalent to a modern-day Burmese Karen's.

.    .    .

Shortly after dawn, someone dropped a pile of thinly sliced onions and whole garlic cloves with the skins still on into a wok of hot soybean oil. As the smell wafted up, I climbed out from under my mosquito net and walked softly out of my room.

Htan Dah—whose name was pronounced, to my unceasing delight, the same as the self-satisfied English interjection "ta-da!"—stood at the gas range, which spat oil at his baggy long-sleeved shirt. He tilted the wok, concentrating harder than he needed to on the swirling oil. Htan Dah was worried about me. As the office manager of Burma Action for the past two years, he'd heard the nighttime weeping of plenty of self-pitying philanthropists, who tended to arrive tired and instantly homesick. The last girl, a Canadian with a lot of luggage, had started sobbing almost as soon as he'd picked her up and couldn't be calmed even by the hours she spent taking calls from her boyfriend back home. She'd cried for days.

Indeed, I'd had a very sad moment the night before when, after my air mattress deflated and my angles pressed into hard floor, and I realized that the ants patrolling the grounds were trekking right through my hair, I actually hoped that I had contracted malaria or Japanese encephalitis from the mosquito bites raging hot and itchy so I would have a legitimate excuse to bail back to the States. That way I wouldn't have to be mad at myself for being too chickenshit to hack it through loneliness and less-than-ideal bathing arrangements. I'd even considered taking the bus back to Bangkok. If there wasn't an immediate flight out, I could just hang out on Khao San Road and read books. I hated Khao San Road, with its hennaed European backpackers and incessant techno and beer specials, but at least it was familiar. I'd realized then that I might start crying, but I was determined not to. Instead, I saved the tearing up for when Htan Dah put another bowl of stick soup in front of me now and asked, "How long are you staying?"

"Six weeks," I said.

"Six weeks!" he hollered. "Why not four months? Or six months?"

"Six weeks is a long time to go out of the country in America," I said. "Besides, I was in Thailand for a month two years ago."

"How many times have you been here?"

"Twice."

"Wow," he said. Then, more softly, "You have traveled a lot. That's nice."

He had no idea, even. "Have you traveled?"

"No, I cannot."

"Why not?"

"Because! I am Karen!"

"So what?"

"So, I cannot go anywhere." He dumped chunks of raw, pink meat into the oil, which sputtered furiously. "If I go outside, I can be arrested."

"Really?"

"Yes! I am refugee!"

Htan Dah's exclamations suggested that none of this should have been news to me—though I soon realized that this was also just how he talked. But my books hadn't said much about refugees or mentioned that most of the Burmese refugees in Thailand were Karen, and Burma Action hadn't told me that my housemates were refugees, and certainly not refugees who'd run away from camp to live and work illegally in that house. I, after all, was the one who'd just figured out that no one here was Korean.

"I'm sorry," I said. "Why would you be arrested because you're a refugee?"

"Because! I don't have Thai ID. I am not Thai citizen, so, I cannot go outside refugee camp."

"Really?"

"Yes! I can be fined, maybe 3,000 baht"—nearly $100 in a country where the average annual income was about $3,000—"I can go to jail, or maybe, be deported . . ." We looked at each other, and he nodded in my silence, emphasizing his point with a sharp dip of his chin. "You have a lot of experience. You have been to a lot of places."

"Did you live in a refugee camp before?"

"Yes. Before I came to BA."

"How long have you lived here?"

"In Thailand?" Htan Dah asked. "I was born in Thailand."

.    .    .

To be a Karen refugee in Thailand is to be unwelcome. The royal Thai government, already sanctuary to evacuees from other Southeast Asian wars by the time the Karen showed up in the eighties, was hardly in a hurry to recognize and protect them as refugees—and, not having signed the 1951 UN Convention Relating to the Status of Refugees, it didn't have to. This is only the latest misfortune in the Karen's long history of troubles. They were massively oppressed and enslaved before Burma became a British colony in 1886, but their relations with the Burmese were nothing so nasty as after they played colonialists' pet and then joined the Allies in World War II. British officers promised the

Karen independence for helping us fight the Burmese and Japan. They lied. The Karen resistance started, and the Karen National Union formed, about as soon as the ink was dry on Burma's postwar independence agreement. Their oath had four parts: *(1) For us surrender is out of the question. (2) Recognition of Karen State must be completed. (3) We shall retain our arms. (4) We shall decide our own political destiny.* The Karen had been well trained and well armed by Westerners. They nearly took the capital in 1949, and when they were pushed back to the eastern hills, they built the largest insurrection (among many) against the Burmese junta. By the eighties, the KNU claimed that its annual income, from taxing smuggled products flowing through the porous Thai border, was in the tens of millions of dollars a year.

The junta responded with Four Cuts. You've never heard of Four Cuts, but it's a Burmese army strategy that every Karen child knows very well: cutting off the enemy's sources of food, finance, intelligence, and recruits (and, some say, their heads). Unfortunately for villagers, these sources of support include the villagers themselves, in addition to their rice and livestock. It's the same strategy the British used to extinguish uprisings back in their day: "We simply wiped out the village and shot everyone we saw," wrote Sir James George Scott, an intrepid administrator who, in addition to killing Burmese, introduced soccer to them. "Burned all their crops and houses." Htan Dah's parents were among the first wave of Karen to flee the wrath of the Burmese army. Today the Burmese camp population in Thailand is 150,000, and the No. 1 answer people give when asked why they left Burma is "running away from soldiers."

·       ·       ·

I asked Htan Dah, on my third day, how many people lived in our office/house. I'd been working on lesson plans all day for the soon-to-start English classes. Men had been working alongside me at the other computers, keeping to themselves.

"Maybe ten," he said.

A lot more dudes than that had been milling around. Many of them were dudes in Che Guevara T-shirts. Htan Dah said that in addition to present staff, there were visitors from other offices and NGOs, plus staff currently "inside"—in Burma.

"Doing what?" I asked.

"Doing interviewww, taking videooo, taking picturrre . . ." he said, drawing out the final syllables. "They go to the village, and they tell about what is going on in Burma, and about how to unite for democracy. Also, they ask, 'Have you seen Burma army? Have they raped you, or shot you, or burned your village?'" This explained the "Human Rights Vocabulary" translation cheat sheet I'd noticed on my first night. I'd since gotten a better look at it, studying the fifteen most-used phrases. One side listed words in Karen script, a train of round characters, with loops that extended lines or swirls above and below the baseline. The other side was in English: (1) Killings (2) Disappearances (3) Torture/inhumane treatments (4) Forced labor (5) Use of child soldiers (6) Forced relocation (7) Confiscation/destruction of property (8) Rape (9) Other sexual violence (10) Forced prostitution (11) Forced marriage (12) Arbitrary/illegal arrest/detention (13) Human trafficking (14) Obstruction of freedom of movement (15) Obstruction of freedom/expression/assembly. These were going to be English classes like no other I'd taken or taught.

"Then what?"

"Then they enter information into Martus."

"Into . . . what?"

"Human rights violation database."

"Then what happens to the information?"

"We can share, with other HRD."

"With other . . ."

"IIuman rights documenter."
"So you guys collect it all . . ."
Htan Dah stared at me.
"And then what? Then it just sits there?"
Htan Dah shrugged.
"How do the guys get to the villages?"
"They walk."
This explained the physique of Htoo Moo, he of the silent *h* and the constant smiling and the never talking to me and the stupefyingly round and hard-looking ass. "How long are they gone?"
"Depends. Maybe three months."
"Do they just hide around the jungle that whole time?"
"Yes!" Htan Dah said. "If they are caught, they could die."

· · ·

Here's how it worked: Somebody had to document what was going on in Burma—and stealthily. One activist who gave an interview to a foreign reporter served seven years in prison. Another was sentenced to twenty-five years for giving an interview critical of the regime to the BBC in 1997. Of the 173 nations in the Reporters Without Borders Press Freedom Index 2008, Burma ranked 170th, behind every other country except the "unchanging hells" of Turkmenistan, North Korea, and Eritrea. Burma has the third most journalists in jail. As for coverage of *eastern* Burma, ground zero of the Karen war . . . forget about it.

So a couple of times a year, Htoo Moo, one of Burma Action's human rights documenters, shouldered a bag carrying what he wasn't wearing of nine shirts, three pairs of pants, two pairs of shorts, four pairs of underwear, and two pairs of socks—plus a tape recorder, six tapes, a notebook, three pens, a digital camera, a battery charger, a kilo of sugar, cold, sinus, and stomach medicines, a bottle of water, and 150 bucks' worth of Thai currency—and trekked clandestinely into his homeland.

His most recent trip had started with a six-hour drive, five hours in a long-tail boat watching the banks of the Salween River and a darkening sky, and two days of walking over mountains and jungle trade paths subsisting on just sugar and found water until he reached a village. Even by Karen standards, this settlement was pretty remote; a fish-paste purchase was a day's walk away. At night, he slept outside on the ground, and during the day he stood thigh-deep in a river, trying—though he couldn't get the hang of the procedure, however effortless the villagers made it look—to net fish while chatting up villagers about abuses by the State Peace and Development Council (SPDC), which is what the government of Burma calls itself.

After a month, Htoo Moo walked two days to interview escaped porters. He took pictures of lesions the straps left in their shoulders—raw, pink holes infested with flies and maggots. The porters told of being starved and dehydrated and repeatedly beaten with fists, kicks, and bamboo, of how prisoners who still fail to get up are shot or left to die, of doing double duty as minesweepers. SPDC offenses can be partially charted by the trail of porters' corpses.

Dodging land mines, Htoo Moo walked to the next small village. He entered it to find that some sort of plague had landed on all ten houses, and most of the people were dying. One house contained a dead boy whose father, the only family member left, was too sick to bury him. The villagers encouraged Htoo Moo to look, to bear witness, and he did, but left after a few days because there was nothing else to be done.

By the time he walked two days to another village, listened to and documented the story of a boy who was shot along with his father and brother by Burmese soldiers while cultivating rice, by the time he'd looked at the fresh bullet holes in the boy's shoulder and ass, and at the bloody track another round had grazed into the side of his head, by the time the boy had explained how he'd sent other villagers back to the field to get his brother and father as soon as he'd staggered home but it was too late, they were already dead, by the time he took pictures of the boy's wounds, which had been treated with only boiled water and cotton dressing, Htoo Moo was ready for a rest.

"The SPDC is coming," the chief told him.

So this is the drill: You flee, carrying everything you can—big heavy loads, as much rice as you can stand on your back in giant baskets, any clothes or anything else you want to own for maybe the rest of your life, your baby. Htoo Moo helped the villagers hide rice, salt, fish paste, and some extra sets of clothing among the surrounding trees before they all took off together in the early evening. He followed the eighty villagers along a path hidden beneath tall grass. Figuring a six-hour walk put them far enough out of harm's way, they stopped at midnight and Htoo Moo slept, finally, on the forest floor.

But the next morning, a scout told them the SPDC was coming; everyone needed to leave. Htoo Moo had slept through breakfast, and there wasn't time to make more. Neighboring villages had evidently joined the flight; there were 200 people in the makeshift camp now. They had with them one KNU soldier. Not wanting to further strain the villagers' rations, Htoo Moo stalked an enormous rat he'd spied lumbering around and killed it with one strike of a piece of bamboo. When he smiled, pleased with his efficiency, an old man next to him laughed. "Before you woke up," he said, "I tried to kill that. I think it was already tired."

The villagers fled until noon. Some of the children with no shoes lost flesh and bled as their feet pounded the ground, and some of them cried silently as they ran. Htoo Moo carried his bag on his back, the dead rat in one hand, his digital camera in the other, occasionally snapping pictures of the exodus. When they stopped, he dug his fingers into the rat's skin and ripped it off. He tore the meat into pieces and went in on lunch with another man, who provided a pot, chilies, and salt. Five minutes later, his belly was full of seared rat meat. He closed his eyes as sleep slowly started to overtake him, and then—gunshots.

*Gunshots.* He clutched his bag and jumped to his feet. Nobody screamed. The boy with the bullet holes started running, new blood rushing from the wound in his ass. Htoo Moo took off, ahead of even the village chief, reaching a flat-out run, crashing shoulder-first through tall croppings of bamboo in his path, before realizing he had no idea where he should be going. He stopped, turned around a couple of times, and considered ditching his camera. What if the SPDC caught him? What if they saw that he'd been taking pictures of gun-shot farmers, prisoner-porters with skin disease, cigarette burns, knife wounds, raw and infected shoulders that bore the permanent scars of carrying over mountains for days or weeks at a time? Though he felt like a coward, he fell back into the middle of the throng. By the time they stopped at nightfall, news had spread through the crowd that one man in the rear had been shot dead.

Htoo Moo listened to the men next to him talking. Of the 200 people, four had guns, four or five rounds apiece. One admitted that he had only three bullets left. "No problem," another told him. "You will just aim very well."

After three days of squatting and swatting bugs in the jungle, Htoo Moo told the chief that he wanted to leave. Sometimes, villagers hide out for weeks because they don't know if it's safe to go back yet. Sometimes, it never is. Htoo Moo needed to get back to work.

"I will take you myself," the chief said. "I am ready." He was in no hurry now. He'd heard over the radio that the soldiers had killed the pigs and the chickens, and then burned the village to the ground. There was nothing to go back to.

To slow down the SPDC advance, the KNU had set up scores of new land mines, and the way in was no longer a safe way out. Htoo Moo and the chief trudged through the jungle for three days to a KNU headquarters, where they shook hands and parted, and Htoo Moo asked a KNU insurgent to guide him the rest of the way. Shortly after they started off, the parasites that had been multiplying in his liver since entering his body via mosquito burst through the cells that hosted them and flooded Htoo Moo's bloodstream. He trekked slowly, through his fever, stopping when the retching brought him to his knees. "Don't rest there!" his guide screamed when he moved toward a smooth patch of soil just to the side of the path. He'd nearly knelt on a land mine. It took another two days to reach the riverbank, where he bought antimalarial tablets with his last few baht and boarded the boat toward Thailand—which had, by default, become home.

•    •    •

"Do you have picture?" Htan Dah asked one evening. "Of your friends?"

"Let's go to the computer room," I replied. Thus were several Karen refugee activists of Mae Sot, Thailand, bestowed with one of democracy's greatest gifts: that of wasting exorbitant amounts of time on social networking websites. I logged in to MySpace, and clicked through some of my pals' profiles, talking about who they were, or where they were, or what they were doing in the pictures. Htoo Moo, working diligently at the next computer, glanced over as nonchalantly as possible. Htan Dah said very little. Once, he asked me to clarify the gender of the girl I was pointing to on the screen. "Are you sure?" he asked. "She looks like a boy." I laughed and told him that she was a lesbian, my ex-girlfriend, actually, which seemed to clear it up for him. Other than that, he mostly just stared at the monitor in stunned silence, for so long that it started to weird me out.

"What do you think?" I asked him when I'd finished the tour.

"Wow," he said quietly.

"So, those are my friends," I said. He made no move to get up or take his eyes off the page.

I asked him if he wanted to see how the website worked. I showed him the browse feature, dropping down the long list of countries whose citizens we could gawk at. "How about Myanmar?" he asked, spying the junta's official name for Burma among the options.

I was surprised it was there, and even more surprised that our first search turned up 3,000 profiles. The junta has some awesome restrictions on owning electronics, especially computers. In 1996, Leo Nichols, former honorary consul for Scandinavian countries and friend of Burmese activists, was sentenced to three years for the illegal possession of fax machines and phones. (Taken into custody, he was tortured and died.) There are Internet cafés, but café workers are required to capture customers' screenshots every five minutes and submit their Web histories, along with home addresses and phone numbers, to the state. Humanitarian geeks in other countries, though, work full time to give Burma's citizens Internet access, with proxy servers that they update when the government figures out how to block them. From the look of it, they were doing their job.

On MySpace, ink-haired Burmese teens and twentysomethings stared at us: the chin-down-sexy-eyes-up shot, the haughty chin up/eyes half-closed look, the profile with eyes askance. Their faces were surrounded by HTML-coded sparkles, animated hearts and stars, slaughtered English colloquialisms. Htan Dah paused long and hard at each picture that came up.

"I don't know them," he said finally.

This conclusion struck me as pretty foregone, since he'd never lived in Burma. "Did you think you would?"

He looked at me, realizing his mistake. "I don't know," he said softly. We made Htan Dah his own profile, and he stayed logged in long after I'd gone to bed.

At dinner the next day, Htan Dah, Htoo Moo, and another refugee, Ta Mla, spent a fair amount of time watching me and muttering to each other in Karen.

"Something on your mind, tiger?" I asked Htan Dah.

"We are talking about your girlfriend," he said.

Yeah, I'd thought that conversation had ended a little too easily. "All right. You can talk about it with me."

"Do you ever have boyfriend?"

"Yes. I've had boyfriends and girlfriends."

This produced a moment of confused silence, which I filled with a lame description of the sexuality continuum, along with an explanation of the somewhat loose sexual mores of modern American gals like myself. Htan Dah responded by telling me that they had heard of gay people, since a visitor to the house had informed them of their existence—last year.

"Last year!" I hollered.

"Yes!" he yelled back. "In Karen culture, we do not have."

"There's never been a gay person in a Karen village in the history of Karen society." All three men shook their heads. "Come on."

"If there was a gay person, they would leave," Htan Dah said. "It is not our culture."

"Let's just say there was a gay person," I said. "Couldn't they stay in the village?"

"No," Htan Dah said. "I would not allow gay people in my village."

"Are you kidding me?!"

Htan Dah held my gaze, though his seemed more uncertain the longer it went on.

"Are you going to make *me* leave?"

"No! For you, in your culture, it is okay," he said. "You are not Karen. But in our culture, it does not belong." Htoo Moo and Ta Mla were nodding, and I scowled at them.

"You're a refugee," I said. "And it sucks. It's ruining your life. But you would force another villager to become a refugee because they were gay?"

Nobody said no. I turned on Htan Dah; I was maddest at him, and he was probably the only one who could follow my fast, heated English. "If there was peace in Burma and you lived in a village and there was a gay Karen person," I asked again, "you would want to make that person another Karen refugee by making them leave?"

That, or my anger, shut him up. "I am interested in your ideas," he said, evenly, after a minute. "I think it is important to keep an open mind."

I shut up, too, and focused on eating rice for a few awkward moments.

"So," I said eventually. "Do you guys have sex?"

Htoo Moo and Ta Mla shook their heads while Htan Dah said, "Sometimes."

"Ever?" I asked Htoo Moo.

"No," he said.

"Why not?"

"Because, I am not married."

"What about you?" I asked Htan Dah.

"Yes," he said, nodding hard once. "I am married."

"You're *married*?"

Htan Dah laughed. "Yes! I am married."

"I didn't know that. Where is your wife?"

"She is in camp. With my kid."

"You have a *kid*?"

Other things I didn't know: that everyone currently in the house—save The Blay and Htan Dah, who were married, apparently—was a virgin. This extended even to kissing. They hailed from the parts of Burma that had been heavily influenced by Christian missionaries, and premarital sex was taboo. Htoo Moo volunteered that he wasn't actively looking for a girlfriend, and that he wouldn't know what do with her even if he found one.

Htan Dah told me I had to show them MySpace again. We crowded around a computer, our cheeks flushed with satiety and humidity and new camaraderie. Htoo Moo interjected burning questions about American life as they came to him.

"Do you eat rice in America?"

"Yes. Usually I eat brown rice."

"Brown rice?"

"It's rice with the hull still on it. Do you know what I'm talking about?"

"No. I don't believe that . . . Have you ever eat tiger?"

"*Eaten* tiger. No."

"Have you ever eat . . . monkey?

" 'Have you ever *eaten* monkey,' you mean. No."

"Are there black lady in America?"

"*Ladies.* Yes . . ."

"What language do they speak?" Htan Dah chimed in.

"English."

"Really?"

I gaped at him, disbelieving, but before I could formulate a response, Htoo Moo said, "In America, you have cream to grow hair." He ran his hand over his baby-smooth jawline.

"Yeah. I think that's true. I think it's generally for people who are bald, though."

"Do you have that?"

"Hair-growing cream? Oh, yeah. I use it on my ass."

The sarcasm seemed to translate, since they laughed for minutes.

We made Ta Mla a MySpace profile, and he and Htan Dah started giving the other guys tutorials as they wandered in. My work here was done.

A few days earlier, when I'd asked my students what they did for fun, I'd had to explain the concept of "fun" for about five minutes before anyone could answer me, and then the answers were "Nothing," "Nothing," "Watch TV," and three "Talk"s. By the time I went upstairs, every computer screen was lit, the guys scrolling through the faces of Burma, a window into a world they considered home but where some had never been and probably none would ever live again.

.  .  .

Htan Dah diligently kept me company during meals. "You are so slow," he said one morning, watching me chew every bit of rice into oblivion. "Why don't you eat fast?"

"Why should I?" I asked. "I'm not in a hurry."

"But what if you are under attack, or have to run away?"

I scoffed at him. "I'm from Ohio."

"Yes, but I am refugee! We are taught to eat fast."

Be that as it may, we were in peacetime Thailand, so this attack seemed like an incredibly hypothetical scenario, and even though Htan Dah had mentioned something about refugee camps getting burned down on the very first day of class, I'd kind of dismissed it.

So boy did I feel like an asshole when he turned in an essay with this intro the next day:

*Having been fallen a sleep at midnight, my parents, sister, aunt and I heard the children's screaming and the voice of the shelling mortars simultaneously came about, and suddenly jumped through the ladder from the top to the bottom of the house to get away from the attacking troops' ammunitions without grabbing any facility.*

For a while, Htan Dah's family and all those other asylum seekers in Thailand were safe, relative to the Karen still in Burma. If they ventured out of the squalid camps, they were subject to harassment and arrest from one of the world's most corrupt police forces, but at least Burmese soldiers were less likely to march into a sovereign country to attack them.

What the Burmese army could do, though, was help a rival Karen faction to do so. They called themselves the Democratic Karen Buddhist Army, or DKBA. There had been discontent within the Christian-led KNU for years, complaints of abuses of power, religious discrimination, and grueling jungle-warfare conditions. In 1994, by which point there were 80,000 Karen living in the Thai camps, a government-allied monk persuaded several hundred Buddhist KNU soldiers to defect. The junta was only too happy to support their cause—which included attacking refugee camps filled with Christian Karen.

The huts at Htan Dah's settlement of Huay Kaloke were cloaked in thick, warm Thai darkness as DKBA soldiers moved in on the 7,000 refugees living there in January 1997. Residents generally went to bed early; there was no electricity, and flammable materials cost money nobody had. But Htan Dah's mother sometimes hired herself out as a laborer, plowing fields for about a dollar a day. That was far less than what the legal Thai workers alongside her made, but she needed money to buy nails—her scavenged-bamboo-and-thatch hut wasn't going to hold itself together—and candles, since she wasn't wild about her kids using homemade lamps, essentially tin cans filled with gasoline.

The small encampment had become overpopulated, so that there wasn't even enough space to play soccer, and Htan Dah barely ever left it. But a Christian organization had donated some books, and NGOs were running a full school system now. Htan Dah had exams the next day; he had stayed up past sundown studying and had been asleep for hours by the time the sound of gunshots reached his family's shelter. Some children somewhere screamed as they leapt out of the elevated hut. They ran, backs and knees bent, low to the dirt, for the surrounding woods as DKBA troops set fire to the camp. The huts burned hot and fast. Htan Dah kept his head down, so that he hardly registered the other people running alongside, not even noticing that some were in their underwear. "Please, God," he prayed. "Oh my God. Save me. Save my life," over and over again. It was a few days before his sixteenth birthday. He prayed and ran until he reached the forest, where, like everyone else, he stopped, turned around, and stood silently watching the camp—bedrooms, books, photos, shoes, a shirt woven by a grandmother—burn to the ground.

The next day, the refugees returned to the smoldering plot and made beds in the ash. They began slowly rebuilding, though none could have any illusions that the Thai security posted at the front gate would protect them. They had long ago noted that the function of the guards was not so much keeping danger out as keeping the refugees in, collecting bribes from those who wanted to leave the camp to work or collect firewood or make a trip to the market. Their attackers met no resistance on their way into Huay Kaloke that night. And less than fourteen months later, when vehicles full of DKBA soldiers drove in again, no one stopped them. Again.

"How do you know the Thai soldiers just let them drive right in through the front gate?" I interrupted Htan Dah as he told me this story on the reading bench in my room. That an army would allow raiding foreign troops unfettered access to 7,000 sleeping civilians—twice—seemed frankly a little far-fetched. "Maybe the soldiers were trying to protect the gate, but the DKBA just went around or something."

Htan Dah had told this story before, and to several foreigners, but never to one rude enough to suggest that he was a liar. He cocked his head. "Because," he said, "There is only one road. The only way into the camp is through the front gate!"

For a second time, Htan Dah awoke in the middle of the night to gunfire and shouting; for a second time, he fled with his family and the clothes he was wearing for the safety of the surrounding trees. But this time, the soldiers also shelled the camp. This time, a pregnant woman was shot dead and two girls from Htan Dah's school who hid in a well suffered burns that killed them. This time a seven-year-old died of shrapnel wounds and dozens were injured—and nearly the whole damn camp was burned down again.

"We accept that we were inactive," the secretary general of Thailand's National Security Council conceded later. Thai authorities decided to close the camp. Htan Dah's family set up a temporary shelter made of sticks and a raincoat, under which they lived while they were waiting to be moved elsewhere.

The trucks didn't arrive for almost a year and a half. When they did, Htan Dah and his family were shipped to a camp in the mountains, where the population in exile eventually became 20,000 strong, where Htan Dah eventually grew up and got married and had a baby of his own, where the cold, wet winds cut through the shacks stacked high in the hills of central Thailand, far away enough to be safer from the DKBA.

•       •       •

My days fell into a strange routine. I taught two classes of English a day, beginner and intermediate. After and between classes, and before the evening of drinking began in earnest, I snacked on coconut-fried cashews I bought at the 7-Eleven while helping the guys translate their HRD interviews or fill out applications for asylum. They kept filling out the applications, even though they had little chance of success—certainly no chance of resettling in the United States, which, under the Patriot Act, had effectively declared all Karen from the contested highlands terrorists for providing "material support" to the "terrorist" KNU.

After class one day, one of the guys wanted to show me a word he saw all the time so I could explain its meaning: marginalized. (He grasped the concept pretty quickly.) He also wanted to know what the thing used to bind people's feet together was called. I told him I didn't think we had a word for that in English. (I was wrong. Though archaic in noun form, the word exists: "fetters.") When Htoo Moo asked me later for the word for systematically slicing open the skin on someone's forearm, I told him I didn't think we had a word for that, either.

Another day, I sat outside holding an impromptu pronunciation lesson on some of the words in an HRD's report.

"Repeat after me," I was saying. *"Rape."*

"Rop."

"Try again. *Rrraaape."*

Another day, a Burma Action staffer I'll call Lah Lah Htoo asked if I wanted to see a video. He loaded a DVD of some footage taken in eastern Burma by aid workers, mostly Karen, some of whom are also medics, called the Free Burma Rangers.

It starts with war footage, guys shooting guns in tall jungle bush and loud rocket fire, and a village burning down and screaming women running for their lives, before moving briefly to photo stills: a picture of villagers standing over a group of dead bodies, a picture of a dead woman with her shirt torn open, a picture of murdered children lined up in a row. Then the camera centers on the face of a seventeen-year-old boy with lifeless, unfocused eyes, a *longyi* (sarong) held up below his neck so he can't see his completely exposed lower leg bone, a bloody white stick still hung with a few slick and glistening black-purple sinews, protruding from a bloody knee—a land-mine wound swarmed by flies. Then he's in a thin hammock, with a man in cheap plastic flip-flops at each end of the bamboo pole from which it swings, and another walking alongside holding an IV drip dangling from another piece of wood, being carried through the mountainous terrain. For four days. Which is how long it takes the Ranger team to get him to a clinic on the border, where a proper amputation can be done.

By that point I'd twisted my face into a permanent wince, and it didn't get any easier to watch. A husband and wife sit next to each other while he explains that their two sons and daughter were taken by Burma army troops. Local Karen leaders negotiated the return of the two boys, but they haven't seen the girl since. "We want her back," the woman says, smiling sadly, before dropping her face to her knees, covering it with her pink sweater, and starting to sob. There are people getting ready to run from an attack, little girls running around talking fast directions to each other while they throw shit in baskets and sacks they strap to their foreheads. A man on his back breathing fast and shallow as Free Burma Ranger medics jab their fingers and instruments into the bloody stump below his knee. Skulls and bones on the ground and a Ranger telling how he brought a bunch of children's presents donated by kids overseas only to find that there are no children in this village anymore. Rangers tearing out infected teeth with pliers. Rangers cleaning the gory, festering wound on a little kid's leg as the child stands still, calm, pantsless. Rangers delivering a baby in the darkness by the green glow of the camera's night mode, on the jungle floor. A shot of a Burma army compound, the camera zooming in shakily on the faces of the boys with rifles, the hiding cameramen whispering breathlessly to each other. A man rocking the tiniest sleeping baby; his wife died in childbirth during their flight through the jungle. He worries he has no idea how to take care of this child without her. Tears streaming hard and quiet down the face of a woman mindlessly fingering her jacket zipper with one hand, standing among the ashes of her old village, in which her husband was killed. A toddler barely old enough to stand picking his way through the jungle as his village flees, carefully parting the brush with his chubby little fingers and stepping through with his bare, scratched legs and feet. A Ranger team leaves a group of internally displaced persons and the IDPs call out please don't leave us, please come back. A man keeps hiding his face contorted with sorrow as he sobs convulsively, "I don't understand why they killed my children. They didn't even know their right hand from their left hand," while the woman next to him weeps silently and gnashes her teeth. The video ends with a quote from Galatians on the screen: *Let us not grow weary while doing good. In due season we shall reap if we don't lose heart.*

"What do you think?" Lah Lah Htoo asked me when it ended.

I thought I might like to close myself in the bathroom so I could punch myself in the chest, just a little, to try to release some of the tightness and weight there.

"Good video?" he asked, because I was taking so long to answer.

"Yeah, it's a good video."

He nodded and waited politely for me to continue, but I just sat quietly, awkwardly, before simply nodding back at him. Eventually, I asked him what they did with the videos they made.

"We send them. To human rights organizations, UN, news."

"Do they ever use them?"

Lah Lah Htoo shrugged.

. . .

Make no mistake: Though most Americans are woefully uninformed about the shit going down in Burma, your federal lawmakers are on it. In 1997, President Bill Clinton barred new U.S. investment in the country. In 2003, Congress introduced the Burmese Freedom and Democracy Act, which banned any Burmese imports, opposed loans to the regime, froze any of its U.S. assets, and denied its leaders entry visas. In 2005, Condoleezza Rice awarded Burma a special designation as an "outpost of tyranny." Bush 43 gave it shout-outs in several State of the Union addresses. ("We will continue to speak out for the cause of freedom in places like Cuba, Belarus, and Burma.") There's a U.S. Senate Women's Caucus on Burma, and Obama just extended sanctions again and said this at his Nobel Peace Prize acceptance: "When there is genocide in Darfur, systematic rape in Congo, repression in Burma—there must be consequences. . . . And the closer we stand together, the less likely we will be faced with the choice between armed intervention and complicity in oppression." Also blacklisting Burma: Australia, which won't sell the regime weapons and has financial sanctions against 463 members of the junta. And the EU has stripped Burma of trading privileges and put an arms embargo in place.

The trouble isn't so much a lack of measures as their total ineffectiveness. Though U.S. investors have had to pull their money out of, say, the garment industry, they can still deal in Burma's oil and gas, which is where the junta's big money comes from. When Congress passed that 1997 law restricting new investment, Unocal got its gas fields grandfathered in. After Chevron absorbed Unocal in 2005, its lobbyists worked tirelessly to ensure that no sanctions would force it to divest. It appeared as though the 2008 Block Burmese JADE (Junta's Anti-Democratic Efforts) Act would finally force Chevron to give up its Burmese holdings, until the Senate Committee on Foreign Relations, chaired by Joe Biden (whose former chief of staff was one Alan Hoffman, once a Unocal lobbyist), stripped out the provision and replaced it with a *suggestion* that the company "consider voluntary divestment over time."

Okay, but if we only fashioned better—and better-targeted—sanctions, advocates say, Burma's economy would collapse and the government might just get packing. But whether or not you believe that sanctions were the straw that broke South Africa's back, you cannot believe that they would have worked in that country if half the world's governments had said, "We're not going to give you money for your stuff anymore" while the other half had said, "Awesome. More for us."

That's the reality in Burma, where China is building an oil pipeline so as to avoid the long trip around the Strait of Malacca. Thailand has the rights to 1.7 trillion cubic feet of natural gas in one concession alone. One Indian firm has signed up for 5 trillion cubic feet. Russia has several firms drilling. A single pipeline operated by France, Thailand, and, yes, Chevron earned the junta more than $1 billion in 2008. The South Korean company Daewoo International plans to earn more than $10 billion over 25 years from its drilling project in Burma's immense Shwe gas reserve; handling Daewoo's exploratory Burma drilling was the American firm Transocean. As a member of the Association of Southeast Asian Nations, Burma is included in a free-trade agreement with India that eliminates tariffs on thousands of products; India plans to invest billions of dollars in two Burmese hydroelectric dams. The EU is discussing a free-trade agreement with ASEAN nations as well, although the United Kingdom swears it won't make a deal that would benefit Burma—it's worth noting the United Kingdom already has oil and gas dealings there. In 2008 Burma saw a 165 percent increase in the number of Chinese multinational companies involved in Burmese mining, oil and gas, and hydropower development. The regime ran a $2.5 billion trade surplus in 2009, with $5 billion in currency reserves.

The United States can better target its sanctions all it wants, but already they've pushed tens of thousands of Burmese textile workers out of factory jobs—and, as even the State Department has admitted, into sex work. And as Chevron has pointed out, if we pull out our remaining investments, someone else—perhaps someone less conscientious—will gladly fill the gap. The international community can't even agree to stop giving the regime weapons. Even if it could get China to play ball on that front, not so much North Korea. As long as there's money to be made in Burma, a cohesive or constructive policy of international financial disengagement—from an energy-rich country neighbored by the world's two most populous, energy-desperate countries—is never going to happen.

You know a situation is dire when its best chance of a good outcome depends on action by the United Nations Security Council. At the 2005 UN World Summit, member nations resolved that if a government perpetuates or allows any of four "atrocity crimes"—war crimes, ethnic cleansing, crimes against humanity, or genocide—the world body is responsible for taking "timely and decisive" action to protect that nation's people. When in 2007 a draft resolution on Burma was brought before the Security Council, some activists felt that there was a strong case for it to include charges of genocide against the Karen. The UN 1948 Convention on the Prevention and Punishment of the Crime of Genocide defines "genocide" as an attempt "to destroy, in whole or in part, a national, ethnical, racial or religious group" with at least one of five methods. One of them the SPDC isn't guilty of: "Forcibly transferring children of the group to another group." But "killing members of the group"? Check. "Causing serious bodily or mental harm to members of the group"? Check. "Deliberately inflicting on the group conditions of life calculated to bring about its physical destruction in whole or in part"? Clearly. "Imposing measures intended to prevent births within the group"? If you count gang-raping and murdering pregnant women, yes. Since the International Criminal Tribunal for Rwanda, systematic rape has been recognized as a key feature of genocide. In Burma, it's systematic, institutionalized, and indoctrinated into soldiers, who are explicitly ordered, "Your blood must be left in the village."

But not one government has officially leveled the charge at Burma, and some academics and even activists argue that these genocidal actions aren't genocide-like enough to count. We can't just be throwing the word around to describe any old horror. Or as my father put it when I tried to impress upon him the seriousness of my BA housemates' situation, "But how does it compare to Sudan?"

If Sudan is the bar against which we're measuring genocide, okay: Burma was alongside Sudan on the list of the world's worst displacement situations for four years running. Sudan's mortality rate for children under five, a common measure of conflict epidemiology, is 109 per 1,000 live births. In eastern Burma, it's 221. In the Darfur genocide, 400,000 civilians have been killed. A junta chairman once estimated that the body count of Burma's civil war—the Karen are only one of seven major minorities that have been involved in dozens of armed insurgencies—"would reach as high as millions."

It comes down to this: A draft resolution that compellingly charges genocide against a country is a draft resolution that's likely to get passed—because no one wants to be the nation that vetoes that. But the 2007 Security Council draft resolution to declare Burma a threat to international peace and security didn't contain charges of genocide. Nor ethnic cleansing, nor crimes against humanity, nor war crimes. China and Russia vetoed it.

●     ●     ●

Since I first arrived at Burma Action's Mae Sot offices, four years ago, some 50,000 Burmese refugees have left Thailand for UN-orchestrated resettlement in Western countries. In 2007, the United States waived its material support prohibition for refugees who'd assisted the KNU and the next year allowed in more than 14,000 refugees, including several BA staff members. In America, they try to make rent with welfare or factory wages and talk, weirdly, about struggling to survive. I apologized to one, after he was moved to a suburb outside cold, gray Cleveland, for his crushing poverty and loneliness and the weather. "It's okay," he replied. "You can never find a good place to live in the world. Only in heaven."

Though some of the documentary activists have emigrated, their footage and reports gather dust in Thailand, awaiting, the human rights community hopes, the day when they might be used at a trial of the junta or in a truth and reconciliation process. Some Burma Action footage made it out and into the opener for *Rambo* part four, whose producers paid—after some hard haggling—about two grand for it.

Lah Lah Htoo is one of those activists who's stayed behind. At a going-away party my last weekend, he sat with a guitar in his lap. On a previous night he'd played a hard-twanging, pentatonic melody on a stringed Karen instrument while he sang, in flowing minor notes, a traditional song about a river, so haunting that I had nearly drunkenly wept. But now the guitar he held was idle, and he tipped his head back and looked at me through half-closed eyes.

"Do you think that we will see each other again?" he asked, one arm dangling over the body of the guitar.

"Of course we'll see each other again," I said. I looked at Htan Dah. "I'll come back to Thailand soon."

"When?" several voices asked.

"Probably next summer. I have to figure it out with work, and money."

"So," one of the guys said, "we will see each other again maybe next year."

"I hope," I said. "Hopefully next year."

"When we see each other again," Lah Lah Htoo said, "it will be in Burma." The other guys cheered. "When we see each other again, you will come to Burma. And you will not *need* a visa to enter. And *I* will pick you up at the airport." His face was barely wide enough for his smile, and he was hollering a bit, over the approving shouts of the other guys. "In a car. In *my* car!" Lah Lah Htoo had left his village when he was a teenager, when he'd run away with the rest of his family and neighbors, and hadn't been back since. A silence settled over his coworkers in the wake of his fantastic predictions, and they all smiled softly and looked off or at the floor or at the wall as they considered cars and airports, and I thought about doomed POWs in movies who know their fate is sealed but talk anyway about how they're going to eat a big cheeseburger when they get back to America, and I kept quiet as long as the guys were quiet, bowing my head as if in reverence of something that had died.

## The New York Times Magazine

WINNER—NEWS AND
DOCUMENTARY
PHOTOGRAPHY

*To commemorate the seventh anniversary of the war in Iraq, The New York Times Magazine devoted fourteen pages to Ashley Gilbertson's photographs of the empty bedrooms of American soldiers killed in Iraq and Afghanistan. It was as though the men and women—children, really—who once lived in these rooms had left just a moment ago. Music posters, sports trophies, stuffed animals, still hung on the walls or sat on shelves. What emerged was a portrait of the young Americans whose lives have been sacrificed in two wars. Equally affecting was the brief essay by Dexter Filkins that accompanied Gilbertson's photographs (the photographs can be viewed on the* New York Times *website). In 600 words, Filkins captured the feel of their life in Iraq, their fear and bravery, the guilt of the survivors. Filkins— whose story "Right at the Edge," about the Taliban in Pakistan, won the National Magazine Award for Reporting for the* Times Magazine *in 2009—remembers. So should we all.*

Dexter Filkins

# *From* The Shrine Down the Hall

J ust kids. You step into the barracks thinking big, burly, and deep-voiced. And what you get are chubby faces and halfhearted mustaches and voices still cracking, boys hurried into uniforms and handed heavy guns. Sept. 11 was junior high, fifth grade even, a half a lifetime ago. Megan Fox is everywhere, plastered above the bunks, the best that Maxim can offer. Junk food, too, sent A.P.O. (Army Post Office) from home: powdered Gatorade and M&M's and teriyaki jerky. Underwear and socks. "Love you, bro," scrawled a sister from California on a care package to Ramadi, Iraq. "Muwah!"

Forty cigarettes and a ten-mile run. Ice cream and cake and twenty-five pull-ups. Who but a kid can punish himself like that? They go on patrol and search a string of houses, then lift weights to heavy metal and sleep away the heat in the afternoon. Their bodies are hard and soft at once, like youth.

Adulthood's a switch. The kids climb into their Humvees and close the clanging doors. They push the clips into their M-4's, pull back the bolts. Safeties off. Only code words and swear words now, no joshing around. Voices drop and eyes go hard. "Movement to contact," someone says. It won't be long now.

Death rides along. In the back seat, in the Humvee, on the bouncing road, in the dark. No one mentions the possibility of death. No one talks about the ambush coming. Nor the bomb in the road ahead, buried under the pile of trash, the one that will explode upward, through the seats.

"What's that up there?" the driver said.

"Hell if I know, move your head," said the other.

"It's nothing," the driver said.

In Helmand Province, in Afghanistan, the bombs were so big that one guy disappeared. He'd been on a foot patrol in a field. After a while they found his leg in a tree; they had to go up and pull it down. The rest of him didn't turn up, so they spent the night in the same place and woke up the next morning and started searching again. He'd floated down a canal.

Sometimes, right after a guy is killed, you feel as if you are in possession of a terrible secret. He's there on the ground, alive only a minute ago, and the only people who know he's dead are standing right there by him. The rest of the world thinks he's alive, as alive as he was when he climbed out of bed that same morning, only a few hours before.

And at that moment, you think about how the word of his death will travel; how it will depart Iraq or Afghanistan and move across the ocean and into the United States and into the town where he lives, Corinth, Miss., say, or Benwood, W. Va., and into the houses and the hearts of the people who love him most in the world. And at that moment, standing there, looking down on the dead man, you can wonder only what the family will do when the terrible news finally arrives, how they will resist it and wrestle with it and suffer from it, and how they will cope and how they will remember.

## National Geographic

WINNER—SINGLE-TOPIC
ISSUE

This short essay by Barbara Kingsolver was the introduction to the special issue of National Geographic entitled "Water: Our Thirsty World." "Water is life," Kingsolver writes. "It's the briny broth of our origins, the pounding circulatory system of the world, a precarious molecular edge on which we survive." A poet, novelist, and essayist, Kingsolver is the author of thirteen books, including The Poisonwood Bible and The Lacuna, her most recent novel, published in 2009. "Water: Our Thirsty World" won the National Magazine Award for Single-Topic Issue, and work from the issue was nominated for awards honoring journalism published online. The issue was also one of the reasons National Geographic was chosen the 2011 Magazine of the Year. "'Water: Our Thirsty World,' is a call to action that cannot be ignored," said the National Magazine Award judges. Or as Kingsolver concluded: "We have been slow to give up on the myth of Earth's infinite generosity. Rather grandly, we have overdrawn our accounts."

Barbara Kingsolver

# Water Is Life

We keep an eye out for wonders, my daughter and I, every morning as we walk down our farm lane to meet the school bus. And wherever we find them, they reflect the magic of water: a spider web drooping with dew like a rhinestone necklace. A rain-colored heron rising from the creek bank. One astonishing morning, we had a visitation of frogs. Dozens of them hurtled up from the grass ahead of our feet, launching themselves, white-bellied, in bouncing arcs, as if we'd been caught in a downpour of amphibians. It seemed to mark the dawning of some new aqueous age. On another day we met a snapping turtle in his primordial olive drab armor. Normally this is a pond-locked creature, but some murky ambition had moved him onto our gravel lane, using the rainy week as a passport from our farm to somewhere else.

The little, nameless creek tumbling through our hollow holds us in thrall. Before we came to southern Appalachia, we lived for years in Arizona, where a permanent runnel of that size would merit a nature preserve. In the Grand Canyon State, every license plate reminded us that water changes the face of the land, splitting open rock desert like a peach, leaving mile-deep gashes of infinite hue. Cities there function like space stations, importing every ounce of fresh water from distant rivers or fossil aquifers. But such is the human inclination to take water as a birthright that public fountains still may bubble in Arizona's town squares and farmers there raise thirsty crops. Retirees from rainier climes irrigate green lawns that impersonate the grasslands they left behind. The truth encroaches on all the fantasies, though, when desert residents wait months between rains, watching cacti tighten their belts and roadrunners skirmish over precious beads from a dripping garden faucet. Water is life. It's the briny broth of our origins, the pounding circulatory system of the world, a precarious molecular edge on which we survive. It makes up two-thirds of our bodies, just like the map of the world; our vital fluids are saline, like the ocean. The apple doesn't fall far from the tree.

Even while we take Mother Water for granted, humans understand in our bones that she is the boss. We stake our civilizations on the coasts and mighty rivers. Our deepest dread is the threat of having too little moisture—or too much. We've lately raised the Earth's average temperature by .74°C (1.3°F), a number that sounds inconsequential. But these words do not: flood, drought, hurricane, rising sea levels, bursting levees. Water is the visible face of climate and, therefore, climate change. Shifting rain patterns flood some regions and dry up others as nature demonstrates a grave physics lesson: Hot air holds more water molecules than cold.

The results are in plain sight along pummeled coasts from Louisiana to the Philippines as superwarmed air above the ocean brews superstorms, the likes of which we have never known. In arid places the same physics amplify evaporation and drought, visible in the dust-dry farms of the Murray-Darling River Basin in Australia. On top of the Himalaya, glaciers whose meltwater sustains vast populations are dwindling. The snapping turtle I met on my lane may have been looking for higher ground. Last summer brought us a string of floods that left tomatoes blighted on the vine and our farmers needing disaster relief for the third consecutive year. The past decade has brought us more extreme storms than ever before, of the kind that dump many inches in a day, laying down crops and utility poles and great sodden oaks whose roots cannot find purchase in the saturated ground. The word "disaster" seems to mock us. After enough repetitions of shocking weather, we can't remain indefinitely shocked.

How can the world shift beneath our feet? All we know is founded on its rhythms: Water will flow from the snowcapped mountains, rain and sun will arrive in their proper seasons. Humans first formed our tongues around language, surely, for the purpose of explaining these constants to our children. What should we tell them now? That "reliable" has been rained out, or died of thirst? When the Earth seems to raise its own voice to the pitch of a gale, have we the ears to listen?

. . .

A world away from my damp hollow, the Bajo Piura Valley is a great bowl of the driest Holocene sands I've ever gotten in my shoes. Stretching from coastal, northwestern Peru into southern Ecuador, the 14,000-square-mile Piura Desert is home to many endemic forms of thorny life. Profiles of this eco-region describe it as dry to drier, and Bajo Piura on its southern edge is what anyone would call driest. Between January and March it might get close to an inch of rain, depending on the whims of El Niño, my driver explained as we bumped over the dry bed of the Río Piura, "but in some years, nothing at all." For hours we passed through white-crusted fields ruined by years of irrigation and then into eye-burning valleys beyond the limits of endurance for anything but sparse stands of the deep-rooted *Prosopis pallida*, arguably nature's most arid-adapted tree. And remarkably, some scattered families of *Homo sapiens*.

They are economic refugees, looking for land that costs nothing. In Bajo Piura they find it, although living there has other costs, and fragile drylands pay their own price too, as people exacerbate desertification by cutting anything living for firewood.

What brought me there, as a journalist, was an innovative refor-estation project. Peruvian conservationists, partnered with the NGO Heifer International, were guiding the population into herding goats, which eat the protein-rich pods of the native mes-quite and disperse its seeds over the desert. In the shade of a stick shelter, a young mother set her dented pot on a dung-fed fire and showed how she curdles goat's milk into white cheese. But milking goats is hard to work into her schedule when she, and every other woman she knows, must walk about eight hours a day to collect water.

Their husbands were digging a well nearby. They worked with hand trowels, a plywood form for lining the shaft with concrete, inch by inch, and a sturdy hand-built crank for lowering a man to the bottom and sending up buckets of sand. A dozen hopeful men in stained straw hats stood back to let me inspect their work, which so far had yielded only a mountain of exhumed sand, dry as dust. I looked down that black hole, then turned and climbed the sand mound to hide my unprofessional tears. I could not fathom this kind of perseverance and wondered how long these beleaguered people would last before they'd had enough of their water woes and moved somewhere else.

Five years later they are still bringing up dry sand, scratching out their fate as a microcosm of life on this planet. There is no-where else. Forty percent of the households in sub-Saharan Africa are more than a half hour from the nearest water, and that dis-tance is growing. Australian farmers can't follow the rainfall pat-terns that have shifted south to fall on the sea. A salmon that runs into a dam when homing in on her natal stream cannot make other plans. Together we dig in, for all we're worth.

Since childhood I've heard it's possible to look up from the bottom of a well and see stars, even in daylight. Aristotle wrote about this, and so did Charles Dickens. On many a dark night the vision of that round slip of sky with stars has comforted me. Here's the only problem: It's not true. Western civilization was in no great hurry to give up this folklore; astronomers believed it for centuries, but a few of them eventually thought to test it and had their illusions dashed by simple observation.

Civilization has been similarly slow to give up on our myth of the Earth's infinite generosity. Declining to look for evidence to the contrary, we just knew it was there. We pumped aquifers and diverted rivers, trusting the twin lucky stars of unrestrained human expansion and endless supply. Now water tables plummet in countries harboring half the world's population. Rather grandly, we have overdrawn our accounts.

In 1968 the ecologist Garrett Hardin wrote a paper called "The Tragedy of the Commons," required reading for biology students ever since. It addresses the problems that can be solved only by "a change in human values or ideas of morality" in situations where rational pursuit of individual self-interest leads to collective ruin. Cattle farmers who share a common pasture, for example, will increase their herds one by one until they destroy the pasture by overgrazing. Agreeing to self-imposed limits instead, unthinkable at first, will become the right thing to do. While our laws imply that morality is fixed, Hardin made the point that "the morality of an act is a function of the state of the system at the time it is performed." Surely it was no sin, once upon a time, to shoot and make pies of passenger pigeons.

Water is the ultimate commons. Watercourses once seemed as boundless as those pigeons that darkened the sky overhead, and the notion of protecting water was as silly as bottling it. But rules change. Time and again, from New Mexico's antique irrigation codes to the UN Convention on International Watercourses, communities have studied water systems and redefined wise use. Now Ecuador has become the first nation on Earth to put the rights of nature in its constitution so that rivers and forests are not simply property but maintain their own right to flourish. Under these laws a citizen might file suit on behalf of an injured watershed, recognizing that its health is crucial to the common good. Other nations may follow Ecuador's lead. Just as legal systems once reeled to comprehend women or former slaves as fully entitled, law schools in the U.S. are now reforming their curricula with an eye to understanding and acknowledging nature's rights.

On my desk, a glass of water has caught the afternoon light, and I'm still looking for wonders. Who owns this water? How can I call it mine when its fate is to run through rivers and living bodies, so many already and so many more to come? It is an ancient, dazzling relic, temporarily quarantined here in my glass, waiting to return to its kind, waiting to move a mountain. It is the gold standard of biological currency, and the good news is that we can conserve it in countless ways. Also, unlike petroleum, water will always be with us. Our trust in Earth's infinite generosity was half right, as every raindrop will run to the ocean, and the ocean will rise into the firmament. And half wrong, because we are not important to water. It's the other way around. Our task is to work out reasonable ways to survive inside its boundaries. We'd be wise to fix our sights on some new stars. The gentle nudge of evidence, the guidance of science, and a heart for protecting the commons: These are the tools of a new century. Taking a wide-eyed look at a watery planet is our way of knowing the stakes, the better to know our place.

# National Magazine Awards 2011
## Finalists and Winners

To view an extended list of the 2011 finalists and winners—including links to content and a searchable database of past award winners—please go to http://asme.magazine.org.

## Magazine of the Year

Honors publications that have achieved excellence both in print and on digital platforms.

*The Atlantic*: James Bennet, editor; Scott Stossel, deputy editor; Bob Cohn, editorial director, Atlantic Digital. For July–August, September, October issues.

*Backpacker*: Jonathan Dorn, editor in chief; Anthony Cerretani, digital director. For March, May, October issues.

*Foreign Policy*: Susan B. Glasser, editor in chief. For May–June, July–August, September–October issues.

*National Geographic* [Winner]: Chris Johns, editor in chief; Rob Covey, digital media editor, NGM.com. For February, April, December issues.

*Wired*: Chris Anderson, editor in chief. For June, August, December issues.

## General Excellence, Print

### *News, Sports, and Entertainment Magazines*

Honors large-circulation weeklies, biweeklies and general-interest monthlies.

*Fast Company*: Robert Safian, editor. For July–August, September, November issues.

*New York* [Winner]: Adam Moss, editor in chief. For April 19, July 12, August 9–16 issues.

*The New Yorker*: David Remnick, editor. For August 2, August 9, October 4 issues.

*People*: Larry Hackett, managing editor. For May 10, September 6, December 20 issues.

*Time*: Richard Stengel, managing editor. For August 9, November 22, December 27, 2010–January 3, 2011 issues.

*Literary, Political, and Professional Magazines*

Honors academic and scholarly publications as well as smaller-circulation general-interest magazines.

*Lapham's Quarterly*: Lewis H. Lapham, editor; Kira Brunner Don, executive editor. For Winter, Spring, Fall issues.

*The Paris Review*: Caitlin Roper, interim editor, for Summer issue. Lorin Stein, editor, for Fall, Winter issues.

*Poetry* [Winner]: Christian Wiman, editor; Don Share, senior editor. For April, September, October issues.

*The Sun*: Sy Safransky, editor and publisher; Tim McKee, managing editor. For March, June, December issues.

*Virginia Quarterly Review*: Ted Genoways, editor. For Winter, Spring, Fall issues.

*Fashion, Service, and Lifestyle Magazines*

Honors women's magazines, including health and fitness magazines and family-centric publications.

*Essence*: Angela Burt-Murray, editor in chief. For July, September, November issues.

*Real Simple*: Kristin van Ogtrop, managing editor. For October, November, December issues.

*Vogue*: Anna Wintour, editor in chief. For March, August, September issues.

*W*: Stefano Tonchi, editor in chief. For September, November, December issues.

*Women's Health* [Winner]: Michele Promaulayko, editor in chief; David Zinczenko, editorial director. For January–February, July–August, October issues.

*Food, Travel and Design Magazines*

Honors shelter magazines as well as lifestyle titles.

*Condé Nast Traveler*: Klara Glowczewska, editor in chief. For May, October, November issues.

*Garden & Gun* [Winner]: Sid Evans, editor in chief. For April–May, June–July, December 2010–January 2011 issues.

*House Beautiful*: Stephen Drucker, editor in chief, for March, April issues. Newell Turner, editor in chief, for July–August issue.

*Martha Stewart Living*: Gael Towey, chief creative and editorial director; Vanessa Holden, editor in chief. For October, November, December issues.

*Saveur*: James Oseland, editor in chief. For August–September, October, December issues.

### Finance, Technology and Lifestyle Magazines

Honors business, science, and active-interest publications.

*Backpacker*: Jonathan Dorn, editor in chief. For March, May, October issues.

*Bloomberg Markets*: Matthew Winkler, editor in chief; Ronald Henkoff, editor. For May, November, December issues.

*GQ*: Jim Nelson, editor in chief. For March, August, September issues.

*Popular Mechanics*: James B. Meigs, editor in chief. For April, June, July issues.

*Scientific American* [Winner]: Mariette DiChristina, editor in chief. For September, November, December issues.

### Special Interest Magazines

Honors magazines serving targeted audiences, including city and regional magazines.

Audubon: David Seideman, editor in chief. For March–April, May–June, September–October issues.

Los Angeles [Winner]: Mary Melton, editor. For February, September, November issues.

San Francisco: Bruce Kelley, editor in chief. For October, November, December issues.

Texas Monthly: Jake Silverstein, editor. For July, November, December issues.

Time Out New York: Michael Freidson, editor in chief. For March 25–31, July 8–14, August 5–11 issues.

## Design

Honors overall excellence in magazine design, including the use of illustrations and photographs.

*Esquire*: David Granger, editor in chief; David Curcurito, design director. For May, October, November issues.

*Fortune*: Andy Serwer, managing editor; John Korpics, creative director. For March 22, May 3, November 1 issues.

*GQ* [Winner]: Jim Nelson, editor in chief; Fred Woodward, design director. For June, August, December issues.

*New York*: Adam Moss, editor in chief; Chris Dixon, design director. For February 22–March 1, April 19, May 17 issues.

*Wired*: Chris Anderson, editor in chief; Scott Dadich, creative director. For June, July, August issues.

## Photography

Honors overall excellence in magazine photography.

*GQ*: Jim Nelson, editor in chief; Dora Somosi, director of photography. For August, November, December issues.

*Martha Stewart Living*: Gael Towey, editorial director; Vanessa Holden, editor in chief; Heloise Goodman, photography director. For August, October, November issues.

*National Geographic*: Chris Johns, editor in chief; Kurt Mutchler, executive editor, photography. For February, April, December issues.

*The New York Times Magazine*: Gerald Marzorati, editor in chief, for February 7, March 21 issues. Hugo Lindgren, editor in chief, for December 12 issue. Kathy Ryan, director of photography.

*W* [Winner]: Stefano Tonchi, editor in chief. For September, October, November issues.

## News and Documentary Photography

Honors photojournalism and photography that documents news, sports, and entertainment events and news-related subjects.

*National Geographic*: Chris Johns, editor in chief. For "Veiled Rebellion," by Elizabeth Rubin; photographs by Lynsey Addario. December.

*The New York Times Magazine* [Winner]: Gerald Marzorati, editor in chief. For "The Shrine Down the Hall," photographs by Ashley Gilbertson; essay by Dexter Filkins. March 21.

*The New York Times Magazine*: Gerald Marzorati, editor in chief. For "Dumping Across the Digital Divide," photographs by Pieter Hugo. August 15.

*Time*: Richard Stengel, managing editor. For "The Perils of Pregnancy: One Woman's Tale of Dying to Give Birth," by Alice Park; photographs by Lynsey Addario. June 14.

*Virginia Quarterly Review*: Ted Genoways, editor. For "The Cocaine Coast," essay and photographs by Marco Vernaschi. Winter.

## Feature Photography

Honors portraiture; fashion, travel, and nature photography; conceptual photography; and photo-illustration.

*AARP The Magazine*: Nancy Perry Graham, editor and vice president. For "The Me I Used to Be," by Frank Yuvancic; photographs by Gregg Segal. November–December.

*ESPN The Magazine* [Winner]: Gary Belsky, editor in chief. For "Bodies We Want," reporting by Morty Ain. October 18.

*National Geographic*: Chris Johns, editor in chief. For "One Cubic Foot," by Edward O. Wilson; photographs by David Littschwager. February.

*The New York Times Magazine*: Hugo Lindgren, editor in chief. For "Fifteen Actors Acting," photographs by Solve Sundsbo; introduction by A. O. Scott. December 12

*W*: Stefano Tonchi, editor in chief. For "The East Enders," by Ted Polhemus; portfolio by Tim Walker. September.

## Single-Topic Issue

Honors magazines that have devoted an issue to the comprehensive examination of a subject.

*Bloomberg Businessweek*: Josh Tyrangiel, editor. For "Year in Review." December 20, 2010–January 2, 2011.

*GQ*: Jim Nelson, editor in chief. For "Comedy Issue." August.

*National Geographic* [Winner]: Chris Johns, editor in chief. For "Water: Our Thirsty World." April.

*New York*: Adam Moss, editor in chief. For "Who Runs New York?" October 4.

*Scientific American*: Mariette DiChristina, editor in chief. For "The End." September

## Magazine Section

Honors a regularly published, clearly branded front- or back-of-the-book department or section.

*Esquire*: David Granger, editor in chief. For "Man at His Best." March, May, June–July issues.

*New York* [Winner]: Adam Moss, editor in chief. For "Strategist." May 24, October 25, December 20–27 issues.

*Real Simple*: Kristin van Ogtrop, managing editor. For "Food." June, October, November issues.

*Real Simple*: Kristin van Ogtrop, managing editor. For "Solutions." July, September, October issues.

*Wired*: Chris Anderson, editor in chief. For "Play." August, October, December issues.

## Personal Service

Honors the superior and consistent use of print to serve readers' needs and aspirations.

*Good Housekeeping*: Rosemary Ellis, editor in chief. For "The (Surprising) Truth About Salt," by Rachael Moeller Gorman. November.

*Men's Health* [Winner]: David Zinczenko, editor in chief; Peter Moore, editor. For "I Want My Prostate Back," by Laurence Roy Stains. March.

*Men's Journal*: Jann S. Wenner, editor in chief; Will Dana, editorial director; Brad Wieners, editor. For a three-part series: "The Complete Guide to Your Knee," by Gretchen Reynolds, March; "The Complete Guide to Your Back," by Catherine Price, April; "The Complete Guide to Your Hip," by Nathanael Johnson, May.

*O, The Oprah Magazine*: Oprah Winfrey, founder and editorial director; Susan Casey, editor in chief. For "My Bra's Too Tight . . . ," January, and "It's Never Too Late . . . ," February, by Paige Williams.

*Wired*: Chris Anderson, editor in chief. For "Blood Simple," by Steven Leckart. December.

## Leisure Interests

Honors the superior and consistent use of print to cover recreational activities and special interests.

*Cooking Light*: Scott Mowbray, editor. For "Oops! The 25 Most Common Cooking Mistakes and How to Avoid Them for Success Every Time," by Ann Taylor Pittman; photographs by Romulo Yanes and Randy Mayor. March.

*Golf Digest*: Jerry Tarde, chairman and editor in chief. For "Why You Can't Putt: The Ultimate Guide to Make You Great on the Greens" by Peter Morrice. October.

*Los Angeles*: Mary Melton, editor. For "A Delicious Guide to Lunch in L.A.," edited by Lesley Bargar Suter. June.

*Men's Journal* [Winner]: Jann S. Wenner, editor in chief; Will Dana, editorial director; Brad Wieners, editor. For "Five Meals Every Man Should Master," by Daniel Duane; photographs by Marcus Nilsson. August.

*Runner's World*: David Willey, editor in chief. For "Pet Project," by Christie Aschwanden and Marc Parent; photographs by Michael Brian. September.

## Public Interest

Honors magazine journalism that illuminates issues of local or national importance.

*The Atlantic*: James Bennet, editor. For "God Help You, You're on Dialysis," by Robin Fields, Propublica. December.

*Marie Claire*: Joanna Coles, editor in chief. For "Still Waiting After All These Years...," by Ralph Blumenthal. September.

*The New Yorker* [Winner]: David Remnick, editor. For "Letting Go," by Atul Gawande. August 2.

*OnEarth*: Douglas S. Barasch, editor in chief. For "What's the Catch?" by Bruce Barcott; photographs by Corey Arnold. Summer.

*Texas Monthly*: Jake Silverstein, editor. For "Innocence Lost," October; and "Innocence Found," January 2011, by Pamela Colloff.

## Reporting

Honors reporting excellence as exemplified by one article or a series of articles.

*Harper's Magazine* [Winner]: Roger D. Hodge, editor. For "The Guantanamo 'Suicides,'" by Scott Horton. March.

*The New York Times Magazine*: Gerald Marzorati, editor in chief. For "The Desert War," by Robert F. Worth. July 11.

*The New Yorker*: David Remnick, editor. For "Covert Operations," by Jane Mayer. August 30.

*Rolling Stone*: Jann S. Wenner, editor and publisher; Will Dana, managing editor. For "The Runaway General," by Michael Hastings. July 8–22.

*Virginia Quarterly Review*: Ted Genoways, editor. For "Digging Out," essay and photographs by Elliott D. Woods. Fall.

## Feature Writing

Honors magazines for original, stylish storytelling.

*The Atlantic*: James Bennet, editor. For "The Wrong Man," by David Freed. May.

*GQ*: Jim Nelson, editor in chief. For "The Suicide Catcher," by Michael Paterniti. May.

*Los Angeles* [Winner]: Mary Melton, editor. For "The End," by Ben Ehrenreich. November.

*Mother Jones*: Monika Bauerlein, editor; Clara Jeffery, editor. For "For Us Surrender Is Out of the Question," by Mac McClelland. March–April.

*The New Yorker*: David Remnick, editor. For "The Mark of a Masterpiece," by David Grann. July 12 and July 19.

## Profile Writing

Honors news or feature stories focused on individuals or groups of closely linked individuals.

*The Atlantic*: James Bennet, editor. For "Autism's First Child," by John Donvan and Caren Zucker. October.

*Harper's Magazine*: Ellen Rosenbush, acting editor. For "Own Goal," by Wells Tower. June.

*New York*: Adam Moss, editor in chief. For "Joan Rivers Always Knew She Was Funny," by Jonathan Van Meter. May 31.

*The New York Times Magazine* [Winner]: Gerald Marzorati, editor in chief. For "The Man the White House Wakes Up To," by Mark Leibovich. April 25.

*The New Yorker*: David Remnick, editor. For "The Unconsoled," by George Packer. September 27.

## Essays and Criticism

Honors long-form journalism that presents the opinions of the writer.

*The American Scholar*: Robert Wilson, editor. For "Solitude and Leadership," by William Deresiewicz. Spring.

*The Antioch Review*: Robert S. Fogarty, editor. For "The Physics of Speed," by William Giraldi. Fall.

*The New Yorker*: David Remnick, editor. For "The Fun Stuff," by James Wood. November 29.

*The Paris Review* [Winner]: Lorin Stein, editor. For "Mister Lytle: An Essay," by John Jeremiah Sullivan. Fall.

*Virginia Quarterly Review*: Ted Genoways, editor. For "Lust, Devotion, and the Binary Code," by Kamin Mohammadi. Summer.

## Columns and Commentary

Honors short-form journalism that presents the views of the writer or publication.

*Esquire*: David Granger, editor in chief. For three "A Thousand Words About Our Culture" columns by Stephen Marche: "What's Your Favorite War?" March; "Why Is Clint Eastwood Still the Man?" November; "Why Can't Kanye West Shut the Hell Up?" December.

*New York*: Adam Moss, editor in chief. For three reviews by Jerry Saltz: "Less Than the Sum of Its Parts," April 5; "A Grand Tour," August 9–16; "Judge Jerry," September 20.

*The New Yorker*: David Remnick, editor. For three "Talk of the Town" columns by Hendrik Hertzberg: "And The Oscar Goes To," February 15–22; "Puppetry," November 29; "Iran and the Bomb," December 13.

*Vanity Fair* [Winner]: Graydon Carter, editor. For three columns by Christopher Hitchens: "Topic of Cancer," September; "Unanswerable Prayers," October; "Miss Manners and the Big C," December.

*Vanity Fair*: Graydon Carter, editor. For three columns by James Wolcott: "The Norman Conquests," June; "Barbarians at the Shore," October; "The Sound of Sanity," December.

## Fiction

Honors the best short stories published in magazines.

*The Atlantic*: James Bennet, editor. For "Bone Hinge," by Katie Williams. May.

*The New Yorker*: David Remnick, editor. For "Foster," by Claire Keegan. February 15–22.

*The New Yorker*: David Remnick, editor. For "Costello," by Jim Gavin. December 6.

*Virginia Quarterly Review* [Winner]: Ted Genoways, editor. For "Minor Watt," by Paul Theroux. Spring.

*Virginia Quarterly Review*: Ted Genoways, editor. For "Uzon," by William Malatinsky. Summer.

# National Magazine Awards for Digital Media 2011 Finalists and Winners

## General Excellence, Digital Media

### News and Opinion

Honors the best general-interest magazines published on digital platforms.

*The Atlantic*: James Bennet, editor; Bob Cohn, editorial director, Atlantic Digital.
*The Daily Beast*: Tina Brown, editor in chief.
*The New York Times Magazine*: Hugo Lindgren, editor in chief.
*Slate* [Winner]: David Plotz, editor.
*Wired.com*: Evan Hansen, editor in chief; Michael Mertens, product manager; Dennis Crothers, UI director.

### Service and Lifestyle

Honors the best fashion, service and lifestyle magazines published on digital platforms.

*Epicurious* [Winner]: Tanya Steel, editor in chief; Jamie Pallot, editorial director.
*Field & Stream*: Anthony Licata, editor; Nate Matthews, online editor.
*POZ*: Regan Hofmann, editor in chief; Oriol Gutierrez, deputy editor.
*Runner's World*: David Willey, editor in chief; Mark Remy, executive editor.
*Self*: Lucy Danziger, editor in chief; Kristen Dollard, digital director.

### Mobile Edition

Honors the best magazines created for mobile devices, including tablets.

*Esquire* [Winner]: David Granger, editor in chief; Peter Griffin, deputy editor; Julian Sancton, associate editor.
*The New Yorker*: David Remnick, editor; Pamela Maffei McCarthy, deputy editor; Blake Eskin, editor, newyorker.com.
*Popular Mechanics*: James B. Meigs, editor in chief; Jerry Beilinson, deputy editor.
*Slate*: David Plotz, editor.
*Sports Illustrated*: Terry McDonell, editor, Time Inc. Sports Group.

### Design

Honors overall excellence in the design of magazine websites and online-only magazines.

*The Daily Beast*: Tina Brown, editor in chief.

New York: Adam Moss, editor in chief; Ben Williams, editorial director, nymag.com; Ian Adelman, director of design and user experience, New York Media/nymag.com.

The New York Times Magazine [Winner]: Hugo Lindgren, editor in chief.

Sports Illustrated: Terry McDonell, editor, Time Inc. Sports Group.

Vogue: Caroline Palmer, editor, vogue.com.

### Photography

Honors overall excellence in the use of photography by magazine websites and online-only magazines.

*Discover Magazine*: Rebecca Horne, photo editor; Gemma Shusterman, web producer; Eliza Strickland, online news editor; Amos Zeeberg, managing editor, online.

*Foreign Policy*: Susan Glasser, editor in chief.

*Life.com* [Winner]: Bill Shapiro, editor; Dawnie Walton, deputy editor; Simon Barnett, director of photography; Ben Cosgrove, deputy editor.

*National Geographic*: Chris Johns, editor in chief.

*Time*: Richard Stengel, managing editor; Jim Frederick, managing editor; Kira Pollack, director of photography; Mark Rykoff, picture editor, TIME.com.

### News Reporting

Honors the timeliness, accuracy, and skill with which news and information are gathered and presented by magazines published on digital platforms.

*The Chronicle of Higher Education*: Jeffrey J. Selingo, editor; Scott Smallwood, managing editor; Ron Coddington, assistant managing editor, Visuals. For reporting on the University of Alabama at Huntsville shooting.

CNET: Declan McCullagh, chief political correspondent; Elinor Mills, senior writer. For reporting on WikiLeaks.

*Foreign Policy* [Winner]: Susan Glasser, editor in chief; Colum Lynch, reporter. For reporting on the United Nations.

*National Geographic*: Chris Johns, editor in chief; Rob Covey, senior vice-president, content/design. For reporting on "The Great Shale Gas Rush."
*Yale Environment 360*: Roger Cohn, editor. For coverage of climate-change issues.

## Blogging

Recognizes excellence in online reporting and commentary published as a blog.

*IEEE Spectrum*: Erico Guizzo, senior associate editor; Harry Goldstein, editorial director, digital; Susan Hassler, editor in chief. For "Automaton."
*Salon*: Glenn Greenwald, contributing writer. For *Glenn Greenwald's Blog*.
*Sports Illustrated*: Terry McDonell, editor, Time Inc. Sports Group; Paul Fichtenbaum, managing editor, SI.com; Joe Posnanski, senior writer. For *Curiously Long Posts*.
*Sunset*: Margo True, food editor. For "One-Block Diet."
*Tablet Magazine* [Winner]: Alana Newhouse, editor in chief; Marc Tracy, staff writer. For *The Scroll*.

## Online Department

Honors a regularly updated, clearly branded department or channel.

*The Daily Beast*: Tina Brown, editor in chief. For "Book Beast."
*Fast Company* [Winner]: Noah Robischon, executive editor; Cliff Kuang, editor; Linda Tischler, senior editor. For "Co. Design."
*Foreign Policy*: Susan Glasser, editor in chief. For "The AfPak Channel."
*National Geographic*: Chris Johns, editor in chief; Rob Covey, senior vice president, content/design. For "Your Shot."
*New York*: Adam Moss, editor in chief; Ben Williams, editorial director, nymag.com; Josh Wolk, entertainment editor, nymag.com. For "Vulture."

## Multimedia Package

Recognizes the use of interactivity and multimedia in the coverage of an event or subject.

*Fast Company*: Robert Safian, editor in chief; Noah Robischon, executive editor; Tyler Gray, deputy editor, digital. For "The Influence Project."

*National Geographic*: Chris Johns, editor in chief; Rob Covey, senior vice president, content/design. For "Water: A Special Issue."

*New York*: Adam Moss, editor in chief; Ben Williams, editorial director, nymag.com. For "New York Fashion Week."

Reason.com and Reason.tv: Nick Gillespie, editor in chief; Paul Feine, producer; Drew Carey, "The Price Is Right." For "Reason Saves Cleveland with Drew Carey."

*Virginia Quarterly Review* [Winner]: Elliott D. Woods, reporter and multimedia production; Jesse Dukes, multimedia and audio production; Bluecadet Interactive, web design and product coordination; Ted Genoways, editor. For "Assignment Afghanistan."

## Interactive Tool

Honors single-purpose interactive utilities that help users perform tasks or manage content.

*The Chronicle of Higher Education*: Jeffrey J. Selingo, editor; Scott Smallwood, managing editor; Ron Coddington, assistant managing editor, visuals. For "Tuition Over Time, 1999–2010" interactive tool.

*Epicurious* [Winner]: Tanya Steel, editor in chief; Jamie Pallot, editorial director. For "*Epicurious* Recipes & Shopping List" iPad app.

*InStyle*: Rosie Amodio, editor, InStyle.com; Kristen Beirne, director of product development, InStyle.com. For "Instant Stylist" online game.

*Marie Claire*: Joanna Coles, editor in chief; Suzanne Sykes, creative director. For "Fall Fashion A to Z" iPad app.

*Real Simple*: Kristin van Ogtrop, managing editor. For "No Time to Cook?" iPad app.

## Podcasting

Honors outstanding audio podcasts on magazine websites and online-only magazines.

*Harvard Business Review*: Adi Ignatius, editor in chief; Eric Hellweg, editor, HBR.org; Sarah Green, associate editor; Adam Buchholz, mutlimedia web producer; Scott Berinato, senior associate editor. For "HBR IdeaCasts."

*The New Yorker*: David Remnick, editor; Pamela Maffei McCarthy, deputy editor; Blake Eskin, editor, newyorker.com. For "*The New Yorker* Out Loud."

*Poetry* [Winner]: Christian Wiman, editor; Don Share, senior editor; Curtis Fox, producer; Ed Herrmann, sound recordist. For "Poetry Magazine Podcast."

*Slate*: David Plotz, editor. For "The *Slate* Culture Gabfest."

*Tablet Magazine*: Alana Newhouse, editor in chief; Julie Subrin, executive producer; Sara Ivry, host. For "Vox Tablet."

## Video

Honors the outstanding use of video by a magazine website or online-only magazine.

*Chow*: Meredith Arthur, executive producer; Blake Smith, producer. For "Chow Video."

*Entertainment Weekly*: Jess Cagle, managing editor; Bill Gannon, managing editor, EW.com. For "Totally Lost."

*The New York Times Magazine*: Hugo Lindgren, editor in chief. For "The Beauty of the Power Game."

*The Oxford American* [Winner]: Warwick Sabin, publisher; Dave Anderson, videographer. For "SoLost."

*Slate*: David Plotz, editor. For "How I Ran an Ad on Fox News."

# National Magazine Awards 2011 Judges

## Judging Chair

Larry Hackett, managing editor, *People*, president, American Society of Magazine Editors

## Judging Leaders

James Bennet, editor, *The Atlantic*
Gayle Goodson Butler, editor in chief, Senior VP, Des Moines, editorial director, *Better Homes and Gardens*
Lucy Danziger, editor in chief, *Self*
Rosemary Ellis, editor in chief, *Good Housekeeping*
David Granger, editor in chief, *Esquire*
Christopher G. Johns, editor in chief, *National Geographic*
Eliot Kaplan, editorial talent director, Hearst Magazines
Ellen Kunes, editor in chief, *Health*
Cynthia Leive, editor in chief, *Glamour*
Anthony Licata, editor, *Field & Stream*
Pamela Maffei McCarthy, deputy editor, *The New Yorker*
Adam Moss, editor in chief, *New York*
Jim Nelson, editor in chief, *GQ*
Barbara O'Dair, executive editor, *Reader's Digest*
Kaitlin Quistgaard, editor in chief, *Yoga Journal*
Lesley Jane Seymour, editor in chief, *More*
Richard Stengel, managing editor, *Time*
Richard David Story, editor in chief, *Departures*
Kristin van Ogtrop, managing editor, *Real Simple*
David Willey, editor in chief, *Runner's World*; editorial director, *Bicycling*, *Running Times*
Betty Wong, editor in chief, *Fitness*
David Zinczenko, SVP, editor in chief, *Men's Health*

## Judges

Julie Vosburgh Agnone, vice president, *National Geographic Kids*
Eric Alterman, columnist, *The Nation*

Andrea Amadio, creative director, *Parents/American Baby*
David A. Andelman, editor, *World Policy Journal*
Lisa Arbetter, deputy managing editor, *InStyle*
Philip Armour, editor in chief, *American Cowboy*
Miriam Arond, director, *Good Housekeeping Research Institute*
John Atwood, deputy editor, *Runner's World*
Matthew Axe, design director, *Whole Living*
Richard Babcock, editor, *Chicago Magazine*
Florian Bachleda, creative director, *Fast Company*
Lisa Bain, executive editor, *Women's Health*
Douglas S. Barasch, editor in chief, *On Earth*
Melina Gerosa Bellows, executive vice president childrens publishing,
    *National Geographic Society*
Gary Belsky, editor in chief, *ESPN The Magazine*
Leigh Belz, senior features director, *Teen Vogue*
Jane Berentson, editor, *Inc.*
Alex Bhattacharji, executive editor, *Details*
Elisabeth Biondi, visuals editor, *The New Yorker*
Debra Birnbaum, editor in chief, *TV Guide Magazine*
Debra Bishop, creative director, *More*
H. Emerson Blake, editor in chief, *Orion*
Kyle Blue, design director, *Dwell*
Dana Bowen, executive editor, *Saveur*
Millie Martini Bratten, editor in chief, *Brides*
Douglas Brod, editor in chief, *Spin*
Daniel Brogan, editor and publisher, *5280 Magazine*
Dudley Brooks, photo director, *Ebony*
Peter G. Brown, editorial consultant
Laurie Glenn Buckle, editor, *Fine Cooking Magazine*
Amid Capeci, design director, *Entertainment Weekly*
Dara Caponigro, editor in chief, *Veranda*
Maile Carpenter, editor in chief, *Food Network Magazine*
Betsy Carter, author
Susan Casey, editor in chief, *O, The Oprah Magazine*
Catherine Cavender, editor, special projects, Hearst Magazines
Andrea L. Chambers, director, Center for Publishing, *New York University*
Janet Chan, editorial consultant
Deborah Chasman, editor, *Boston Review*
Melissa Chessher, chair, Magazine Department, Newhouse School
Jody Churchfield, Art director, *Martha Stewart Weddings*

David Clarke, editor, *Golf Magazine*
Ana Connery, director, Print Content, Strategy and Design, The Parenting
    Group
Stephen D. Corey, editor, *The Georgia Review*
Judith Coyne, executive editor, *More*
Paul Crawford, creative director, *Golf Magazine*
Jonathan Dahl, editor in chief, *SmartMoney*
Will Dana, managing editor, *Rolling Stone*
Maxine Davidowitz, creative consultant, Maxine Davidowitz Design
Bob Der, managing editor and publisher, *Sports Illustrated for Kids* and
    *Time for Kids*
Mariette DiChristina, editor in chief, *Scientific American*
Karen Dillon, editor, *Harvard Business Review*
Chris Dixon, design director, *New York*
Suzanne Donaldson, photo director, *Glamour*
Jonathan Dorn, VP, AIM Outdoor Group; editor in chief, *Backpacker*
Amy DuBois Barnett, editor in chief, *Ebony*
Simon Dumenco, media columnist, *Advertising Age*
Andrea Dunham, design director, *People*
Arem Duplessis, design director, *The New York Times Magazine*
Rene Ebersole, features editor, *Audubon*
Milton Esterow, editor and publisher, *ARTnews*
Sid Evans, VP, editor in chief, *Garden and Gun*
Ellen Fair, managing editor, *Art + Auction, Modern Painters*
Barbara Fairchild, columnist, *Real Eats Magazine*
Linda Fears, editor in chief, *Family Circle*
Ruth Feldman, VP, international editorial director, Martha Stewart
    Living Omnimedia
John Fennell, associate professor, Meredith Chair for Service Journalism,
    Missouri School of Journalism
Steve Fennessy, editor, *Atlanta*
Dan Ferrara, deputy editor, *Inc.*
Peter Finch, senior editor, *Golf Digest*
Steve Fine, director of photography, *Sports Illustrated*
Rose Fiorentino, creative director, *TV Guide Magazine*
Peter Flax, editor in chief, *Bicycling*
Stephen Frailey, chair, Photography Department, School of Visual Arts;
    editor in chief, *Dear Dave*
Carla Frank, creative director, *Cooking Light*
Lisa Lee Freeman, editor in chief, *ShopSmart Magazine*

David Friend, editor of creative development, *Vanity Fair*

Janet Froelich, creative director, *Real Simple*

Anne Fulenwider, executive editor, *Marie Claire*

David Garlock, senior lecturer and Magazine Program head, University of Texas

Sheri Geller, design director, *Country Living*

Ted Genoways, editor, *Virginia Quarterly Review*

Rip Georges, creative director, *LA Times Magazine*

Susan Glasser, editor in chief, *Foreign Policy*

Klara Glowczewska, editor in chief, *Condé Nast Traveler*

Jon Gluck, deputy editor, *New York*

Henry Goldblatt, deputy managing editor, *Entertainment Weekly*

Susan Goodall, editorial development director, *Glamour*

Heloise Goodman, photography director, Martha Stewart Living Omnimedia

Meryl Gordon, director, magazine writing, Arthur L. Carter Journalism Institute

Lisa Gosselin, editorial director, EatingWell Media Group, *EatingWell Magazine*

Nancy Perry Graham, editor in chief, *AARP The Magazine*

Sam Grawe, editor in chief, *Dwell*

Eleanor Griffin, VP, brand development, *Southern Living*

Edward Grinnan, editor in chief and vice president, *Guideposts*

Oriol R. Gutierrez Jr., deputy editor, *POZ*

Tish Hamilton, executive editor, *Runner's World*

Melissa Harris, editor in chief, *Aperture*

Susan Hassler, editor in chief, *IEEE Spectrum*

Luke Hayman, partner, *Pentagram*

Ronald Henkoff, editor, *Bloomberg Markets*

Jill Herzig, editor in chief, *Redbook*

Lindy Hess, director, Columbia Publishing Course, Columbia School of Journalism

Geraldine Hessler, design director, *Glamour*

Mary C. Hickey, channel editor, AARP.org

Aaron Hicklin, editor in chief, *Out*

Roger D. Hodge

Gary Hoenig, general manager/editorial director, ESPN Publishing

Regan Hofmann, editor in chief, *POZ*

Carol Holstead, associate professor, University of Kansas

Elizabeth Hummer, d esign director, *Harper's Bazaar*

Christopher Hunt, assistant managing editor, *Sports Illustrated*

Samir A. Husni, director, Magazine Innovation Center, The University
    of Mississippi
Joe Hutchinson, art director, *Rolling Stone*
Adi Ignatius, editor in chief, *Harvard Business Review Group*
William H. Inman, editor in chief, *Institutional Investor*
Clara Jeffery, coeditor, *Mother Jones*
Sammye Johnson, Carlos Augustus de Lozano Chair in Journalism,
    Trinity University
Laurie Jones, managing editor, *Vogue*
Dorothy Kalins, director, Dorothy Kalins Ink
James Kaminsky, media consultant
Susan Kane, editorial consultant
Janice Kaplan, consultant
Peter Kaplan, editorial director, Fairchild Fashion Group
Susan Kaufman, editor, *People StyleWatch*
Brandon Kavulla, creative director, *Wired Magazine*
Michael Kinsley
Rik Kirkland, senior managing editor, McKinsey & Company, Inc.
Kimberly D. Kleman, editor in chief, deputy editorial director,
    *Consumer Reports*
Deirdre Koribanick, design director, *Food Network Magazine*
Laurie Kratochvil, director of photography, *Nomad Editions*
Steven Lagerfeld, editor, *The Wilson Quarterly*
Frank Lalli, chief content officer, The Rooster Group
Chi Lam, design director, *Everyday Food*
Anna Last, editor in chief, *Everyday Food*
Valerie Latona, editor
Sally Lee, SVP/NY editorial director, Meredith Corporation; editor in
    chief, *Ladies' Home Journal*
Ellen Levine, editorial director, Hearst Magazines
Joe Levy, editorial director, *Maxim*
Carla Rohlfing Levy, editorial director, *Self*
Hugo Lindgren, editor in chief, *The New York Times Magazine*
Karmen Lizzul, creative director, *Family Circle*
Joe Lorio, senior editor, *Automobile*
Belinda Luscombe, editor at large, *Time*
Eve MacSweeney, features director, *Vogue*
Paul Maidment, principal and editor in chief, *Bystander Media*
James Marcus, deputy editor, *Harper's Magazine*
Jacqueline Marino, assistant professor, Kent State University

Hannah McCaughey, design and photography director, *Outside*
Kevin S. McKean, vice president/editorial director, *Consumers Union*
Liz McMillen, editor, *The Chronicle Review*
Mary Melton, editor, *Los Angeles Magazine*
Rachel Davis Mersey, assistant professor, Medill School of Journalism
Francesca Messina, senior group art director, McGraw-Hill
Jason Meyers, executive editor, *Entrepreneur*
Brenda Milis, director of photography, *Men's Health*
Sarah Gray Miller, editor in chief, *Country Living*
Christian Millman, executive editor, *Taste of Home*
Marilyn Milloy, deputy editor, *AARP The Magazine*
Luke Mitchell, deputy editor, *Popular Science*
Peg Moline, editor in chief, *Fit Pregnancy/Natural Health*
Ted Moncreiff, executive editor, *W*
Gregory Monfries, creative director, *Essence*
Terence Monmaney, executive editor, *Smithsonian Magazine*
Peter Moore, editor, *Men's Health*
Kitty Morgan, executive editor, *Better Homes and Gardens*
Don Morris, creative director, *Don Morris Design*
Courtney Murphy, creative director, *Good Housekeeping*
Christopher Napolitano, creative director, Indian Country Today
    Media Network
Silvana Nardone, editor in chief, *DishTowelDiaries.com*
Victor Navasky, Delacorte Professor, Columbia University Graduate School
    of Journalism
Martha Nelson, editorial director, Time Inc.
Robert Newman, The Man, Robert Newman Design
Sue Ng, design director, *SmartMoney*
Catriona Ni Aolain, director of photography, *ESPN The Magazine*
Pam O'Brien, executive editor, *Fitness*
James Oseland,editor in chief, editorial director, *Saveur, Garden Design*
Deborah Paul, editorial director, *Emmis Publishing*
Abe Peck, professor emeritus in service; director, business to business
    communication, Medill School of Journalism, Northwestern University
Jodi Peckman, creative director, *Rolling Stone*
Abigail Pesta, editor at large, *Marie Claire*
Andrea Pitzer, editor, *Nieman Storyboard*
Sean Plottner, editor, *Dartmouth Alumni Magazine*
Dana Points, editor in chief, *Parents and American Baby*
Kira Pollack, director of photography, *Time*

Eric Pooley, deputy editor, *Bloomberg BusinessWeek*
Victoria Pope, deputy editor, *National Geographic*
Lynn Povich
Corey S. Powell, editor in chief, *Discover*
Robert Priest, creative director, *Priest + Grace*
Michele Promaulayko, editor in chief, *Women's Health*
Katherine Pushkar, lifestyle editor, *Better Homes and Gardens*
John Rasmus
Michael W. Robbins, editor, *Military History*
Kerry Robertson, *Market Design*
Meredith Kahn Rollins, executive editor, *Redbook*
David Rotman, editor, *Technology Review*
Sarah Rozen, director of photography, *Women's Health*
Kathy Ryan, director of photography, *The New York Times Magazine*
Robert Safian, editor, *Fast Company*
Ina Saltz, Principal, Saltz Design
Bernard Scharf, creative director, *Travel + Leisure*
Manny Schiffres, executive editor, *Kiplinger's Personal Finance*
Eric Schurenberg, editor in chief, BNET, editorial director, *CBS MoneyWatch.com*
Carol Schwalbe, a ssociate professor, Arizona State University School of Journalism
Scot Schy, creative director, *House Beautiful*
Cynthia Hall Searight, creative director, *Self*
David Seideman, editor in chief, *Audubon*
Andrew Serwer, managing editor, *Fortune*
Bill Shapiro, editor in chief, *Life.com*
Jake Silverstein, editor, *Texas Monthly*
Dora Somosi, director of photography, *GQ*
Nancy Soriano, publisher/director, Craft F&W Media
David Speranza, design director, *Bicycling*
Ted Spiker, associate professor, University of Florida
Lorin Stein, editor, *The Paris Review*
Fredrika Stjarne, director of photography, *Food & Wine*
Jay Stowe, editor, *Cincinnati Magazine*
Matt Strelecki, art director, *Successful Farming*
Bill Stump, SVP/editorial director, *Prevention, Organic Gardening*
John Swansburg, culture editor, *Slate*
Catherine Talese, photography editor/consultant
Katie Tamony, V.P./editor in chief, *Sunset*

# National Magazine Awards for Digital Media

## Judging Chair

Peggy Northrop, VP and global editor in chief, *Reader's Digest*; vice
president, American Society of Magazine Editors

## Judging Leaders

Chris Anderson, editor in chief, *Wired*
Bob Cohn, editorial director, Atlantic Digital
Dana Cowin, editor in chief, *Food & Wine*
Doug Crichton, director, Mobile Engagement, Meredith Corporation
Hugh Delehanty, Senior VP and editor in chief, AARP Media Properties
Paul Fichtenbaum, managing editor, SI.com
Mark Jannot, editor in chief, *Popular Science*, editorial director, Bonnier
Technology Group
James B. Meigs, editor in chief, *Popular Mechanics*
John Papanek, SVP, editor at large, ESPN
Eric Schurenberg, editor in chief, BNET
Sree Sreenivasan, dean of student affairs and professor of professional
practice, the School of Journalism, Columbia University
Cyndi Stivers, development editor, Time Inc. Style & Entertainment Group
Digital

## Judges

Ian Adelman, director of design and user experience, *New York Media/
nymag.com*
Rosie Amodio, editor, *InStyle.com*
Jenn Andrlik, editor, *marthastewart.com*
Ebelinda Antigua, creative director, *Working Mother Magazine*
Liz Armstrong, Online director, *ReadyMade*
James Baker, executive editor, *Condé Nast Traveler*
Mark Bautz, editor in chief, *Spin.com*
Rich Beattie, executive editor, *TravelandLeisure.com*
Giselle Benatar, editor in chief, New Media, *ConsumerReports.org*
Benjamin Berentson, digital managing director, *Glamour*

Roger Black, Roger Black Studio

Trisha Blackmar, senior editor, *Sports Illustrated*

Denise Brodey, general manager, Your Life, *USA Today/usatoday.com*

Merrill Brown, principal, MMB Media LLC

Anatole Burkin, VP, digital content, Taunton Press

Christina Caldwell, online director, *W*

Eric Capossela, design director, *Atlanta Magazine*

Janice Castro, senior director, Graduate Education and Teaching Excellence, Medill School of Journalism

Nick Catucci, editor in chief, *rollingstone.com*

Roger Cohn, editor, *Yale Environment 360*

James Oliver Cury, web director, *Hearst Digital Media*

Scott Dadich, executive director, editorial development, *Condé Nast*

Angela Diegel, online director, *Popular Mechanics*

Alfred A. Edmond Jr., SVP/editor at large, *Black Enterprise*

Daniel Eisenberg, executive editor, *Time.com*

Blake Eskin, editor, *newyorker.com*

Rachel Fishman Feddersen, editorial director, digital, The Parenting Group

Robbyn Footlick, executive editor/executive producer, *ESPN The Magazine*/ESPN Insider

Nick Gillespie, editor in chief, *Reason.com and Reason.tv*

Harry Goldstein, editorial director, digital, *IEEE Spectrum*

Devin Gordon, senior editor, *GQ Magazine*

David Griffin, executive editor, e-publishing, *National Geographic*

Evan Hansen, editor in chief, *Wired.com*

Douglas Harbrecht, director, new media, *Kiplinger.com*

Kathleen Harris, managing editor, *RealSimple.com*

Eric Hellweg, editor, *Harvard Business Review Online*

Melinda Henneberger, editor in chief, *Politics Daily*

Mike Hofman, editor, *Inc.com*

Michael Hogan, executive Digital editor, *Vanity Fair*

Holly Stuart Hughes, editor in chief, *Photo District News*

Jimmy Jellinek, chief content officer/editorial director, Playboy Enterprises, Inc.

Peter Kafka, senior editor, *All Things Digital*

Michael Kress, executive editor, *Parents.com*

Kate Lawler, executive editor, *Ladies' Home Journal*

Jacqueline Leo, editor in chief, *The Fiscal Times*

Michael Martin, editor in chief, *Time Out New York*

Gerald Marzorati, Assistant managing editor, new ventures, *The New York Times*
Craig Matters, managing editor, *Money*
Celeste McCauley, Senior editor, special projects, *Guideposts*
Noah Michelson, Associate editor, *Out*
Scott Mowbray, editor, *Cooking Light*
Alana Newhouse, editor in chief, *Tablet Magazine*
Bernard Ohanian, VP/editor, *AARP Digital*
Scott Omelianuk, editor, *This Old House, thisoldhouse.com*
Janet Paskin, editor, *SmartMoney.com*
Chris Peacock, executive editor, *CNNMoney*
Brandon Perlman, Digital editor, *Departures*
Bill Phillips, executive editor, *Men's Health*; editor, *MensHealth.com*
David Plotz, editor, *Slate*
Cliff Ransom, executive editor, *Popular Science*
Mark Remy, executive editor online, *Runner's World*
Suzanne Riss, editor in chief, *Working Mother Magazine*
Noah Robischon, executive editor, *Fast Company*
Ann Shoket, editor in chief, *Seventeen*
Dirk Standen, editor in chief, *Style.com*
Tanya Steel, editor in chief, *Epicurious.com*
Michael Steele, editor in chief, *Us Weekly*
Matt Sullivan, web director, *Esquire*
Andrew Sullivan, Senior editor, *The Atlantic Monthly*
Ganda Suthivarakom, Website director, *Saveur.com and GardenDesign.com*
Brian D. Sweany, deputy editor, *Texas Monthly*
Gael Towey, chief editorial and creative director, Martha Stewart Living Omnimedia, Inc.
Mark Weinberg, VP, programming and product strategy, Hearst Digital Media
Emil Wilbekin, managing editor, *Essence.com*
Deborah Wilburn, executive editor online, *Prevention.com*
Ben Williams, editorial director, *nymag.com*
Philip Yam, managing editor, online, *Scientific American*
Amos Zeeberg, managing editor, online, *Discover*

Affiliations listed are at time of judging

# Permissions

# Contributors

**JOEL BROUWER** is the author of three books of poems, including *And So* (Four Way Books, 2009). He teaches at the University of Alabama.

**PAMELA COLLOFF** is an executive editor at *Texas Monthly* and has been writing for the magazine since 1997. Her work has also appeared in *The New Yorker* and has been anthologized in three editions of *Best American Crime Reporting*. Colloff has been a finalist for two National Magazine Awards, first in 2001 for her article on school prayer, "They Haven't Got a Prayer," and again in 2011 for her two-part series, "Innocence Lost" and "Innocence Found." Colloff holds a bachelor's degree in English literature from Brown University and was raised in New York City. She lives in Austin with her husband and son.

**JOHN DONVAN:** "I first began to focus on autism and to understand its long tangled story of parents struggling in the dark to reach, grow, and protect their children when I met my wife. She was an established journalist then but about to respond to a lifelong urge by applying to medical school. She had lots of reasons, but one of them had to do with her brother. Only eighteen months younger than she, he had severe autism, and it had marked her life. She shared many stories of her family rolling with the punches—from initial misdiagnosis, to the classic labeling of her mother as the culprit, to the fight for an education and the misunderstanding of a public that either ignored her brother or feared him. My wife went on to get her M.D., and I went on to make reporting on autism an avocation. I've served as a London correspondent for CNN, while for ABC News I've held the posts of White House correspondent, as well as in Moscow, Jerusalem, and Amman. Based in Washington for the past decade, I have reported primarily for *Nightline* but contribute to virtually all of ABC's broadcast and online platforms. My work has won three Emmy awards and several nominations beyond that. For more than a decade, autism has been the topic to which I return again and again. I have been a frequent speaker before the World Affairs Council, an occasional substitute host for NPR, and for the past three years the full-time host and moderator of *Intelligence Squared*, a series of Oxford-style debates on Bloomberg Television."

**BEN EHRENREICH** is a freelance journalist and novelist. His first novel, *The Suitors*, was published in 2006 and his second, *Ether*, will be published in the fall of 2011 by City Lights Books. Ehrenreich's articles, essays, and short fiction have been published in *Los Angeles*, *Harper's*, *L.A. Weekly*, *The London Review of Books*, *McSweeney's*, and many other publications. He lives in Los Angeles.

**DEXTER FILKINS** Before joining *The New Yorker* in January 2011, Dexter Filkins had been with the *New York Times* since 2000, reporting from Afghanistan, Pakistan, New York, and Iraq, where he was based from 2003 to 2006. He had also worked for the *Miami Herald* and the *Los Angeles Times*, where he was chief of the paper's New Delhi bureau. In 2009, he won a Pulitzer Prize as part of a team of *New York Times* reporters in Pakistan and Afghanistan. He was a Nieman Fellow at Harvard University in 2006 and 2007 and a fellow at the Carr Center for Human Rights Policy at Harvard's Kennedy School of Government in 2007 and 2008. He has received numerous prizes, including two George Polk Awards and three Overseas Press Club Awards. His 2008 book, *The Forever War*, won the National Book Critics Circle Award for Best Nonfiction Book and was named a best book of the year by the *Boston Globe*, the *New York Times*, the *Washington Post*, and *Time*.

**ATUL GAWANDE** became a staff writer at *The New Yorker* in 1998. He completed his surgical residency at Brigham and Women's Hospital, Boston, in 2003, and joined the faculty as a general and endocrine surgeon. He is an associate professor of surgery at Harvard Medical School, an associate professor in the Department of Health Policy and Management at the Harvard School of Public Health, and the associate director of the B.W.H. Center for Surgery and Public Health. Gawande has published research studies in areas ranging from surgical technique to U.S. military care for the wounded and error and performance in medicine. He is the director of the World Health Organization's global campaign to reduce surgical deaths and complications. From 1992 to 1993, he served as a senior health-policy adviser in Bill Clinton's presidential campaign and in the White House. Gawande's essays have been selected twice for the annual *Best American Essays* collection and six times for the *Best American Science Writing*, and he was the editor of the *Best American Science Writing* for 2006. His book *Complications: A Surgeon's Notes on an Imperfect Science* was a finalist for the National Book Award in 2002. His most recent book, *The Checklist Manifesto: How to Get Things Right*, was published in December 2009. His previous book, *Better: A Surgeon's Notes on Performance*, was published in April 2007. In 2006 he received the MacArthur Award in recognition of his research and writing.

**WILLIAM GIRALDI'S** first book, *Busy Monsters*, was published in August 2011 by W. W. Norton. He teaches in the Writing Program at Boston University and is a senior editor for the journal *Agni*. His work has appeared recently in *The American Scholar, The Believer, Bookforum, Georgia Review, Kenyon Review, The New York Times Book Review, Poets & Writers, Salmagundi, Southern Review*, and *Yale Review*.

**MICHAEL HASTINGS** is a contributing editor to *Rolling Stone* and the author of *I Lost My Love in Baghdad: A Modern War Story*. For the past six years, he's covered the wars in Iraq and Afghanistan. In 2010, he was awarded the prestigious George Polk Award for journalism and named a Huffington Post Game Changer. At the age of twenty-five, he was named *Newsweek*'s Baghdad correspondent, where he served from 2005 through 2007. In 2008, he covered the U.S. presidential elections for *Newsweek*. He's written for *Foreign Policy, GQ,* the *L.A. Times, Salon, Slate,* the *Washington Post,* and numerous other publications. His next book, *The Operators: The Wild and Terrifying Inside Story of America's War in Afghanistan,* is scheduled for release later this year.

**CHRISTOPHER HITCHENS** joined *Vanity Fair* as a contributing editor in September 1992 and writes a monthly column. Hitchens began his journalism career in 1973 as a staff writer at *The New Statesman* and since then has written for the *Evening Standard* of London and served as a foreign correspondent for London's *Daily Express* and as foreign editor of *The New Statesman.* Hitchens wrote a biweekly column for *The Nation* from 1982 to 2002. He has also served as Washington editor for *Harper's* and as U.S. correspondent for *The Spectator* and the *Times Literary Supplement.* Additionally, he was the book critic at *New York Newsday* from 1986 to 1992. Hitchens is the author of numerous books, including *Hostage to History: Cyprus from the Ottomans to Kissinger* (1984), *Prepared for the Worst* (1988), *The Missionary Position* (1994), *No One Left to Lie To* (1999), *The Trial of Henry Kissinger* (2001), *Letters to a Young Contrarian* (2001), *Why Orwell Matters* (2002), *Hitch 22: A Memoir* (2010), and *Arguably: Essays by Christopher Hitchens* (2011). He has also written and presented a number of documentaries for British television.

**SCOTT HORTON** is a contributing editor of *Harper's* and writes "No Comment" for the *Harper's* website. A New York attorney known for his work in emerging markets and international law, especially human-rights law and the law of armed conflict, Horton lectures at Columbia Law School. A lifelong human-rights advocate, Horton served as counsel to Andrei Sakharov and Elena Bonner, among other activists in the former Soviet Union. He is a cofounder of the American University in Central Asia and has been involved in some of the most significant foreign-investment projects in the Central Eurasian region. Horton recently led a number of studies of abuse issues associated with the conduct of the war on terror for the New York City Bar Association, where he has chaired several committees, including, most recently, the Committee on International Law. He is also a member of the board of the National Institute of Military Justice, the Andrei Sakharov Foundation, the EurasiaGroup, and the American Branch of the International Law Association.

BARBARA KINGSOLVER's thirteen books of fiction, poetry, and creative nonfiction include the novels *The Bean Trees*, *The Poisonwood Bible*, and her most recent, *The Lacuna*, winner of the Orange Prize for Fiction. Translated into more than twenty languages, her work has won a devoted worldwide readership and many awards, including the National Humanities Medal. Many of her books have been incorporated into the core English literature curriculum of colleges throughout the country. She lives with her husband and daughter on their farm in southwest Virginia.

MARK LEIBOVICH is a national political reporter for the *New York Times* based in the Washington, D.C., bureau. He is a regular contributor to the *New York Times Magazine*, where he specializes in the intersection of politics, media, and culture. Leibovich's April 2008 profile of MSNBC's Chris Matthews was a finalist for a National Magazine Award in 2009. Leibovich wrote about national politics for the *Washington Post*'s Style section. He previously covered the U.S. technology sector for the *Post*'s Business section, which led to the publication of his first book, *The New Imperialists: How Five Restless Kids Grew Up to Virtually Rule Your World*. He has also worked at the *San Jose Mercury News* and the *Boston*

*Phoenix.* Leibovich grew up in the Boston area and lives in Washington, D.C., with his wife, Meridith Kolbrener, and his three daughters, Nell, Eliza, and Frances.

**STEPHEN MARCHE**, a columnist for *Esquire*, is the author, most recently, of *How Shakespeare Changed Everything.*

**JANE MAYER** joined *The New Yorker* as a staff writer in March 1995. Based in Washington, D.C., she writes about politics for the magazine and has been covering the war on terror. Recent subjects include Alberto Mora, the Pentagon's secret torture policy, the prison at Guantánamo Bay, and the legality of CIA interrogations. She has also written about George W. Bush, the Bin Laden family, Sarah Palin, and the television show *24.* Before joining *The New Yorker*, Mayer was for twelve years a reporter at the *Wall Street Journal.* In 1984, she became the *Journal*'s first female White House correspondent. Mayer has won of the John Chancellor Award for Excellence in Journalism, a Guggenheim Foundation Fellowship, the Edward Weintal Prize, and the Ridenhour Book Prize. She was a nominee for a 2008 National Book Critics Circle Award, a 2008 L.A. *Times* Book Prize, and the 2009 Helen Bernstein Award. She has twice been a finalist for a National Magazine Award and was nominated twice by the *Journal* for a Pulitzer Prize in the feature-writing category. Before joining the *Journal*, Mayer worked as a metropolitan reporter for the *Washington Star.* She began her career in journalism as a stringer for *Time* while still a student in college. She has also written for a number of other publications, including the *Los Angeles Times*, the *New York Review of Books*, and the *Washington Post.* Mayer is the author of the best-selling 2008 book *The Dark Side: The Inside Story of How the War on Terror Turned Into a War on American Ideals.* She is also the coauthor of two other best-selling books: *Strange Justice*, with Jill Abramson, and *Landslide: The Unmaking of the President, 1984–1988*, with Doyle McManus. Mayer, who was born in New York, graduated with honors from Yale in 1977 and continued her studies in history at Oxford. She lives in Washington with her husband and daughter.

**MAC MCCLELLAND** is human rights reporter at *Mother Jones,* writer of the blog *The Rights Stuff,* and the author of *For Us Surrender Is Out of the Question: A Story From Burma's Never-Ending War.*

**MICHAEL PATERNITI** is the author of *Driving Mr. Albert: A Trip Across America with Einstein's Brain,* which has been translated in twenty countries, and is the winner of a National Magazine Award for Feature Writing. His work appears regularly in *GQ,* where he is a writer at large; his work has also appeared in *Harper's, Details, Esquire,* the *New York Times Magazine,* and *Outside.* He lives in Portland, Maine, with his wife and son.

**JOE POSNANSKI** is a senior writer at *Sports Illustrated.* He was sports columnist at the *Kansas City Star* from 1996 to 2009, and during that time he was twice named the best sports columnist in America by the Associated Press Sports Editors. He was also nominated for twenty-one awards by the APSE and won additional first-place national awards in feature and project writing. Joe continues to write columns for the *Star.* He has written three books; the latest, *The Machine: The Story of the 1975 Cincinnati Reds,* was published in September 2009. He previously wrote *The Good Stuff,* a collection of columns, and *The Soul of Baseball: A Road Trip Through Buck O'Neil's America,* which won the Casey Award for the Best Baseball Book of the Year in 2007. He has written essays for several books, including *The Hardball Times Annual,* ESPN's bestselling *College Football Encyclopedia,* and *Football and Philosophy: Going Deep.* His work twice has been anthologized in *The Best American Sportswriting.* Posnanski previously worked as sports columnist for the *Cincinnati Post* and the *Augusta Chronicle* and started his career as a multi-use reporter and editor at the *Charlotte*

*Observer.* Posnanski grew up in Cleveland and now lives in Charlotte with his wife, Margo, and their two daughters, Elizabeth and Katie.

**LAURENCE ROY STAINS:** "Like a lot of writers, I started early. I grew up in a small town outside Buffalo, New York, and began writing bad science fiction when I was eight. In high school, I edited the student newspaper, wrote poetry during my callow undergraduate years. After a brief stint in newspapers, I gravitated towards magazines. As an editor, I started up two magazines for Rodale Press: *New Shelter,* which briefly flourished during the oil crisis of 1978 through 1982, and *Men's Health,* which has enjoyed a better run. I was also on staff at *Philadelphia* from 1987 to 1992. As a writer I've freelanced for many national publications: *AARP Magazine, Better Homes & Gardens, Child, GQ, Men's Health* and its latest spin-off, *Best Life, Money,* the *New York Times Magazine, Philadelphia, Rolling Stone, Sports Illustrated, This Old House, USA Weekend,* the *Washington Post,* and *Worth.* I've been a coauthor of five books and a finalist twice in the National Magazine Awards. I came late to teaching. I first taught magazine article writing as an adjunct professor at Temple University in the spring of 2001. Eighteen months later I was teaching full-time—I was hooked. My teaching schedule also includes a rotation of the following courses: Magazine Article Writing, Advanced Magazine Writing, Magazine Editing and Design, and the graduate courses the American Magazine and Magazine Writing."

**JOHN JEREMIAH SULLIVAN** is a writer for the *New York Times Magazine,* the southern editor of *The Paris Review,* and the author of *Pulphead: Essays* (2011). He lives in North Carolina with his wife and daughters.

**PAUL THEROUX** is the author of more than forty books, including the nonfiction works *The Great Railway Bazaar, The Old Patago-*

*nian Express, Riding the Iron Rooster,* and *Ghost Train to the Eastern Star.* His novels include *Blinding Light, Hotel Honolulu, My Other Life, Kowloon Tong, The Mosquito Coast,* and, most recently, *A Dead Hand: A Crime in Calcutta.* He lives in Hawaii and on Cape Cod.

**MARC TRACY** is a staff writer at *Tablet Magazine.*

**JONATHAN VAN METER** is a contributing editor at *New York* and *Vogue* as well as the founding editor of *Vibe.* He is the author of *The Last Good Time: Skinny D'Amato, the Notorious 500 Club, and the Rise and Fall of Atlantic City* and is at work on *Ladies' Man,* a memoir of writing about women.

**JONAH WEINER** is *Slate*'s pop critic and a contributing editor at *Rolling Stone.* His writing has also appeared in *Details, Men's Journal,* the *New York Times,* and the *New York Times Magazine.* He was born in Brooklyn and lives there today.

**PAIGE WILLIAMS** won the National Magazine Award for Feature Writing in 2008 and shared a nomination the following year. She's written long-form features for a range of magazines and newspapers and teaches narrative writing at the Nieman Foundation for Journalism at Harvard.

**CAREN ZUCKER:** "I am a television producer and journalist with over twenty-five years of experience and have reported domestically and internationally for ABC's *World News Tonight* and *Nightline.* I've covered breaking news and reported on a wide range of issues, including politics, business, health, and foreign policy. These experiences, however, reveal only a small fragment of my life experience as a news producer. My story begins on the birth date of a child with autism, Mickey McGuinness, my son and my first, born May 3, 1994. Mickey would guide my career path and have an impact on the stories I chose to cover. But most of all, his existence would create in me—as his mother—an advocate, a seeker of answers, and a more compassionate human being. And so, over the past dozen years, I have carved out a niche in a very special kind of reporting. By passion, and somewhat by default, but mostly for love, covering autism has become my mission. Together with my friend and coauthor, ABC correspondent John Donvan, we created and launched "Echoes of Autism," a continuing series for ABC News exploring the science, treatment, social issues, and debate that surround this condition. We were often the first team to tell many of the most important stories in autism and bring them to millions of viewers."